# Healing

# Your

# Spiritual

# Traumas

# Kim Michaels

# Healing

# Your

# Spiritual

# Traumas

Kim Michaels
More to Life

Healing Your Spiritual Traumas

MORE TO LIFE PUBLISHING

www.morepublish.com

For foreign and translation rights,

contact: info@ morepublish.com

ISBN: 978-87-93297-48-7

# Content

# INTRODUCTION

This book is the workbook companion to the novel *My Lives with Lucifer, Satan, Hitler and Jesus*. The novel introduces the idea that many spiritual people have come to earth as volunteers or "avatars." We have then received deep spiritual traumas as a result of what we have experienced here. Many of us still carry these traumas with us, and it can explain why we sometimes can feel as if we are not making progress on the spiritual path or why there are certain issues we cannot overcome.

This book contains further teachings on these concepts as well as practical tools for helping you heal the traumas and overcome any negativity in your attitude to life on this planet. Please note that it is recommended that you read the novel before using this book. The reason is that the novel contains many important teachings that can help you start the healing process. This book will then give you the practical tools to continue and complete the process.

This book contains a number of invocations that you are meant to give aloud. If you are not familiar with giving such invocations, you can find further teachings and instructions on the website *www.transcendencetoolbox.com*. You can also give the invocations along with a recording and you can purchase recordings of the invocations in this book on the website *www.morepublish.com*.

# 1 | CAN YOU LOVE YOURSELF?

Kim: We are going to say several times: "Mother Mary, I love you."

**All: Mother Mary, I love you. Mother Mary, I love you. Mother Mary, I love you. Mother Mary, I love you. Mother Mary, I love you.**

[Mother Mary:] My beloved hearts, I am indeed the Ascended Master Mother Mary.

I…love…you. I love you, each and every one of you. Can you believe that I love you?

**Several: Yes.**

Can you *all* believe that I love you?

**All: Yes.**

Can you *truly* believe that I love you?

**All: Yes.**


Can you believe with your *heart* and not with your *mouth* that I love you?

**All: Yes.**


Then, answer me in your hearts and not with your mouths, for it is so easy to say the things you are expected to say, to do the things you are expected to do, to feel the things you are expected to feel, to think the thoughts you are expected to think and to see yourself as what you are expected to think you are.

Now, you can *believe* that I love you. You can *feel* that you love me. You can, some of you, feel my love for you, but the big question that I put before you tonight is: "Can you love yourself? Can you *truly* love yourself? Can you love your 'self,' not yourself?"


## The two selves

Do you see the need to make a distinction? You all think of yourself as "yourself," but you need to realize that there is an outer personality, an outer self, and there is the inner being, the inner self. Then, you can begin to accept that you can love your "self," not the outer personality, but the self that you are.

Why do I ask you to make this distinction? Because so few people in the world, and certainly so few people on the European continent, make the distinction between the outer self and the pure self, the pure Being. Why do they not make this distinction? Because they have been pro-grammed – over many, many lifetimes – by the fallen beings not to make this distinction.

What is the characteristic of fallen beings? They cannot make the dis-tinction between the outer self and the real self. They are identified with the outer self, the separate self. If they were able to make the distinction, they would know they are not the outer self. They would know they are part of the One Self of God. Therefore, they would not be completely trapped in the fallen consciousness.

They want all of you to see yourselves as they see themselves. This is the definition of the spiritual false hierarchy, the so-called power elite.

These are beings that long ago rejected the idea that God loves them. I could appear to such beings and tell them that I love them, but they would not be able to accept it, for if they were to accept it, they would be transformed by my love. They do not want to be transformed so their only option is to reject my love.

## The lie of conditional love

What have they done to you? They have made you believe that my love is conditional, is conditioned upon you living up to certain conditions that they have defined. Thereby, they have made themselves like God because they have said: "We are capable of defining the conditions that even God must obey before he gives love to the human beings in embodiment on earth." This, of course, is all a lie, all an illusion, but how will you see this? How will the people of Europe see this when their leaders, for so many centuries, have been telling them something different?

You, of course, have started to see this. I am well aware of this, but what I want to point out to you is that there are still certain pockets in your being. This goes for all of you with no exception, including the messenger who is speaking these words. You have pockets in your being where you cannot fully love yourself. This is what I would like to address.

I have had you make the distinction between the inner self and the outer, or the separate, self. We do this for a reason. We realize that, because of the heavy programming, we cannot start you out having you love the outer self. You have been programmed, conditioned, to think that God's love is conditional. You think you could not possibly love the outer self, that God could not possibly love the outer self.

You look at me as Mother Mary, as an ascended being, as the representative of the Divine Mother, and in your minds you elevate me to being above you either in position or at least in consciousness. In a certain sense I am, of course, above you because I hold a position in the cosmic hierarchy that is higher than any unascended being can hold. I also, of course, have ascended so my consciousness is higher. But I am not higher in the sense of the fallen beings and their value judgments. I am one with the One Mind, the All, and you are one with that One Mind. You have been programmed by those who deny this reality to think that you are not, and so you elevate me in your minds.

## A new view of the outer self

You may look at the idea that I hold the immaculate concept for you, and you may feel or think that I look at the highest possible vision, at your highest potential, at how you would be in the fullness of your Christhood. You may think this is what I see and what I love. Many of you have an often-unrecognized desire to hide aspects of your human self from me because you think that if I saw that aspect of the human self, then I could not love that human self. You might even think that I would condemn you, reject you, scold you or spank you (or however you see the Mother). You see, my beloved, what I would like to do in this discourse is to challenge the view you have of me and of yourself.

It is true that you have to start out by realizing that you are more than the outer self, the outer personality. You have to start separating yourself from that outer personality because that is how you connect to your higher self. Most of you have started this process. Some of you have made good progress in this process. What I give you here is the next step up. This is where you start looking at the outer self differently. You do not look at it as an enemy of your spiritual growth. You do not look at it as something so bad, evil or impure that I would condemn you for having it.

It is perfectly valid that we have given you the impression that your ego is opposing your spiritual growth and you need to get beyond it, to transcend it. We have in earlier teachings given you the concept of the "dweller on the threshold" that needs to be bound and slain. These are all valid concepts. I am not here invalidating anything said previously, but I am pointing out to you that in the process of progressive revelation, in the process of a progressive spiritual path, there are stages.

There comes a point where you need to question the teaching that you have used at a lower level of the path. It is not that you come to see it as wrong or invalid. You realize that any teaching given in words can only have certain limitations. It can so easily be interpreted in ways that can take you only so far on the path. It is as if that teaching can take you to a certain level, but it cannot take you beyond that level. It can actually become a closed circle that keeps you at a certain level. I want to give you a new way of looking at yourself—your outer self and your inner self. You may have situations in your daily life where you get upset over certain things. You may get irritated, you may get angry, you may be afraid, you may have other patterns. You feel that this is not your highest potential, not the way you ideally should be. You feel that you would rather that I not see you in those situations. Many of you have compartmentalized your lives a little bit. This is seen in an extreme form, for example, in many Christians, who – as the popular saying goes – go to church on Sunday and confess their sins, and then they can go out and sin with good conscience the other six days of the week. Almost all of the people in embodiment have done this to some degree. You separate church and state, so to speak. You separate your spiritual quest from your daily life.

## Transcending self-judgment

You all have a routine, or at least most of you have a routine, of giving certain decrees and invocations. Many of you have gotten good at setting aside the time, going into a separate space, giving your decrees and invocations. When you feel you are in this controlled environment where you are doing something spiritual, then you would like me to be there and watch you. When you are yelling at the kids or losing your harmony at work, you would prefer that I was not there, that I did not see it. Why do *you* make this distinction? Do you think that *I* make a distinction? Do you think that I can stand here and say that I love you and my love is unconditional, yet there are some situations where you do something that is not according to your vision of what a spiritual person should do, and in those situations I no longer love you? Yes, that is how many of you think because that is how the ego thinks. That is how the outer self is programmed to think. It can see only conditional love.

I make no such distinction. I have no value judgments, at least not what you call value judgments. What I desire to give you is this concept that you need to start looking at yourself, your outer self, your normal daily behavior, in a different way. Try to break down the separation so that you allow yourself to be free from this tendency to judge yourself. Try to ask yourself why you judge, why you have an idea that as a spiritual person, as an ascended master student, you should always behave such and such, and you should never do this or that.

You understand, my beloved, that I have been in physical embodiment on earth. You may have a wonderful image based on the many portraits of me where I sit with this immaculate baby on my lap that is the Christ Child. You may think, based on these glorified images, that when I was in embodiment —when Jesus was little, when there were other children in the house – my house was always perfectly clean, perfectly orderly, and I never raised my voice to the children. You may think so, but that was not the case. I was in my last embodiment at the time, as many of you are. I had considerable spiritual attainment, but I can assure you that there were times when I lost my head, so to speak. I got irritated with the children, I got irritated with Joseph, and sometimes I yelled at them.

This may shock you, but what I am pointing out to you is that I was a human being in embodiment on a very dense planet in a very tense situation. You are also in a very tense situation in these very intense decades where we are transitioning between the Age of Pisces and the Age of Aquarius. I can assure you that anybody who is a spiritual person, who is striving for a higher consciousness, is being subjected to a tremendous pressure, a tremendous amount of projections, in this time.

There are forces that do not want you to succeed. They do not want you to raise your consciousness. They do not want you to manifest your Christhood. They are desperate to make you hold on to some idea that – because of some flaw you have, because of some mistake you made yesterday or 30 years ago – you are not worthy to represent the ascended masters, to express your Christhood, to take a stand for anything that will improve life on earth. They are desperate to make you hold on to that illusion.

I ask you to look at your outer self differently. As I said, there is a period on the path where it is constructive to look at your ego, the outer self, as something that opposes your growth, that holds back your growth, that needs to be dealt with. You need to make the calls for the energies to be transmuted. You need to come to see the illusions. You may need to make the calls for Archangel Michael to bind your dweller, to bind your ego, to bind all kinds of dark forces attacking you through that ego and through that dweller.

These are all legitimate steps to take, but when you have taken those steps and you come to the next level, this is no longer constructive. It is not that your outer self and your ego are no longer opposing your path. They *are*—if you let them. That is what I want to communicate to you: "Stop letting them."

## Making the ego inconsequential

The way to do this is to look at your outer self, your ego, not as an *enemy* of your spiritual growth, not as an *ally* of your spiritual growth but as *inconsequential* for your spiritual growth. You need to look at them and say: "I acknowledge that I have this tendency. I see that this is part of my outer self, but it is not who I am. It is not going to define me, and it is not going to hold me back on my path. It is *not* going to make me hide from Mother Mary."

You see, my beloved, I am in complete acceptance of the Law of Free Will and your individual free will. If you say: "Mother Mary, I don't want you to look at me in this situation," then I will not look at you. But when I do not look at you, I cannot help you, my beloved. I cannot look away from you and hold the immaculate concept for you at the same time. You are asking me, in effect, *not* to hold that immaculate concept for you precisely in the situations where you need me to do so.

Do you see? When you are in perfect harmony and perfectly at peace, you do not really need me to hold the immaculate concept for you, do you? It is when you are out of harmony that you need me to hold the balance for you. In those situations you so often, without realizing it, are saying: "Oh, Mother Mary, don't look now. Leave me alone." You think that, if I saw you in that state, I would not love you.

When I say: "I love you," I do not make the distinction between the outer and the inner self. Of course, I know who you are. I know that the inner self is real. I know that the outer self is unreal, but right now it is part of your total being, and I love you as a totality, as the total being that you are.

I recognize a very simple fact, which I have from my own experience: When we are in embodiment in an unascended sphere, especially on a planet as dense as earth, we cannot avoid having an outer self. You cannot be in embodiment on a planet like earth and be completely free of an outer self because you could not stand being here. There are so many things happening on this planet right now that, if you were to fully acknowledge them, you simply could not handle being in embodiment. Your compassion would literally almost scatter your aura because you would want to help all of these people who are suffering.

Your outer self is almost like a protection so that you can be on this planet. You can function in terms of your daily life, but also in terms of focusing on raising your own consciousness. In order to do this on a planet like this, you need to have a shield around you. You almost need to have blinders on so that you do not see all of the things that are going on. It is simply a necessary defense mechanism.

## Why you need to love the human self

Of course, I also know that, when you have this outer self, the outer self is what it is. It is born of the duality consciousness. It has an internal conflict, it has an internal division, and this will pull you in different directions. There will be outer situations where it just gets too much for you. It is just too overwhelming when the children are screaming and will not listen, and it is so easy to get irritated. I did it myself, my beloved.

I do not know what you really imagine about the beings who have ascended from a planet like earth. You may think that Jesus was the perfect human being when he was in embodiment, but I have told you before that he was not. He could also get out of harmony. He could also lose his temper. He could be very short, very direct, almost irritable, when people approached him. I understand why. He was so focused within that, when someone pulled on his attention, it was too much for him to bridge the two worlds.

You may think that El Morya, or Master MORE, in his last embodiment was always cool, calm and collected. If you look at some of his previous embodiments, you see that he would also sometimes get overwhelmed by the energies and react in various ways. You have all thought about Saint Germain as the Wonderman of Europe. Yes, when he did get a dispensation to manifest a physical body, he was in the ascended state of consciousness, and he was always cool, calm and collected. But that was after he had qualified for his ascension. Before that, he was not always in total harmony.

None of us who have ascended have done so by being perfect according to some standard defined by the fallen beings. We have ascended by coming to a point where we realized that this fallen standard is not going to define me anymore, and that means only one thing: Whatever human self you have left, you need to love it. There comes a point where you need to love your human self, your outer self, your ego, your dweller on the threshold, whatever you want to call it. As I said, there is a stage on the path where you need to see it as the opponent of your spiritual growth. You need to separate yourself from it. When you have separated yourself from it to a certain degree, if you still at that point continue to see it as an opponent, as an enemy, you are still letting it define you. When you are completely blinded by your outer self, it is defining you, but when you are opposing it, seeing it as an enemy of your spiritual growth, it is also defining you, although in a different way.

You come to this point where you realize that the next step is that you no longer see it as an enemy. You realize it cannot define you, cannot stop your path. At that point, if you do not see it as an enemy, your logical step is to love it. Surely it is difficult to love something that you see as your enemy. In order to be completely free of that enemy, you have to come to a point where you do what Jesus told people to do 2,000 years ago: love your enemies. Then, they cannot define you.

What is it that defines you, my beloved? You are spiritual beings; what is a spiritual being? A spiritual being in embodiment is ideally an open door for unconditional love. What happens when you think you have an enemy, and you say: "I cannot love that enemy, I cannot express love towards that enemy?" You are letting the enemy cause you to shut off the flow of unconditional love through you. You are letting that enemy *define* you because now you are no longer a spiritual being who sees yourself as an open door for unconditional love. You see yourself as something else, something lesser.

Love your enemies—then you will be free from them and the consciousness they represent. You will be free to be what you are: an open door for unconditional love. You will be free to accept fully, with all of your being, that God loves you, that *I* love you. Then you can love yourself. You can love both the "your" part and the "self" part.

## Making peace with having an outer self

There comes a point where you are making a distinction between the outer self and the real self, between what is real and what is unreal. You no longer need to hide the unreal self from me or from yourself. You see it as unreal, you see that it does not define you, but you are not threatened by it. You are not even really concerned about it. It is not even really important. You may say with the linear mind that I am contradicting myself and what

I said earlier, but when you go beyond the linear mind, you see that I am talking about a progression. There is a stage where you need to separate yourself from the outer self, and you do that by seeing yourself as distinct from the outer self. There also comes a point where you need to transcend the outer self, and, my beloved, contrary to what most of you tend to think, this does not mean that you have no outer self.

It means that you come to the point where the outer self you have left is just enough to keep you in embodiment. Therefore, it is no longer a threat to your spiritual progress or to your service to other people. At that point, you do not need to be concerned with it anymore. You do not need to continue to analyze it and try to expose it and try to find out: "What is my ego? What is going on? What is it I am believing?" All of these tools are valid, but there comes a point where it is no longer necessary to be so concerned with and focused on them.

There is, of course, a balance to be found. We do not want you to go back into being identified with the outer self and not seeing things you need to overcome. You can come to the point where you have made peace with the fact that, as long as you are in embodiment, you have certain aspects of the outer self. If you once in a while fall into that pattern, then you do not need to condemn yourself.

You do not need to think the whole epic mindset that now, you have made a mistake that you can never overcome. Now, Mother Mary is not going to love you, she is not going to approach you for three months, or whatever you think. You do not need to punish yourself. You do not need to impose some kind of penance on yourself: "Now I have to recite 350 Hail Marys because I yelled at the children," or whatever people do. They think they can somehow compensate, and then I will suddenly love them again once they have done this mechanical thing or lit so many candles in the church.

You need to come to the point where you realize that this is not how I think, this is not how I feel, this is not how I look at you. I am an ascended master. I am not a fallen being. I do not look at you as the fallen beings do. Please, if you love me, stop projecting onto me that I look at you as the fallen beings do, because I do not!

Do I sound stern? It is because I want to cut through this resistance of the outer self, which will not acknowledge that I am not like the image of me created by the fallen beings. I am an ascended being. I refuse to conform to the images of the fallen beings. I absolutely refuse. Therefore, when I have a messenger who is willing to be the open door, I will speak in the physical. Billions of people need to hear: I am a God-free being. I am not bound by the consciousness of human beings in embodiment or fallen beings in and out of embodiment. I am free of it. I want you to be free of it. You cannot be completely free – I cannot help you to the maximum degree – if you will not realize that I am not affected by this.

## Rejecting unconditional love

My love is *not* conditional. There are people who absolutely refuse to acknowledge unconditional love. They are found everywhere in churches and spiritual movements and elsewhere. Either they are fallen beings in embodiment or they are totally blinded by the fallen consciousness. There is no other explanation. God never has and never will conform to the consciousness of the fallen beings or unascended beings.

One of the most severe manifestations of anti-love is to think that someone in embodiment on a planet as dense as earth can define how God is going to act, think or look at life. It is complete and utter spiritual pride. There are fallen beings in embodiment and in the astral plane, in the mental plane and in the identity realm of planet earth who think they are high and sophisticated beings. As Jesus said: "By their fruits ye shall know them."

Just look at what is happening on planet earth, and you will see that this cannot be a very high planet. If it is not a very high planet, then none of the fallen beings associated with earth can be very sophisticated beings— except in their own minds. It is not rocket science to see that on a planet with so many manifestations of anti-love, so much war, so much conflict, those who are creating this cannot be very sophisticated beings. So stop following them.

Stop thinking that they have the capacity or the authority to define how the ascended masters think or feel, or what the ascended masters should say or should not say, or through which messenger they should speak or through which messenger they should not speak.

I cannot help those who, even though they acknowledge me as an ascended master, are projecting a fallen image onto me. I cannot help you because I cannot and will not violate your free will, even though it is not a conscious decision you are making. Therefore, I cannot hold the immaculate concept for you in the situations where you need it the most. There are people who believe they are spiritual, even ascended master students, who are almost constantly in a state of consciousness that is not their highest potential. They need me to hold the immaculate concept for them, but they will not let me do so. The consequence is that their consciousness becomes a self-reinforcing closed spiral. They believe they are making progress. They believe they are going to make their ascension in this life. They are exactly like the Christians who believe that Jesus will save them at the end of this lifetime, and they will go to heaven because they have been good Christians.

## Shifting consciousness and the ascension

If you have not shifted your consciousness, how can you enter the ascended realm? There is no other criterion, my beloved, than your state of consciousness. There is no outer thing you could do to qualify. Do you not understand this?

This is a consequence of the fact that God's love is unconditional. This also means there is nothing you could do on earth, there is no condition you could define and live up to on earth, that would force God to let you into the Kingdom. You will enter the Kingdom when you stop trying to force God to let you in and accept that God will let you in when you no longer have any conditions in your mind that define how you or God should behave.

I am not here saying that you can do anything you want. When you are in oneness with your I AM Presence and your higher self, you will not want to do most of the things that human beings do. It will not be because you are forcing yourself to *not* do it based on some spiritual ideal. It will be because you naturally do not choose to do it. There is no artificial evaluation on your part based on what you *should* or *should not* do. You are simply flowing with your self, with your higher self.

## Moving on instead of analyzing

This is a dense planet. Life gets messy sometimes, and you have these situations where, even though you may have reached a high level of the spiritual path, you still fall below. You still get irritated. You still get out of sorts. What I am saying is that there is a period on the path where you need to look at these situations and the pattern and find out what the pattern is and go after it. There comes a higher stage where you need to allow yourself to, once in a while, be imperfect. Then, instead of condemning yourself, instead of over-analyzing: "Why did I do this?" you just simply move on. You just move on.

If you are out walking and it starts raining and you come into the house with drops of water on your coat, do you condemn yourself for having water on your coat? Do you over-analyze why this water would stick to your coat, or do you just simply shake it off, hang up your coat, and get on with your daily business?

My beloved, please stop thinking that I look at you and judge you as you judge yourself. I judge no man and no woman. I have no judgment towards any being, even the darkest fallen being you could imagine. I have no judgment. I love you without any conditions. I love the totality of who you are. I realize that part of the path of growth in an unascended sphere, especially on a planet as dense as earth, is that you go into the human consciousness and live it out until you have had enough of the experience. Then you separate yourself from it and say: "I no longer want this. This is no longer me. This does not define me."

This is just part of the path, my beloved. Give yourself freedom from always judging, evaluating, analyzing. Work towards a point where you can see yourself do something that was not perfect but, instead of condemning and analyzing yourself, you just look at it and say: "So what?" Then, you move on.

Now, if you listen carefully, my beloved, you will hear all of the demons in the astral plane howling at you right now that you must not accept what I am saying: "You must not believe this. This must be a false teaching. This cannot be right." They are desperate to make you reject what I am saying because your rejection of unconditional love is the only hold they have over you. If you can let go of this illusion, most of you will be free in a way you have never been before. You will be free just to be yourselves.

Why do you think I want you to be someone else? Why do you think I want you to live up to some norm, some image, of how an ascended master student, a spiritual person, should be? I see that God has given you, each one of you, a unique individuality. I want you to express that individuality to the greatest extent possible in your daily lives. I want you to bring the gift to this planet that you decided you wanted to bring before you came into embodiment.

I do not want you to conform to some outer standard of what a spiritual person should be. I want you to be who you are. You cannot be who you are if you are always judging and analyzing and thinking you should live up to some outer standard and norm. I cannot hold the immaculate concept for you if you think that I am the one who has imposed this standard upon you.

Please, my beloved, stop thinking you have to hide anything from me. I am a very experienced mother. I have seen everything that naughty children could possibly do, absolutely everything, starting with Jesus who could be extremely naughty. Do not think you can surprise me. Do not think you can make me turn away from you.

I wish there were words that I could say that could reach into your mind and turn the dial of consciousness so that it would just click and you would be free. I know there are no such words. Therefore, I have to give you words you can hear, hoping that over time you will allow them to sprout and grow to the point that the rose of the heart unfolds and you can accept the love behind the words. This is the love that cannot be carried by the words and the love that cannot be confined to the words, the love that I AM.

*I love you.* Will you love yourself as I love you?

# 2 | INVOKING FREEDOM
# FROM ANTI-LOVE

In the name I AM THAT I AM, Jesus Christ, I call to all representatives of the Divine Mother, especially Mother Mary, to help me overcome the illusions of anti-love. Help me see the lies and wounds that prevent me from accepting the unconditional love of the Divine Mother, including...

[Make personal calls.]

*Part 1*

1. Mother Mary, help me know you as an ascended master and know that you are the Divine Mother for me.

O blessed Mary, Mother mine,
there is no greater love than thine,
as we are one in heart and mind,
my place in hierarchy I find.

**O Mother Mary, generate,**
**the song that does accelerate,**
**the earth into a higher state,**
**all matter does now scintillate.**

2. Mother Mary, help me know and truly experience that you love me.

I came to earth from heaven sent,
as I am in embodiment,
I use Divine authority,
commanding you to set earth free.

**O Mother Mary, generate,**
**the song that does accelerate,**
**the earth into a higher state,**
**all matter does now scintillate.**

3. Mother Mary, help me feel your love for me and then use that as a foundation for loving myself.

I call now in God's sacred name,
for you to use your Mother Flame,
to burn all fear-based energy,
restoring sacred harmony.

**O Mother Mary, generate,**
**the song that does accelerate,**
**the earth into a higher state,**
**all matter does now scintillate.**

4. Mother Mary, help me make a distinction between the outer personality, the outer self, and the inner being, the inner self.

Your sacred name I hereby praise,
collective consciousness you raise,
no more of fear and doubt and shame,
consume it with your Mother Flame.

**O Mother Mary, generate,**
**the song that does accelerate,**
**the earth into a higher state,**
**all matter does now scintillate.**

5. Mother Mary, help me begin to accept that I can love the self, not the outer personality, but the self that I am.

All darkness from the earth you purge,
your light moves as a mighty surge,
no force of darkness can now stop,
the spiral that goes only up.

**O Mother Mary, generate,**
**the song that does accelerate,**
**the earth into a higher state,**
**all matter does now scintillate.**

6. Mother Mary, help me overcome the programming from the fallen beings that prevents me from knowing that I am more than the outer self.

All elemental life you bless,
removing from them man-made stress,
the nature spirits are now free,
outpicturing Divine decree.

**O Mother Mary, generate,**
**the song that does accelerate,**
**the earth into a higher state,**
**all matter does now scintillate.**

7. Mother Mary, I call forth the judgment of the Divine Mother upon the fallen beings who are identified with the separate self and reject the truth that they are part of the One Self of God.

I raise my voice and take my stand,
a stop to war I do command,
no more shall warring scar the earth,
a golden age is given birth.

**O Mother Mary, generate,**
**the song that does accelerate,**
**the earth into a higher state,**
**all matter does now scintillate.**

8. Mother Mary, I call forth the judgment of the Divine Mother upon the spiritual false hierarchy, the power elite, the beings who have rejected the idea that God loves them.

As Mother earth is free at last,
disasters belong to the past,
your Mother Light is so intense,
that matter is now far less dense.

**O Mother Mary, generate,**
**the song that does accelerate,**
**the earth into a higher state,**
**all matter does now scintillate.**

9. Mother Mary, I call forth the judgment of the Divine Mother upon the fallen beings who have made themselves like God because they have said: "We are capable of defining the conditions that even God must obey before he gives love to the human beings in embodiment on earth."

In Mother Light the earth is pure,
the upward spiral will endure,
prosperity is now the norm,
God's vision manifest as form.

**O Mother Mary, generate,**
**the song that does accelerate,**
**the earth into a higher state,**
**all matter does now scintillate.**

## Part 2

1. Mother Mary, help me transcend the lie of the fallen beings that God's love is conditional, is conditioned upon me living up to certain conditions that they have defined.

> O blessed Mary, Mother mine,
> there is no greater love than thine,
> as we are one in heart and mind,
> my place in hierarchy I find.
>
> **O Mother Mary, generate,**
> **the song that does accelerate,**
> **the earth into a higher state,**
> **all matter does now scintillate.**

2. Mother Mary, help me resolve the pockets in my being where I cannot fully love myself.

> I came to earth from heaven sent,
> as I am in embodiment,
> I use Divine authority,
> commanding you to set earth free.
>
> **O Mother Mary, generate,**
> **the song that does accelerate,**
> **the earth into a higher state,**
> **all matter does now scintillate.**

3. Mother Mary, help me overcome the sense that you are so much higher than me based on the dualistic scale of the fallen beings. Help me know that we are all one with the One Mind of God.

> I call now in God's sacred name,
> for you to use your Mother Flame,
> to burn all fear-based energy,
> restoring sacred harmony.

**O Mother Mary, generate,**
**the song that does accelerate,**
**the earth into a higher state,**
**all matter does now scintillate.**

4. Mother Mary, help me overcome all desires to hide aspects of my human self from you because I think that if you saw that aspect of the human self, then you could not love that outer self.

Your sacred name I hereby praise,
collective consciousness you raise,
no more of fear and doubt and shame,
consume it with your Mother Flame.

**O Mother Mary, generate,**
**the song that does accelerate,**
**the earth into a higher state,**
**all matter does now scintillate.**

5. Mother Mary, help me overcome the sense that you would condemn me, reject me, scold me or spank me. Help me start separating myself from the outer personality and connect to my higher self.

All darkness from the earth you purge,
your light moves as a mighty surge,
no force of darkness can now stop,
the spiral that goes only up.

**O Mother Mary, generate,**
**the song that does accelerate,**
**the earth into a higher state,**
**all matter does now scintillate.**

6. Mother Mary, help me start looking at the outer self differently so I do not see it as an enemy of my spiritual growth. I do not look at it as something so bad, evil or impure that you would condemn me for having it.

All elemental life you bless,
removing from them man-made stress,

the nature spirits are now free,
outpicturing Divine decree.

**O Mother Mary, generate,**
**the song that does accelerate,**
**the earth into a higher state,**
**all matter does now scintillate.**

7. Mother Mary, help me overcome the tendency to compartmentalize my life and want to hide certain things from you because I do not accept that your love truly is without conditions.

I raise my voice and take my stand,
a stop to war I do command,
no more shall warring scar the earth,
a golden age is given birth.

**O Mother Mary, generate,**
**the song that does accelerate,**
**the earth into a higher state,**
**all matter does now scintillate.**

8. Mother Mary, help me allow myself to be free from the tendency to judge myself. Help me see why I judge and why I have the idea that I have to judge my behavior according to an outer standard.

As Mother earth is free at last,
disasters belong to the past,
your Mother Light is so intense,
that matter is now far less dense.

**O Mother Mary, generate,**
**the song that does accelerate,**
**the earth into a higher state,**
**all matter does now scintillate.**

9. Mother Mary, help me see that I live in a very tense situation where the planet is transitioning between the Age of Pisces and the Age of Aquarius. I am being subjected to a tremendous pressure, a tremendous amount of projections.

> In Mother Light the earth is pure,
> the upward spiral will endure,
> prosperity is now the norm,
> God's vision manifest as form.
>
> **O Mother Mary, generate,**
> **the song that does accelerate,**
> **the earth into a higher state,**
> **all matter does now scintillate.**

## Part 3

1. Mother Mary, help me see that there are forces that do not want me to succeed. They are desperate to make me hold on to some idea that – because of some flaw I have or some mistake I made – I am not worthy to take a stand for anything that will improve life on earth.

> O blessed Mary, Mother mine,
> there is no greater love than thine,
> as we are one in heart and mind,
> my place in hierarchy I find.
>
> **O Mother Mary, generate,**
> **the song that does accelerate,**
> **the earth into a higher state,**
> **all matter does now scintillate.**

2. Mother Mary, help me look at my outer self, my ego, not as an enemy of my spiritual growth, not as an ally of my spiritual growth, but as inconsequential for my spiritual growth.

I came to earth from heaven sent,
as I am in embodiment,
I use Divine authority,
commanding you to set earth free.

**O Mother Mary, generate,**
**the song that does accelerate,**
**the earth into a higher state,**
**all matter does now scintillate.**

3. Mother Mary, I now say: "I acknowledge that I have this tendency. I see that this is part of my outer self, but it is not who I am. It is not going to define me, and it is not going to hold me back on my path. It is not going to make me hide from Mother Mary."

I call now in God's sacred name,
for you to use your Mother Flame,
to burn all fear-based energy,
restoring sacred harmony.

**O Mother Mary, generate,**
**the song that does accelerate,**
**the earth into a higher state,**
**all matter does now scintillate.**

4. Mother Mary, help me see that you will respect my choice to hide from you, but then you cannot help me overcome the outer self.

Your sacred name I hereby praise,
collective consciousness you raise,
no more of fear and doubt and shame,
consume it with your Mother Flame.

**O Mother Mary, generate,**
**the song that does accelerate,**
**the earth into a higher state,**
**all matter does now scintillate.**

5. Mother Mary, help me stop rejecting your help in the situations where I need it the most, the situations where I am not in harmony.

> All darkness from the earth you purge,
> your light moves as a mighty surge,
> no force of darkness can now stop,
> the spiral that goes only up.

> **O Mother Mary, generate,**
> **the song that does accelerate,**
> **the earth into a higher state,**
> **all matter does now scintillate.**

6. Mother Mary, help me see that when you say that you love me, you do not make the distinction between the outer and the inner self. You love me as a totality, as the total being that I am.

> All elemental life you bless,
> removing from them man-made stress,
> the nature spirits are now free,
> outpicturing Divine decree.

> **O Mother Mary, generate,**
> **the song that does accelerate,**
> **the earth into a higher state,**
> **all matter does now scintillate.**

7. Mother Mary, help me accept that when I am in embodiment in an unascended sphere, especially on a planet as dense as earth, I cannot avoid having an outer self.

> I raise my voice and take my stand,
> a stop to war I do command,
> no more shall warring scar the earth,
> a golden age is given birth.

**O Mother Mary, generate,**
**the song that does accelerate,**
**the earth into a higher state,**
**all matter does now scintillate.**

8. Mother Mary, help me see that the outer self is almost like a protection so that I can be on this planet and function in terms of my daily life. The outer self is a necessary defense mechanism.

As Mother earth is free at last,
disasters belong to the past,
your Mother Light is so intense,
that matter is now far less dense.

**O Mother Mary, generate,**
**the song that does accelerate,**
**the earth into a higher state,**
**all matter does now scintillate.**

9. Mother Mary, help me see that no person who has ever ascended has done so by being perfect according to some standard defined by the fallen beings. They have ascended by deciding that this fallen standard is not going to define them anymore.

In Mother Light the earth is pure,
the upward spiral will endure,
prosperity is now the norm,
God's vision manifest as form.

**O Mother Mary, generate,**
**the song that does accelerate,**
**the earth into a higher state,**
**all matter does now scintillate.**

*Part 4*

1. Mother Mary, help me see that when I have separated myself from the human self to some degree, then whatever human self I have left, I need to love it.

> O blessed Mary, Mother mine,
> there is no greater love than thine,
> as we are one in heart and mind,
> my place in hierarchy I find.
>
> **O Mother Mary, generate,**
> **the song that does accelerate,**
> **the earth into a higher state,**
> **all matter does now scintillate.**

2. Mother Mary, help me see that when I am completely blinded by the outer self, it is defining me. When I am seeing it as an enemy of my spiritual growth, it is also defining me. I need to stop letting it define me.

> I came to earth from heaven sent,
> as I am in embodiment,
> I use Divine authority,
> commanding you to set earth free.
>
> **O Mother Mary, generate,**
> **the song that does accelerate,**
> **the earth into a higher state,**
> **all matter does now scintillate.**

3. Mother Mary, help me see that when I no longer see the outer self as an enemy, the next logical step is to love it.

> I call now in God's sacred name,
> for you to use your Mother Flame,
> to burn all fear-based energy,
> restoring sacred harmony.

**O Mother Mary, generate,**
**the song that does accelerate,**
**the earth into a higher state,**
**all matter does now scintillate.**

4. Mother Mary, help me see that I am a spiritual being. A spiritual being in embodiment is ideally an open door for unconditional love.

Your sacred name I hereby praise,
collective consciousness you raise,
no more of fear and doubt and shame,
consume it with your Mother Flame.

**O Mother Mary, generate,**
**the song that does accelerate,**
**the earth into a higher state,**
**all matter does now scintillate.**

5. Mother Mary, help me see that when I think I have an enemy that I cannot love, I am letting that enemy cut off the flow of unconditional love through my being. The enemy defines me by making me feel I am no longer a spiritual beings who is open to unconditional love.

All darkness from the earth you purge,
your light moves as a mighty surge,
no force of darkness can now stop,
the spiral that goes only up.

**O Mother Mary, generate,**
**the song that does accelerate,**
**the earth into a higher state,**
**all matter does now scintillate.**

6. Mother Mary, help me see that only by loving my enemies will I be free from the consciousness they represent. I will be free to be what I am, an open door for unconditional love.

All elemental life you bless,
removing from them man-made stress,

the nature spirits are now free,
outpicturing Divine decree.

**O Mother Mary, generate,**
**the song that does accelerate,**
**the earth into a higher state,**
**all matter does now scintillate.**

7. Mother Mary, help me accept fully that God loves me, that you love me.
Help me love myself, both the "my" part and the "self" part.

I raise my voice and take my stand,
a stop to war I do command,
no more shall warring scar the earth,
a golden age is given birth.

**O Mother Mary, generate,**
**the song that does accelerate,**
**the earth into a higher state,**
**all matter does now scintillate.**

8. Mother Mary, help me see that I no longer need to hide the unreal self
from you or from myself. Help me see it as unreal, see that it does not
define me. Help me no longer feel threatened by it, no longer see it as
important.

As Mother earth is free at last,
disasters belong to the past,
your Mother Light is so intense,
that matter is now far less dense.

**O Mother Mary, generate,**
**the song that does accelerate,**
**the earth into a higher state,**
**all matter does now scintillate.**

9. Mother Mary, help me see that transcending the outer self does not
mean that I have no outer self. It means that the outer self I have left is just
enough to keep me in embodiment. It does not define me.

In Mother Light the earth is pure,
the upward spiral will endure,
prosperity is now the norm,
God's vision manifest as form.

**O Mother Mary, generate,
the song that does accelerate,
the earth into a higher state,
all matter does now scintillate.**

## Part 5

1. Mother Mary, help me overcome the epic mindset that because I made a mistake, I can never overcome it and you are not going to love me.

O blessed Mary, Mother mine,
there is no greater love than thine,
as we are one in heart and mind,
my place in hierarchy I find.

**O Mother Mary, generate,
the song that does accelerate,
the earth into a higher state,
all matter does now scintillate.**

2. Mother Mary, help me overcome the mindset that if I punish myself and do a penance, you will love me again.

I came to earth from heaven sent,
as I am in embodiment,
I use Divine authority,
commanding you to set earth free.

**O Mother Mary, generate,
the song that does accelerate,
the earth into a higher state,
all matter does now scintillate.**

3. Mother Mary, help me realize that you do not think this way because you are an ascended master, not a fallen being.

> I call now in God's sacred name,
> for you to use your Mother Flame,
> to burn all fear-based energy,
> restoring sacred harmony.
>
> **O Mother Mary, generate,**
> **the song that does accelerate,**
> **the earth into a higher state,**
> **all matter does now scintillate.**

4. Mother Mary, I will stop projecting onto you that you look at me as the fallen beings do.

> Your sacred name I hereby praise,
> collective consciousness you raise,
> no more of fear and doubt and shame,
> consume it with your Mother Flame.
>
> **O Mother Mary, generate,**
> **the song that does accelerate,**
> **the earth into a higher state,**
> **all matter does now scintillate.**

5. Mother Mary, help me see through the resistance of the outer self and acknowledge that you are not like the image of God created by the fallen beings. You are an ascended being and you refuse to conform to the images of the fallen beings.

> All darkness from the earth you purge,
> your light moves as a mighty surge,
> no force of darkness can now stop,
> the spiral that goes only up.

**O Mother Mary, generate,**
**the song that does accelerate,**
**the earth into a higher state,**
**all matter does now scintillate.**

6. Mother Mary, help me know that you are a God-free being. You are not bound by the consciousness of human beings in embodiment or fallen beings in and out of embodiment.

All elemental life you bless,
removing from them man-made stress,
the nature spirits are now free,
outpicturing Divine decree.

**O Mother Mary, generate,**
**the song that does accelerate,**
**the earth into a higher state,**
**all matter does now scintillate.**

7. Mother Mary, help me see that you are free of the fallen consciousness. You want me to be free of it, but I cannot be completely free if I do not realize that you are not affected by the fallen consciousness.

I raise my voice and take my stand,
a stop to war I do command,
no more shall warring scar the earth,
a golden age is given birth.

**O Mother Mary, generate,**
**the song that does accelerate,**
**the earth into a higher state,**
**all matter does now scintillate.**

8. Mother Mary, help me see that your love is not conditional. People who refuse to acknowledge unconditional love are either fallen beings in embodiment or totally blinded by the fallen consciousness.

As Mother earth is free at last,
disasters belong to the past,

your Mother Light is so intense,
that matter is now far less dense.

**O Mother Mary, generate,**
**the song that does accelerate,**
**the earth into a higher state,**
**all matter does now scintillate.**

9. Mother Mary, help me see that God never has and never will conform to the consciousness of the fallen beings or unascended beings.

In Mother Light the earth is pure,
the upward spiral will endure,
prosperity is now the norm,
God's vision manifest as form.

**O Mother Mary, generate,**
**the song that does accelerate,**
**the earth into a higher state,**
**all matter does now scintillate.**

*Part 6*

1. Mother Mary, help me see that one of the most severe manifestations of anti-love is to think that someone in embodiment on a planet as dense as earth can define how God is going to act, think or look at life.

O blessed Mary, Mother mine,
there is no greater love than thine,
as we are one in heart and mind,
my place in hierarchy I find.

**O Mother Mary, generate,**
**the song that does accelerate,**
**the earth into a higher state,**
**all matter does now scintillate.**

2. Mother Mary, help me see that earth is not a very high planet and none of the fallen beings associated with earth are very sophisticated beings. This is proven by the many manifestations of anti-love, such as war and conflict. Help me to stop following the fallen beings.

> I came to earth from heaven sent,
> as I am in embodiment,
> I use Divine authority,
> commanding you to set earth free.
>
> **O Mother Mary, generate,**
> **the song that does accelerate,**
> **the earth into a higher state,**
> **all matter does now scintillate.**

3. Mother Mary, help me stop projecting a fallen image upon you so I can stop rejecting your help when I need it the most.

> I call now in God's sacred name,
> for you to use your Mother Flame,
> to burn all fear-based energy,
> restoring sacred harmony.
>
> **O Mother Mary, generate,**
> **the song that does accelerate,**
> **the earth into a higher state,**
> **all matter does now scintillate.**

4. Mother Mary, help me see that the only way to enter the ascended realm is to shift my consciousness. Nothing else will qualify me for salvation or the ascension.

> Your sacred name I hereby praise,
> collective consciousness you raise,
> no more of fear and doubt and shame,
> consume it with your Mother Flame.
>
> **O Mother Mary, generate,**
> **the song that does accelerate,**

**the earth into a higher state,
all matter does now scintillate.**

5. Mother Mary, help me see that because God's love is unconditional, there is nothing I could do on earth, there is no condition I could define and live up to, that would force God to let me into the Kingdom.

All darkness from the earth you purge,
your light moves as a mighty surge,
no force of darkness can now stop,
the spiral that goes only up.

**O Mother Mary, generate,
the song that does accelerate,
the earth into a higher state,
all matter does now scintillate.**

6. Mother Mary, help me see that I will enter the Kingdom when I stop trying to force God to let me in. Help me accept that God will let me in when I no longer have any conditions in my mind that define how I or God should behave.

All elemental life you bless,
removing from them man-made stress,
the nature spirits are now free,
outpicturing Divine decree.

**O Mother Mary, generate,
the song that does accelerate,
the earth into a higher state,
all matter does now scintillate.**

7. Mother Mary, help me come to the point of naturally acting based on oneness instead of trying to force myself to live up to an ideal defined by the fallen beings.

I raise my voice and take my stand,
a stop to war I do command,

no more shall warring scar the earth,
a golden age is given birth.

**O Mother Mary, generate,**
**the song that does accelerate,**
**the earth into a higher state,**
**all matter does now scintillate.**

8. Mother Mary, help me allow myself to, once in a while, be imperfect and instead of condemning myself or over-analyzing, I simply move on.

As Mother earth is free at last,
disasters belong to the past,
your Mother Light is so intense,
that matter is now far less dense.

**O Mother Mary, generate,**
**the song that does accelerate,**
**the earth into a higher state,**
**all matter does now scintillate.**

9. Mother Mary, help me realize that part of the path of growth in an unascended sphere, especially on a planet as dense as earth, is that I go into the human consciousness and live it out until I have had enough of the experience. Then, I separate myself from it and say: "I no longer want this. This is no longer me. This does not define me."

In Mother Light the earth is pure,
the upward spiral will endure,
prosperity is now the norm,
God's vision manifest as form.

**O Mother Mary, generate,**
**the song that does accelerate,**
**the earth into a higher state,**
**all matter does now scintillate.**

*Part 7*

1. Mother Mary, help me give myself freedom from always judging, evaluating and analyzing.

> O blessed Mary, Mother mine,
> there is no greater love than thine,
> as we are one in heart and mind,
> my place in hierarchy I find.
>
> **O Mother Mary, generate,**
> **the song that does accelerate,**
> **the earth into a higher state,**
> **all matter does now scintillate.**

2. Mother Mary, help me reach the point where I can see myself do something that was not perfect but, instead of condemning and analyzing myself, I just look at it and say: "So what?" And then I move on.

> I came to earth from heaven sent,
> as I am in embodiment,
> I use Divine authority,
> commanding you to set earth free.
>
> **O Mother Mary, generate,**
> **the song that does accelerate,**
> **the earth into a higher state,**
> **all matter does now scintillate.**

3. Mother Mary, help me see that the fallen beings are desperate to make me reject what you are saying because my rejection of unconditional love is the only hold they have over me.

> I call now in God's sacred name,
> for you to use your Mother Flame,
> to burn all fear-based energy,
> restoring sacred harmony.

**O Mother Mary, generate,**
**the song that does accelerate,**
**the earth into a higher state,**
**all matter does now scintillate.**

4. Mother Mary, help me let go of this illusion and be free in a way I have never been before. Help me be free just to be myself.

Your sacred name I hereby praise,
collective consciousness you raise,
no more of fear and doubt and shame,
consume it with your Mother Flame.

**O Mother Mary, generate,**
**the song that does accelerate,**
**the earth into a higher state,**
**all matter does now scintillate.**

5. Mother Mary, help me realize that you do not want me to be someone else. You do not want me to live up to some image of how a spiritual person should be.

All darkness from the earth you purge,
your light moves as a mighty surge,
no force of darkness can now stop,
the spiral that goes only up.

**O Mother Mary, generate,**
**the song that does accelerate,**
**the earth into a higher state,**
**all matter does now scintillate.**

6. Mother Mary, help me see that God has given me a unique individuality. You want me to express that individuality to the greatest extent possible in my daily life.

All elemental life you bless,
removing from them man-made stress,

the nature spirits are now free,
outpicturing Divine decree.

**O Mother Mary, generate,
the song that does accelerate,
the earth into a higher state,
all matter does now scintillate.**

7. Mother Mary, help me bring the gift to this planet that I wanted to bring before I came into embodiment.

I raise my voice and take my stand,
a stop to war I do command,
no more shall warring scar the earth,
a golden age is given birth.

**O Mother Mary, generate,
the song that does accelerate,
the earth into a higher state,
all matter does now scintillate.**

8. Mother Mary, help me see that you want me to be who I am. I cannot be who I am if I am always judging, analyzing and thinking I should live up to some outer standard and norm. Help me see that you have not imposed this standard upon me.

As Mother earth is free at last,
disasters belong to the past,
your Mother Light is so intense,
that matter is now far less dense.

**O Mother Mary, generate,
the song that does accelerate,
the earth into a higher state,
all matter does now scintillate.**

9. Mother Mary, help me turn the dial of consciousness so that it will click and I am free. Help me have the rose of the heart unfold until I can accept your love, the love that cannot be carried by words or confined to words, the love that you *are*. Help me love myself as you love me.

> In Mother Light the earth is pure,
> the upward spiral will endure,
> prosperity is now the norm,
> God's vision manifest as form.

> **O Mother Mary, generate,**
> **the song that does accelerate,**
> **the earth into a higher state,**
> **all matter does now scintillate.**

## Sealing

In the name of the Divine Mother, I call to Mother Mary for the sealing of myself and all people in my circle of influence in the creative flow of the Divine Mother, the River of Life. I call for the multiplication of my calls by all representatives of the Divine Mother, so that we form the perfect figure-eight flow of "As Above, so below." Thus, I accept that this is fully manifest, because the mouth of the Lord, the Divine Mother that I AM, has spoken it. Amen.

# 3 | YOUR ORIGINAL BIRTH

# TRAUMA

I AM indeed the Ascended Master MORE or, as I have been known in the past, M, Morya, El Morya, Bapu, or other names. What is in a name? I am more than any name. I am more than Master MORE. I am more than ever before. What could hold an ascended master to any image that can exist in the physical octave on a planet like earth? Nothing! Nothing, my beloved, could ever hold me. Whatever image anyone projects upon me, be they fallen beings or ascended master students – not that those two are necessarily mutually exclusive – I will be more than that image.

You will never reach me if you hold on to an image from the past. What is the past? One second ago is the past, my beloved. As quickly as you can think, it is the past. Do you realize that the human mind has a certain interval where it is capable of distinguishing time? It is very close to what you call a second, but you can actually distinguish shorter intervals.

*That* is the past. When that interval has passed, everything before is in the past. Now, you may say: "That interval is so short that my conscious mind cannot keep up. I cannot consciously think, 'Oh, this is in the past. Now I am in the present.'" Nay, you cannot, but why do you need to distinguish between past and present and future? Why does there need to be anything but now?

## *Why do you need time?*

Why do you need this separation, this division of time into past, present and future? Flow with the eternal now. Then you are being more than ever before, even though there is no before, there is no after, there is only now. This is the true joy of being in the flow of the River of Life.

The manifestations of anti-love are the ones that want to separate everything, divide everything up into these separate categories. Then they want to say that what happened in the past will affect the now and will determine the future.

Think about the Indian concept of karma where everything that happens in your life is predetermined by your karma from past lives. If that was the case, my beloved, what would be the entire purpose of life? Is it not to expand your consciousness? How do you expand your consciousness? By making choices. If everything in your present is determined by the past where is the room for choices?

You may say: "But my karma was created by me making choices in the past." Yes, that is true, but if your past choices could take away your ability to make choices in the now where would be the learning? Where would be the purpose of life? Would a loving God create a universe where you could make one choice that would take away your ability to undo that choice by making another choice? What kind of God would do this? Certainly not the God that I know.

It may be the god that the fallen beings have invented and that many people on earth worship because they think this god needs worshiping. My beloved, the false god created by the fallen beings *needs* to be worshiped by human beings because that god has no reality and therefore cannot receive the energy from the ascended realm that I am feeling flowing through me constantly. It needs energy from human beings, and that is why it needs to be worshiped. How could a formless God ever need anything from human beings on earth? Yes, the formless God needs one thing: It needs to give of itself, and it needs those who are willing to receive. That is what closes the figure-eight flow. *That,* the real God desires. Deity desires to flow, to become more through you when you are becoming more.

## How God becomes more

The Creator of the universe has already attained the Creator consciousness. It cannot become more by being more of a Creator. It becomes more by creating extensions of itself and sending them into the unascended sphere. Then, as they grow in consciousness, the Creator becomes more through you. Why would the Creator create a universe where you cannot become more, where there is a limitation to how much you can become more, where there is a limitation to what you can transcend? No God would do this—except the false god that has no reality.

I no longer pay any attention to those false gods. Why would you? Why would you think you need to?

Look at yourselves, my beloved, and be honest with yourselves. Almost every one of you has some false image of god that you are carrying with you, not only in this lifetime but from past lifetimes. I am not blaming you for this. It is almost inevitable, living on this planet for several lifetimes, to be indoctrinated, programmed with this false image of god.

I am not trying to find fault. I am not asking you to find fault with yourself. I am just asking you to recognize: "Oh, yes, I do tend to look at God a certain way, and obviously this is not the real God." Then decide you are willing to let it go. You are willing to be free of these images.

## Where you really came from

My beloved, how do the fallen beings keep you trapped in a separate self, in the duality consciousness? Do you realize that there was a time for most of you when you were in the etheric realm, looking at earth? Most of you who are spiritual people were not created to take your first embodiment on earth. You had embodied on other planets before.

You had come to a point where you had the free-will choice that you did not have to go back to your old planet. You could embody on another planet. You looked at earth and you saw the need because you saw how the original inhabitants had all been trapped in this veil, in this downward spiral. You saw that the only realistic way to change this was that someone would embody who was not trapped in the spiral, who had a higher level of consciousness and therefore could pull the inhabitants up. You looked at earth at whatever stage that was, and you decided that you wanted to come here and take embodiment.

For some people on earth, this is their first embodiment on this planet. Even some of the spiritual people that are mature souls, it is their first embodiment on this planet. Many souls have embodied for the first time on earth at this specific time because they wanted to help bring about the transition from Pisces to Aquarius, and they wanted to help Saint Germain manifest the Golden Age. Many of you have helped Saint Germain manifest a Golden Age on other planets before earth, and so you wanted to be part of it. There are also many of you who have been on this planet for many lifetimes.

Nevertheless, there came a point where you descended into embodiment for the first time on this planet. I can assure you – and I *need* to assure you because you have all suppressed the memory – that being in the etheric octave and looking down on earth is one thing. Yes, you can, of course, see that there are problems on earth. You can see there are many conditions that are not the way they should be. That is why you wanted to come and help. There is no way from the etheric octave that you can actually know how dense it is to be in embodiment on earth. It is impossible.

## The shock of taking embodiment

The moment you take physical embodiment for the first time, and the moment you become more conscious of what is happening on this planet, you will experience a shock. There is not one person who has taken embodiment (after the earth started its downward spiral) who has not experienced a severe shock at being in embodiment for the first time. You may know that there are people who talk about the shock of being born physically in this lifetime. Most people have suppressed it, and you can go back and re-experience it and thereby overcome this birth trauma. I am talking about a birth trauma of taking embodiment for the first time.

The fallen beings, at least some of them, are aware of what is going on. Some of them have the ability to track when a new lifestream comes into embodiment for the first time on earth. Those fallen beings are in the identity realm, but they have a hierarchy below them, a false hierarchy below them, that goes into the mental, the emotional and the physical. They have some ability to tune in to your lifestream, what kind of lifestream you are. Then they can instruct those below them, going all the way to the physical, to expose you to a situation that for you is the most severe, appalling, repulsive situation you could possibly imagine. They know exactly what is your worst-case scenario, and they will use their underlings, as we might call them, to put you in a physical situation where you are exposed to what you consider the worst thing that could happen to you.

Many people have been exposed to war, torture and other forms of abuse. This is a manifestation of anti-love that is a perversion of the first ray of power. The fallen beings in all four octaves cause you to be exposed to such an abuse of power that you find it absolutely appalling and shocking. You feel this should not happen to anybody. This simply should not be happening.

When you react this way, this is when you go into a state of shock. While you were in the etheric octave, you could see that there were things happening on the planet, but you were not in them, and you knew that you were not affected by what happened in the physical octave. When you come into physical embodiment, it is almost inevitable that you forget that you are a spiritual being who cannot be affected by what happens in the physical octave. When you are in the physical body, you are experiencing the pain, the trauma, the suffering of the physical body. You cannot keep the awareness that: "Oh, I am a spiritual being, and nothing that happens to the body defines me." There comes a point where the body is exposed to such torture, such pain, that it is virtually impossible for anyone to stay non-attached to this.

## The wound of total pain

There comes that point where the fallen beings have exposed you to such trauma that they force you to experience the full pain of it. You cannot remain non-attached. There is that state of total pain that we have all experienced the first time we took embodiment on this planet. This becomes a wound in your being, a wound in your soul, in your four lower bodies. It is a pain that seemed overwhelming to you at the time, and it *was* overwhelming to you, given your level of consciousness at the time.

I am not in any way blaming you. I reacted the same way when I first took embodiment. So did all who have taken embodiment. What I am seeking here is to help you acknowledge this cosmic birth trauma and free yourself from it. Some of you will have a sense of what this is. Some of you will be able to look at: "What is it that disturbs me the most on earth? What is the condition I really would like to eradicate? What is it I really feel should not be happening?"

You may not have been exposed to it in this lifetime, but you have seen other people be exposed to it and you are saying: "This really should not be going on." Well, this will tie into what happened to you in your first embodiment. If you will contemplate it, you will gain greater clarity on what it is in you.

Of course, it is not enough to contemplate. You need to recognize that there is a certain amount of energy that has been qualified through that wound. You need to make the calls to us, invoke the light to consume it, so that you come to the point where you can begin to look at it. I tell you truly: There is only one way to be free from this trauma. It is to do what neither your ego, nor the fallen beings, nor most human beings would want you to do—and that is to go straight back into it and re-experience it.

## The need to re-experience the trauma

There is no way to be free of any experience you have had on earth by running away from that experience and the pain that it caused. You cannot be free from anything by running away from it. You can be free only by going right into it and then experiencing that, because you have moved on in consciousness, it no longer defines you. You are no longer identified with it. You are no longer imprisoned by it. What the fallen beings want you to believe, what your ego wants you to believe, is that if you go into this original pain, you will die. You will be overwhelmed again. It will be too much for you. But, you see, you have moved on since you first came to this planet. Most of you have moved on way beyond in consciousness, and therefore it is the same as being an adult who goes back into a childhood trauma or birth trauma.

You can deal with it now because you realize that you are not having the same experience as you had the first time. You are not being overwhelmed. You are not completely going into the pain. You can distance yourself from it. When you go into it, you experience: "I'm still here. I'm still alive. I didn't die. I didn't become destroyed. I didn't become swallowed up by the pain. I am just standing here and looking at the swirling energy, and I am looking at the beliefs, and I am looking at all these beings in the astral plane, and I am realizing this is not me. This is just something that a part of me, the outer self, experienced. But I am more than this experience, and therefore I can look at it and say: 'You no longer own me. You no longer define me. This is not who I am. Get thee behind me, Satan, for I see your unreality, and I see and experience my own reality and the reality of the ascended masters.'"

## The masters will assist us

We are not saying you have to do this all by yourself. Whichever masters are close to your heart, we are here to assist you with this. We will assist you very far along the way. There does come a point when we cannot assist you anymore, where you must take that step on your own, that final step of confronting your own demons, as the popular saying goes, and seeing that they are not real.

You understand that what I am giving you here is the key to how the fallen beings trap people. They abuse the power they have in the physical octave to expose you to this trauma, this unreality that you think is reality, this idea that because of what happened to you in the past, this is determining, defining your present experience of life and what will happen to you in the future. That is what I aim to shatter in you—that illusion.

They are really saying that what you did with your will in the past has suspended what you can do with your will in the present and for all eternity. *That* is a manifestation of anti-love. I am determined to see you free from it if you are willing, but you have to supply the will. I cannot will for you.

Once you have willed, I can reinforce your choice. I can help you, but I cannot will you to make the choice. It is *your* choice to make, but you need to know. This is what I can do for you, give you the absolute knowledge that there is no choice that cannot be undone by making a higher choice. That is the eternal law. That is why it is possible to take a planet into the low state that you see on earth right now because there is no limitation to free will. This works both ways.

## We can uncreate what we have created

You can create any kind of misery you want, even the misery you do not consciously want. You can also *uncreate* any kind of misery you have created. You can be free from it.

I am free from any misery on earth. I am free from my birth trauma that followed me to my last embodiment, make no mistake of it. This will be the last thing you overcome before you are free to ascend because it was the first thing that trapped you in the lower state of consciousness. The challenge, the trap that they spring upon you, is that when you were exposed to this birth trauma, this first trauma, you were obviously experiencing that it was some outside force that forced this experience upon you. Indeed, it *was* an outside force in the physical that forced it upon you, namely, the fallen beings and their henchmen.

What the fallen beings have projected upon you is that you are here to overcome, to banish the forces that exposed you to this trauma so that other people are not exposed to it. They project upon you that you have to engage in some kind of struggle, some kind of battle, with these external forces. They want you to believe that once those forces are removed from the earth, you will be free of your trauma.

You see, my beloved, you did not invite those forces to come to earth. They were invited here by other choices, other beings who made choices. You cannot undo the choices of those other beings. What *can* you do? You can undo your own choices. You can realize that: "I am here to make a positive difference on this planet. But I do not make a positive difference by fighting the fallen beings and the forces of darkness. I make a positive difference by transcending their state of consciousness. How do I do this? By transcending the consciousness in myself that caused me to react to them in such a way that it gave me this original trauma."

This is your highest service on earth. When you free yourself from that state of consciousness, then you will pull up on the collective and pull up on all other people in embodiment. That is what you came here to do. Was it wrong, was it bad, that you reacted the way you did? Nay, you took it on, but you did not take it on to carry it with you forever. You did not take it on in order to have the impetus to fight the fallen beings. You took it on in order to demonstrate that whatever you have taken on – a condition in this world – you can transcend it. You can transcend it by your will power, your will to be free, your will to be more.

## Wanting us to be more

I am the Ascended Master MORE. All I want for you is for you to be more. When you have the will to be more, you are inviting me to come into your life and give you maximum help and support. I do not want to force you in any way. I just want you to know that I am here for you whenever you make the decision: "I will to be MORE."

As Mother Mary said – which is one of the most profound teachings you will ever hear – when you are not willing to be more, you are subconsciously saying: "Master MORE, leave me alone. I'm not done with experiencing what is less. I'm not ready for more yet." The moment you decide that you are ready for more, that is when I can truly assist you in a way that you cannot possibly dream about today.

I put no limitations on what can happen or how much more you can become. There can never, ever come a point where I would want to hold you back from becoming more. I am not afraid of you surpassing me, as many parents and teachers on earth are. I love nothing more than seeing you become more.

Also, I have no comparison. You cannot become more than me because you can only become more *than* yourself, more *of* yourself. That is how we all grow to realize that we are infinite beings. It is not a matter of comparison. In the ascended realm all comparisons and value judgments fall away. I am not more than Saint Germain. I am MORE and he is Germain, but one is not more than the other. I become more MORE and he becomes more Germain, and that is how it should be. There is no threat there. You become more *you*.

That is my desire for you. You have been so programmed on earth to think that you are less, that you should be less, that you have to be less, that you can only be less, that you are not allowed to be more. I tell you: "*You are!* You are allowed to be more." How can I say this? Because I am the Chohan of the First Ray. I am the one who determines how the First Ray can be expressed on earth, and I am giving you permission to be more. I am the only one who can give you that permission because that is my position in hierarchy, and I am giving you permission to be more than ever before.

With that, my beloved, I thank you for your attention, for your love, for your deep love that I feel that so many ascended master students have for me. Whatever name they choose to use, I respond to all of them. I still want you to know I am also more than all of them, as you are more than your name. For what can hold Spirit? Certainly not anything on a planet like earth.

Truly, I am Spirit, and so are you. In that awareness we are one. In fact, we are more than one because even oneness is a concept that can be said to have an opposite. What we really are can have no opposite. It just *is*.

# 4 | INVOKING FREEDOM FROM YOUR BIRTH TRAUMA

In the name I AM THAT I AM, Jesus Christ, I call to Master MORE and Mother Mary to heal me of the original birth trauma I encountered when I first took embodiment on earth and was exposed to the fallen consciousness. Help me overcome all wounds and illusions that prevent me from fulfilling my original reason for coming here, including...

[Make personal calls.]

*Part 1*

1. Master MORE, help me awaken to the reality that the manifestations of anti-love want to separate everything, divide everything up into separate categories. Then, they want to say that what happened in the past will affect the now and will determine the future.

Master MORE, come to the fore,
we will absorb your flame of MORE.
Master MORE, our will so strong,
our power centers cleared by song.

**Master MORE, your Sacred Heart,
from this we will no more depart,
we are forever in your flow,
of Diamond Will that you bestow.**

2. Master MORE, help me awaken to the reality that the purpose of life is to expand my consciousness. I expand my consciousness by making choices. If everything in the present is determined by the past where is the room for choices?

Master MORE, your wisdom flows,
as our attunement ever grows.
Master MORE, we have a tie,
that helps us see through Serpent's lie.

**Master MORE, your Sacred Heart,
from this we will no more depart,
we are forever in your flow,
of Diamond Will that you bestow.**

3. Master MORE, help me awaken to the reality that the fallen beings have invented a false god that many people on earth worship because they think this god needs worshiping.

Master MORE, your love so pink,
there is no purer love, we think.
Master MORE, you set us free,
from all conditionality.

**Master MORE, your Sacred Heart,
from this we will no more depart,
we are forever in your flow,
of Diamond Will that you bestow.**

4. Master MORE, help me awaken to the reality that the false god created by the fallen beings needs to be worshiped by human beings because that god has no reality and therefore cannot receive energy from the ascended realm.

> Master MORE, we will endure,
> your discipline that makes us pure.
> Master MORE, intentions true,
> as we are always one with you.

> **Master MORE, your Sacred Heart,**
> **from this we will no more depart,**
> **we are forever in your flow,**
> **of Diamond Will that you bestow.**

5. Master MORE, help me awaken to the reality that a formless God never needs anything from human beings on earth. The formless God needs to give of itself, and it needs those who are willing to receive.

> Master MORE, our vision raised,
> the will of God is always praised.
> Master MORE, creative will,
> raising all life higher still.

> **Master MORE, your Sacred Heart,**
> **from this we will no more depart,**
> **we are forever in your flow,**
> **of Diamond Will that you bestow.**

6. Master MORE, help me awaken to the reality that when we receive God, we close the figure-eight flow. Deity desires to flow, to become more through me when I am becoming more.

> Master MORE, your peace is power,
> the demons of war it will devour.
> Master MORE, we serve all life,
> our flames consuming war and strife.

**Master MORE, your Sacred Heart,
from this we will no more depart,
we are forever in your flow,
of Diamond Will that you bestow.**

7. Master MORE, help me awaken to the reality that the Creator consciousness becomes more by creating extensions of itself and sending them into the unascended sphere. As I grow in consciousness, the Creator becomes more through me.

Master MORE, we are so free,
eternal bond from you we see.
Master MORE, we find rebirth,
in flow of your eternal mirth.

**Master MORE, your Sacred Heart,
from this we will no more depart,
we are forever in your flow,
of Diamond Will that you bestow.**

8. Master MORE, help me awaken to the reality that the Creator has not created a universe where I cannot become more, where there is a limit to how much I can become more, where there is a limit to what I can transcend.

Master MORE, you balance all,
the seven rays upon our call.
Master MORE, forever MORE,
we are the Spirit's open door.

**Master MORE, your Sacred Heart,
from this we will no more depart,
we are forever in your flow,
of Diamond Will that you bestow.**

9. Master MORE, help me awaken to the reality that I do not need to pay attention to the false gods who need energy from me.

Master MORE, your Presence here,
filling up the inner sphere.
Life is now a sacred flow,
God Power we on all bestow.

**Master MORE, your Sacred Heart,
from this we will no more depart,
we are forever in your flow,
of Diamond Will that you bestow.**

## Part 2

1. Master MORE, help me awaken to the reality that I have some false image of God, not only from this lifetime but from past lifetimes. I have been indoctrinated and programmed with this false image of God.

Master MORE, come to the fore,
we will absorb your flame of MORE.
Master MORE, our will so strong,
our power centers cleared by song.

**Master MORE, your Sacred Heart,
from this we will no more depart,
we are forever in your flow,
of Diamond Will that you bestow.**

2. Master MORE, help me awaken to the reality that I tend to look at God a certain way, but that I can be free of these images.

Master MORE, your wisdom flows,
as our attunement ever grows.
Master MORE, we have a tie,
that helps us see through Serpent's lie.

**Master MORE, your Sacred Heart,
from this we will no more depart,
we are forever in your flow,
of Diamond Will that you bestow.**

3. Master MORE, help me awaken to the reality that I am a spiritual being who was not created to take my first embodiment on earth. I have embodied on other planets before.

Master MORE, your love so pink,
there is no purer love, we think.
Master MORE, you set us free,
from all conditionality.

**Master MORE, your Sacred Heart,
from this we will no more depart,
we are forever in your flow,
of Diamond Will that you bestow.**

4. Master MORE, help me awaken to the reality that at some point I looked at earth and saw how the original inhabitants had all been trapped in this veil, in this downward spiral. I saw that the only realistic way to change this was that someone would embody who was not trapped in the spiral.

Master MORE, we will endure,
your discipline that makes us pure.
Master MORE, intentions true,
as we are always one with you.

**Master MORE, your Sacred Heart,
from this we will no more depart,
we are forever in your flow,
of Diamond Will that you bestow.**

5. Master MORE, help me awaken to the reality that I have embodied on earth at this specific time because I wanted to help bring about the transition from Pisces to Aquarius, and I wanted to help Saint Germain manifest the Golden Age.

Master MORE, our vision raised,
the will of God is always praised.
Master MORE, creative will,
raising all life higher still.

**Master MORE, your Sacred Heart,
from this we will no more depart,
we are forever in your flow,
of Diamond Will that you bestow.**

6. Master MORE, help me awaken to the reality that when I first embodied on earth, and became more conscious of what is happening on this planet, I experienced a severe shock, a birth trauma.

Master MORE, your peace is power,
the demons of war it will devour.
Master MORE, we serve all life,
our flames consuming war and strife.

**Master MORE, your Sacred Heart,
from this we will no more depart,
we are forever in your flow,
of Diamond Will that you bestow.**

7. Master MORE, help me awaken to the reality that some of the fallen beings tracked me when I first took embodiment. They tuned in to my lifestream, and they instructed those below them in the false hierarchy to expose me to a situation that was the most severe, appalling, repulsive situation I could possibly imagine.

Master MORE, we are so free,
eternal bond from you we see.
Master MORE, we find rebirth,
in flow of your eternal mirth.

**Master MORE, your Sacred Heart,
from this we will no more depart,
we are forever in your flow,
of Diamond Will that you bestow.**

8. Master MORE, help me awaken to the reality that the fallen beings knew exactly what was my worst-case scenario. They used their underlings to put me in a physical situation where I was exposed to what I considered the worst thing that could happen to me.

Master MORE, you balance all,
the seven rays upon our call.
Master MORE, forever MORE,
we are the Spirit's open door.

**Master MORE, your Sacred Heart,**
**from this we will no more depart,**
**we are forever in your flow,**
**of Diamond Will that you bestow.**

9. Master MORE, help me awaken to the reality that when I first took embodiment, the fallen beings in all four octaves caused me to be exposed to such an abuse of power that I found it absolutely appalling and shocking. I felt this should not happen to anybody.

Master MORE, your Presence here,
filling up the inner sphere.
Life is now a sacred flow,
God Power we on all bestow.

**Master MORE, your Sacred Heart,**
**from this we will no more depart,**
**we are forever in your flow,**
**of Diamond Will that you bestow.**

*Part 3*

1. Master MORE, help me awaken to the reality that when I reacted this way, I went into a state of shock.

Master MORE, come to the fore,
we will absorb your flame of MORE.

Master MORE, our will so strong,
our power centers cleared by song.

**Master MORE, your Sacred Heart,
from this we will no more depart,
we are forever in your flow,
of Diamond Will that you bestow.**

2. Master MORE, help me awaken to the reality that while I was in the etheric octave, I could see that there were things happening on the planet, but I was not in them, and I knew I was not affected by what happened in the physical octave.

Master MORE, your wisdom flows,
as our attunement ever grows.
Master MORE, we have a tie,
that helps us see through Serpent's lie.

**Master MORE, your Sacred Heart,
from this we will no more depart,
we are forever in your flow,
of Diamond Will that you bestow.**

3. Master MORE, help me awaken to the reality that when I came into physical embodiment, it was almost inevitable that I forgot that I am a spiritual being who cannot be affected by what happens in the physical octave.

Master MORE, your love so pink,
there is no purer love, we think.
Master MORE, you set us free,
from all conditionality.

**Master MORE, your Sacred Heart,
from this we will no more depart,
we are forever in your flow,
of Diamond Will that you bestow.**

4. Master MORE, help me awaken to the reality that when I was in the physical body, I experienced the pain, the trauma, the suffering, of the physical body. I could not keep the awareness that: "Oh, I am a spiritual being, and nothing that happens to the body defines me."

Master MORE, we will endure,
your discipline that makes us pure.
Master MORE, intentions true,
as we are always one with you.

**Master MORE, your Sacred Heart,
from this we will no more depart,
we are forever in your flow,
of Diamond Will that you bestow.**

5. Master MORE, help me awaken to the reality that there came a point where the body was exposed to such torture, such pain, that it was virtually impossible for me to stay non-attached to this.

Master MORE, our vision raised,
the will of God is always praised.
Master MORE, creative will,
raising all life higher still.

**Master MORE, your Sacred Heart,
from this we will no more depart,
we are forever in your flow,
of Diamond Will that you bestow.**

6. Master MORE, help me awaken to the reality that there came a point where the fallen beings had exposed me to such trauma that they forced me to experience the full pain of it. I could not remain non-attached.

Master MORE, your peace is power,
the demons of war it will devour.
Master MORE, we serve all life,
our flames consuming war and strife.

**Master MORE, your Sacred Heart,**
**from this we will no more depart,**
**we are forever in your flow,**
**of Diamond Will that you bestow.**

7. Master MORE, help me awaken to the reality that there was a state of total pain that I experienced the first time I took embodiment on this planet.

Master MORE, we are so free,
eternal bond from you we see.
Master MORE, we find rebirth,
in flow of your eternal mirth.

**Master MORE, your Sacred Heart,**
**from this we will no more depart,**
**we are forever in your flow,**
**of Diamond Will that you bestow.**

8. Master MORE, help me awaken to the reality that this became a wound in my being, a wound in my soul, in my four lower bodies. It was a pain that seemed overwhelming to me at the time, and it *was* overwhelming to me, given my level of consciousness at the time.

Master MORE, you balance all,
the seven rays upon our call.
Master MORE, forever MORE,
we are the Spirit's open door.

**Master MORE, your Sacred Heart,**
**from this we will no more depart,**
**we are forever in your flow,**
**of Diamond Will that you bestow.**

9. Master MORE, help me awaken to the reality that I need to acknowledge this cosmic birth trauma and free myself from it.

Master MORE, your Presence here,
filling up the inner sphere.

Life is now a sacred flow,
God Power we on all bestow.

**Master MORE, your Sacred Heart,
from this we will no more depart,
we are forever in your flow,
of Diamond Will that you bestow.**

## Part 4

1. Master MORE, help me awaken to the reality that my individual birth trauma relates to what disturbs me the most on earth, the condition I would most like to eradicate.

Master MORE, come to the fore,
we will absorb your flame of MORE.
Master MORE, our will so strong,
our power centers cleared by song.

**Master MORE, your Sacred Heart,
from this we will no more depart,
we are forever in your flow,
of Diamond Will that you bestow.**

2. Master MORE, help me awaken to the need to make calls for the consumption of the misqualified energy produced through the filter of my birth trauma.

Master MORE, your wisdom flows,
as our attunement ever grows.
Master MORE, we have a tie,
that helps us see through Serpent's lie.

**Master MORE, your Sacred Heart,
from this we will no more depart,
we are forever in your flow,
of Diamond Will that you bestow.**

3. Master MORE, help me awaken to the reality that there is only one way to be free from this trauma, and that is to go straight back into it and re-experience it.

> Master MORE, your love so pink,
> there is no purer love, we think.
> Master MORE, you set us free,
> from all conditionality.

> **Master MORE, your Sacred Heart,**
> **from this we will no more depart,**
> **we are forever in your flow,**
> **of Diamond Will that you bestow.**

4. Master MORE, help me awaken to the reality that there is no way to be free of any experience I have had on earth by running away from that experience and the pain that it caused.

> Master MORE, we will endure,
> your discipline that makes us pure.
> Master MORE, intentions true,
> as we are always one with you.

> **Master MORE, your Sacred Heart,**
> **from this we will no more depart,**
> **we are forever in your flow,**
> **of Diamond Will that you bestow.**

5. Master MORE, help me awaken to the reality that I cannot be free from anything by running away from it. I can be free only by going right into it and then experiencing that, because I have moved on in consciousness, it no longer defines me.

> Master MORE, our vision raised,
> the will of God is always praised.
> Master MORE, creative will,
> raising all life higher still.

**Master MORE, your Sacred Heart,
from this we will no more depart,
we are forever in your flow,
of Diamond Will that you bestow.**

6. Master MORE, help me awaken to the reality that what the fallen beings want me to believe, what my ego wants me to believe, is that if I go into this original pain, I will die. I will be overwhelmed again. It will be too much for me.

Master MORE, your peace is power,
the demons of war it will devour.
Master MORE, we serve all life,
our flames consuming war and strife.

**Master MORE, your Sacred Heart,
from this we will no more depart,
we are forever in your flow,
of Diamond Will that you bestow.**

7. Master MORE, help me awaken to the reality that I have moved on in consciousness since I first came to this planet. I can deal with it now because I am not having the same experience as I had the first time. I am not being overwhelmed.

Master MORE, we are so free,
eternal bond from you we see.
Master MORE, we find rebirth,
in flow of your eternal mirth.

**Master MORE, your Sacred Heart,
from this we will no more depart,
we are forever in your flow,
of Diamond Will that you bestow.**

8. Master MORE, help me awaken to the reality that I can distance myself from the pain by going into it and experiencing that it will not destroy me.

Master MORE, you balance all,
the seven rays upon our call.
Master MORE, forever MORE,
we are the Spirit's open door.

**Master MORE, your Sacred Heart,**
**from this we will no more depart,**
**we are forever in your flow,**
**of Diamond Will that you bestow.**

9. Master MORE, help me awaken to the reality that I can look at the
swirling energy, look at the beliefs, look at the beings in the astral plane,
and I can realize: "This is not me. This is just something the outer self
experienced. I am more than this experience, and therefore I can look at
it and say: 'You no longer own me. You no longer define me. This is not
who I am. Get thee behind me, Satan, for I see your unreality, and I see
and experience my own reality and the reality of the ascended masters.'"

Master MORE, your Presence here,
filling up the inner sphere.
Life is now a sacred flow,
God Power we on all bestow.

**Master MORE, your Sacred Heart,**
**from this we will no more depart,**
**we are forever in your flow,**
**of Diamond Will that you bestow.**

*Part 5*

1. Master MORE, help me awaken to the reality that I am not alone in
dealing with my birth trauma. You are close to my heart and will help me
in dealing with it.

Master MORE, come to the fore,
we will absorb your flame of MORE.

Master MORE, our will so strong,
our power centers cleared by song.

**Master MORE, your Sacred Heart,
from this we will no more depart,
we are forever in your flow,
of Diamond Will that you bestow.**

2. Master MORE, help me awaken to the reality that there does come a point when you cannot assist me anymore. I must take that final step of confronting my own demons and seeing that they are not real.

Master MORE, your wisdom flows,
as our attunement ever grows.
Master MORE, we have a tie,
that helps us see through Serpent's lie.

**Master MORE, your Sacred Heart,
from this we will no more depart,
we are forever in your flow,
of Diamond Will that you bestow.**

3. Master MORE, help me awaken to the reality that the fallen beings trapped me by abusing the power they had in the physical octave to expose me to this trauma, this unreality that I thought was reality.

Master MORE, your love so pink,
there is no purer love, we think.
Master MORE, you set us free,
from all conditionality.

**Master MORE, your Sacred Heart,
from this we will no more depart,
we are forever in your flow,
of Diamond Will that you bestow.**

4. Master MORE, help me awaken to the reality that the fallen beings trap me by using the idea that what happened to me in the past is defining, my present experience of life and what will happen to me in the future.

Master MORE, we will endure,
your discipline that makes us pure.
Master MORE, intentions true,
as we are always one with you.

**Master MORE, your Sacred Heart,**
**from this we will no more depart,**
**we are forever in your flow,**
**of Diamond Will that you bestow.**

5. Master MORE, help me awaken to the reality that the fallen beings are saying that what I did with my will in the past has suspended what I can do with my will in the present and for all eternity.

Master MORE, our vision raised,
the will of God is always praised.
Master MORE, creative will,
raising all life higher still.

**Master MORE, your Sacred Heart,**
**from this we will no more depart,**
**we are forever in your flow,**
**of Diamond Will that you bestow.**

6. Master MORE, help me shatter this illusion and see that it is a manifestation of anti-love. Help me have the will to be free from this illusion so I can receive your help.

Master MORE, your peace is power,
the demons of war it will devour.
Master MORE, we serve all life,
our flames consuming war and strife.

**Master MORE, your Sacred Heart,**
**from this we will no more depart,**
**we are forever in your flow,**
**of Diamond Will that you bestow.**

7. Master MORE, help me awaken to the reality that there is no choice that cannot be undone by making a higher choice. It is the eternal law that there is no limitation to free will, and this works both ways.

Master MORE, we are so free,
eternal bond from you we see.
Master MORE, we find rebirth,
in flow of your eternal mirth.

**Master MORE, your Sacred Heart,
from this we will no more depart,
we are forever in your flow,
of Diamond Will that you bestow.**

8. Master MORE, help me awaken to the reality that I can create any kind of misery I want, even the misery I don't consciously want. I can also *uncreate* any kind of misery I have created. I can be free from it.

Master MORE, you balance all,
the seven rays upon our call.
Master MORE, forever MORE,
we are the Spirit's open door.

**Master MORE, your Sacred Heart,
from this we will no more depart,
we are forever in your flow,
of Diamond Will that you bestow.**

9. Master MORE, help me awaken to the reality that the birth trauma will be the last thing I overcome before I am free to ascend because it was the first thing that trapped me in the lower state of consciousness.

Master MORE, your Presence here,
filling up the inner sphere.
Life is now a sacred flow,
God Power we on all bestow.

**Master MORE, your Sacred Heart,**
**from this we will no more depart,**
**we are forever in your flow,**
**of Diamond Will that you bestow.**

*Part 6*

1. Master MORE, help me awaken to the reality that the trap used by the fallen beings is that when I was exposed to this birth trauma, I was experiencing that it was some outside force that forced this experience upon me.

Master MORE, come to the fore,
we will absorb your flame of MORE.
Master MORE, our will so strong,
our power centers cleared by song.

**Master MORE, your Sacred Heart,**
**from this we will no more depart,**
**we are forever in your flow,**
**of Diamond Will that you bestow.**

2. Master MORE, help me awaken to the reality that the fallen beings project on me that I am here to overcome, to banish, the forces that exposed me to this trauma so that other people are not exposed to it.

Master MORE, your wisdom flows,
as our attunement ever grows.
Master MORE, we have a tie,
that helps us see through Serpent's lie.

**Master MORE, your Sacred Heart,**
**from this we will no more depart,**
**we are forever in your flow,**
**of Diamond Will that you bestow.**

3. Master MORE, help me awaken to the reality that the fallen beings project upon me that I have to engage in a struggle with these external forces. They want me to believe that once those forces are removed from the earth, I will be free of my trauma.

> Master MORE, your love so pink,
> there is no purer love, we think.
> Master MORE, you set us free,
> from all conditionality.

> **Master MORE, your Sacred Heart,**
> **from this we will no more depart,**
> **we are forever in your flow,**
> **of Diamond Will that you bestow.**

4. Master MORE, help me awaken to the reality that the fallen beings were invited to earth by other beings and I cannot undo their choices. What I *can* do is to undo my own choices.

> Master MORE, we will endure,
> your discipline that makes us pure.
> Master MORE, intentions true,
> as we are always one with you.

> **Master MORE, your Sacred Heart,**
> **from this we will no more depart,**
> **we are forever in your flow,**
> **of Diamond Will that you bestow.**

5. Master MORE, help me awaken to the reality that I am here to make a positive difference on this planet, but I do not make a positive difference by fighting the fallen beings and the forces of darkness. I make a positive difference by transcending their state of consciousness.

> Master MORE, our vision raised,
> the will of God is always praised.
> Master MORE, creative will,
> raising all life higher still.

**Master MORE, your Sacred Heart,
from this we will no more depart,
we are forever in your flow,
of Diamond Will that you bestow.**

6. Master MORE, help me awaken to the reality that I transcend the fallen consciousness only by transcending the consciousness in myself that caused me to react to them in such a way that it gave me this original trauma.

Master MORE, your peace is power,
the demons of war it will devour.
Master MORE, we serve all life,
our flames consuming war and strife.

**Master MORE, your Sacred Heart,
from this we will no more depart,
we are forever in your flow,
of Diamond Will that you bestow.**

7. Master MORE, help me awaken to the reality that my highest service on earth is to free myself from the fallen state of consciousness, and then pull up on the collective and pull up on all other people in embodiment. That is what I came here to do.

Master MORE, we are so free,
eternal bond from you we see.
Master MORE, we find rebirth,
in flow of your eternal mirth.

**Master MORE, your Sacred Heart,
from this we will no more depart,
we are forever in your flow,
of Diamond Will that you bestow.**

8. Master MORE, help me awaken to the reality that it was not wrong or bad that I reacted the way I did. I took on part of the fallen consciousness, but I do not have to carry it with me forever.

Master MORE, you balance all,
the seven rays upon our call.
Master MORE, forever MORE,
we are the Spirit's open door.

**Master MORE, your Sacred Heart,
from this we will no more depart,
we are forever in your flow,
of Diamond Will that you bestow.**

9. Master MORE, help me awaken to the reality that I did not take on the fallen consciousness in order to fight the fallen beings. I took it on in order to demonstrate that whatever I have taken on, I can transcend it. I can transcend it by my will power, my will to be free, my will to be more.

Master MORE, your Presence here,
filling up the inner sphere.
Life is now a sacred flow,
God Power we on all bestow.

**Master MORE, your Sacred Heart,
from this we will no more depart,
we are forever in your flow,
of Diamond Will that you bestow.**

*Part 7*

1. Master MORE, help me awaken to the reality that you only want me to be more.

Master MORE, come to the fore,
we will absorb your flame of MORE.
Master MORE, our will so strong,
our power centers cleared by song.

**Master MORE, your Sacred Heart,**
**from this we will no more depart,**
**we are forever in your flow,**
**of Diamond Will that you bestow.**

2. Master MORE, help me awaken to the reality that when I have the will to be more, I am inviting you to come into my life and give me maximum help and support.

Master MORE, your wisdom flows,
as our attunement ever grows.
Master MORE, we have a tie,
that helps us see through Serpent's lie.

**Master MORE, your Sacred Heart,**
**from this we will no more depart,**
**we are forever in your flow,**
**of Diamond Will that you bestow.**

3. Master MORE, help me awaken to the reality that you do not want to force me. You want me to know that you are here for me whenever I make the decision: "I will to be MORE."

Master MORE, your love so pink,
there is no purer love, we think.
Master MORE, you set us free,
from all conditionality.

**Master MORE, your Sacred Heart,**
**from this we will no more depart,**
**we are forever in your flow,**
**of Diamond Will that you bestow.**

4. Master MORE, help me awaken to the reality that when I am *not* willing to be more, I am subconsciously saying: "Master MORE, leave me alone. I'm not done with experiencing what is less. I'm not ready for more yet."

Master MORE, we will endure,
your discipline that makes us pure.

Master MORE, intentions true,
as we are always one with you.

**Master MORE, your Sacred Heart,
from this we will no more depart,
we are forever in your flow,
of Diamond Will that you bestow.**

5. Master MORE, help me awaken to the reality that the moment I decide
that I am ready for more, that is when you can truly assist me in a way that
I cannot dream about today.

Master MORE, our vision raised,
the will of God is always praised.
Master MORE, creative will,
raising all life higher still.

**Master MORE, your Sacred Heart,
from this we will no more depart,
we are forever in your flow,
of Diamond Will that you bestow.**

6. Master MORE, help me awaken to the reality that you put no limitations
on what can happen or how much more I can become. There can never
come a point where you would want to hold me back from becoming
more. You love nothing more than seeing me become more.

Master MORE, your peace is power,
the demons of war it will devour.
Master MORE, we serve all life,
our flames consuming war and strife.

**Master MORE, your Sacred Heart,
from this we will no more depart,
we are forever in your flow,
of Diamond Will that you bestow.**

7. Master MORE, help me awaken to the reality that I have been programmed to think that I am less, that I should be less, that I have to be less,
that I can only be less, that I am not allowed to be more.

Master MORE, we are so free,
eternal bond from you we see.
Master MORE, we find rebirth,
in flow of your eternal mirth.

**Master MORE, your Sacred Heart,
from this we will no more depart,
we are forever in your flow,
of Diamond Will that you bestow.**

8. Master MORE, help me awaken to the reality that I am allowed to be
more, that you are giving me permission to be more.

Master MORE, you balance all,
the seven rays upon our call.
Master MORE, forever MORE,
we are the Spirit's open door.

**Master MORE, your Sacred Heart,
from this we will no more depart,
we are forever in your flow,
of Diamond Will that you bestow.**

9. Master MORE, help me awaken to the reality that you are a Spirit, and
so am I. In that awareness, we are one.

Master MORE, your Presence here,
filling up the inner sphere.
Life is now a sacred flow,
God Power we on all bestow.

**Master MORE, your Sacred Heart,
from this we will no more depart,
we are forever in your flow,
of Diamond Will that you bestow.**

## *Sealing*

In the name of the Divine Mother, I call to Mother Mary for the sealing of myself and all people in my circle of influence in the creative flow of the Divine Mother, the River of Life. I call for the multiplication of my calls by all representatives of the Divine Mother, so that we form the perfect figure-eight flow of "As Above, so below." Thus, I accept that this is fully manifest, because the mouth of the Lord, the Divine Mother that I AM, has spoken it. Amen.

# 5 | A TOOL FOR HEALING

# PSYCHOLOGICAL

# TRAUMA

I AM the Ascended Master Mother Mary, the representative of the Divine Mother for earth. It is my intent with this release to give you a tool that can be used over and over again for healing any kind of psychological issue or trauma. It is specifically designed to help you heal what we have called the "cosmic birth trauma." This is a tool that should be acknowledged as being for people who have reached a certain level of the spiritual path. It is not a tool that should be used out of any human ambition, of wanting to seem to be an advanced student or wanting to think you are ready for anything.

You should be familiar with our teachings on the cosmic birth trauma, you should be familiar with our teachings on dark forces and you need to invoke protection [from Archangel Michael] each time you use this tool. You also need, after having gone through the visualization I will give you, to use an invocation that might be appropriate for whatever psychological issue you are dealing with. We have a large number of invocations for different aspects of psychology [see *www.transcendencetoolbox.com*], but I suggest, to begin with, that you give an invocation for helping people love themselves. You can also create a vigil out of this exercise where you give the exercise once a day and after each visualization, you give one of the invocations from my *Course in Abundance* [see *www.morepublish.com*], as they work well together with the purpose of healing your psychological issues.

This is a tool, that should not be used by those who have severe psychological issues that require professional attention. You should not be using this if you are in a deeply unbalanced state. This is not because the tool itself is dangerous, but because it is a visualization that takes you deeper into your psychology. It can uncover unbalances that you cannot necessarily deal with if you are not in a somewhat balanced state. Having given you these cautions, it is, of course, my joy to present you with a tool that can help you heal your psychology and attain what our beloved Saint Germain has called "mental freedom." We will now begin the visualization.

[NOTE: You can give the visualization by using the book and reading one section at a time, then closing your eyes and visualizing. However, you might find it helpful to use an audio recording so you can keep your eyes closed. Recordings of the exercises in this book are available from *www. morepublish.com*.]

## Beginning the visualization

Visualize that you are standing in front of a wall. It is a very tall wall. You cannot even see the top. It extends to both sides and you cannot see where it ends. You can see that the wall is very thick, made of stone, but it is not stone as you know it from earth. It is a substance that vibrates at a higher level.

You realize, therefore, that this wall forms an impenetrable barrier for any of the lower energies that you encounter on earth. Nothing on earth can penetrate that wall. Once you go beyond the wall, you will be protected, completely protected and sealed, from any negative energy that might be burdening you, that might have burdened you in this lifetime or in past lifetimes.

You now visualize that there is a gate. The gate, seemingly without anyone opening it, swings open before you. You now need to make a decision whether you will enter that gate or whether you will stay where you are and not participate in the visualization.

I now assume that if you are participating, you have made the choice to enter the gate. You hear the door close behind you and you now know that you are protected and sealed from any negative energies on earth, in the emotional realm, the mental or identity realm.

## The base chakra

You now look around and you see a beautiful garden. It has wide lawns, sparkling green, with trees in the background, flowerbeds laid out in curving forms filled with flowers. There are birds that are singing in the background but otherwise it is quiet. When you walk across the grass, it is so soft that you almost sink into it. I ask you, when you are giving this exercise on your own, to explore this garden for as long as you like, [pause the recording as necessary] and taking your time to explore the garden.

As you go around on your journey of discovery, there will come a point where you come to a tall hedge and there is an opening in the hedge. This doorway is covered by a gate. It is an open gate, like you see in some gardens, made out of a metal lattice work that allows air to flow through.

You realize that you can pass through that gate. There is an opening that is big enough to let you through, but you cannot pass through as long as you have any backpack on your back.

You now become aware that you do have a pack strapped to your back. This is some concern you have about the world, or some trauma you have experienced in this lifetime.

I ask you now to tune in to your base chakra and to see if there is any concern you have about the world, about yourself, about your own life, or any trauma you have experienced in your own life that comes to your mind when you tune in to your base chakra.

I am not asking you to go deeply into this but just get an impression. You realize that this concern or this trauma, is what you are carrying on your back. In order to pass through the gate, you need to take off that backpack and leave it outside the gate.

You do not need to analyze or go into this or be overwhelmed by it. You simply see it and then you decide: "I am willing to set this aside for now so I can enter this gate and see what is on the other side."

You now visualize that you take off the backpack, leave it outside the door and then you pass through the opening in the gate.

## The seat of the soul chakra

You now find yourself in another garden, even more intimate than the first. This garden is filled with flowers that seem to actually radiate light. It is a wonderful garden, it is a garden made for the play of children. You can hear the laughter of children somewhere in the background. You might even feel like taking some time for exploring the garden and exploring what it feels like to be in this playful vibration of the child.

When you are ready, you will find that, as you are walking around the garden, you come to another gate in another hedge. As with the first one, there is an opening that you can pass through. Now, you see that you have another backpack on your back.

I now ask you to tune in to the seat of the soul chakra and again, look for any concern or trauma that relates to the seat of the soul, the creativity of the soul, the playfulness of the child. Then, you simply look at this and then you decide: "Yes, I want to pass through the gate so I will leave this backpack outside."

You visualize taking off the pack and then you again pass through the opening that is smaller than the first opening, for somehow you have become a little bit smaller compared to when you started.

## The solar plexus chakra

Another garden opens up. This one is completely quiet, there is not even the sound of birds. It is calmness itself.

As you walk around this garden, you realize that not even your footsteps are making a sound. You find yourself listening to your breath, but not even your breath makes a sound. It is as if the garden absorbs sound and you feel what a freedom it is to not have the noise of the world with you.

After some time, you come to another gate. I now ask you to tune in to your solar plexus chakra. Again, tune in to any concern, any trauma you can identify. Simply be aware of it and then be aware that it is residing in another backpack that has somehow appeared on your back.

Again, you decide: "I will not go into this, I will set the backpack aside because I want to pass through the next gate."

You visualize putting the backpack next to the gate, passing through the opening that is a little bit smaller, as you have now become smaller.

## The heart chakra

Now, you have entered a garden that has a beautiful rose-pink light. It is filled with roses, pink roses but in all kinds of shapes and sizes. It is beautiful, it is peaceful.

You sense that there is a vibration here almost—*almost* like love, but it is not like any love you have known on earth. It is *unconditional* love.

Again, you may explore the garden as you need to, but at some point you come back and now you discover that there is another gate. This time I ask you to tune in to your heart chakra and again look for any concern or burden, any trauma relating to the heart, to love, to being disappointed in love, to feeling your love rejected.

You just see that it is there; you do not go into it. You realize that it is again in the backpack that you are carrying with you and the backpack cannot pass through the gate. You decide again: "I want to pass through the gate." You put aside the backpack and now an even smaller version of you is passing through the gate.

## The throat chakra

Behind that gate is another garden, but this is not a garden of plants. It is a garden of jewels, beautiful blue crystals everywhere, in all kinds of shapes and sizes. There is a light shining into the garden and it is reflected by all these crystals and creates all kinds of patterns.

There are walkways between these, almost like flowerbeds of crystals. As you walk into it, you can again take time to explore.

At some point, you find another gate. This time you need to tune in to your throat chakra and again see any trauma, any concern you have related to life, related to speaking out or not speaking out, related to organization, government or any such concern.

Once again, of course, you see that these concerns are not filling your mind, they are filling your backpack, the backpack that has again appeared. Again, the backpack cannot pass through but you can pass through. You decide to set aside this backpack also, and then you pass through the opening in the gate, finding yourself smaller because you are lighter, you are more innocent, you are more childlike.

## The third eye chakra

Now, you see another garden and this one, to your surprise, is huge. It has wide views of expansive vistas and meadows with flowers, cloud formations and all kinds of beautiful wide scenarios.

You can again explore and this time you can move faster, you can move at the speed of light and see all kinds of things. You can explore at your leisure.

At some point, you again find another gate. This time you tune in to your third eye chakra and you see any situation, any concern, any trauma that comes up related to vision, your ability to see, your ability to know and understand.

Again, you realize that this concern or trauma is confined to the backpack so it is not taking over your mind. Again, you decide to take off the backpack and you pass through the opening in the gate.

## The crown chakra

This time, you see an intimate garden. In the center of the garden is a Buddha figure, sitting in perfect calmness. He is sitting on a thousand-petaled lotus flower that floats on the water of a still pond. You are amazed at the beauty and the tranquility of the scene.

Again, there are pathways for you to explore if you desire and you can explore them for a time.

There again comes a point where you find another gate and you realize that you need to tune in to your crown chakra and see any concerns, any traumas you have related to knowing, to wisdom, to being at peace in knowing that everything is the Buddha nature.

You realize, again, that it is all confined to the backpack. It does not take over your mind, and you decide to put aside the backpack and again you pass through the gate.

## With Mother Mary

On the other side of the gate is not a garden, for suddenly you feel yourself being in the body of an infant, sitting on my lap. You now visualize that you are an infant child and I am holding you on my lap. It is warm, you are totally protected, totally surrounded by the nurturing Presence of the Divine Mother.

You have left your cares behind and you are now an innocent child, lying on the lap of the Divine Mother. If you desire, I will rock you back and forth, I will sing you a lullaby. If you desire to drink from my breasts, you are welcome to do so for I am not uncomfortable about the physical body and your need for nurturing. You may drink in the pure nurturance of the Divine Mother until you are full.

I now ask you to visualize, however you can, that we are reversing the birth process that brought you into physical embodiment. You are entering again this narrow confined space that is the birth canal, and you are feeling squeezed on all sides. Instead of what can be the traumatic push of being pushed out, you are now effortlessly gliding backwards into the birth canal, towards a safe space, a warm space, a nurturing space that is the womb of the Divine Mother.

You are now in the womb of the Divine Mother—in my womb. This symbolizes that we have moved beyond your present embodiment, we have moved beyond all of the attachments and concerns that normally keep you so focused on your current physical body, your current life and the world in which you live. We have left them behind outside the gate.

We are now nurtured, we feel safe and therefore we are ready to walk down a tunnel that opens up before us. It is a tunnel that leads towards your past lives on this planet.

## Exploring past lives

As we walk through this tunnel hand in hand, me guiding you, making you feel safe, we are aware that there are doorways on the side of the tunnel. They are open doorways and they lead into your past lives.

It may be that at some future time, when you use this exercise, you will feel prompted to enter one of these doorways and see something that

happened in that lifetime. Should you do this in the future, you can use the technique I will give you later, to resolve any trauma from a particular lifetime. My purpose of this exercise is to bring you back in time and that is why we do not go into any of the doors. I am aware that sometimes we come to a door and there seems to be almost a magnetic force pulling on your attention to enter that door. That is when I put my arm around you and say "Not now, we have other things to look at further down the tunnel."

We walk on past doorway after doorway. None of them have such a pull on you that I cannot guide you past them. We simply let them fall away. They are not important, but we go further and further back in what you call time. Truly, we are just moving, almost like you would move on earth where you can move freely in any direction. We are just choosing to move in the direction that points back towards the first time you took embodiment on this planet earth.

## The theater

After some time, we suddenly find ourselves at the end of the tunnel. There are no more doorways on the side, but there is an opening at the end of the tunnel.

As we go through this opening, we find ourselves in a theatre. There are rows of seats, there is a central walkway that leads down towards the stage. Up front is the stage. There are some elaborate set pieces and decorations.

I now take your hand and we sit down on one of these seats. As we sit there, it is as if a performance suddenly starts playing. Characters appear on the sides, they play different roles, a scenario is acted out.

You are not going into this in any way; you are just observing it. It is playing out. You may not even see any particular performance going on, you may just have certain sensations, certain feelings.

It may be that the first time you do this exercise, you are not quite ready to see in detail. Whatever you see, whatever you perceive, whatever you experience, whatever you sense, it attunes you somehow to a situation that was the very first trauma you encountered after taking embodiment on this planet.

You may feel some emotion, you may have some thoughts, you may be perfectly calm. It is all okay, for I am here with you. I am guiding you, I am guarding you and nothing will overwhelm you, nothing bad will happen to you. Whatever happened to you back then, cannot happen again, my beloved. It cannot happen to you now, for you are not the person that it happened to back then.

You may be able to see that there is a person on the stage who is being exposed to some traumatic situation, but you do not really identify with that person. You see the scenario, but you are not pulled into it. You are not on the stage observing this happening, you are sitting with me next to you observing it from without.

After some time, the scenario will have outplayed itself. It is as if all of the characters that appeared on the stage are now frozen in place. You might imagine a theatre where suddenly all of the actors on the stage froze, almost like you froze a movie into a still picture.

At this point, I take you by the hand. We walk down the central isle. We walk to one side of the stage and here is a curtain that we pull aside and now we walk behind the stage.

You are now backstage with me and you see that what seemed very real when seen from the front, is now just set pieces and props that only look real when they are seen from a certain perspective. When they are seen from the front, then it seems like it is a real world you are looking at. Now that you are backstage, you see that it is all just set up and nothing of it is actually real. It is all make-believe, it is all a play that is being outplayed.


## On the stage

Now, of course, we walk onto the stage. Again, I am holding you. If you like, I will carry you. We walk up to the central character that was exposed to some traumatic event.

We see that the trauma was so great that it was actually the trauma that caused the person to be frozen. The person, the being, is still frozen there and has been frozen ever since this happened.

All of the other characters are also frozen, but we realize that they are not real characters that are frozen in time, they are a perception of the central person. Even though there were other beings that performed these actions back then, they have moved on in time. What remains in the theatre is the way that the person perceived these characters and what they did to it.

We now walk up to this person and I give you time to adjust. It is almost like you are looking at a stranger but there is something familiar about it. You look up at me with question marks in your eyes. I kneel down beside you, put my arm around your shoulder and I say: "Can you see that at one time, this was how you identified yourself and can you see that you are so much more today?" Suddenly, you are a little bit shaken and your body jolts because you realize that this was *you* at one point. Although it seems scary, I am here with you and you also realize: "But this is not who I am anymore. I have moved on in so many ways."

Now, I tell you that this theatre exists in your consciousness, in the energy field of your consciousness. Your consciousness, your total consciousness, is so much more today. You say: "How do I know this?" I say: " Did you not walk through the seven gardens? Those gardens are your consciousness, the consciousness that you have built since your first embodiment on earth. Consider the beauty of those gardens, and you can see that you are so much more today than that person who first embodied on this earth."

Now you see that this first traumatic event was extremely shocking to you because of the contrast between what you had known before you came to earth and the severity of what you experienced on this planet. Even though it was shocking back then, you realize that now you know so much more, have experienced so much more on this planet, have had many positive experiences on this planet, have built your attainment on this planet. Your mastery on the seven rays has built these beautiful gardens that you have seen.

Truly, this initial event, as shocking as it was, no longer defines you. You are no longer the being that is frozen in time. It is just that this being is part of you. It is still part of you because it was frozen in time and you have never gone back and looked at it.

Now that you are here with me, looking at it, you see that you are so much more. Therefore, you can look at this original trauma. In fact, you can go into it and re-experience it. You will not have the same experience of it as you had the first time.

Then, you realize that in order to be free of the trauma, you actually need to allow yourself to go inside the person that is frozen in time on the stage. You are first apprehensive: "But Mother Mary, can I ever get out of it again?" I say: "But you can hold my hand the entire time, and if you cannot get out on your own, I will pull you out. *That*, I promise you."

You look into my eyes and I see the shift that you determine: "It has been long enough that I have carried this trauma with me and therefore I will go into it and re-experience it."

Suddenly, you slip into that original character, that original person, and now you are re-experiencing a traumatic event. At this point it may not come to you in detail, but there may be a feeling that is intense. There may be a pain, there may be a pull on you and you allow yourself to experience it for some time. It may be a second, it may be a few seconds, it may be longer. When you are ready, you feel that I am pulling on your hand. As you suddenly direct your attention away from the pain, away from the trauma, and towards me, you feel how you effortlessly slip out of that character. I do not even have to pull you because you effortlessly slip out.

Again, you are like a child sitting on my lap. I am comforting you, I am holding you and suddenly you are able to look at the situation with complete peace. You look at the situation and you realize it was just an event, like so many other events. "There are so many other events on earth that have not had an impact on me, that have not defined me. And in my mind I have made this event out to be special, to be so much worse, but it is just an event, it is just something that happened."

"Therefore, I realize, that there are so many other events that I have just let go of and surely I can let go of this also. I can let go of it, I do not have to hold on to it. I do not have to grasp it anymore. It has no place in my being, I do not want it, I do not need it. I want to be free of it. I want to play in the gardens without being burdened and being pulled back towards this event."

"It is as if the real situation is not there anymore. It has been changed by time, it has moved totally on and is not there. It is only in my mind that it is there, it is only in my mind that it exists. I don't want it in my mind anymore and I have power to change my mind. I can change whatever happens in my mind."

You suddenly get excited and you say: "Mother Mary, help me be free of this, help me be free of this entire scenario." I say: "Surely, I will help you."

First, I need you to go back into that character that was hurt and then I need you to love that character, to love yourself as you were back then, to love yourself as you feel that I love you. You love your reaction.


Suddenly, you realize that after that situation, the pain was so intense that you actually blamed yourself for reacting that way. You blamed yourself for reacting to the situation in a way that caused you pain. You blame yourself and think you should have been able to experience this situation without having pain, without reacting.

My beloved, none of us could avoid reacting to the severe trauma of taking embodiment for the first time on this planet, none of us ever could and you do not have to. Whatever was your reaction, you can be free of it. You can be free of it by loving the self that reacted.

As you go into that self and love it, then you feel how the character that was frozen in time suddenly begins to thaw, to melt, to become liquid. It is no longer stiff, it is no longer a hardened shell. It becomes liquid, it is flowing and then you see that it becomes so liquid that it is suddenly a pool of liquid on the floor.

Then, you become aware that I am handing you a piece of cloth and I say: "Wipe up the liquid and give it to me." You wipe up the liquid from the floor and you hand me the wet cloth. I take it into my heart chakra and transform it.

You feel how there is a burden that lifts from you and you feel a pull on your being to go back into one of these gardens and explore the beautiful scenario. You also become aware that even though you feel that you are somehow freer, you realize that you are still on that stage because the other characters are still frozen in time.

You look at me and ask: "But why am I still here? Why are these other characters still there if they were only perceptions in my mind?" I tell you it is because when the original trauma happened, you fixated your mind on a particular view of yourself, which is what you have just dissolved. You also fixated your mind on a particular view of the beings who were doing this to you and that view is still frozen in time.

Therefore, you need to do a little bit more mop-up work. What you need to do and what I guide you to do is that you sit on the stage. You look at one character that comes to your mind, one image. It may not be detailed but there is a sense that there is something there, that it is dangerous, that it is a threat to you, that it wants to do you harm.

Now, you realize that you are not the being who was there originally. You are not afraid; you are here with me. You are free in yourself and therefore you can look at the image you have in your mind, the image you formed in your mind back then, and you can love that image. You can send love to it. As you do this, you see how the hardened shell begins to soften, to melt, to become liquid. Again, it ends up as a pool of liquid on the stage. I give you another piece of cloth, and you again mop up the liquid, give it to me and I consume it in my heart chakra.

There may be other characters that are on the stage and as you do this exercise again, each time a different character may come to your mind. Now, you know the formula. You love it until it melts, becomes liquid and you mop it up and you give it to me—and I consume it.

## Using the exercise on other traumas

There may come a time where you do this exercise and there are no more characters that come to your mind, the stage is empty. At that point, you are ready to leave the theatre behind. You may still do the exercise and you may find that one of the other doors in the tunnel has a pull on you. You can go in and you will see another stage with another scenario. You can follow the same formula to go into that character and realize it is not you. You fill it with love, melt it and then you can see if there are other characters. You can realize that they are also just frozen in time and you are melting them and mopping them up, so to speak.

There may come a point where you can walk through this tunnel and nothing pulls on you. Then, there is no need to repeat the exercise. I am, in the first part, concerned about you going back to the original trauma and truly dissolving all of the characters that hurt you in that scenario. When you are free of the original birth trauma, it will be so much easier for you to resolve any trauma you received in any succeeding embodiment.

This is why I have taken you directly to the beginning, rather than starting to dissolve some of the other traumas that may be later, closer to your current embodiment and therefore in a sense have more of a pull on you. They may even be easier in some ways to dissolve, but they are not easier to dissolve if you have not resolved the original trauma. All other traumas are related to it, they all built on it. Therefore, by going to the source, my beloved, and resolving that, we set the stage for the resolution of all else.

## Leaving the theater

Now, I ask you to visualize that we are on the stage and at least for now no other character comes to your mind. It is time to leave the theatre behind and we again walk out the door, walk through the tunnel. Suddenly, we are back and now you are going through the birth experience again. This time there is no pain, you do not even feel confined in the birth canal.

You are suddenly back in embodiment as a little child sitting on my lap. You may stay on my lap, as a meditation, for as long as you like before you complete this exercise and give the final invocation. I will hold you for as long as you desire, until you feel you are ready, you are whole, you are healed enough to go back into your physical body and the awareness of this lifetime. You do this, of course, by going through the gates representing your chakras.

You may, at the gate, again pick up the backpack that you left behind. You may not be aware that you are doing this and this is okay, but you may also find at some point that you suddenly hesitate and you realize you have a choice: "Will I pick up the backpack or will I leave it there?" Then, you might decide to leave it and come back to your normal awareness with a lighter feeling of not carrying so much weight.

You may at some point even find that you have dissolved the backpack, that you have no backpacks. You can again do the exercise and walk through the doors without having to leave anything behind because you have already transformed it.

## Accepting Divine love

What I want to leave you with is that the most difficult part of being in embodiment on earth is that we cannot truly accept Divine love. Many times this is because that original birth trauma was so shocking to us that it made us feel that if God really loved us, he should not have allowed us to go through this trauma. He should not have allowed us receive such a trauma, he should somehow have protected us.

It is an enigma. It is an enigma that takes some contemplation, some acceleration, some challenging your paradigms, some challenging the ideas that the fallen beings have put out there about an angry God, or a remote God, or no God, until you realize that you *chose* to come into embodiment.

You knew the conditions on this planet. You had a sense that it would be difficult, you could not know exactly how difficult because we cannot know how we experience a situation by projecting into the future. You cannot know, until you experience it, exactly how you will react.

The reason you chose to go into this situation was, of course, first of all, that you had a positive purpose for coming to earth. It was also because you knew that whatever trauma you might receive from coming into embodiment on earth, you could be free of it again. It could not truly destroy you, change you or touch you. It might be in your perception that it would touch you, but it could not touch the formless being that you truly are. Therefore, you knew that whatever happened could be undone by you, when you had the knowledge and you had the help. You also knew that there would be ascended masters and representatives of the Divine Mother who were ready to help you, as it has now been my privilege to offer my help to you.

Therefore, you knew, as Shakespeare said: "All the world's a stage." You knew that what happens in the material realm of earth is just like what is going on in a theatre. It is not real. You know that when you are in a theatre, you may be deeply affected by the play. You may have an emotional reaction, it may stir thoughts in your mind. But you are not identified with the play, you do not think you are one of the players on the stage.

Even if you are in a performance and you are one of the actors, you may live yourself into the character but you know that once you leave the stage, you will come out of it again. The reason you have been identified with earth was that the original birth trauma was so severe that it caused you to think it had changed you and that you had now become this wounded being. This has caused you to identify yourself with the character you have played in all of your embodiments.

What you can accomplish by using this exercise a sufficient number of times, is to come to the point where you no longer identify yourself with the original character that was hurt in the original birth trauma. Neither do you identify yourself with any of the other roles you have played in other embodiments. Neither do you fully identify yourself with the role you are playing in this embodiment.

When you come to that point, then you gain a new mental freedom where you realize that, yes you were born into a certain family, a certain nation, a certain culture. This has a certain history that goes back in time. You were affected by your environment, you were affected by your genes. Beyond this, you have also had many past lifetimes that have affected you, but all of this has now been resolved to a point where it is not going to define the course of the rest of your time in embodiment. You are free to choose whom you will be for the rest of this lifetime.

It is my greatest joy to offer my help to bring you to that point of mental, emotional, identity and physical freedom. Mother Mary I AM, and I am forever your Divine Mother.

# 6 | INVOCATION FOR HEALING SPIRITUAL TRAUMA

In the name I AM THAT I AM, Jesus Christ, I call to all representatives of the Divine Mother, especially Mother Mary, to help me overcome any trauma I have received in my past. Help me forgive myself and all people involved so I can liquefy all selves and rise above my past selves, including...

[Make personal calls.]

*Part 1*

1. Mother Mary, help me tune in to my base chakra and see any concern I have about the world, about myself, about my own life. Help me tune in to any trauma I have experienced in my own life that is stored in my base chakra.

Archangel Michael, light so blue,
my heart has room for only you.
My mind is one, no longer two,
your love for me is ever true.

**Archangel Michael, you are here,**
**your light consumes all doubt and fear.**
**Your Presence is forever near,**
**you are to me so very dear.**

2. Mother Mary, send the Light of the Divine Mother into my base chakra to consume this condition. Help me see any underlying beliefs and surrender them.

Archangel Michael, I will be,
all one with your reality.
No fear can hold me as I see,
this world no power has o'er me.

**Archangel Michael, you are here,**
**your light consumes all doubt and fear.**
**Your Presence is forever near,**
**you are to me so very dear.**

3. Mother Mary, help me tune in to my seat of the soul chakra and see any concern I have about the world, about myself, about my own life. Help me tune in to any trauma I have experienced in my own life that is stored in my seat of the soul chakra.

Archangel Michael, hold me tight,
shatter now the darkest night.
Clear my chakras with your light,
restore to me my inner sight.

**Archangel Michael, you are here,**
**your light consumes all doubt and fear.**
**Your Presence is forever near,**
**you are to me so very dear.**

4. Mother Mary, send the Light of the Divine Mother into my seat of the soul chakra to consume this condition. Help me see any underlying beliefs and surrender them.

> Archangel Michael, now I stand,
> with you the light I do command.
> My heart I ever will expand,
> till highest truth I understand.
>
> **Archangel Michael, you are here,**
> **your light consumes all doubt and fear.**
> **Your Presence is forever near,**
> **you are to me so very dear.**

5. Mother Mary, help me tune in to my solar plexus chakra and see any concern I have about the world, about myself, about my own life. Help me tune in to any trauma I have experienced in my own life that is stored in my solar plexus chakra.

> Archangel Michael, in my heart,
> from me you never will depart.
> Of hierarchy I am a part,
> I now accept a fresh new start.
>
> **Archangel Michael, you are here,**
> **your light consumes all doubt and fear.**
> **Your Presence is forever near,**
> **you are to me so very dear.**

6. Mother Mary, send the Light of the Divine Mother into my solar plexus chakra to consume this condition. Help me see any underlying beliefs and surrender them.

> Archangel Michael, sword of blue,
> all darkness you are cutting through.
> My Christhood I do now pursue,
> discernment shows me what is true.

**Archangel Michael, you are here,**
**your light consumes all doubt and fear.**
**Your Presence is forever near,**
**you are to me so very dear.**

7. Mother Mary, help me tune in to my heart chakra and see any concern I have about the world, about myself, about my own life. Help me tune in to any trauma I have experienced in my own life that is stored in my heart chakra.

Archangel Michael, in your wings,
I now let go of lesser things.
God's homing call in my heart rings,
my heart with yours forever sings.

**Archangel Michael, you are here,**
**your light consumes all doubt and fear.**
**Your Presence is forever near,**
**you are to me so very dear.**

8. Mother Mary, send the Light of the Divine Mother into my heart chakra to consume this condition. Help me see any underlying beliefs and surrender them.

Archangel Michael, take me home,
in higher spheres I want to roam.
I am reborn from cosmic foam,
my life is now a sacred poem.

**Archangel Michael, you are here,**
**your light consumes all doubt and fear.**
**Your Presence is forever near,**
**you are to me so very dear.**

9. Mother Mary, help me tune in to my throat chakra and see any concern I have about the world, about myself, about my own life. Help me tune in to any trauma I have experienced in my own life that is stored in my throat chakra.

Archangel Michael, light you are,
shining like the bluest star.
You are a cosmic avatar,
with you I will go very far.

**Archangel Michael, you are here,**
**your light consumes all doubt and fear.**
**Your Presence is forever near,**
**you are to me so very dear.**

## Part 2

1. Mother Mary, send the Light of the Divine Mother into my throat chakra to consume this condition. Help me see any underlying beliefs and surrender them.

Archangel Michael, light so blue,
my heart has room for only you.
My mind is one, no longer two,
your love for me is ever true.

**Archangel Michael, you are here,**
**your light consumes all doubt and fear.**
**Your Presence is forever near,**
**you are to me so very dear.**

2. Mother Mary, help me tune in to my third eye chakra and see any concern I have about the world, about myself, about my own life. Help me tune in to any trauma I have experienced in my own life that is stored in my third eye chakra.

Archangel Michael, I will be,
all one with your reality.
No fear can hold me as I see,
this world no power has o'er me.

**Archangel Michael, you are here,**
**your light consumes all doubt and fear.**
**Your Presence is forever near,**
**you are to me so very dear.**

3. Mother Mary, send the Light of the Divine Mother into my third eye chakra to consume this condition. Help me see any underlying beliefs and surrender them.

Archangel Michael, hold me tight,
shatter now the darkest night.
Clear my chakras with your light,
restore to me my inner sight.

**Archangel Michael, you are here,**
**your light consumes all doubt and fear.**
**Your Presence is forever near,**
**you are to me so very dear.**

4. Mother Mary, help me tune in to my crown chakra and see any concern I have about the world, about myself, about my own life. Help me tune in to any trauma I have experienced in my own life that is stored in my crown chakra.

Archangel Michael, now I stand,
with you the light I do command.
My heart I ever will expand,
till highest truth I understand.

**Archangel Michael, you are here,**
**your light consumes all doubt and fear.**
**Your Presence is forever near,**
**you are to me so very dear.**

5. Mother Mary, send the Light of the Divine Mother into my crown chakra to consume this condition. Help me see any underlying beliefs and surrender them.

Archangel Michael, in my heart,
from me you never will depart.
Of hierarchy I am a part,
I now accept a fresh new start.

**Archangel Michael, you are here,**
**your light consumes all doubt and fear.**
**Your Presence is forever near,**
**you are to me so very dear.**

6. Mother Mary, I accept that as I am sitting on your lab, I am totally protected, totally surrounded by the nurturing Presence of the Divine Mother.

Archangel Michael, sword of blue,
all darkness you are cutting through.
My Christhood I do now pursue,
discernment shows me what is true.

**Archangel Michael, you are here,**
**your light consumes all doubt and fear.**
**Your Presence is forever near,**
**you are to me so very dear.**

7. Mother Mary, I have left my cares behind and I am now an innocent child, lying on the lap of the Divine Mother. I am absorbing the nurturance of the Divine Mother and I am full.

Archangel Michael, in your wings,
I now let go of lesser things.
God's homing call in my heart rings,
my heart with yours forever sings.

**Archangel Michael, you are here,**
**your light consumes all doubt and fear.**
**Your Presence is forever near,**
**you are to me so very dear.**

8. Mother Mary, we are reversing the birth process that brought me into physical embodiment. I am now effortlessly gliding backwards into the birth canal, towards a safe space, a warm space, a nurturing space that is the womb of the Divine Mother.

> Archangel Michael, take me home,
> in higher spheres I want to roam.
> I am reborn from cosmic foam,
> my life is now a sacred poem.

> **Archangel Michael, you are here,**
> **your light consumes all doubt and fear.**
> **Your Presence is forever near,**
> **you are to me so very dear.**

9. Mother Mary, I am now in the womb of the Divine Mother—in your womb. I am beyond my present embodiment, beyond all of the attachments and concerns that normally keep me so focused on my current physical body, my current life and the world in which I live. I have left them behind outside the gate.

> Archangel Michael, light you are,
> shining like the bluest star.
> You are a cosmic avatar,
> with you I will go very far.

> **Archangel Michael, you are here,**
> **your light consumes all doubt and fear.**
> **Your Presence is forever near,**
> **you are to me so very dear.**

## Part 3

1. Mother Mary, I am now nurtured, I feel safe and therefore I am ready to walk with you down the tunnel that leads towards my past lives on this planet.

O Blessed Mary's Song of Life,
consuming every form of strife.
As I attune to sound so fair,
each cell is healthy, I declare.

**O Mother Mary, generate,**
**the song that does accelerate,**
**my mind into a peaceful state,**
**God's perfect love I radiate.**

2. As I walk with you, I feel attracted to a doorway that leads to a specific past life.

As life's own song I ever hear,
it does consume all sense of fear.
In tune with Mother's symphony,
from all diseases I AM free.

**O Mother Mary, generate,**
**the song that does accelerate,**
**my mind into a peaceful state,**
**God's perfect love I radiate.**

3. Mother Mary, as we go through the opening, we find ourselves in a theatre and up front is a stage.

In Mother's love I do transcend,
and all my struggles hereby end.
For when with Mother's eye I see,
no imperfection touches me.

**O Mother Mary, generate,**
**the song that does accelerate,**
**my mind into a peaceful state,**
**God's perfect love I radiate.**

4. Mother Mary, I now take your hand and we sit down. A performance starts playing, characters appear on the sides, they play different roles, a scenario is acted out.

I see that healing must begin
by finding Living Christ within.
For as I see with single eye,
each cell the light does amplify.

**O Mother Mary, generate,**
**the song that does accelerate,**
**my mind into a peaceful state,**
**God's perfect love I radiate.**

5. Mother Mary, I am not going into this in any way; I am just observing it. As it is playing out, I have certain sensations, certain feelings.

In Mother's music I am free,
from memories of a lesser me.
My vision in a perfect state,
that all my cells regenerate.

**O Mother Mary, generate,**
**the song that does accelerate,**
**my mind into a peaceful state,**
**God's perfect love I radiate.**

6. Mother Mary, I am attuning to a situation from a past life that was traumatic to me.

O Mother's Love, sweet melody,
from imperfections I AM free.
O Mother Mary, sound of sounds,
within my heart your love abounds.

**O Mother Mary, generate,**
**the song that does accelerate,**
**my mind into a peaceful state,**
**God's perfect love I radiate.**

7. Mother Mary, I feel the emotion, I have some thoughts, but I am perfectly calm. It is all okay for you are here with me. You are guiding me and nothing will overwhelm me, nothing bad will happen to me.

Through Mother's beauty so sublime,
transcending bounds of space and time.
All cells beyond the mortal tomb,
as they are whole in Mother's womb.

**O Mother Mary, generate,**
**the song that does accelerate,**
**my mind into a peaceful state,**
**God's perfect love I radiate.**

8. Mother Mary, I know that whatever happened to me back then, cannot happen again. It cannot happen to me because I am not the person that it happened to back then.

In resonance with life's own song,
in life's harmonics I belong.
The blueprint of my perfect state
does every cell reconsecrate.

**O Mother Mary, generate,**
**the song that does accelerate,**
**my mind into a peaceful state,**
**God's perfect love I radiate.**

9. Mother Mary, I see that there is a person on the stage who is being exposed to a traumatic situation, but I do not really identify with that person. I see the scenario, but I am not pulled into it. I am not on the stage observing this happening, I am sitting with you next to me observing it from without.

The tuning fork in every cell
is now attuned to Mother's bell.
From curse of death I AM now free,
I claim my immortality.

**O Mother Mary, generate,**
**the song that does accelerate,**
**my mind into a peaceful state,**
**God's perfect love I radiate.**

*Part 4*

1. Mother Mary, the scenario has now outplayed itself and the characters on the stage are now frozen in place.

> O Blessed Mary's Song of Life,
> consuming every form of strife.
> As I attune to sound so fair,
> each cell is healthy, I declare.
>
> **O Mother Mary, generate,**
> **the song that does accelerate,**
> **my mind into a peaceful state,**
> **God's perfect love I radiate.**

2. Mother Mary, I take your hand and we walk behind the stage.

> As life's own song I ever hear,
> it does consume all sense of fear.
> In tune with Mother's symphony,
> from all diseases I AM free.
>
> **O Mother Mary, generate,**
> **the song that does accelerate,**
> **my mind into a peaceful state,**
> **God's perfect love I radiate.**

3. Mother Mary, we are now backstage and I see that what seemed very real when seen from the front, is now just set pieces and props that only look real when they are seen from a certain perspective. Now that we are backstage, I see that it is all just a set-up and none of it is actually real. It is all make-believe, it is all a play that is being outplayed.

> In Mother's love I do transcend,
> and all my struggles hereby end.
> For when with Mother's eye I see,
> no imperfection touches me.

**O Mother Mary, generate,**
**the song that does accelerate,**
**my mind into a peaceful state,**
**God's perfect love I radiate.**

4. Mother Mary, we walk onto the stage and you are holding me. We walk up to the central character that was exposed to some traumatic event.

I see that healing must begin
by finding Living Christ within.
For as I see with single eye,
each cell the light does amplify.

**O Mother Mary, generate,**
**the song that does accelerate,**
**my mind into a peaceful state,**
**God's perfect love I radiate.**

5. Mother Mary, we see that the trauma was so great that it caused the person to be frozen. The person, the being, is still frozen there and has been frozen ever since this happened.

In Mother's music I am free,
from memories of a lesser me.
My vision in a perfect state,
that all my cells regenerate.

**O Mother Mary, generate,**
**the song that does accelerate,**
**my mind into a peaceful state,**
**God's perfect love I radiate.**

6. Mother Mary, all of the other characters are also frozen, but I realize that they are not real characters that are frozen in time, they are a perception of the central person.

O Mother's Love, sweet melody,
from imperfections I AM free.

O Mother Mary, sound of sounds,
within my heart your love abounds.

**O Mother Mary, generate,**
**the song that does accelerate,**
**my mind into a peaceful state,**
**God's perfect love I radiate.**

7. Mother Mary, I see that even though there were other beings that performed these actions back then, they have moved on in time. What remains in the theatre is the way that the person perceived these characters and what they did to it.

Through Mother's beauty so sublime,
transcending bounds of space and time.
All cells beyond the mortal tomb,
as they are whole in Mother's womb.

**O Mother Mary, generate,**
**the song that does accelerate,**
**my mind into a peaceful state,**
**God's perfect love I radiate.**

8. Mother Mary, we now walk up to this person and you give me time to adjust. It is almost like I am looking at a stranger but there is something familiar about it.

In resonance with life's own song,
in life's harmonics I belong.
The blueprint of my perfect state
does every cell reconsecrate.

**O Mother Mary, generate,**
**the song that does accelerate,**
**my mind into a peaceful state,**
**God's perfect love I radiate.**

9. Mother Mary, enveloped in your love, I see this was how I identified myself back then. I also see that I am so much more today.

The tuning fork in every cell
is now attuned to Mother's bell.
From curse of death I AM now free,
I claim my immortality.

**O Mother Mary, generate,**
**the song that does accelerate,**
**my mind into a peaceful state,**
**God's perfect love I radiate.**

## Part 5

1. Mother Mary, I realize that this was me at one point. I also realize that this is not who I am anymore. I have moved on in so many ways.

O Blessed Mary's Song of Life,
consuming every form of strife.
As I attune to sound so fair,
each cell is healthy, I declare.

**O Mother Mary, generate,**
**the song that does accelerate,**
**my mind into a peaceful state,**
**God's perfect love I radiate.**

2. Mother Mary, I realize that this theatre exists in my consciousness, in the energy field of my consciousness. I know that my consciousness, my total consciousness, is so much more today. I am so much more today than the person who embodied in that past life.

As life's own song I ever hear,
it does consume all sense of fear.
In tune with Mother's symphony,
from all diseases I AM free.

**O Mother Mary, generate,
the song that does accelerate,
my mind into a peaceful state,
God's perfect love I radiate.**

3. Mother Mary, I see that the traumatic event was extremely shocking to me because of the contrast between what I had known before I came to earth and the severity of what I experienced on this planet.

In Mother's love I do transcend,
and all my struggles hereby end.
For when with Mother's eye I see,
no imperfection touches me.

**O Mother Mary, generate,
the song that does accelerate,
my mind into a peaceful state,
God's perfect love I radiate.**

4. Mother Mary, I realize that even though it was shocking back then, I am so much more. I have experienced so much more on this planet, have had many positive experiences, have built my attainment, my mastery on the seven rays.

I see that healing must begin
by finding Living Christ within.
For as I see with single eye,
each cell the light does amplify.

**O Mother Mary, generate,
the song that does accelerate,
my mind into a peaceful state,
God's perfect love I radiate.**

5. Mother Mary, the previous event, as shocking as it was, no longer defines me. I am no longer the being that is frozen in time. It is just that this being is part of me. It is still part of me because it was frozen in time and I have never gone back and looked at it.

In Mother's music I am free,
from memories of a lesser me.
My vision in a perfect state,
that all my cells regenerate.

**O Mother Mary, generate,**
**the song that does accelerate,**
**my mind into a peaceful state,**
**God's perfect love I radiate.**

6. Mother Mary, now that you are here with me, I see I am so much more. Therefore, I can look at this past trauma. I can go into it and re-experience it. I will not have the same experience of it as I had the first time.

O Mother's Love, sweet melody,
from imperfections I AM free.
O Mother Mary, sound of sounds,
within my heart your love abounds.

**O Mother Mary, generate,**
**the song that does accelerate,**
**my mind into a peaceful state,**
**God's perfect love I radiate.**

7. Mother Mary, I realize that in order to be free of the trauma, I need to allow myself to go inside the person that is frozen in time on the stage.

Through Mother's beauty so sublime,
transcending bounds of space and time.
All cells beyond the mortal tomb,
as they are whole in Mother's womb.

**O Mother Mary, generate,**
**the song that does accelerate,**
**my mind into a peaceful state,**
**God's perfect love I radiate.**

8. Mother Mary, I know I can get out of it again because I will hold your hand the entire time. If I cannot get out on my own, you will pull me out.

In resonance with life's own song,
in life's harmonics I belong.
The blueprint of my perfect state
does every cell reconsecrate.

**O Mother Mary, generate,**
**the song that does accelerate,**
**my mind into a peaceful state,**
**God's perfect love I radiate.**

9. Mother Mary, I determine: "It has been long enough that I have carried this trauma with me and therefore I will go into it and re-experience it."

The tuning fork in every cell
is now attuned to Mother's bell.
From curse of death I AM now free,
I claim my immortality.

**O Mother Mary, generate,**
**the song that does accelerate,**
**my mind into a peaceful state,**
**God's perfect love I radiate.**

## Part 6

1. Mother Mary, I slip into that original character, that original person, and now I am re-experiencing the traumatic event. I allow myself to experience the feelings and thoughts that come to me.

O Blessed Mary's Song of Life,
consuming every form of strife.
As I attune to sound so fair,
each cell is healthy, I declare.

**O Mother Mary, generate,**
**the song that does accelerate,**
**my mind into a peaceful state,**
**God's perfect love I radiate.**

2. Mother Mary, I feel that you are pulling on my hand and I direct my attention away from the pain, away from the trauma, and towards you. I now effortlessly slip out of that character.

As life's own song I ever hear,
it does consume all sense of fear.
In tune with Mother's symphony,
from all diseases I AM free.

**O Mother Mary, generate,**
**the song that does accelerate,**
**my mind into a peaceful state,**
**God's perfect love I radiate.**

3. Mother Mary, I am like a child, sitting on your lap. You are comforting me, you are holding me. Suddenly, I am able to look at the situation with complete peace. I look at the situation and I realize it was just an event, like so many other events.

In Mother's love I do transcend,
and all my struggles hereby end.
For when with Mother's eye I see,
no imperfection touches me.

**O Mother Mary, generate,**
**the song that does accelerate,**
**my mind into a peaceful state,**
**God's perfect love I radiate.**

4. Mother Mary, I realize there are so many other events on earth that have not had an impact on me, that have not defined me. In my mind, I have made this event out to be special, to be so much worse, but it is just an event. It is just something that happened.

I see that healing must begin
by finding Living Christ within.
For as I see with single eye,
each cell the light does amplify.

**O Mother Mary, generate,
the song that does accelerate,
my mind into a peaceful state,
God's perfect love I radiate.**

5. Mother Mary, I realize, that there are so many other events that I have just let go of and surely I can let go of this also. I can let go of it, I do not have to hold on to it. I do not have to grasp it anymore. It has no place in my being, I do not want it, I do not need it. I want to be free of it. I want to play in the gardens without being burdened and being pulled back towards this event.

In Mother's music I am free,
from memories of a lesser me.
My vision in a perfect state,
that all my cells regenerate.

**O Mother Mary, generate,
the song that does accelerate,
my mind into a peaceful state,
God's perfect love I radiate.**

6. Mother Mary, it is as if the real situation is not there anymore. It has been changed by time, it has moved totally on and is not there. It is only in my mind that it is there, it is only in my mind that it exists. I don't want it in my mind anymore and I have power to change my mind. I can change whatever happens in my mind.

O Mother's Love, sweet melody,
from imperfections I AM free.
O Mother Mary, sound of sounds,
within my heart your love abounds.

**O Mother Mary, generate,**
**the song that does accelerate,**
**my mind into a peaceful state,**
**God's perfect love I radiate.**

7. Mother Mary, help me be free of this, help me be free of this entire scenario.

Through Mother's beauty so sublime,
transcending bounds of space and time.
All cells beyond the mortal tomb,
as they are whole in Mother's womb.

**O Mother Mary, generate,**
**the song that does accelerate,**
**my mind into a peaceful state,**
**God's perfect love I radiate.**

8. Mother Mary, I now go back into the character that was hurt and then I love that character, I love myself as I was back then, I love myself as I feel that you love me. I love my reaction.

In resonance with life's own song,
in life's harmonics I belong.
The blueprint of my perfect state
does every cell reconsecrate.

**O Mother Mary, generate,**
**the song that does accelerate,**
**my mind into a peaceful state,**
**God's perfect love I radiate.**

9. Mother Mary, I realize that after that situation, the pain was so intense that I actually blamed myself for reacting that way. I blamed myself for reacting to the situation in a way that caused me pain. I blame myself and think I should have been able to experience this situation without having pain, without reacting.

The tuning fork in every cell
is now attuned to Mother's bell.
From curse of death I AM now free,
I claim my immortality.

**O Mother Mary, generate,**
**the song that does accelerate,**
**my mind into a peaceful state,**
**God's perfect love I radiate.**

## Part 7

1. Mother Mary, I see that I could not avoid reacting to such severe trauma and I do not have to. Whatever was my reaction, I can be free of it. I can be free of it by loving the self that reacted.

Astrea, loving Being white,
your Presence is my pure delight,
your sword and circle white and blue,
the astral plane is cutting through.

**Astrea, come accelerate,**
**with purity I do vibrate,**
**release the fire so blue and white,**
**my aura filled with vibrant light.**

2. Mother Mary, I go into that self and love it, and then I feel how the character that was frozen in time suddenly begins to thaw, to melt, to become liquid. It is no longer stiff, it is no longer a hardened shell, it becomes liquid, it is flowing. Then, I see that it becomes so liquid that it is suddenly a pool of liquid on the floor.

Astrea, calm the raging storm,
so purity will be the norm,
my aura filled with blue and white,
with shining armor, like a knight.

**Astrea, come accelerate,**
**with purity I do vibrate,**
**release the fire so blue and white,**
**my aura filled with vibrant light.**

3. Mother Mary, I take the piece of cloth you give me, and I wipe up the liquid from the floor and hand you the wet cloth. You take it into your heart chakra and transform it.

Astrea, come and cut me free,
from every binding entity,
let astral forces all be bound,
true freedom I have surely found.

**Astrea, come accelerate,**
**with purity I do vibrate,**
**release the fire so blue and white,**
**my aura filled with vibrant light.**

4. Mother Mary, I feel how there is a burden that lifts from me. Yet I am still on the stage because the other characters are still frozen in time.

Astrea, I sincerely urge,
from demons all, do me purge,
consume them all and take me higher,
I will endure your cleansing fire.

**Astrea, come accelerate,**
**with purity I do vibrate,**
**release the fire so blue and white,**
**my aura filled with vibrant light.**

5. Mother Mary, I realize that when the original trauma happened, I fixated my mind on a particular view of myself and of the beings who were doing this to me. That view is still frozen in time.

Astrea, do all spirits bind,
so that I am no longer blind,

I see the spirit and its twin,
the victory of Christ I win.

**Astrea, come accelerate,**
**with purity I do vibrate,**
**release the fire so blue and white,**
**my aura filled with vibrant light.**

6. Mother Mary, I sit on the stage and I look at one character that comes to my mind, one image. I realize that I am not the being who was there originally. I am not afraid; I am here with you.

Astrea, clear my every cell,
from energies of death and hell,
my body is now free to grow,
each cell emits an inner glow.

**Astrea, come accelerate,**
**with purity I do vibrate,**
**release the fire so blue and white,**
**my aura filled with vibrant light.**

7. Mother Mary, I am free in myself and therefore I look at the image I formed in my mind back then, and I love that image. I send love to it and the hardened shell begins to soften, to melt, to become liquid. Again, it ends up as a pool of liquid on the stage.

Astrea, clear my feeling mind,
in purity my peace I find,
with higher feeling you release,
I co-create in perfect peace.

**Astrea, come accelerate,**
**with purity I do vibrate,**
**release the fire so blue and white,**
**my aura filled with vibrant light.**

8. Mother Mary, I take another piece of cloth from you, and I mop up the liquid, give it to you and you consume it in your heart chakra.

Astrea, clear my mental realm,
my Christ self always at the helm,
I see now how to manifest,
the matrix that for all is best.

**Astrea, come accelerate,**
**with purity I do vibrate,**
**release the fire so blue and white,**
**my aura filled with vibrant light.**

9. Mother Mary, we are on the stage and at least for now, no other character comes to my mind. We walk out the door, walk through the tunnel.

Astrea, with great clarity,
I claim a new identity,
etheric blueprint I now see,
I co-create more consciously.

**Astrea, come accelerate,**
**with purity I do vibrate,**
**release the fire so blue and white,**
**my aura filled with vibrant light.**

## Part 8

1. Mother Mary, we are back and I am going through the birth experience again. This time there is no pain, I do not even feel confined in the birth canal.

Astrea, loving Being white,
your Presence is my pure delight,
your sword and circle white and blue,
the astral plane is cutting through.

**Astrea, come accelerate,**
**with purity I do vibrate,**
**release the fire so blue and white,**
**my aura filled with vibrant light.**

2. Mother Mary, I am back in embodiment as a little child sitting on your lap, feeling embraced by and enveloped in your unconditional love.

Astrea, calm the raging storm,
so purity will be the norm,
my aura filled with blue and white,
with shining armor, like a knight.

**Astrea, come accelerate,**
**with purity I do vibrate,**
**release the fire so blue and white,**
**my aura filled with vibrant light.**

3. Mother Mary, I am ready, I am whole, I am healed enough to go back into my physical body and the awareness of this lifetime. I do this by going through the gates representing my chakras.

Astrea, come and cut me free,
from every binding entity,
let astral forces all be bound,
true freedom I have surely found.

**Astrea, come accelerate,**
**with purity I do vibrate,**
**release the fire so blue and white,**
**my aura filled with vibrant light.**

4. Mother Mary, I realize that before I came into embodiment, I knew the conditions on this planet and I had a sense that it would be difficult. I also I knew that whatever trauma I might receive, I could be free of it again. It could not truly destroy me, change me or touch me.

Astrea, I sincerely urge,
from demons all, do me purge,

consume them all and take me higher,
I will endure your cleansing fire.

**Astrea, come accelerate,**
**with purity I do vibrate,**
**release the fire so blue and white,**
**my aura filled with vibrant light.**

5. Mother Mary, I realize that what happens in the material realm of earth is just like what is going on in a theatre. It is not real.

Astrea, do all spirits bind,
so that I am no longer blind,
I see the spirit and its twin,
the victory of Christ I win.

**Astrea, come accelerate,**
**with purity I do vibrate,**
**release the fire so blue and white,**
**my aura filled with vibrant light.**

6. Mother Mary, I realize that the reason I have been identified with earth was that the original birth trauma caused me to think it had changed me and that I had now become this wounded being. This has caused me to identify myself with the character I have played in all of my embodiments.

Astrea, clear my every cell,
from energies of death and hell,
my body is now free to grow,
each cell emits an inner glow.

**Astrea, come accelerate,**
**with purity I do vibrate,**
**release the fire so blue and white,**
**my aura filled with vibrant light.**

7. Mother Mary, I no longer identify myself with that original character that was hurt in the original birth trauma. Neither do I identify myself with any of the other roles I have played in other embodiments. Neither do I fully identify myself with the role I am playing in this embodiment.

> Astrea, clear my feeling mind,
> in purity my peace I find,
> with higher feeling you release,
> I co-create in perfect peace.

> **Astrea, come accelerate,**
> **with purity I do vibrate,**
> **release the fire so blue and white,**
> **my aura filled with vibrant light.**

8. Mother Mary, I realize that I was born into a certain family, a certain nation, a certain culture. This has a certain history that goes back in time. I was affected by my environment, I was affected by my genes. Beyond this, I have also had many past lifetimes that have affected me.

> Astrea, clear my mental realm,
> my Christ self always at the helm,
> I see now how to manifest,
> the matrix that for all is best.

> **Astrea, come accelerate,**
> **with purity I do vibrate,**
> **release the fire so blue and white,**
> **my aura filled with vibrant light.**

9. Mother Mary, I now gain a new mental freedom because all of this has now been resolved to a point where it is not going to define the course of the rest of my time in embodiment. I am free to choose whom I will be for the rest of this lifetime.

> Astrea, with great clarity,
> I claim a new identity,
> etheric blueprint I now see,
> I co-create more consciously.

**Astrea, come accelerate,**
**with purity I do vibrate,**
**release the fire so blue and white,**
**my aura filled with vibrant light.**


## Sealing

In the name of the Divine Mother, I call to Mother Mary for the sealing of myself and all people in my circle of influence in the creative flow of the Divine Mother, the River of Life. I call for the multiplication of my calls by all representatives of the Divine Mother, so that we form the perfect figure-eight flow of "As Above, so below." Thus, I accept that this is fully manifest, because the mouth of the Lord, the Divine Mother that I AM, has spoken it. Amen.

# 7 |A HEALING EXERCISE

# IN DIVINE LOVE

I AM the Presence of Love. You may have noticed that when you receive a dictation from the ascended masters, they often present themselves as: I AM the Ascended Master so-and-so. I am naturally a Being in the ascended realm, but I choose not to present myself as an ascended master, for I have not ascended from earth or even from the sphere in which you exist. I ascended in a previous sphere and therefore, I hold a higher position in the cosmic hierarchy than any of the ascended masters that you have so far heard from.

This is to let you know where I am in the cosmic hierarchy. It gives you the understanding that, as part of what we have called progressive revelation, there can come those points where a particular dispensation, where the ascended masters who have released light on earth, can reach a level where the students of that dispensation have been willing to study and apply the teaching to the point where they can receive a teaching from a higher level of the cosmic hierarchy than has been released before on earth.

I come in recognition of the fact that so many people have taken the teachings that have been given in this dispensation about non-duality and duality, about the epic mindset, about the ego, and about love and unconditional and conditional love. I come in recognition of the fact that enough people have applied these teachings, have sincerely looked at themselves, looked at the conditions they have, and struggled with what all ascended beings go through: struggling to come to see what is what, what is *real*, what is *unreal*, what is the ego, what is not the ego. All of these questions that it is natural for beings to have, especially on a planet as dark as earth.

## What is anti-love?

Why is the earth so dark? Well, in large part because it has been so affected by anti-love. Now, my beloved, what is anti-love? In a sense, we could say that here we hit against the limitations of earth, the limitations that this planet has such a low level of consciousness that even words have become charged with duality, infused with duality. When you hear the word "anti-love," you think that anti-love must be in opposition to love.

Of course, there can be no opposition to real love. It has no opposite. This is one of the illusions that the ascended masters have taught you. It is brought about by the fallen beings who seek to define an opposite to love and then they say that the opposite is anti-love but "love" is love, is real love. Of course, in defining an opposite, you are not defining one opposite; you are defining two. What most people, the vast majority of people on earth, call love, is not Divine love. It is the opposite of anti-love and both have been defined by the dualistic mindset and the fallen beings.

What I come to give you is not just a teaching, but also a tool and an exercise whereby I will offer my assistance to anyone who gives this exercise, who listens to this dictation, reads it, applies the exercise. I will be there with you anytime you do so, for I am naturally not restricted by time and space. Now, the very purpose of this exercise is to help you shift your mind so that you come to be free of one of the major issues that people on earth face. This is a complex issue, but it all revolves around the love from God the Father.

## The father image of God

Many of you have grown up in the West where God has been portrayed as being exclusively male, a man, often an old man, often an angry, judgmental man sitting on a throne in the sky, willing to condemn you to an eternity of torment in hell if you do not obey his commands. Is it possible to love such a God with all your heart, mind and soul? Well, there are those, for example in the Christian movement, who claim that you should be able to love this God, and if you cannot, he may send you to hell.

They are not willing to recognize that the image of God that they have taken over was not given to them by Jesus. It came from the fallen beings who defined the image of the angry, judgmental God in the sky simply as a means to get people on earth to obey them. People were so afraid of being punished by the angry God that they were willing to follow the fallen beings in embodiment and even those in the three higher realms. So you have a completely false image of God.

What is the reality, my beloved? We have, for example in this magnificent invocation you have just given, the concept of God the Father and God the Mother [*Invocation for Loving Yourself*, available on *www. transcendencetoolbox.com*]. As the ascended masters have explained to you, God the Father is the Creator, the Being who created this world of form. Therefore, as the Creator, as the one out of which the entire world of form sprang, as the one who has embedded its Being in the entire world of form, this is the active principle in the sense that it was the Creator who started the entire world of form. Therefore, when you apply the feminine/ masculine polarity, which is what people can fathom on earth, then God the Creator is the father principle.

## A realistic view of God

Does the Creator love you? Well, first of all, you need to recognize that the Creator is not the God of official Christianity, of Judaism or of Islam. Nor is it truly the God of any other religion, including the Hindu Brahma. They are all seen as these remote gods. Is God remote? Is there a place in the highest realm where the Creator sits on a white throne, looking down upon its creation from on high? There is not, my beloved. How could there be? I am the Presence of Love. I am existing in a sphere that is higher than not only earth, but any aspect of this material universe or the four realms of this sphere in which you live. I can tell you that from my perspective, there is a vast distance in vibration between the earth and the place where I normally reside, or rather the sphere where I reside. From where I reside to the Creator, there is an even greater distance.

Where I go with this is to give you, not the sense that the Creator is so remote from you, but to give you the realistic assessment that earth is a planet with a very low level of collective consciousness compared to the vibration of the Creator. Therefore, if the Creator's light was to be focused on earth, it is not simply that the earth would be blown apart by the intensity of the light. It is that matter itself, the very atoms and molecules of the earth, would be annihilated because it would be raised in vibration instantly. All of the matrices that have been put upon the Mother light in order to create the earth in its present form, would be obliterated in an instant and the light would be freed.

You understand that the Creator cannot manifest itself on earth. This means that you need to come to the realistic assessment that there is absolutely no image that you could ever create on earth that gives you an adequate or an accurate depiction of the Creator. That is why I say, my beloved, that there is no place where the Creator sits in a discernible form. The Creator is the originator of form and, as such, either has no form or has every form. You see the difficulty in taking the linear mindset on earth and wanting to apply it to the Creator.

You sense that there is something higher than the earth. People have projected that there must be some kind of progression, and this progression must end up in some highest point, like you see in a pyramid. There is a point, a single point at the top, and that must be where the Creator sits, then, and looks down on everything below it. In reality, these are just images that is all that you can fathom with the linear mindset that dominates earth. They have no bearing on the Creator, whatsoever. What I ask you to contemplate, not simply now but in general, is that the Creator has no specific form and there is no form on earth whatsoever that can in any way represent the Creator. There is no form you can imagine with the consciousness that you have on earth that could represent the Creator.

## *The Creator is more than any form*

I also ask you to contemplate the enigma, in a sense, that the Creator is the originator of all form. Now, in a sense the Creator, when creating a form, does not become that form, yet the form is created out of the Creator's Being. The Creator is in the form. It is just that a form must of necessity have limitations in order to be defined, and even though the Creator can create a defined form, this does not mean that the Creator's Being is limited to that form. Since the Creator is all there is and since the Creator creates everything out of its own Being, then the Creator is the form but is also more than form. It is not defined by the form, even though it has defined the form.

This, my beloved, is the essential principle of creation. You create a form. Your being is in the form but your being is not confined to the form because your being is more. This, my beloved, is also the essential principle of co-creation where you are individual lifestreams created out of the Creator's Being. Even though you were not created directly by the Creator, you have come out of a lineage that all comes from the One Mind of the Creator. That is why we say that you are co-creating because you are co-creating within the sphere defined by the Creator. Still, though you are co-creating, the principle applies to your co-creation.

## What you have created

You define a form. In order to manifest it, you must endow it with your own being. You are therefore – your being is – in the form, but your being is more than the form. It is not the form. It is not confined to the form. What is the form you have created, my beloved? Is it your physical body? Nay, it is your four lower bodies; not the physical, but the mind. The mind in the identity level, the mind in the mental, the mind in the emotional and the mind that is associated with the body. This is your creation.

You have created it over many lifetimes. Many of you in other places than earth, but many of you have been here on earth for many lifetimes. You have created the four lower bodies, the soul vehicle, the self that allows you to function on earth, to relate to earth. It even allows you to be here without going completely insane, for it is a planet that can drive beings to insanity.

What I give you is the image that you have created your lower vehicle out of your being. Your being is in it but your being is not exclusively it. Your being is more. What has happened is, my beloved, that over time, especially on this dark planet, you have been manipulated and fooled by the fallen beings.

I want to give you the image here that when you first descended into embodiment on earth, your entire being was not invested in your four lower bodies. Now, what I say here applied not to the lifestreams that were originally created to be on earth. I am talking specifically about those who came after the earth had descended into duality. The lifestreams who were on earth had at that point already become identified with their four lower bodies. Most of you came here on what we might call some rescue mission where you volunteered to come here to raise the earth up.

When you came here, you created the vehicle of your four lower bodies out of your being. We might say here that your being at that time, depending on your experience, had a certain quantity of consciousness. This, what I am giving you is not an absolute concept; it is a somewhat artificial concept. I am giving it to help you understand that when you first came to earth, my beloved, only a small portion of the quantity of your entire being was invested into creating your four lower bodies. There was a portion of your being that was invested into creating your soul vehicle because you cannot create anything without creating it out of your being and thereby investing a portion of your being in the form you are creating.

When a relatively small portion of your being is invested in your four lower bodies, it is easy for you to realize that you are *not* the four lower bodies. You are *more* than the four lower bodies, and therefore you are not fully identified with the four lower bodies. You are not so fully invested in experiencing and taking seriously everything that happens to the four lower bodies, everything that happens on earth. You were *in* the world, but not *of* the world. You knew that you were here and you knew that the fallen beings could not control you. They could not destroy you. You could not be destroyed by anything on earth. You knew this.

## The cosmic birth trauma

What happened when you went through what Mother Mary called the cosmic birth trauma was that the fallen beings exposed you to such severe abuse that it shocked you so much that in order to deal with this shock, you had to create a more complex four lower bodies. You had to create structures in your identity body. You had to create structures in your mental body and in your emotional body. This even affected how you related to the physical body and how you, in future lifetimes, saw the need to create more dense physical bodies in order to withstand even the energies on earth. After this initial birth trauma, you started creating a much more complicated soul vehicle as a reaction to what you were exposed to on earth.

My beloved, there is no blame here. We all understand that this was an unavoidable reaction to what you were exposed to. What I am only pointing out is that in order to create this more complex soul vehicle, you invested a greater portion of your being into it. The greater the portion of your being that is invested in your soul vehicle, the more your sense of identity will be focused there. You identify more and more with the soul vehicle and therefore, you are no longer quite as aware, quite as conscious, that you are not the soul vehicle, that you are more than the soul vehicle, that you are a spiritual being who came from a higher realm. You are therefore not trapped on earth, you are not trapped in duality, and you are not forced to react to duality. You see, my beloved, how the fallen beings deliberately and gradually managed to expose you to such abuse that in order to deal with this, you created this more and more complex soul vehicle.

We have given you an image, or the ascended masters have given you an image, that there is a dividing line between the material universe and the spiritual. Above that dividing line is your I AM Presence, and right on the dividing line is a single point. There is a figure-eight flow of energy that goes from the upper half, the I AM Presence, through that single point, into the four lower bodies. When you multiply the energy with love, it can flow back up and, therefore, you receive more.

What we have given you is that you have a Conscious You. The real meaning of giving you this concept is that it is to help you see that regardless of how complex of a soul vehicle you have created, you still have the possibility to step outside of that soul vehicle and reconnect to your I AM Presence. It is the point of contact that can never be lost. Now, you may say that for many people on earth, the Conscious You is just like a single point. It is a point of awareness, a point of contact, but this is because you have created this very complex soul vehicle that has drawn all of your attention, all of your sense of identity, so that there is very little left for the I AM Presence.

## Understanding the figure-eight flow

Now, you might say, my beloved, that when you originally came to earth and when you first created your four lower bodies (before you had been abused by the fallen beings), the figure-eight flow between your I AM Presence Above and your lower being below was actually lower down than it is today. There was a part of your I AM Presence, a part of your higher being, that was in the identity octave. It was much closer to you, and therefore it was easier for you to connect to it. It was easier for you to know that you are more than the four lower bodies. What happened was that as you created the more complex soul vehicle and began to identify more with it, well, you could not have that conscious contact with the I AM Presence. That is why the I AM Presence, so to speak, had to withdraw up so that it could not be affected by what was happening to you on earth. That is why the nexus of the figure-eight flow is now at the borderline between the spiritual realm and the sphere in which you are focused.

What can actually happen is that, as you walk the path, you again create the opening where your I AM Presence can begin to extend a part of itself into the higher levels of your identity body, and even gradually further down. That is how you can become one with your I AM Presence. I know that the ascended masters have given you various images over time, and sometimes that you become an open door for the I AM Presence and the I AM Presence expressing itself through you. This is one valid concept, but it is still a linear concept. You could just as easily say that as you become the open door, your I AM Presence can extend itself into your four lower bodies, further and further down until it can even take some command over the physical body.

These are not incompatible ways of describing the process, my beloved. They are just different ways and one is more adapted to the linear mindset where what I am given you is more of a spherical vision that is not so linear. Thus, it might require some contemplation by you, depending on how attached you still are to the linear way of looking at everything.

You see, my beloved, when we give revelation, we must give it adapted to a certain level of consciousness and that means we have had to give our revelation to the linear mindset that is so dominant on earth. As we give progressive revelation, we can give you less linear concepts, more spherical concepts. This is given for those who are beginning to move out of their identification with the linear mindset and realize they are not the linear mind, and that not everything can be explained in a way that the linear mind can grasp.

## What is the I AM Presence?

Certainly, it is an enigma. Certainly, there is a challenge in the concept of the I AM Presence. What exactly is the I AM Presence? How does it relate to you? It is possible to take the image of the remote God and transfer it to the I AM Presence, as many students of ascended masters have done. It is also possible to go beyond it and realize that you cannot truly grasp your I AM Presence with the linear mind. Why is this so, my beloved? Because the linear mind creates mental images and it projects them upon the phenomenon that you are seeking to understand. When you are seeking to understand the I AM Presence, your linear mind creates a mental image. It is the only thing it can do. Your outer mind, your linear mind, creates a mental image and then it projects it onto the I AM Presence and says: "This is how the Presence should be."

This is what people and the fallen beings do with ideas. You create an idea and you project it upon reality. Then, you seek to study reality through the filter of the idea, which means you are actually wanting reality to conform to your vision, to validate your vision. My beloved, we have not given you the concept of the I AM Presence for the purpose that you should study the I AM Presence at a distance and come to *understand* it with linear mind. We have given you the concept for the purpose that you should come to the point where you can directly experience the I AM Presence and this resolves the enigmas of the linear mind.

The Conscious You is a concept we have given you. It is also an enigma. What exactly is the Conscious You? What does it mean that it is pure awareness? Well, it means, in one simple sense, that it is not dualistic. It is not always operating with two opposites and therefore having to explain everything within that dualistic mindset. It has the potential to connect to the I AM Presence, to the ascended masters, to the non-linear mind, to the non-dualistic mind. It can experience this directly—and *you* can experience the non-linear reality directly.

What was it you have talked about with communication from the heart? It is not linear communication. It is non-linear. It is spherical because it connects rather than divides. Linear thinking can only divide because linear thinking wants to define a form by setting it apart from other forms.

## Linear thinking and co-creation

What, then, is the difference between linear thinking and co-creation? Have I not just said that you co-create by envisioning a form and endowing it with your own being? Is there a difference? Well, there is. Is it subtle? *Yes.* Is it easy to understand? Not with the linear mind! You cannot *understand* it. But even though you create a form that has existence in time and space and is therefore limited to something that seems linear to you, the form itself is not created by the linear mind. You see, my beloved, you have a mental body. Most of you will say that you think with the mental body. You would, therefore, say that your linear mind must be a natural part of your mental body. This is the limitation. The linear mind is *not* a natural part of your mental body. The linear mind is a product of the fall into duality. The linear mind can only see time and space as linear phenomena. That is why you see time moving in increments in a particular direction that is irreversible. That is why you see space and that you can move from one place to another in space. Now, it is not so that the linear mind is evil. It is just that the linear mind is limited to thinking in linear terms and therefore, it sets everything apart from everything else. It can only define forms as being different.

Now, listen carefully. The linear mind needs the differences between a triangle and a circle in order to set the two forms apart and identify them. So far, so good. Nothing inherently problematic about this. When you have created a certain form, you have set that form apart from other forms and then you endow it with your being. You see, when you are not in duality, you know that the form was created out of your being, which is part of the greater Being of the One Mind of the Creator and of all life. Therefore, the form is not separate from its source. To the linear mind, there is no such thing as one source, one mind and therefore, the linear mind sees forms as different.

My beloved, when you first co-created, you did not create out of the linear mind. Your mental body, before you descended into duality, did not think in linear terms, did not have what you call the linear mind now. This is something that came in after the descent into duality, and this means that there is a range of phenomena on earth that are affected by the linear mind. I am not saying they are created out of the linear mind, for they are not. The linear mind cannot create, but the linear mind can form a filter so that you use that to envision certain forms and then you endow them with your being and bring them into physical manifestation.

Humankind has created certain phenomena that are affected by the linear mind. This, of course, is what the ascended masters have told you has caused even the densification of matter—the creation of so many inharmonious, imbalanced manifestations that are at war with each other, that are breaking each other down—the creation of diseases, the creation of what you call natural disasters. All of these unbalanced manifestations are affected by the linear mind, but why is this so? Why is there conflict between certain forms on earth? Why is there conflict between groups of people? It is because the linear mind can only look at differences and then it defines one form as being separate from another. The higher mind, the spherical mind, of course, sees the differences between different forms. It is not that, from the ascended level, we cannot see the difference between a circle and a triangle. We also see that they are not separate forms that are just floating around in space, for they came from the same source. They are endowed with the same consciousness, and this is what unites everything.

## Identifying with your soul vehicle

When human beings started creating these more complex soul vehicles, they invested more and more of their beings into these soul vehicles, and suddenly they came to identify themselves with the soul vehicles. Those soul vehicles were affected by the linear mindset because the fallen beings had managed to make the linear mindset dominant on earth. You created the soul vehicle in response to the linear mindset of the fallen beings and that is why, when the soul vehicle had reached a certain complexity (where the majority of the quantity of your being was invested in it), you shifted and started identifying yourself as a linear being.

This is what has caused people to identify themselves based on the outer divisions you see on earth: the two sexes, men and women, racial groups, ethnic groups, religious groups, political affiliations, national affiliations. That is why people are so invested in these outer divisions that they cannot communicate at the heart level. They cannot come to an understanding; they cannot come to an acceptance of each other. They can only see conflict and that is why there cannot be true unity.

Then, what is the only element that can bridge this, that can overcome this? It is love. It is love in the Divine sense. We have called it unconditional love to set it apart from the dualistic love of the dualistic mind, the dualistic love defined by the fallen beings. They have defined what they say: "This is true love. And then: "This is the opposite of love, this is anti-love." There is love, and what is the opposite? Hatred. Well, both hatred and love are defined by the fallen beings out of the dualistic mind and have nothing to do with Divine love.

Your Conscious You can experience Divine love regardless of how complex your soul vehicle is, regardless of how much of your being is invested in it, regardless of how identified you are with it. You can step outside of that soul vehicle, even for a split second, and experience Divine love. When you experience that Divine love, it will transform you. It will transform the way you look at everything, my beloved.

## What all people have in common

The only way for Europe to reach a higher union (that is a true union, rather than the forced union you have attempted to create), is that more and more people begin to connect to this love. Therefore, they become aware that: "Even though we have grown up in different nations, we have something in common. We share something in common." Many people call it "humanity." Well, whatever people need to call it, the important thing is that they recognize: "We have something in common and this something is more important to us than the outer divisions." Why? Because when you experience that inner source, when you connect to your source personally, and when you meet another person who is connected to his or her source, then you can feel something happening between you when you are together. Suddenly, there is more.

There is an old saying that sometimes when people meet, sweet music arises. You recognize that you come together and in your union there is more than you had alone. What does this do? It makes you feel better and it makes you feel better about yourself. That is why people want to experience it. As Mother Mary has been saying, there are more and more people who are aware of the value of this, who are becoming more conscious of it. They want this genuine connection to something higher, however they choose to see it or choose to label it. They want it, and that really is an expression of love: it is a manifestation of love. It somehow transcends the level of consciousness, the sense of self, that people have, and suddenly they experience something more. This is what you experience if you open yourself to the Presence of the ascended masters, to each other at a conference like this.

## Experiencing God's love

When you connect to that love, you go beyond the linear mind, and therefore you do not need to see the Creator through the linear mind. You do not need to see love through the linear mind. Therefore, you can begin to resolve these enigmas that I talked about. Does the Creator love you? Well, my beloved, the Creator does love you with an unconditional and infinite love, but you see, the Creator has given you free will and the Creator has absolute respect for that free will. Therefore, the Creator will never, *ever* impose itself upon you. You can experience the Creator's Being, the Creator's love, but you have to open yourself to it.

This messenger had this experience, as he has described, and it was because he opened himself to the experience. He was willing to process the experience afterwards and come to the point of overcoming the linear view of God, the linear view of love, and therefore being able to accept that what he experienced was the Creator's love. He also, thereby, came to understand and experience that the love of the Creator is a love for you, but from your perspective, you will experience it as an impersonal love. This is not because the Creator is impersonal, but this is the only way you can experience God's love while you are still in a dense environment and in the four lower bodies that you have on earth.

Even though you can experience the Creator's Being and experience that you are connected to the Creator (you are out of the Creator, and the Creator has love for you), you will, because of the limitations on earth, experience it as impersonal. That is why, as it also says in this *Invocation for Loving Yourself,* that we have given you the image that God the Mother gives you the personal love, the nurturing love. Of course, what is God the Mother? Well, in a sense everything is the Mother in polarity with the Creator as the Father element. For you, even though you are an aspect of the Mother, what gives you Divine love is first and foremost the ascended masters who are working with earth. They are willing to give you Divine love, meaning a very personal Mother flame, a nurturing love for you individually. It is, as I said, because of the limitations on earth, impossible to experience the Creator's love as personal, but it is possible to experience the love of an ascended master as very personal, very individual. As one person expressed last night, you can create such a relationship to an ascended master that the master virtually becomes your personal psychotherapist. You can ask and talk to the master about everything and ask all kinds of questions. You will get an answer when you keep in mind that the master is not answering your questions exactly as they are asked because often you ask questions from the linear mind. The goal of the master is to set you free from the linear mind and your identification with your four lower bodies. These are the kind of answers you will get: answers that liberate you. They do not necessarily answer your question in a linear way. Often, by answering your question in a linear way, the ascended master would only reinforce the linear mindset and your identification with your four lower bodies.

## Spiritual concepts are not linear

Perhaps, it would be important for many of you to consider that it is not the goal of studying a spiritual teaching that you understand spiritual concepts with the linear mind. Many, many, many ascended master students over the decades have been trapped into thinking that they need to study the teaching with the linear mind so that they can understand the teaching, categorize the teaching, label the teaching. They can always come up with a quote from the teaching and recite the teaching to others, and seemingly it fits every situation. This is actually a blind alley on the spiritual path. It does not help you and it can actually take you into the false path where you connect to the false masters in the mental realm. They will gladly make you feel that you are one of the most sophisticated spiritual students on the planet because you can grasp all these concepts with the linear mind.

The real purpose of an ascended master teaching is not to give you understanding, but to give you a direct experience: a direct experience of your I AM Presence, the Presence of an ascended master or the Presence of the Creator, of the non-linear reality that is beyond the earth. It is this experience that is love. It is this experience that shifts you. You can see that when people come together and they experience the love between them, it shifts and now they can suddenly solve outer problems and conflicts that they could not solve before.

## A healing exercise

My beloved, I know that I have already tested your endurance but I am still not done with my discourse. I trust that you will be able to stay with me as I take you through an exercise that is the real dispensation I want to give you. I will be with you every time you repeat it. It may also help you that you, before the exercise, listen to the dictation because these concepts I have given you are, of course, not coincidental. They set the stage for the success of the exercise.

I ask you to consider, my beloved, that your goal is to feel good about yourself. Naturally, you can look at the earth and you can apply various models that describe the current conditions on it. You could very well apply the model and say that all of the problems on earth, all of the conflicts between human beings, are caused by the simple fact that most people do not feel good about themselves. In order to compensate for this, instead of changing themselves and their inner beings, they are trying to change the world and they are trying to change other people. In their desperate attempt to feel good about themselves by controlling their environment, you have the creation of all of these conflicts.

You could even say that this applies to the fallen beings who, from the moment they fell, have not felt good about themselves regardless of the fact that some of them have incredible spiritual pride. If you actually look at a fallen being, they do not feel good about themselves. They have managed, here on earth, to take dominion over the earth by making everybody else feel not good about themselves. This is the only problem on earth from a certain perspective.

The goal here is to feel good about yourself and the goal of the exercise is to help you have an experience of that spherical part of your being. How do you feel good about yourself, really? Not by having any particular conditions fulfilled on earth, but by connecting to who you really are, connecting to your higher being. There is no way that your I AM Presence can make you feel bad about yourself. There is no way that experiencing the Presence of an ascended master can make you feel bad about yourself. There is no way that experiencing Divine love can make you feel bad about yourself. You may have a reaction afterwards that stirs up something in your psychology that then comes out and that makes you feel bad about yourself, but it was not the experience of Divine love because while you are in it, you do feel good about yourself because your outer self falls away. Your goal is to feel better about yourself than you feel right now.

## A visualization

I ask you to visualize that you are walking through a forest. Dense trees on both sides but you are not paying attention to them. There is a trail in front of you. You are walking through the forest. You come to a clearing in the forest and here is one of these observation towers that you have seen many places where you can walk up and then you are above the treetops, and then you can look out over a broad landscape. You are now standing at the foot of this observation tower and it has several levels. There is a staircase that leads up to a platform. From that platform, another staircase leads up. You are, therefore, standing at the ground level. In front of you is a staircase that leads up to the first platform. Do not worry about the top of the tower. You are only looking at the first platform. On that platform stands an ascended master. It is individual for each one of you. Whomever you feel is closest to your heart, that master is standing on the first platform. That master is standing there with open arms. You know that if you walk up the stairs to that platform, the master will embrace you and you know you will feel better about yourself when you are given a hug by an ascended master.

Somehow, you cannot lift your feet from the ground. You are trying with all your might, but both your feet are stuck to the ground. You become aware that it is because you are carrying a weight. You are carrying a burden and it prevents you from walking up the stairs. I am not asking you to look at this burden in detail. You may get an impression of what it is, you may not; but do not spend mental energy on trying to figure out what this is. Just tune in to the fact that you have a shoulder bag hanging on one shoulder that is weighing you down.

Now, you look up at the master and now you have to make a decision, my beloved: "Do I want to ascend that staircase and embrace the master? Because then I have to take that shoulder bag and simply lift it off my shoulder and let it slide off and fall to the ground."

Now, you realize that you actually have the power to do this. You can push that shoulder bag, lower your shoulder, push the band of that shoulder bag and you can let it slide off your arm and it falls to the ground. Now, you can ascend that first staircase.

If you are willing, you are feeling that the weight falls off of you and you grab the handles and you ascend the staircase, and there is that ascended master embracing you. You are embracing that master and you are feeling the love of that master. You are feeling enveloped in that love and right now, nothing else matters.

Now, as you give this exercise at later times, you may want to stay at this level. There is absolutely nothing wrong with staying at the first level, embracing that ascended master for as long you like. You may even give this exercise many times and still go to the first level and embrace that master.

For the sake of the exercise, I now make you aware that you are on a platform and there is another staircase that leads to a second platform above you. As you walk to the staircase, you see that there is another ascended master, again individual for each one of you, that is waiting for you with open arms. Again, your feet are stuck to the platform because you have another bag that is hanging on your shoulder.

Again, you realize that if you are willing, you have the power to just gently push it out so that it slides off your arm, falls to the ground and you are again free to walk up the stairs. There is the second ascended master embracing you. Again, you feel the love of that master. You feel good about yourself. You feel enveloped in that nurturing love of the Mother coming from this master. Whether you see it as a male or female master, it is still the nurturing love of the Mother that is coming to you. It is very personal for you.

This master knows you, loves you, does not judge or criticize you, loves you exactly like you are right now. No conditions, except your willingness to embrace the master and your willingness to, at least temporarily, set aside some of the weight you are normally carrying in order to open yourself to the master's embrace. Why do you need to open yourself? Because otherwise, you could not feel the love of the master. It is not that the master is not radiating it to you, but you cannot feel it.

After some time, you become aware that there is another staircase, leading to the third level and there is another master. Again, there is a weight that you can slide off. I am not specifying what these weights are because they are individual to you personally. As you give this exercise, the weights may even shift. They may be different. You may get a clearer and clearer vision, or a different vision from time to time. That is why I am not giving you a specific vision of what it is. It is simply a weight that you feel at the moment, and it prevents you from ascending that third staircase, and you let it slide off. You walk up and you again embrace the next master.

After some time in that master's embrace, there is the fourth staircase, leading up to the fourth platform, and a fourth master is waiting for you. You again become aware that there is a weight and you just let it slide off because now it becomes easier. You let it slide off. You walk up and you embrace the fourth master. Yes, you may, if you choose, see these masters as being associated with the rays, but it is not necessary to be so linear.

Again, whatever comes to you (and it may be a different master for every time you give the exercise), you walk up the staircase and embrace the fourth master and you feel the love of that master. You begin to recognize that each master has a certain quality of Divine love. Each master is giving you something different that is exactly what you need to heal some aspect of your psychology. You are enjoying the embrace of that master for a time; and as you give the exercise yourself, you can take however much time you want at a certain level.

There comes that point where you become aware that there is another staircase, leading to the fifth level. Again, there is a weight. You become aware of it. You let it slide off. You ascend the stairs and you embrace that master, which again is giving you a slightly different quality of Divine love, a slightly different form of nurturance. You again feel better, lighter, more loved, more cared for.

After some time at the fifth level, well there is staircase number six, and again there is a weight. You let it slide off. You ascend that staircase. Now, you are at the sixth level, embracing that master who gives you another unique quality of the nurturing love of the Divine Mother. You feel even more loved, even more whole, even more embraced in this sense that, not only is there someone who cares for you, but actually the entire universe cares for you, personally.

The entire universe, the entire Mother realm, you are beginning to feel, wants to nurture you, individually, and give you what you truly need in order to walk the path that you have defined for yourself in your Divine plan. You feel that nurturance.

You feel that the Mother is not your enemy. The Mother actually wants to give you what you need. The universe wants to give you what you need—not necessarily what your ego and your outer mind think you need, such as a flashy new car or this or that, but they want to give you what you need in order to grow.

After some time of this accepting that you actually live in a friendly universe, you realize there is staircase number seven. Again, there is a burden, you allow it to slide off of you. You ascend that staircase. There is a master waiting for you, but the master is not right at the top of the staircase because there is now a bigger platform. As you come up to that level, you are suddenly struck by the fact that you are above the trees. You are above all of the things on earth that seem to have concern for you. It is almost like you are not even on earth. You are in an entirely different realm.

You are looking down on earth from a great height and you see the earth down there. You see your four lower bodies. You see your life. You see all of the people and the circumstances around you from such a distance. Suddenly, you realize: "Oh, are they really that insignificant from a cosmic perspective? Is everything I'm going through and that is burdening me and that seems so important to me—is it really so insignificant when seen from this high a perspective?"

If you are willing, you can allow yourself to feel as if suddenly waves upon waves of energy are rolling upon you and your consciousness is expanded and expanded and expanded. You realize that what is going on on earth – what seems so important from your daily perspective – from a cosmic perspective, it is just so insignificant. It is incredibly insignificant. Not in the sense that it does not matter, but in the sense that compared to who you really are, the conditions on earth have so little power over your real Being, over who you really are. It is only your identification with these circumstances that make them seem so important and that make them have power over you. From the perspective of your I AM Presence, they have no power over your I AM Presence whatsoever. They are utterly insignificant, utterly indecisive in defining you.

Then, you become aware that there is a shocking gap between the perspective of your I AM Presence and the perspective you have when you are in the four lower bodies. You realize that your I AM Presence feels so good about itself and you. You feel so good about yourself when you see things from the perspective of your I AM Presence. You want that feeling. You really would like to carry at least some of that feeling with you when you go back into your four lower bodies, and you are thinking: "How could I possibly do this? How can I bridge this gap? How can I have just a little bit of the feeling, that my I AM Presence has, with me in the body?"

## Be open to receiving

Then, you become aware that there is an ascended master standing on the platform with his or her finger up, saying: "May I be of some assistance? May I be allowed to help you with this enigma?" If you are willing, you can then turn to that master and you can say: "Help me see what it is in my psychology, in my attitude, in my beliefs, what it is in my four lower bodies, that blocks me from carrying some of the feeling, some of the perspective, of my I AM Presence with me when I go back into my four lower bodies." Depending on your openness, the master will give you some impulse. It may not be some intellectual, linear, mental understanding. Depending on your openness, the master will give you some impulse.

Whatever it is that you receive from that master, in the beginning it may be difficult to grasp. It certainly may be difficult for your linear mind to grasp it because the master is seeking to help you experience the perspective of your I AM Presence and your I AM Presence is not seeing life through the linear mind. The master cannot give you a linear understanding and concept because the linear mind, when you come back into your four lower bodies, will only use it to create another mental image. The master is seeking to give you something that you can grasp and you can carry with you. I ask you to be open and to receive whatever the master gives you, and to hold on to it, and to carry it with you as you descend that staircase.

In the beginning, you may want to just descend the staircase without paying attention to the other masters, and then go back into your four lower bodies. As you become more experienced with the exercise, you may find that you can stop at each level and each master will give you something that will help you.

You are walking down the steps of the tower, and you now come to the ground level. Now, you are back in your four lower bodies. You walk back towards the forest, and as you walk through that forest, you gradually come back to your four lower bodies, and you are now sitting in your chair in your normal waking awareness.

## A different perspective

Hopefully, you can carry something with you from this exercise that will give you a different perspective. It will help you start the process of resolving something in your psychology so that you can gradually come to the point where you can have the perspective of your I AM Presence while you are still in the four lower bodies. Therefore, nothing on earth truly has power over you again. Nothing can define you. There is nothing you are completely identified with. There is nothing you take so seriously that you feel forced to always react to it and to always react the same way.

You realize you can choose your reactions. You can choose *not* to react. You can come to a point where you have transcended the elements in your consciousness that cause you to react to certain other people or certain circumstances. I assure you that when you have transcended a certain level of consciousness, you will no longer attract to you the people or the circumstances that caused you to react. Then, as you no longer are trapped in these reactionary patterns, it will be easier for you to tune in to your I AM Presence, tune in to the ascended master, and feel the love that is beyond earth and therefore, truly makes everything on earth less important than experiencing and even expressing the love.

## Divine love is the ultimate perspective

Once you have a glimpse of Divine love, nothing on earth can truly be important, compared to Divine love. Not that anything on earth can be compared to Divine love, but the feeling you have from experiencing Divine love is beyond anything you can experience on earth. This then, pulls you into experiencing it more and more, and the more you experience Divine love, the more you disassociate, dis-identify yourself with your four lower bodies.

What does this mean? It means you are now freeing a portion of your being to not be invested in the four lower bodies because you are dissolving the self that you had created in reaction to the world and that caused that portion of your being to be trapped in the four lower bodies. As you free it, you begin to have much more of an awareness of your I AM Presence. You begin to have a completely different relationship to your I AM Presence. The I AM Presence is not up there and you are down here, but certainly sometimes you can float up there and sometimes you feel that your I AM Presence is extending itself to where you are. All of a sudden, the barriers begin to break down and even the concept of the figure-eight flow is not so much a figure-eight flow that flows from one sphere to another. It is actually not even a flow. It is simply an awareness, a sense of oneness. The flow only comes in when you are the open door for letting the energy flow to other people and therefore, you become Divine love in action.

My beloved, you will recognize, I am sure, that when a being who is at my level speaks, I have no limitations of time and space. I do not pay as much attention to the limitations of your physical body and I know that it has been a long discourse. I am very grateful that you have been willing to endure this, that you have been willing to be the open doors also for radiating the energies and the concepts from my Being, from my Presence, into the collective consciousness. Truly, it is setting the foundation for a greater unity among people and among nations.

This is certainly one condition for bringing forth Saint Germain's Golden Age. Surely, the golden age that Saint Germain envisions cannot be forced. It can only be brought through love. It can only be brought when people choose it because it makes them feel better than what they have now.

Truly, how many people feel good about the political situation and the economic situation you have right now? What is the real goal? Is it to change the outer conditions? Nay, it is to change the inner feeling so that people realize that there are certain conditions, certain visions, that can make them feel better. This becomes the motivation—not an outer, linear motivation, not a self-centered motivation. It becomes the motivation that: "I want to feel better about myself and I want other people to feel the same. When we all feel better about ourselves and we come together, we can come to feel even better together than we feel separately." This is the true way to manifest a golden age.

My gratitude and my complete acceptance of each one of you personally, whoever you are, wherever you are, however you see yourself. I do not see you as you see yourself. I see the totality of your being and I accept every aspect of your being, every aspect of who you are right now and your potential to be more.

# 8 | INVOKING DIVINE LOVE

In the name I AM THAT I AM, Jesus Christ, I call to the Presence of Love, to help me overcome any trauma I have received in my past and be able to feel and accept Divine Love. Help me overcome all blocks that prevent me from tuning in to my I AM Presence, including…

[Make personal calls.]

*Part 1*

1. O Presence of Love, I want to feel good about myself and I am willing to know what prevents me from feeling good about myself.

O Presence of Love from higher sphere,
manifest your Presence here,
as you descend now from Above,
you do consume all less than love.

**O Presence of Love, release your flow,**
**for I now have the will to grow,**
**all lesser love I do transcend,**
**as to your heart I do ascend.**

2. O Presence of Love, I feel good about myself not by having any particular conditions fulfilled on earth, but by connecting to who I really am, connecting to my I AM Presence.

O Presence of Love, now cut me free,
unburdened by my past to be,
I lovingly submit to you,
my mind is one, no longer two.

**O Presence of Love, release your flow,**
**for I now have the will to grow,**
**all lesser love I do transcend,**
**as to your heart I do ascend.**

3. O Presence of Love, I am walking through a forest with trees on both sides but I am not paying attention to them.

O Presence of Love, my peace restore,
by cleansing now my bodies four,
help me now recreate them all,
so I can follow higher call.

**O Presence of Love, release your flow,**
**for I now have the will to grow,**
**all lesser love I do transcend,**
**as to your heart I do ascend.**

4. O Presence of Love, I come to a clearing in the forest and here is an observation tower where I can walk up to look out over the landscape.

O Presence of Love, with you I see
that love remains forever free,
for no conditions can it hold,
as love will always break the mold.

**O Presence of Love, release your flow,
for I now have the will to grow,
all lesser love I do transcend,
as to your heart I do ascend.**

5. O Presence of Love, I visualize myself standing at the foot of a staircase, leading to a platform. On the platform stands the ascended master who is closest to my heart.

O Presence of Love, in your great light,
I do ascend to greater height,
in nexus of the figure-eight,
I see my Presence oh so great.

**O Presence of Love, release your flow,
for I now have the will to grow,
all lesser love I do transcend,
as to your heart I do ascend.**

6. O Presence of Love, I realize I cannot walk up the staircase because a heavy bag is holding me down. I am willing to see that burden.

O Presence of Love, now fill my cup,
to Presence mine, I open up,
the veil of matter is no more,
as I am now the open door.

**O Presence of Love, release your flow,
for I now have the will to grow,
all lesser love I do transcend,
as to your heart I do ascend.**

7. O Presence of Love, I now make the decision that I want to ascend the staircase and embrace the master. Therefore, I take the bag and lift it off my shoulder. I let it slide off and fall to the ground.

O Presence of Love, now I am free,
from soul-defined identity.

I recreate my bodies four,
so they become forever more.

**O Presence of Love, release your flow,
for I now have the will to grow,
all lesser love I do transcend,
as to your heart I do ascend.**

8. O Presence of Love, I feel how the weight falls off and I grab the handles and I ascend the staircase. There, I am embracing the master and I am feeling the love of the master. I am feeling enveloped in that love and right now, nothing else matters.

O Presence of Love, I truly see
that no conditions come from thee,
no thing on earth defines your love,
forever streaming from Above.

**O Presence of Love, release your flow,
for I now have the will to grow,
all lesser love I do transcend,
as to your heart I do ascend.**

9. O Presence of Love, I now see that there is another staircase that leads to a second platform. There is another ascended master waiting for me with open arms.

O Presence of Love, I now conceive
of how I can your love receive,
as I am centered in my heart,
your love to me you do impart.

**O Presence of Love, release your flow,
for I now have the will to grow,
all lesser love I do transcend,
as to your heart I do ascend.**

## Part 2

1. O Presence of Love, I see I have another bag hanging on my shoulder. I gently push it out so that it slides off my arm. I am free to walk up the stairs.

O Presence of Love from higher sphere,
manifest your Presence here,
as you descend now from Above,
you do consume all less than love.

**O Presence of Love, release your flow,**
**for I now have the will to grow,**
**all lesser love I do transcend,**
**as to your heart I do ascend.**

2. O Presence of Love, there is the second ascended master embracing me. I feel the love of that master. I feel good about myself. I feel enveloped in the nurturing love of the Mother coming from this master.

O Presence of Love, now cut me free,
unburdened by my past to be,
I lovingly submit to you,
my mind is one, no longer two.

**O Presence of Love, release your flow,**
**for I now have the will to grow,**
**all lesser love I do transcend,**
**as to your heart I do ascend.**

3. O Presence of Love, I feel how this master knows me, loves me, does not judge or criticize me, loves me exactly as I am right now. No conditions, except my willingness to embrace the master and my willingness to set aside some of the weight I am normally carrying.

O Presence of Love, my peace restore,
by cleansing now my bodies four,

help me now recreate them all,
so I can follow higher call.

**O Presence of Love, release your flow,**
**for I now have the will to grow,**
**all lesser love I do transcend,**
**as to your heart I do ascend.**

4. O Presence of Love, I now see that there is another staircase, leading to
the third level and there is another master.

O Presence of Love, with you I see
that love remains forever free,
for no conditions can it hold,
as love will always break the mold.

**O Presence of Love, release your flow,**
**for I now have the will to grow,**
**all lesser love I do transcend,**
**as to your heart I do ascend.**

5. O Presence of Love, I feel a weight, and I let it slide off. I walk up and
I embrace the next master.

O Presence of Love, in your great light,
I do ascend to greater height,
in nexus of the figure-eight,
I see my Presence oh so great.

**O Presence of Love, release your flow,**
**for I now have the will to grow,**
**all lesser love I do transcend,**
**as to your heart I do ascend.**

6. O Presence of Love, I am enjoying the embrace of this master as if time
does not exist.

O Presence of Love, now fill my cup,
to Presence mine, I open up,

the veil of matter is no more,
as I am now the open door.

**O Presence of Love, release your flow,**
**for I now have the will to grow,**
**all lesser love I do transcend,**
**as to your heart I do ascend.**

7. O Presence of Love, I now see that there is another staircase leading to
the fourth level and another master waiting for me with open arms.

O Presence of Love, now I am free,
from soul-defined identity.
I recreate my bodies four,
so they become forever more.

**O Presence of Love, release your flow,**
**for I now have the will to grow,**
**all lesser love I do transcend,**
**as to your heart I do ascend.**

8. O Presence of Love, I become aware that there is a weight and I just
let it slide off because now it becomes easier. I walk up and I embrace the
fourth master.

O Presence of Love, I truly see
that no conditions come from thee,
no thing on earth defines your love,
forever streaming from Above.

**O Presence of Love, release your flow,**
**for I now have the will to grow,**
**all lesser love I do transcend,**
**as to your heart I do ascend.**

9. O Presence of Love, I feel that each master has a certain quality of
Divine love. Each master is giving me something different that is exactly
what I need to heal some aspect of my psychology.

O Presence of Love, I now conceive
of how I can your love receive,
as I am centered in my heart,
your love to me you do impart.

**O Presence of Love, release your flow,
for I now have the will to grow,
all lesser love I do transcend,
as to your heart I do ascend.**

## Part 3

1. O Presence of Love, I now become aware that there is another staircase,
leading to the fifth level and a new master.

O Presence of Love from higher sphere,
manifest your Presence here,
as you descend now from Above,
you do consume all less than love.

**O Presence of Love, release your flow,
for I now have the will to grow,
all lesser love I do transcend,
as to your heart I do ascend.**

2. O Presence of Love, I feel that there is a weight. I become aware of it. I
let it slide off. I ascend the stairs and I embrace that master.

O Presence of Love, now cut me free,
unburdened by my past to be,
I lovingly submit to you,
my mind is one, no longer two.

**O Presence of Love, release your flow,
for I now have the will to grow,
all lesser love I do transcend,
as to your heart I do ascend.**

3. O Presence of Love, this master is giving me a slightly different quality of Divine love, a slightly different form of nurturance. I again feel better, lighter, more loved, more cared for.

> O Presence of Love, my peace restore,
> by cleansing now my bodies four,
> help me now recreate them all,
> so I can follow higher call.

> **O Presence of Love, release your flow,**
> **for I now have the will to grow,**
> **all lesser love I do transcend,**
> **as to your heart I do ascend.**

4. O Presence of Love, I now see staircase number six and another master waiting to embrace me.

> O Presence of Love, with you I see
> that love remains forever free,
> for no conditions can it hold,
> as love will always break the mold.

> **O Presence of Love, release your flow,**
> **for I now have the will to grow,**
> **all lesser love I do transcend,**
> **as to your heart I do ascend.**

5. O Presence of Love, again there is a weight. I let it slide off. I ascend that staircase to the sixth level, embracing that master.

> O Presence of Love, in your great light,
> I do ascend to greater height,
> in nexus of the figure-eight,
> I see my Presence oh so great.

> **O Presence of Love, release your flow,**
> **for I now have the will to grow,**
> **all lesser love I do transcend,**
> **as to your heart I do ascend.**

6. O Presence of Love, I feel how this master gives me another unique quality of the nurturing love of the Divine Mother. I feel even more loved, even more whole, even more embraced. I feel that, not only is there someone who cares for me, but actually the entire universe cares for me, personally.

> O Presence of Love, now fill my cup,
> to Presence mine, I open up,
> the veil of matter is no more,
> as I am now the open door.

> **O Presence of Love, release your flow,**
> **for I now have the will to grow,**
> **all lesser love I do transcend,**
> **as to your heart I do ascend.**

7. O Presence of Love, I am beginning to feel how the entire universe, the entire Mother realm, wants to nurture me, individually, and give me what I truly need in order to walk the path that I have defined for myself in my Divine plan. I feel that nurturance.

> O Presence of Love, now I am free,
> from soul-defined identity.
> I recreate my bodies four,
> so they become forever more.

> **O Presence of Love, release your flow,**
> **for I now have the will to grow,**
> **all lesser love I do transcend,**
> **as to your heart I do ascend.**

8. O Presence of Love, I feel that the Mother is not my enemy. The Mother actually wants to give me what I need. The universe wants to give me what I need—not necessarily what my ego and my outer mind think I need, but they want to give me what I need in order to grow.

> O Presence of Love, I truly see
> that no conditions come from thee,

no thing on earth defines your love,
forever streaming from Above.

**O Presence of Love, release your flow,**
**for I now have the will to grow,**
**all lesser love I do transcend,**
**as to your heart I do ascend.**

9. O Presence of Love, after some time of accepting that I actually live in a friendly universe, I realize there is staircase number seven and another master.

O Presence of Love, I now conceive
of how I can your love receive,
as I am centered in my heart,
your love to me you do impart.

**O Presence of Love, release your flow,**
**for I now have the will to grow,**
**all lesser love I do transcend,**
**as to your heart I do ascend.**

## Part 4

1. O Presence of Love, again, there is a burden, and I allow it to slide off. I ascend that staircase.

O Presence of Love from higher sphere,
manifest your Presence here,
as you descend now from Above,
you do consume all less than love.

**O Presence of Love, release your flow,**
**for I now have the will to grow,**
**all lesser love I do transcend,**
**as to your heart I do ascend.**

2. O Presence of Love, there is a master waiting for me, but the master is not right at the top of the staircase because there is now a bigger platform. As I come up to that level, I am struck by the fact that I am above all of the things on earth that seem to have concern for me. It is almost like I am not even on earth. I am in an entirely different realm.

> O Presence of Love, now cut me free,
> unburdened by my past to be,
> I lovingly submit to you,
> my mind is one, no longer two.

> **O Presence of Love, release your flow,**
> **for I now have the will to grow,**
> **all lesser love I do transcend,**
> **as to your heart I do ascend.**

3. O Presence of Love, I am looking down on earth from a great height, and I see the earth down there, and I see my four lower bodies. I see my life, including all of the people and the circumstances around me, from a distance and I realize: "Oh, are they really that insignificant from a cosmic perspective? Is everything I'm going through and that is burdening me and that seems so important to me—is it really so insignificant when seen from this high a perspective?"

> O Presence of Love, my peace restore,
> by cleansing now my bodies four,
> help me now recreate them all,
> so I can follow higher call.

> **O Presence of Love, release your flow,**
> **for I now have the will to grow,**
> **all lesser love I do transcend,**
> **as to your heart I do ascend.**

4. O Presence of Love, I allow myself to feel as if waves upon waves of energy are rolling upon me and my consciousness is expanded and expanded and expanded.

O Presence of Love, with you I see
that love remains forever free,
for no conditions can it hold,
as love will always break the mold.

**O Presence of Love, release your flow,
for I now have the will to grow,
all lesser love I do transcend,
as to your heart I do ascend.**

5. O Presence of Love, I realize that what is happening on earth – and what seems so important from my daily perspective – from a cosmic perspective, it is just so insignificant. It is incredibly insignificant.

O Presence of Love, in your great light,
I do ascend to greater height,
in nexus of the figure-eight,
I see my Presence oh so great.

**O Presence of Love, release your flow,
for I now have the will to grow,
all lesser love I do transcend,
as to your heart I do ascend.**

6. O Presence of Love, compared to who I really am, the conditions on earth have so little power over my real being, over who I really am.

O Presence of Love, now fill my cup,
to Presence mine, I open up,
the veil of matter is no more,
as I am now the open door.

**O Presence of Love, release your flow,
for I now have the will to grow,
all lesser love I do transcend,
as to your heart I do ascend.**

7. O Presence of Love, it is only my identification with these circumstances that make them seem so important and that make them have power over me.

> O Presence of Love, now I am free,
> from soul-defined identity.
> I recreate my bodies four,
> so they become forever more.

> **O Presence of Love, release your flow,**
> **for I now have the will to grow,**
> **all lesser love I do transcend,**
> **as to your heart I do ascend.**

8. O Presence of Love, from the perspective of my I AM Presence, they have no power over my I AM Presence whatsoever. They are utterly insignificant, utterly indecisive in defining me.

> O Presence of Love, I truly see
> that no conditions come from thee,
> no thing on earth defines your love,
> forever streaming from Above.

> **O Presence of Love, release your flow,**
> **for I now have the will to grow,**
> **all lesser love I do transcend,**
> **as to your heart I do ascend.**

9. O Presence of Love, I see that there is a shocking gap between the perspective of my I AM Presence and the perspective I have when I am in the four lower bodies.

> O Presence of Love, I now conceive
> of how I can your love receive,
> as I am centered in my heart,
> your love to me you do impart.

**O Presence of Love, release your flow,**
**for I now have the will to grow,**
**all lesser love I do transcend,**
**as to your heart I do ascend.**

## Part 5

1. O Presence of Love, I realize that my I AM Presence feels so good about itself and me. I feel so good about myself when I see things from the perspective of my I AM Presence.

O Presence of Love from higher sphere,
manifest your Presence here,
as you descend now from Above,
you do consume all less than love.

**O Presence of Love, release your flow,**
**for I now have the will to grow,**
**all lesser love I do transcend,**
**as to your heart I do ascend.**

2. O Presence of Love, I want that feeling. I really would like to carry some of that feeling with me when I go back into my four lower bodies. I want to bridge this gap.

O Presence of Love, now cut me free,
unburdened by my past to be,
I lovingly submit to you,
my mind is one, no longer two.

**O Presence of Love, release your flow,**
**for I now have the will to grow,**
**all lesser love I do transcend,**
**as to your heart I do ascend.**

3. O Presence of Love, I become aware that there is an ascended master standing on the platform, saying: "May I be of some assistance? May I be allowed to help you with this enigma?"

> O Presence of Love, my peace restore,
> by cleansing now my bodies four,
> help me now recreate them all,
> so I can follow higher call.

> **O Presence of Love, release your flow,**
> **for I now have the will to grow,**
> **all lesser love I do transcend,**
> **as to your heart I do ascend.**

4. O Presence of Love, I turn to that master and I say: "Help me see what it is in my psychology, in my attitude, in my beliefs, what it is in my four lower bodies, that blocks me from carrying some of the feeling, some of the perspective, of my I AM Presence with me when I go back into my four lower bodies."

> O Presence of Love, with you I see
> that love remains forever free,
> for no conditions can it hold,
> as love will always break the mold.

> **O Presence of Love, release your flow,**
> **for I now have the will to grow,**
> **all lesser love I do transcend,**
> **as to your heart I do ascend.**

5. O Presence of Love, the master gives me some impulse that I can grasp and I can carry with me. I am open and I receive what the master gives me, and I hold on to it, I carry it with me as I descend the staircase.

> O Presence of Love, in your great light,
> I do ascend to greater height,
> in nexus of the figure-eight,
> I see my Presence oh so great.

**O Presence of Love, release your flow,**
**for I now have the will to grow,**
**all lesser love I do transcend,**
**as to your heart I do ascend.**

6. O Presence of Love, I am walking down the steps of the tower, and I now come to the ground level. I am back in my four lower bodies. I walk back through the forest, and I gradually come back to my four lower bodies. I am now sitting in my chair in my normal waking awareness.

O Presence of Love, now fill my cup,
to Presence mine, I open up,
the veil of matter is no more,
as I am now the open door.

**O Presence of Love, release your flow,**
**for I now have the will to grow,**
**all lesser love I do transcend,**
**as to your heart I do ascend.**

7. O Presence of Love, I am resolving something in my psychology so that I can have the perspective of my I AM Presence while I am still in the four lower bodies.

O Presence of Love, now I am free,
from soul-defined identity.
I recreate my bodies four,
so they become forever more.

**O Presence of Love, release your flow,**
**for I now have the will to grow,**
**all lesser love I do transcend,**
**as to your heart I do ascend.**

8. O Presence of Love, nothing on earth truly has power over me again. Nothing can define me. There is nothing I am completely identified with. There is nothing I take so seriously that I feel forced to always react to it and to always react the same way.

O Presence of Love, I truly see
that no conditions come from thee,
no thing on earth defines your love,
forever streaming from Above.

**O Presence of Love, release your flow,
for I now have the will to grow,
all lesser love I do transcend,
as to your heart I do ascend.**

9. O Presence of Love, I realize I can choose my reactions. I can choose *not* to react.

O Presence of Love, I now conceive
of how I can your love receive,
as I am centered in my heart,
your love to me you do impart.

**O Presence of Love, release your flow,
for I now have the will to grow,
all lesser love I do transcend,
as to your heart I do ascend.**

*Part 6*

1. O Presence of Love, I transcend the elements in my consciousness that cause me to react to certain other people or certain circumstances.

O Presence of Love from higher sphere,
manifest your Presence here,
as you descend now from Above,
you do consume all less than love.

**O Presence of Love, release your flow,
for I now have the will to grow,
all lesser love I do transcend,
as to your heart I do ascend.**

2. O Presence of Love, I tune in to my I AM Presence, tune in to the ascended master, and I feel the love that is beyond earth and therefore makes everything on earth less important than experiencing and even expressing the love.

O Presence of Love, now cut me free,
unburdened by my past to be,
I lovingly submit to you,
my mind is one, no longer two.

**O Presence of Love, release your flow,**
**for I now have the will to grow,**
**all lesser love I do transcend,**
**as to your heart I do ascend.**

3. O Presence of Love, nothing on earth is truly important, compared to Divine love. The feeling I have from experiencing Divine love is beyond anything I can experience on earth.

O Presence of Love, my peace restore,
by cleansing now my bodies four,
help me now recreate them all,
so I can follow higher call.

**O Presence of Love, release your flow,**
**for I now have the will to grow,**
**all lesser love I do transcend,**
**as to your heart I do ascend.**

4. O Presence of Love, the more I experience Divine love, the more I dis-associate, dis-identify myself with my four lower bodies.

O Presence of Love, with you I see
that love remains forever free,
for no conditions can it hold,
as love will always break the mold.

**O Presence of Love, release your flow,**
**for I now have the will to grow,**
**all lesser love I do transcend,**
**as to your heart I do ascend.**

5. O Presence of Love, I am freeing a portion of my being to not be invested in the four lower bodies because I am dissolving the self that I had created in reaction to the world and that caused that portion of my being to be trapped in the four lower bodies.

O Presence of Love, in your great light,
I do ascend to greater height,
in nexus of the figure-eight,
I see my Presence oh so great.

**O Presence of Love, release your flow,**
**for I now have the will to grow,**
**all lesser love I do transcend,**
**as to your heart I do ascend.**

6. O Presence of Love, as I free it, I have much more of an awareness of my I AM Presence. I have a completely different relationship to my I AM Presence. The I AM Presence is not up there and I am down here.

O Presence of Love, now fill my cup,
to Presence mine, I open up,
the veil of matter is no more,
as I am now the open door.

**O Presence of Love, release your flow,**
**for I now have the will to grow,**
**all lesser love I do transcend,**
**as to your heart I do ascend.**

7. O Presence of Love, I float up and feel that my I AM Presence is extending itself to where I am. The barriers break down and even the concept of the figure-eight flow is not so much a figure-eight flow that flows from one sphere to another.

O Presence of Love, now I am free,
from soul-defined identity.
I recreate my bodies four,
so they become forever more.

**O Presence of Love, release your flow,
for I now have the will to grow,
all lesser love I do transcend,
as to your heart I do ascend.**

8. O Presence of Love, it is simply an awareness, a sense of oneness and the flow only comes in when I am the open door for letting the energy flow to other people and therefore, I become Divine love in action.

O Presence of Love, I truly see
that no conditions come from thee,
no thing on earth defines your love,
forever streaming from Above.

**O Presence of Love, release your flow,
for I now have the will to grow,
all lesser love I do transcend,
as to your heart I do ascend.**

9. O Presence of Love, I want to feel better about myself and I want other people to feel the same. When we all feel better about ourselves and we come together, we can come to feel even better together than we feel separately. This is the true way to manifest the golden age.

O Presence of Love, I now conceive
of how I can your love receive,
as I am centered in my heart,
your love to me you do impart.

**O Presence of Love, release your flow,
for I now have the will to grow,
all lesser love I do transcend,
as to your heart I do ascend.**

## Sealing

In the name of the Divine Mother, I call to Mother Mary for the sealing of myself and all people in my circle of influence in the creative flow of the Divine Mother, the River of Life. I call for the multiplication of my calls by all representatives of the Divine Mother, so that we form the perfect figure-eight flow of "As Above, so below." Thus, I accept that this is fully manifest, because the mouth of the Lord, the Divine Mother that I AM, has spoken it. Amen.

# 9 | UNDERSTANDING WHY YOU CANNOT UNDERSTAND CHRISTHOOD

I AM the Ascended Master Jesus Christ. It was not my intention to speak at this conference, having had my say last time. But because of the many questions you asked the messenger about Christhood, I decided it would be helpful for you to give you a discourse on this topic.

## The greatest threat to dark forces

My beloved, the first thing we need to recognize is that personal Christhood, where you personally put on the Christ consciousness, is the greatest threat to the dark forces and the false teachers on this planet. They have, therefore, done everything they could possibly think of to prevent people from knowing about Christhood, seeing it as a realistic possibility for themselves and understanding the process of attaining Christhood and what it means.

They have done everything they could think of to create all kinds of diversionary tactics where they set other spiritual goals that are perhaps in some cases leading to a heightened state of awareness but are not as much of a threat to them as Christhood. They have also done everything they could think of to define Christhood in a certain way so that people attain, or strive for, an ultimate goal and then suddenly think that now they have attained it and do not need to go further.

## There is no ultimate state

My beloved, the most important thing you can realize about Christhood is that it is an ongoing process. You can attain Christhood while being in physical embodiment, but there is no ultimate state of Christhood that you could attain while in physical embodiment. We may say that there is no ultimate state of Christhood in the sense that there is no ultimate state of consciousness, except perhaps the Creator consciousness, but even that is transcending itself as it is creating. You need to recognize here that there is no ultimate state.

Life, awareness, self-awareness is an ongoing process. There is always the possibility of self-transcendence. There never was – *never was* – a static state in the world. There never *was* a static state in the world and there never *will be*. There never was a beginning and there never will be an ending. There can be a beginning of a cycle and the ending of a cycle, but there was no ultimate beginning before which there was nothing. There was a beginning of our world of form where the Creator existed in itself but this was not the ultimate beginning, for there never has been an ultimate beginning. There never will be an ultimate ending.

## You cannot understand Christhood

This is something that the linear mind finds it very difficult to grasp and that is why you need to understand that you cannot *understand* Christhood. You can, however, come to understand that you cannot *understand* Christhood. When you understand that you cannot *understand* Christhood and why you cannot understand Christhood, then you may begin to grasp at least glimpses of what Christhood is.

You need to recognize here that most people on earth have been programmed to think through the linear, analytical, rational mind. This mind cannot understand, grasp or deal with Christhood. Christhood goes beyond what the linear mind can deal with. That is why you also need to understand that the way you look at Christhood now is not the ultimate way to look at Christhood. It is not possible for me, even as an ascended master, to give you an ultimate discourse on Christhood because Christhood is a process of gradually raising your consciousness.

We have given you the knowledge that there are 144 levels of consciousness that are possible on earth. We can therefore say that Christhood is the process where you start at the 48th level and then raise your consciousness gradually to the 144th level. At the 144th level, you have attained the highest degree of Christhood that is possible on earth in its current state.

This means, my beloved, that when you start at the 48th level, you can have a certain understanding of Christhood but it is not the full understanding. As you grow towards higher levels of consciousness, your understanding of (your grasp of, your experience of) Christhood will change. You will not gain the full grasp of what Christhood is until you reach the 144th level. Therefore, you can see that it is not possible to give a definition of Christhood that can be grasped by all the many levels of consciousness between the 48th and the 144th level.

Why am I saying that this begins at the 48th level? Because for those who are below the 48th level, they cannot grasp Christhood. They may, of course, hear the concept of Christhood. They may also decide that they want to attain Christhood, but they cannot grasp what Christhood truly means. Therefore, they can build some kind of intellectual, rational, linear perception of what Christhood is. They may even think they are making progress towards this goal but they are not, my beloved. You can raise your consciousness from the lowest level to the 48th level, and you are making progress in a spiritual sense, but you are not even beginning the process of putting on Christhood.

The reason for this is that you are still too tied to the outer mind that thinks it can understand everything by creating these labels, and then adding a value judgment to the label they have created based on the dualistic mindset. Then, they think they can define Christhood based on a set of outer criteria. They think they can set up a list that says: When you live up to this criteria, put a check mark. Then go on to the next criteria, put a check mark. When you have completed the list and you have a check mark at every point, then you have attained Christhood. This is the only way they can conceive of it, those who are below the 48th level.

There are many false teachers in the world who attempt to give you some kind of path that leads to some kind of goal. They may not call it Christhood, they may call it higher awareness, cosmic consciousness, enlightenment, whatever. But it is all a mechanical path, an outer path. By performing certain exercises or rituals, or studying certain teachings, learning them by heart, they think they can qualify for entry into heaven by living up to a set of criteria defined here on earth.

## *The beginning of Christhood*

Now, my beloved, when you go above the 48th level of consciousness, you can begin the process of Christhood. You still may have many misconceptions about Christhood, but you will, in order to go above the 48th level, have the essential quality that is the beginning of the process of Christhood, and that is your willingness to listen to your intuition, even when your rational, linear mind tells you something different. In other words, what happens at the 48th level is that you begin to follow your intuition in certain cases and therefore you ignore, put aside or neutralize your rational, linear, logical, intellectual, analytical mind.

You will see, all of you who are here – and you are all above the 48th level of consciousness or you would not be here – you will see that there are decisions you have made to engage in the spiritual path. Your friends or family find it difficult to understand you because they have a rational, linear reasoning that says that you should not be doing what you are doing, or believing or accepting what you are accepting. You may not be able to give them a rational, linear understanding that they can accept for why you are doing what you are doing. You just *know* that this is the right thing for you.

This, then, is the essence of Christhood between the 48th and the 96th level. You are rising higher in consciousness by dealing with the Seven Rays as we have described in the course of self-mastery (See *www.morepublish.com*) where the Chohans give you a gradual path. As you do this, you are increasing your intuition, which is truly your connection to your I AM Presence and your ascended teachers. This means that you become more and more willing to ignore your own rational mind, but also to ignore the impulses, the projections, that are coming to you from without, whether it be from other people (such as family or friends), from society, the mass consciousness, dark forces or whatever it may be.

As you rise higher, there will be more of these projections but you get better and better at not letting them affect you. As you rise towards the 96th level, you increase your ability to read vibration, to read the energetic level of another person who is talking to you, an idea that comes to you or even a projection that comes to you from the lower forces. You get better at reading the vibrational level, and then you get better at sensing when it vibrates below a certain level and when it vibrates above it.

## Learning to read vibration

Now, my beloved, what I am telling you here is that when you go above the 48th level of consciousness, you have established in your own being, in your heart, a certain vibration that you know is higher than the fear-based vibrations of the world. It is sort of the highest vibration you are capable of recognizing with your level of consciousness. At the 48th level, for example, you have a certain base vibration you can recognize. Therefore, you can recognize that there are things that are very clearly vibrating below that level, and some that are vibrating above that level. You may have difficulty recognizing something that is too far above. You may also have difficulty distinguishing between your base vibration and something that is slightly below it, but you can clearly sense the difference between your base vibration and something that is very far below it.

Now, as you go higher on the levels towards the 96th level, you raise the vibration you are able to recognize. This means that you can now recognize higher and higher vibrations. Of course, you do not forget the base vibration you had at the 48th level so you can now recognize a greater and greater span of higher vibrations. This also means that you become better at distinguishing those vibrations that are slightly below the 48th level, and therefore it becomes more and more difficult for the dark forces to fool you.

There comes that point when you reach the 96th level where you have achieved the ability to read any vibration that the fallen beings can throw at you from beneath the 48th level. In other words, you cannot be fooled by a vibration that is below the 48th level, no matter how cleverly it is disguised.

You can recognize the vibration alone. This, however, does not mean that you have attained the fullness of Christhood. In fact, it is actually the preliminary stages of Christhood, and the real process of attaining personal Christhood – becoming the Living Christ – starts above the 96th level.

## The initiation at the 96th level

However, at the 96th level, you do face a crucial initiation, and this is an initiation that you saw me go through at the beginning of my mission. It is not depicted particularly well in the scriptures, but you do have, for example, the situation at the wedding in Cana where my mother had to push me into turning the water into wine and thereby stepping forward to begin my public mission. There are also other hints in the scriptures, such as the baptism by John the Baptist, and there are other more subtle hints.

The point here is that when you are the 96th level, you face a crucial decision. You can continue to pursue spiritual growth in order to elevate yourself and your own state of consciousness, or you can make the choice that from this point forward, you are pursuing spiritual growth not to elevate yourself but to serve in elevating the whole.

The difference may seem subtle. It *seems* subtle because it *is* subtle. In fact, most people below the 96th level will not be able to grasp the subtlety and those below the 48th will not be able to grasp it at all. They will not even be able to see why there should be such a choice. My beloved, Christhood at the higher levels of consciousness is not about raising your own consciousness, your own self. Do you understand, my beloved, that between the 48th to the 96th level of consciousness, you are raising your individuality, as you see it, above the pull of the mass consciousness?

As the mass consciousness is on earth today, there is no way you can manifest a higher state of consciousness while you are influenced by the mass consciousness. Therefore, at the 48th level, you come to the realization that you have the potential as an individual to raise yourself up above the mass consciousness. At the 48th level, you have a certain sense of self, a certain sense of identity, a mental understanding of who you are, an emotional grasp of who you are, and a physical, conscious understanding of who you are. As you see yourself at the 48th level, this is the self you begin to raise.

Now, of course, that self is transformed as you move towards the 96th level, but you are still fundamentally conceiving of yourself as an individual human being who is walking a spiritual path and raising your level of consciousness. It is inevitable, it is necessary – and there is nothing wrong with it – that you have a motivation for why you want to raise yourself, why you want to attain a higher level of consciousness.

However, this also gives room for the false teachers to influence you in subtle ways, and they have done this by, for example, portraying Christhood, enlightenment or cosmic consciousness as a supernatural state where you attain some supernatural abilities, such as turning the water into wine, walking on water or raising the dead—whatever you have. They make you think that you become a super-human that has supernatural abilities. There are many people who have a desire to have such abilities and who have a desire to go out and demonstrate these abilities to other people. They may have a seemingly benign desire to attract people to the spiritual path, but behind it is always this self-centered motivation of elevating themselves above others. In other words, there is always an element of the self-centered as you are walking the path from the 48th to the 96th level.

The initiation you face at the 96th level is: Will you abandon this self-motivated desire for growth? Will you step up to a higher motivation where you realize that the real goal of attaining your ascension is to now begin to dismantle the self that you have used as a vehicle for rising from the 48th to the 96th level?

Now, you may liken this to a space rocket, my beloved, that has two stages. One is the motor with a huge fuel tank that is needed to carry the rocket beyond the gravitational pull of the earth. It is necessary to have that self between the 48th and the 96th level. I am not blaming anyone. There is nothing wrong with this. It is necessary but as you see with the rocket, once the rocket has gone into space, it does not need that huge booster and fuel tank because it was only needed to take it to that stage. Therefore, the rocket must separate itself from it and let it fall away.

The crucial distinction at the 96th level is between those who grasp this and those who do not. There are those who, at the 96th level, continue to seek to elevate themselves. Then, there are those who see the need to actually let go of the self they have at the 96th level. This does not mean that they can instantly let go of it, for there is always a certain need for continuity so you can function in the material realm. Therefore, what I am saying is that, once you get to the 96th level and grasp what the higher stage of Christhood is about, you engage in a process that step-by-step leads you from the 96th to the 144th level. This process is not about elevating yourself, giving yourself some special abilities, making yourself superior to other people. It is actually about dismantling the self that separates you from other people.

## Progressive views of Christhood

Do you see, my beloved, it may seem contradictory that you need a certain self to pull yourself above the mass consciousness. Then, once you have done that, you need to dismantle that self and strive for oneness with all people. The fact of the matter is that while you are affected by the mass consciousness, you are not in oneness with other people, you are not in oneness with your I AM Presence, you are not in oneness with the ascended masters. You are simply in this mechanization state where we have said that the fallen beings have attempted to make everyone the same. *That,* my beloved, is not oneness.

It may be *sameness,* but it is not *oneness.* You see, oneness in a spiritual sense is where you recognize your divine, your spiritual, individuality but your spiritual individuality does not set you apart from others. We who are ascended masters recognize our individuality. I recognize my own individuality as distinct from Master MORE's or Saint Germain's, but we are not in conflict or competition with each other. We have achieved a degree of oneness that you cannot fathom in the unascended state. But you can begin to fathom it as you move closer to the 144th level.

These are the two main stages of Christhood and that is why, when you are below the 96th level, you can have a certain view of Christhood, a certain grasp, a certain understanding of what you think it is. Once you go above the 96th level, you begin to realize that it is much more. It is something, in fact, completely different from what you thought at your previous level of consciousness. It is extremely – *extremely* – important that whatever level you are at, you adopt the conscious attitude that you do not, at your present level, have the full grasp of what Christhood is. Therefore, you will not look at a particular definition or view of Christhood and say: "This is what Christhood is" and therefore you close your mind to a higher view, a higher understanding, a higher experience.

While you are below the 96th level, you will still think that Christhood is something you can *understand.* I am asking you to be aware that even though you may have a certain understanding of Christhood, there will come a point where that understanding needs to be dismissed. Now, instead of *understanding* Christhood, you are focused on *experiencing* it.

There is a difference between understanding and experience in the sense that while you are understanding something, you are looking at it from a distance. You are saying: "Christhood is up there and I am understanding what it is, and I am understanding how to get closer to it." What is implied in this is that you are not there.

## Experiencing Christhood

As you come to the 96th level and as you make that conscious decision to shift away from being focused on yourself, to be focused on something beyond the self, then you can begin to *experience* Christhood. This again does not mean you experience the fullness of it, but you experience Christhood at a certain stage. This is where, as the messenger described, you need to come to that point where you are consciously willing to accept that you have achieved a degree of Christhood. If you do not make that acceptance, then you cannot actually, truly, begin the process of experiencing higher and higher expressions of Christhood.

You may think you are the Christ below the 96th level, and we continually see some students who think they can declare that they have attained Christhood while they are still below the 96th level or at the 96th level. My beloved, they are declaring this with the outer mind and this is not what I am talking about. I am talking about a very delicate shift that is not based on the outer mind. It is not making a decision with the outer mind but it is recognizing that you cannot *deny* Christhood either.

You are recognizing that there is always, in the human ego, a dynamic of inferiority and superiority. You recognize that there is a tendency, there is an element of your ego, that wants to inflate your own sense of self-importance. Therefore, you recognize that those who are affected by this level of ego, they are declaring that they are the Christ before they are actually ready for it, before they have made that decision to stop focusing on self. They are trying to use Christhood as a way to elevate the separate self to some ultimate status.

Then, on the other hand, you also see that there are those who are caught in the inferiority aspect of the ego and they are thinking that they should not recognize that they have reached a certain stage of the path. They should be humble, they should not bring attention to themselves. They should be so concerned about not being prideful that they actually switch to the opposite extreme of being prideful because they are so humble and not declaring themselves to have reached any certain stage. You see, pride can be expressed as both *inferiority* and *superiority*.

## Acknowledging Christhood

When you recognize this, you recognize that it is necessary to look at yourself, to look at your psychology, to look at both aspects of the ego, the inferiority aspect, the superiority aspect, to come to see how they have affected your self. Then, as you go through this process of exposing this dynamic of the ego, there comes that point where you have seen through it, and you see that you are more than this. This is not who you are, this does not define you. Then, you see that you actually want to go completely beyond this ego dynamic because you want oneness with your I AM Presence, you want oneness with the ascended master who is closest to your heart. You want that more than any status you could have here on earth.

That is when you can come to that spontaneous inner realization that you cannot declare your Christhood prematurely, but neither can you deny it, or ignore it, beyond the level where you actually are at in consciousness. Then, you come to the realization that it is necessary for you to acknowledge that you have made progress on the spiritual path, you have reached a certain level of consciousness. You have reached a level of Christhood that is above the 96th level because you recognize that you are no longer focused on that separate self. You have aspects of it but you are not focused on it. It is not defining you, it is not defining your path.

That is when you acknowledge that you have attained a degree of Christhood, but you also acknowledge that it is not the highest degree of Christhood. You realize that between the 96th and the 144th levels, this is a process that is not the way many people think it is. This is not the stage where you attain some supernatural ability. Supernatural abilities are not an essential part of Christhood. There are people who have attained Christhood, who have qualified for their ascension, without ever displaying any supernatural abilities, without ever being recognized by others. Those who are below the 48th level cannot even recognize people at the higher levels, and most people below the 96th level cannot recognize them very easily either.

At this stage, you are not focused on the world in the sense that you are focused on living up to certain images or expectations. You are not seeking to impress the world. You are not seeking validation from the world.

You have attained what you might term a higher sense of spiritual self-sufficiency where you do not need the recognition or the validation of other people or the world. You do not need to be validated by others because you are validated from within yourself by your experience of a greater degree of oneness than you had before. You can still remember how it was when you did not have the sense of oneness with your I AM Presence or with the ascended masters that you now have. Therefore, you are not looking at the degree of oneness you have as some theoretical goal that you see from a distance. You are experiencing it, and you experience that, as you continually look at yourself and see more limitations, more limiting beliefs, and let them go, then you achieve a higher degree of oneness.

## Continual self-observation

You realize that the path between the 96th and the 144th level is actually a path of continual self-observation. In every situation, you are observing your own reactions. Whenever you see a reaction that you know vibrates below the level that is the base vibration you now recognize, then you look at it openly and honestly. You are not seeking to hide it from yourself, you are not seeking to excuse it. Neither are you condemning yourself because you have gone beyond the need to condemn yourself in any way. You are not finding fault with others, you are not finding fault with yourself, you are not judging with that dualistic value judgment. You are simply observing. You observe that there is something here that is limiting you and then you look at what it is until you discover the mechanism. Then, you realize how you let that self die and you rise to a higher level.

You see, my beloved, below the 96th level, striving for Christhood is based on the perception you have with the outer self. It is based on raising yourself beyond the pull of the mass consciousness. Now, as you go above the 96th level, and in fact, *in order* to go above the 96th level, you need to pass the initiation that I described when I said that if you seek to save your life, you shall lose it, but those who are willing to lose their lives for my sake, shall find it. What is meant by this is that you now need to start letting go of aspects of your life, meaning your outer self, the self that brought you to the 96th level. You need to let elements of that self die because you experience (you feel, you see) that it is more important for you to come one step higher in the process of attaining oneness with your I AM Presence or oneness with the ascended master that is closest to your heart. It may be me; it may be any other master you desire. It is a process of attaining oneness and you attain oneness with your higher self, with your I AM Presence, only by letting the outer self die step by step, element by element, increment by increment.

## Continual dying

This is a process where, in a way, it could be said, it is a continual process of dying because you are dying to the world. You are letting the worldly self die so that the prince of this world comes and has less and less in you until he finally comes and has *nothing* in you. You have let that worldly self die, and there is nothing left of it. At that point, there is also nothing that keeps you in embodiment and that is why you will move into the ascension process. It is important for you to keep in mind that it is a matter of letting the outer self die.

Now my beloved, I call it a form of death because most people see death as some final stage where something disappears, something dies, something is no more. This is literally what happens to your outer self: it dies. There is a certain self, a certain element of it, and as Hilarion explained in his book (*The Mystical Initiations of Vision*), for each of the levels of consciousness, there is a certain illusion. We could also say that there is a certain self that you need to let die at the 96th level in order to ascend to the 97th level. Then, there is a self at the 97th level that you allow to die in order to ascend to the 98th and so on. It is something final.

Now this, of course, you are also doing between the 48th and the 96th levels, but you are not conscious of it, in most cases. As you go above that 96th level and make that first decision to let the self die, then you become more and more conscious of this. You see that something is actually dying. It is no more, you are completely letting it go. At that point, you begin to realize that death is not something that happens to you that you are not in control of. Death is actually you consciously letting go of the self that no longer serves you. It is a process over which you are in control, my beloved. You are consciously letting that self die and you see it as a final act where the self is no more after you have let it go.

## Glamorous images of Christhood

You see, my beloved, there are many people who will listen to or read this discourse and they will feel a certain sense of disappointment because suddenly what I am describing as Christhood does not sound nearly as glamorous as they see it right now. This only demonstrates to you that you have adopted, to some degree, one of these false images presented by the false teachers of what it means to reach some higher state of consciousness.

There is especially one aspect I would like to bring to your attention. It is so typical for spiritual movements (whether it be the major religions or smaller spiritual movements centered around a certain guru) that they look up to the leader of the movement as being somehow above other people. You will see, for example, how there are many modern spiritual organizations that were started by a certain person and the people in the movement think that this person is enlightened. They have some, often very unclear, view of what it means to be enlightened but they clearly think that the person who is enlightened is somehow above others.

If enlightenment has any meaning as a concept, it would be the same as Christhood. What is Christhood? It is that as you go closer and closer to the 144th level, you begin to see that behind all of the phenomena found in the world, there is an underlying oneness. This means that you begin to see yourself, first of all, in oneness with your I AM Presence and with the ascended masters above you. You see that you are part of this ongoing flow of energy from Spirit—the upper part of the figure-eight. Then, as you come closer and closer to that nexus, you begin to see your oneness with all that is below, not with the fallen beings, with the duality consciousness but with those who are the self-aware extensions of God, the sons and daughters of God. You see your oneness with all people. As you go closer and closer to this oneness, all value judgments, all comparisons, completely fade away, my beloved.

In a sense, it is necessary to say that as you get closer to the 144th level of consciousness, of course you are at a higher level of consciousness than those who are at the 48th level, for example. Naturally, you have risen, through a very determined effort, very high above the 48th level. This does not mean that you now see yourself as better or more important than others. On the contrary, your value judgments fade away and it gives no meaning for you to compare yourself to others. In fact, it gives no meaning to even compare yourself to any scale. You consider less and less where you are at on the scale of consciousness. You are simply focused on being who you are, expressing your Divine plan as you are beginning to see it more clearly and serving other people, serving the cause of the ascended masters of raising all life. This is your focus.

You understand, my beloved, the more enlightened a person is, the less he or she wants to be seen as enlightened when people see an enlightened person as being above them. You realize that if other people see you as being above them, they cannot see you as an example to follow. They see a gap between you and themselves and therefore you cannot inspire them fully to follow the path that you have followed. You see, my beloved, if a person sets himself or herself up as being fundamentally above others, then that person cannot be enlightened. If the person was enlightened, he or she would not want other people to put them up there on a pedestal. Instead, the enlightened person would do everything possible to prevent people from seeing a gap. The person wants people to see that all have the potential to follow the same path and reach these higher levels of consciousness. Here, all of the comparisons, all of the value judgments, fade away and as a result of this, you attain a greater and greater degree of inner peace. There is nothing you have to live up to in the world. There is nothing you have to strive for. There is nothing you have to condemn yourself for. You do not have to judge or evaluate other people.

You see, my beloved, when I said: "For judgment I am come," it did not mean that I was come to judge and evaluate and criticize other people. It meant that I came to allow other people to judge themselves by the way they acted towards me. The ultimate judgment was that they killed my physical body and thereby attempted to kill the Living Christ.

Now, fortunately we live in an age where the fallen beings find it increasingly difficult to kill the Living Christ and therefore you obviously do not have to go through that experience—I sincerely hope for you. You understand here that the idea is that I did not come to judge and criticize and evaluate anybody, as many people think. As we have said before, we of the ascended masters are not sitting up here watching your every action, your every word, your every thought and feeling. We are not criticizing, condemning, evaluating and judging you, my beloved. We are only seeking to raise you up.

## Raising others instead of yourself

This is what you do when you come closer and closer to the 144th level. You become less and less concerned about creating a sense that you are elevated above others. In fact, you become more and more concerned about helping other people raise their consciousness. You are more concerned about raising up others than raising yourself, and therefore you do what you can to avoid people putting you up on a pedestal.

My beloved, these are my thoughts for now. Obviously this is not meant to be the final word on Christhood, but it is what I determined would be valuable to you, based on the questions you have been asking and that many people around the world have been asking. Therefore, I give you thanks for listening and for being the open doors, for again, I could use your chakras to radiate an impetus into Korea and into the world – the mass consciousness of the world – to reach those who have the potential to step forward and recognize their Christhood and begin those higher stages above the 96th level.

My beloved, I want to express my deep gratitude for those of you here in Korea who have studied our teachings, who have given our invocations and who have been so instrumental in bringing the changes you have seen in these past ten months since our last conference and obviously even before that conference. We are grateful and we do, my beloved, recognize your efforts. We are, of course, not in any way seeking to make you feel superior to others but you understand, my beloved, that when you get beyond that inferiority-superiority dynamic, it is valid to recognize that you have made an effort, it has produced results and you have made a difference in your nation by what you are doing. Therefore, you can, of course, continue to make a difference. As you rise to higher levels of consciousness, you can make more and more of a difference. Of course, as you rise towards that 96th level, you become more and more of an open door for the impulses and energies from your I AM Presences and the ascended masters. It is this inflow of energy that will make the ultimate difference in raising the earth into the golden age.

You might say that as you come closer and closer to the fullness of Christhood at the 144th level, you become more and more of an open door for radiating the golden age consciousness into the world. This means that in many cases you may have to do less and less on the outer and that is why you have seen some people who have withdrawn to a cave and sat there and held the spiritual balance. Of course, in this day and age, it is also very important that most of the people who are striving for Christhood engage themselves actively in society and therefore, you become the examples. As we have said many times, the matrix where there is one person who is seen as the example was a Piscean phenomenon and in the Aquarian Age we need many people to be the examples.

That is why an Aquarian-age organization does not elevate one leader to some supreme status but sees that all people have the potential to serve as examples and be the open doors. Thus, my beloved, my gratitude for your willingness to be the open doors for my release of light this day.

# 10 | SOLVING THE
# ENIGMAS OF THE PATH
# TO BUDDHAHOOD

The Buddha I AM, Gautama is my name. I would like to take this opportunity to talk about some topics that may not seem to be saying anything about Korea. Perhaps in not saying anything about Korea, I shall nevertheless be saying something about Korea for those who are able to grasp it.

If you study the magnificent discourse given by Jesus on the Path to Christhood, you will see, my beloved, that there are certain stages of this path. Especially, when you approach and go beyond the 96th level, then there will be some challenges that you will be facing, that you will have to deal with, in order to climb higher towards the 144th level. We can consider these challenges as certain paradoxes, as certain enigmas, that you will need to resolve before you can rise to a higher level of the path. There are a number of these enigmas, and I will not go into all of them but I will comment on some of them.

## *Seeing contradictions or seeing beyond them*

Now, you see my beloved, when we of the ascended masters approach unascended humankind and attempt to give you a teaching, then we face a very specific challenge that few people in embodiment have understood. The fact of the matter is that when you are an ascended master, you have transcended the linear, dualistic, analytical mind. Therefore, you have a more spherical awareness; you do not see everything through this filter of polarities, of extremes, of value judgments and a value scale. You do not have a linear mind that compares one statement to another and perhaps sees a contradiction because the two do not seem to be saying the same.

We know, of course, that people who are unascended are indeed in this state of mind of very easily seeing contradictions because they interpret everything with the linear mind. They think they have to take *this* statement literally, they think they have to take *that* statement literally; and when you take two statements literally, they seem to be in contradiction. Now my beloved, there are many spiritual students who have begun to study spiritual, or for that matter religious, teachings and then they have seen what they perceived to be contradictions. Many in the western world have used the seeming contradictions of religious scriptures to reason with science or materialism that all religion is made up and that none of it really makes sense.

This, of course, is the extreme outcome of using the linear mind. Even many religious or spiritual people do find contradictions, often between two different spiritual teachings. This makes them think they have to reason that one of them is *right* and the other one is *wrong*. There are even those who begin to see contradictions within one spiritual teaching and it confuses them, it even causes some to give up on the path. My purpose here is to give you some remarks that can help you get beyond this stage, for it is indeed a stage on the path. In a certain sense, you have risen above the linear mind but you have not consciously broken through and freed your conscious mind from the linear way of thinking. You are not consciously seeing the limitations of the linear way of thinking, and therefore you can still be disturbed by these seeming contradictions.

At a very general level, my beloved, I can tell you that, of course, there can be certain instances where there may be statements that are contradictory. We cannot, when we bring forth a teaching through an unascended messenger, guarantee that there could not be certain errors that creep in and there might be a few contradictions here and there. When you come to a more mature level of the path, you will not let one error or one contradiction cause you to reject the part of the teaching that is still valid. That having been said, in the vast majority of cases, what seems like a contradiction only *seems* like a contradiction because it is viewed through the filter of the linear mind. The constructive response when you see a contradiction is to say: "I need to raise my consciousness so I can gain a higher perspective on the issue. There must be something I have not seen, something I have not understood. When I see it, it will resolve what right now seems like a contradiction." Then, you open yourself up to direct, intuitive guidance from the ascended masters, from your I AM Presence, from your Christ Self to resolve the enigma. Or you study further teachings because you realize there may be other teachings that could help you resolve the enigma.

## Misunderstanding non-attachment

As one example of what many people have seen as contradictory, you can take the mission of the Buddha itself. I taught, even 2,500 years ago, that the goal of my teaching was to give you a path that could help you rise above the normal state of consciousness by attaining complete non-attachment. Yet my beloved, if I personally had achieved complete non-attachment, why would I bother to teach?

In other words, many people interpret the concept of non-attachment to mean that you do not care what happens on earth. They reason that if the Buddha truly had non-attachment, he should not care what happened to other people so why bother to go out and give them a teaching that might help them escape the wheel of suffering? Why would the Buddha not simply be non-attached and move on, leaving people to make the same discovery he had made and thereby free themselves if they could. If they could not, he would leave them to continue on the wheel of rebirth, suffering until they had finally had enough and awakened themselves.

You see my beloved, non-attachment is not the same as not caring. It is, however, not a caring that is a *human* caring. It is not based on fear. It is not based on wanting to force other people or wanting to force a change in the world. The fact that you are non-attached does not mean that you will choose to do nothing. It means that you might choose to do something to help others, or you can choose to move on. If you choose to help others, you are not coming from the human level of wanting to see a specific result. You are actually not teaching for a specific purpose, you are not seeking to achieve a specific result from your teaching. You are teaching because you want to share what you have discovered, you want to share who you are. You are therefore not seeking to force others; you are offering them an alternative to the prevalent state of consciousness on earth.

There are those for whom this will seem like a subtle, perhaps even nonsensical, distinction. This, I recognize, is the case. I cannot help you resolve these paradoxes if you are not at the level where you are willing to do what I just described and raise your consciousness. If you are always projecting out that the problem is "out there," that the problem is with the teaching or the teacher, then you cannot resolve these paradoxes. You will then have to enter the School of Hard Knocks and receive a sufficient number of knocks until you become willing to say: "Perhaps it is me that needs to change, perhaps the block is in my consciousness rather than being a fault with the teacher, the teaching, other people or the world?"

## Seeing the limits of the linear mind

Some of you might know the story told about my life that after I had qualified for Buddhahood, after I had entered nirvana and considered going out of nirvana in order to teach, I was confronted with the entire force of this world, saying that there was no point in me going out and teaching. The state of consciousness I had reached was so fundamentally different from the state of consciousness that all people are in, that there was no way they could understand or grasp my teaching. In other words, it could not make a difference.

My response to this was: *"Some* will understand." During the past 2,500 years, *some* have understood but only *a few.* We are, however, now at a point in time where many more are ready to understand and that is, of course, why I now present myself as an ascended master, as one among many ascended masters, and attempt to give you a teaching that is adapted to the modern age.

Again, before I decided to do this, I had to face this force that is not a conscious being. It is simply that when you, as an ascended master, consider what you can do for unascended mankind, you need to tune in to where mankind is at in consciousness. Then, you are confronted with the difference between the collective consciousness and your own state of consciousness and there is a certain moment where you feel the impossibility of bridging the gap. Therefore, you have to deal with that, you have to, in your mind, find a way around it. You look at where people are at in consciousness and you consider ways of helping them rise above that and tune in to some aspect of your Presence, your Being.

This dictation is one expression of this, as all of my other dictations have been and as all dictations from ascended masters are. What I am seeking here is to help you see the limitations of the linear mind because the linear, rational, analytical mind is indeed much more dominant in today's world than it was 2,500 years ago.

## When enlightenment blocks enlightenment

I would like to give you another example. One of the concepts I gave to the world back then was the concept that when you walk the eight-fold path, you can attain a higher state of consciousness that I called enlightenment. Now, I attempted back then to tell people how to attain enlightenment and how to avoid having the concept of enlightenment block their enlightenment. Very few people have understood this and especially in the modern age very few people have grasped it, precisely because of the influence of the linear mind.

You see, my beloved, we have given you the concept of a spiritual path. We have talked about the 144 levels of consciousness, of how you can consciously begin the path at the 48th level and you can plot your course as you rise up towards the 96th level. You can follow a series of logical steps that take you in a linear process of gradually raising your consciousness. We have also told you that you can go beyond the 96th level and you again go up through a series of steps until you reach the 144th level. This is, of course, a linear process, but the spiritual path, or the process of attaining enlightenment, does not have to be described in a *linear* fashion. It could also be described in a *spherical* fashion. It is simply that what we give you in this age is adapted to the fact that you have a linear way of thinking. We, of course, also adapt our teachings in such a way, design them in such a way, that you will gradually escape the blindness of the linear mind and come to see beyond it by daring to follow your intuition, which is not linear.

I still want to express some idea here about this concept of enlightenment. In order to fully understand this, we need to step back a little bit. I attempted to give this teaching 2,500 years ago, but it was actually more difficult to give it back then. Ironically, you might say, it was more difficult because people did not think in such a linear way back then as they do now.

It is not so, my beloved, that it was better or that people were more open to a spiritual teaching back then than they are today. It is not that I am trying to say here that the development of the linear mind has been a backwards step. It is only a backwards step when it is taken to the extreme. The development of the linear mind in its higher form is indeed designed by the ascended masters. It is a logical step up from the kind of more mythological, magical thinking that people were in before the modern age. Precisely because you have a more linear mind, it is actually possible to give you a new perspective on what enlightenment is and how your concept of enlightenment can block your enlightenment.

## The limitations of understanding

You have, in the modern mindset, this concept of *understanding* something. You have the idea that there is a lower level of understanding where you do not have enough knowledge and insight. Then, you can follow a process of gaining greater and greater understanding and insight until you see something that you cannot see when you do not have the more advanced knowledge. This has actually made it easier for us to present a logical path where we can make people lock in to the desire they have to progress. We can give them a very gradual, step-by-step process for progressing in their knowledge and understanding of the spiritual side to life. Yet what you also can understand here, even with the linear mind, is that there are levels of understanding. This is easy to see.

A few hundred years ago, even scientists had a far more simple and primitive understanding of the material universe than they have today. Today, they have a more sophisticated, more detailed, more in-depth understanding. There is a progression here, but what you can switch to understand with the linear mind is that it is not so that advancing your knowledge can be done in only one way or within one system.

As a simple example of this, my beloved, you can take the concept of atoms. All matter is made of atoms and even atoms are made of smaller parts, called elementary particles. I have just described this knowledge to you in very simple terms but it took scientists centuries to develop this knowledge. Now, I have just described this knowledge to you in a language called English, but you could also describe this same knowledge in a language called Korean, Chinese or French or any other language. It is the same knowledge but it is expressed with different words.

You can also see with the linear mind that science in general is attempting to describe how the material universe works but there is not just one branch of science. You have, for example, physics and you have chemistry. When you take a physical perspective on how matter works, you describe the workings of matter in one way. When you take a chemical perspective, you describe it in another way.

It is not that these two are mutually exclusive or incompatible. They are different ways to describe essentially the same phenomena. Then, you can look a little broader and see that what you call life on earth is more than just physical matter. There is also what you call biological life and this is described by the science of biology. It is not that biology is incompatible with physics or chemistry. It is perhaps looking at slightly different phenomena but it is mainly describing life in a different way. Then you can go even beyond this and see that many of the physical sciences are attempting to express their findings in the language of mathematics. Now, you see that there is an everyday language, which human beings use to communicate in their everyday lives, and there is a mathematical language that scientists use to describe certain phenomena that are beyond what you deal with in your normal life.

You cannot really say that the language of mathematics is incompatible with everyday language. They are two different ways to describe, in many cases, the same phenomena. Of course, mathematics can describe certain phenomena or describe them with greater precision than everyday language. On the other hand, my beloved, everyday language is very useful for many practical applications. As a silly example, try to go into McDonald's and order a hamburger by using a mathematical formula and who knows what you will get. You see here that with the linear mind that people have today, it is actually possible to see that the different branches of science are parallel ways to describe the same phenomena.

You even have the concept, developed by some people based on the findings of science, that there are parallel realities, parallel universes, parallel dimensions that might exist inside each other. You have now the most advanced branch of physics, called string theory, which talks about these tiny vibrating strings that exist in eleven dimensions. You are beginning to see that even the linear mind can be used to expand people's understanding of spiritual concepts when you realize that a spiritual teaching (not necessarily a doctrinal religion but a more *universal* spiritual teaching) is simply a language. It is not just a language of words but a language of concepts. When science describes a certain phenomenon as a vibrating string and a spiritual teaching describes it as an elemental being, these are not incompatible descriptions but parallel descriptions of the same phenomena. This may not be acceptable to science but those who are open to a spiritual teaching can see here that there can be different ways of describing the same phenomenon. Some ways cause you to focus on certain aspects of the phenomenon and others cause you to focus on other aspects.

## Enlightenment is not a concept

Now, I set out this long discourse saying I would explain how giving you the concept of enlightenment can block your enlightenment. We now need to take my remarks to the point where we realize that, as physics describes matter in one way and chemistry in another and a spiritual teaching can describe it in a third way, what all of these teachings have in common is, my beloved, that they give you a *concept* that your mind can use to create an internal image of the phenomenon. You cannot, with your physical eyes, see an atom so when you read the description of atoms given by physics, that description does not give you a direct experience of the atom. It enables you to create a mental image of the atom. Now, this mental image can be useful because it can give you the sense that you *understand* the phenomenon. It can also be useful in practical terms in the sense that it can allow you to do something in your everyday life.

Why is it, for example, that the modern world has created a much more comfortable material lifestyle where people are, on a routine basis, doing things that people could not even dream of doing a thousand years ago? It is because, as the linear mind has developed and as the scientific mindset has given you a certain understanding of the world, you have become able to solve problems that could not be solved with the understanding people had five hundred or a thousand years ago. This has been useful because you can do something in the practical world and therefore you can create a better standard of living for yourself and for most people.

It is for this reason that Saint Germain has sponsored so much technology that is based on the knowledge of science. It has enabled people to create a more comfortable form of living where they actually can have their minds freed to pursue the spiritual side of life instead of having all their energy consumed by making a living. My beloved, this is a positive development, clearly, but everything in the material universe (at least as long as so many people are trapped in the sense of separation, the consciousness of duality) has a price. There is always a downside, as they say. The downside is that people can become so attached to these scientific concepts that they cannot see that the concept that is describing the phenomenon is not the same as the phenomenon. This has one very important limitation. Many people in the modern world have lost the idea (that at least a few people had in previous times) that the mind has abilities that are beyond the linear, analytical aspect of the mind. What we have told you in our teachings is that consciousness always comes before the physical manifestation. For every physical phenomenon that exists in the material world, there is a certain matrix of consciousness that exists in the identity, mental, and emotional realms. Your outer mind, your physical senses, the part of the mind that is so tied to the physical senses, can only experience the material phenomenon, not the consciousness behind it.

There are other aspects of your mind that have the potential to experience the consciousness behind any physical phenomenon. When you experience that consciousness, you gain a more direct experience of the totality of the phenomenon. Now, this does not mean, my beloved, that you still do not need the linear understanding. In order to live your lives in practical everyday situations, you need to have that linear understanding. It is important for you to realize, as spiritual students, that when we, even as ascended masters, give you a concept about some spiritual phenomenon, your linear mind will immediately create an internal image of the phenomenon.

This is what Jesus described in a different way in his dictation about Christhood where he said that when you are at the 48th level of consciousness, you form a certain concept of what Christhood is but it cannot be the fullness of Christhood. Therefore, you cannot rise to the higher levels of Christhood unless you are willing to look beyond your present concept of Christhood and experience a higher reality. He also said that when you go beyond the 96th level, you are no longer so concerned about understanding with the linear mind but more concerned about experiencing. It is exactly the same with enlightenment.

When I gave the concept of enlightenment, I attempted to express this and I knew that few people would understand it. You see my beloved, the concept of enlightenment is just that: a concept. For all people who are at a lower state of consciousness, it *can only be* a concept. They form a mental image of what it means to be enlightened, they want to set up some external criteria. They want to set up an automatic, mechanical path that says: "If I follow these steps and do everything that has been described exactly as it was described, then I should automatically end up being enlightened. When I am enlightened, when a person is enlightened, that person has *this* characteristic and *that* characteristic. The person behaves like *this,* does not behave like *that,* it speaks like *this,* it does not speak like *that."* This is what the linear mind wants to do.

My beloved, does this mean the linear mind is not useful on the spiritual path? Of course not. As Jesus also described, there is a certain point where you need to follow a very linear, logical path. It can be very, very useful for people, who become aware that life has a spiritual side, to be presented with a linear path where they go through certain stages, certain progressive initiations that gradually raise their consciousness. The linear path *does* raise your consciousness, but a linear path where you keep taking one step at a time can *only* take you to a certain level. It can take you beyond the 96th level but, my beloved, listen carefully.

We have said there are 144 levels of consciousness so logically, when you come to the 139th level of consciousness, you need to take one step up and you are at the 140th level. Then you take another step and you are the 141st level and so on. You see my beloved, the strict linearity that you saw between the 48th and the 96th level becomes less and less important as you go beyond the 96th level.

It is as if the concept of a path becomes less important to you. You are not so focused on evaluating: "What level am I at? What initiation do I need to pass in order to take the next level up, what are the characteristics of a person at that level?" You simply are not so concerned about where you are at because now, instead of being focused on the single steps, you are focused on the process. It is, as we might say, instead of being focused on still images of the river, you are focused on the movement of the river, the process itself.

My point is that as long as you, in your mind, have the concept of a path that will lead you step-by-step to nirvana or to enlightenment, then you will never reach the goal. It may seem contradictory that I am telling you that in order to reach enlightenment you have to follow a gradual path, but that as long as you have the concept of this path, you cannot reach enlightenment. The reason for this, my beloved, is that enlightenment is not a linear phenomenon, it is not a physical phenomenon, it is not even a state of consciousness. It is not so that you can say that at the 143rd level you are *not* enlightened but at the 144th level you *are.* There is actually a lower stage where, at some point above the 96th level, you reach a state that you can call enlightenment because now you understand that the only thing that really matters is that you free your mind from all of the concepts it has that are based on the conditions in this world. That is when you also realize that your concept of enlightenment is just that: a *concept* not an *experience*. Therefore, you can switch your mind so that instead of striving to fulfill the criteria defined by your concept of enlightenment, you are free of the image, free of the concept. Therefore, you experience what I called enlightenment, a different perspective where your mind is not identified with its own concepts of material phenomena.

There are certain phenomena in the material world that were not exclusively created by your mind. As we have said before, all material phenomena are created by a mind, originally created by the minds of the Elohim. Since humankind started embodying on the planet, humankind has co-created certain phenomena that exist today. While you are still at the lower levels of consciousness, you are not experiencing the material world as it is, you are experiencing it through the concepts of the mind, the concepts you have created in your mind. While your mind, your individual mind, has not created the material phenomena, it has created your images, your concepts of those phenomena; what they are, how they work what you *can* do with them, what you *cannot* do with them.

In other words, your mind is defining how you see the material world's ability to limit your mind. You understand, my beloved? There are certain material phenomena, but what limits you is not so much the material phenomena as the images, the concepts in your mind. The path of attaining what we have called mastery of mind over matter is freeing your mind from the concept, created by the mind, that limits your direct experience of matter.

The enlightened state is not a state of perfection. It is not even a final state. It is possible to receive what I as the Buddha termed enlightenment and still not be at the 144th level, still have levels of enlightenment to go through before you ascend. The, so to speak, lowest level of enlightenment is where you stop identifying yourself with the images and concepts that your own mind has created. You become aware that everything you have in your mind that relates to the material world (and for that matter most of what you have in your mind that relates to the spiritual world) is just concepts created by the mind. By becoming non-attached to these concepts, non-attached to these images, by not identifying yourself with the images, you can free your mind from the limitations defined by those images.

## Mind over matter

Many of you have accepted these very subtle images that your mind cannot change matter. As long as you believe in, identify with, as long as you
are attached to, these images, then your mind cannot change matter. When
you free your mind from these images, then your mind can begin to change
matter. Then, your mind begins to see that the physical phenomenon is
an expression of the matrices of consciousness in the three higher levels.
Your mind *does* have the ability to influence these consciousness matrices.

Therefore, your mind is not trapped by the phenomena and it is not
trapped by your images of these phenomena. This ties in with what I
started out saying because you could look at a contradiction or a seeming contradiction in even the teachings we have given you at these two
conferences. For example, you have all of these dictations by the masters
who pointed out to you that here is a particular issue in your society that
you need to make the calls on in your invocations so that you invoke light
from the ascended masters and so that the masters can step in and bring
about change in your society. On the other hand, you have a dictation
from me at the last conference where I told you to focus on being in the
now and appreciating the now, not always being so concerned about the
past and the future. You could say: "Well, is there not a contradiction
here?" You see, my beloved, the resolution to this seeming paradox is to
realize that there is a difference between the fear-based, dualistic perspective of human beings and the love-based non-dualistic perspective of the
ascended masters.

It is perfectly true, my beloved, that the ascended masters want to see
a linear, progressive change that improves the living conditions for the
people on earth. This, however, is not incompatible with the consciousness of the Buddha. I came out of nirvana in order to teach people because
I also desire to see a linear, progressive improvement of the living conditions on earth. The difference is that we are not attached to seeing particular changes at a particular time. We are, as we have said earlier, not so
focused on a particular change because our overall goal is to raise the consciousness of our unascended brothers and sisters so that you can begin to
become more conscious of the process of co-creation.

You see, my beloved, I am not telling you to *not* care about what happens in the future. I am not telling you to ignore what happened in the
past. You need to be aware of what happened in the past in order to
understand the mechanisms that caused certain problems that have caused

certain limitations in your society. You need to see the underlying consciousness so you can free yourself from it and help other people be free
of it.

When I am telling you to focus more on being in the now, I am not
saying that you should force your mind to ignore the past, force your mind
to ignore the future. I am telling you to overcome the wounds you had in
the past whereby you overcome your attachment to the past so that the
past cannot pull you into these reactionary patterns that actually prevent
you from 1) enjoying the moment and 2) being free to make a decision to
change the course of your life for the future.

I am also telling you to resolve your psychology so that you are not
trapped in the pattern where you are constantly looking to get away from
the present moment into some imagined future that you think will be better. In other words, I am telling you to not strive towards the future in
order to escape dealing with your own psychology, which is the reason so
many people get trapped in dreaming about a better future. I am telling
you to actually free yourself from this escapism of dreaming about a better
future and instead focus on resolving your psychology so that you can be
focused in the now. It is only in the now that you can make the conscious
choices that will actually enable you, *empower* you, to co-create a better
future.

## Attaining mental freedom from the past

If you look at my last discourse, you will see how I gave you the example
that when you are trapped in a reactionary pattern, it seems like there is
only one course your life can follow. So many people are trapped in the
patterns where they feel that outer circumstances have boxed them in so
that there is only one choice they can make in the present situation. The
choice they make has an inevitable consequence, and it brings them to
another situation where it seems like there is only one choice, again, they
can make. This produces another consequence and that is what you call
the Sea of Samsara or the wheel of suffering because you are constantly
feeling like there is only one thing you can do. You have no options, you
have no freedom of choice. Whatever you do creates a consequence that
makes your life even more stressful, gives you even more suffering, makes
you feel even more boxed in. This is why, as some of the lady masters said,
many people in the Asian culture (because of the predefined roles of men

and women) feel that once they have gotten married and once their initial euphoria is over, they feel like their lives are locked on a track and they can only follow that track. It gives them stress and it gives them suffering but they see no way out of it. What I was telling you in my last discourse is not to focus in the now as a form of escapism but to resolve the patterns of your past and to transcend the longing for a better future so that you are free in your psychology to see that there is never a situation where you have only one choice, one option. There is always the option to look at your reactionary patterns, change your reaction to the situation. Once you change your reaction, overcome that attachment, then you will be able to see that you have at least two choices. You may not have unlimited choices but you have an alternative to what you previously considered the only choice. When you choose that alternative, you may still create consequences but they will not be as severe or as limiting as previously.

This means that in your new situation, you can again look at your reactions. When you overcome a reactionary pattern, you will see three choices in your new situation. As you choose the highest of those choices, you will bring yourself in a situation where now you have more choices with less severe consequences. This is how you gradually attain the freedom where you see that, as I said in my last discourse, you are standing in the center of an open plain and you can choose any course you want.

## Everything is appearances

This, my beloved, is a degree of mental freedom that you attain above the 96th level. This is still not the same as enlightenment, although when you attain this degree of mental freedom, it becomes much easier to switch to the state of enlightenment. As you attain freedom in the mind, what is it that creates this freedom? It is that you stop identifying with the mental images that your own mind had created of what the world is like and how the world limits you. *That* makes it much easier to then switch to the point where you see (as I also attempted to explain those many years ago) that everything in the world is just a phenomenon. It is an *appearance,* it is not a *reality* that is set in stone or in atoms.

Everything is a product of a matrix in consciousness. That was what I attempted to explain those many years ago but found it difficult to explain because people did not even have the concept of consciousness or of parallel realities or different languages that I have given you in this discourse.

Once you realize that everything is a phenomenon, everything is an appearance that can be changed (when you tune in to the consciousness behind the phenomenon and work on changing the matrices in the emotional, mental and identity realm), then you gain an entirely new perspective on life. You can also gain an entirely new perspective on what we have told you.

My beloved, what did we tell you last time? What did Saint Germain discourse on in terms of the tendency in the Asian culture to take life very seriously? He said that you will not create the Golden Age by working harder but by playing more. Co-creation is an act of playfulness, not an act of taking life so seriously that you want to control every aspect of life.

## Taking the teachings too seriously

We have in previous ascended master organizations seen this clear tendency that the students used our teachings to suddenly begin to take life, the spiritual path and themselves very seriously. They suddenly saw that there is a potential to create a much better age in the world. In some previous organization (where they were still trapped in dualistic thinking), they thought that the goal of being an ascended master student was to prevent some major calamity, such as a nuclear war. They got so focused on how serious it was that the world could face this calamity and they were the only ones who could prevent it. Therefore, they needed to take this task so seriously that they needed to decree all of the time and they needed to behave according to a very strict code.

My beloved, it got to the point where all joy was squeezed out of their lives and you could safely say that they were much more happy and joyful before they entered an ascended master teaching than after. Many of these people had relatives who could see this and who attempted to tell them this, but the people would not even listen to it because they were so serious about "saving the world for Saint Germain."

My beloved, we, of course, do not desire to see you repeat those patterns and that is why we have attempted to give you a higher vision (perhaps even between the lines of our words, but I have attempted in this discourse to be fairly direct in my words). What I desire you to see is that it is possible to switch the mind where you realize that, naturally, we of the ascended masters want you to make the calls, we want you to raise your consciousness and we do see you as the key to improving life in your society. You can make the calls that give us the authority to remove some of these dark forces and dark energies that will help other people awaken and embrace these new ideas.

You *are* important to us, but my beloved, precisely because you are important to us, we do not want you to be burdened or stressed out by this. We want you to switch your minds so that you realize that this is not some duty or obligation that we are putting upon you. It is a part of your Divine plan that you chose before coming into embodiment, and we do not want you to take this so seriously that there is no room for joy. We want you to actually see this as an act of playfulness. It is not so difficult for you to switch, although it may require a process, partly because you need to deal with the collective mindset in your part of the world that takes everything so seriously.

We want you to realize here, my beloved, that it is possible to make this shift where you are not attached to producing specific results in your society. Naturally, we have outlined some goals that we would like to see changed in Korea. Of course, we do. Who does not want to see these goals, these improvements, made? We are not attached to seeing those improvements come about in a particular way, at a particular time through particular people. We are always mindful of free will. In other words, we do not want to force this upon the Korean people. We want to free them so that they can, as we have said now so many times, spontaneously awaken and suddenly it is obvious to them that this is the next step, this is what they actually want.

The switch we want you to make in your minds is that your role is to make the calls that allow us to step in and do our work. When you have made the calls, you do not need to be attached to what happens in society, what other people do. *You* set them free because *we* are setting people free. We are not seeking to force anyone. We also set you free and we want you to set yourselves free so that you realize that the work you are doing must not become a burden that stresses you out and prevents you from fulfilling the daily obligations in your life or prevents you from enjoying your daily life.

We ask to always strive to find enjoyment in your service and in your daily life. This is truly the eightfold path that I attempted to give people 2,500 years ago but that many people could not grasp because for them enlightenment or the path became another obligation, another goal to be pursued. It became a source of stress because they either felt they were not up to the task, or they felt they were far behind, or they felt they had to work harder, or they felt that now that they had worked so hard they were clearly above other people and so they became prideful.

## The trap on each stage of the path

What I am telling you here could be expressed in a very simple way, namely that the spiritual path has stages and the dark forces do not want you to take the step from one stage to the next. For each stage of the path, they have set a trap for you. They want you to go into that trap so that you stay at that level. Therefore, we simply give you the concept that the spiritual path can be seen as a kind of game. At each stage you know that the dark forces have set a trap for you. You just need to be aware and look out for the trap by looking at your own reactions, by looking at the reactions of other spiritual people and saying: "Oh, now I see the trap and I am not going to put my foot there."

When you realize this, you realize that you do not even have to take the dark forces seriously, for whereas *you* can come to see through their traps, *they* cannot. They are trapped by their own limited imagination. You are not trapped by a limited imagination and when you have our teachings and apply them, it is not so difficult to avoid these traps. Therefore, you can come to that point where your path is not a source of *stress;* it is a source of *joy.* You walk the path in a joyful manner and if you make a mistake, *so what,* my beloved? You have learned from that mistake, and then you just move on from there. You realize that there is really, as we have said before, no choice you could make that could cause you to be trapped forever. Any choice can be undone by making a more enlightened choice, a more aware choice.

## Enlightenment is not a goal

What I would like to say as a closing remark is that enlightenment is not a stage on the path of the 144 levels of consciousness. Enlightenment is not the end goal of the eightfold path. Enlightenment is not a goal, it is not a concept, it is not a mental image. It is an *experience* of not being trapped in mental images. The only way to ever reach enlightenment is to switch out of the mental images and allow yourself to experience. Where do you experience enlightenment? Not in the *past,* not in the *future,* only in the *now.* You can experience enlightenment in any now that could ever appear to you. Keep these concepts in mind until there comes a now where it suddenly becomes obvious to you and you say: *"Now,* I am there!" You do not even say: "Now, I see it" because you are not *seeing* it as a concept that is removed from yourself. You are *experiencing* it as your new reality.

My beloved, again a long discourse that may have stretched your body's ability to sit on a hard chair. It may have stretched your emotional body's ability to avoid going into some kind of reaction to something I said. It may have stretched your mental body's capacity to keep focusing on these very tricky concepts I have thrown at you. It may have stretched your identity body and made you wonder: "Well, based on what the Buddha said, Who am I? What kind of being am I?" Of course, my beloved, this is the ultimate challenge because any sense of identity you have in this world is just a mental image. It has no ultimate reality and you cannot take it with you into the ascended state. You do not need to let go of your sense of identity now, you let go of it in increments. You only have that final surrender of the last aspect of your worldly identity when you are ready to ascend. Otherwise, what would keep you in the body? What would keep you focused on serving life—which is, after all, very much part of your path?

Do not believe, my beloved, that the path is only about raising your level of consciousness and getting rid of the outer self. You chose to come into this world because you wanted to have certain experiences and you wanted to co-create a better world. You wanted to make a contribution to the upward progression of this world.

It is not so, my beloved that your service to life, your expression of life, your enjoyment of life, your experiences in life, are contrary to spiritual growth. That is why I said many years ago that enlightenment is the same as the unenlightened consciousness. When you free yourself from the concepts that make up the unenlightened consciousness and free yourself from the concept of enlightenment, then you realize that the world is not an enemy of your spiritual growth; it is the vehicle for your spiritual growth. Your path to Buddhahood was not actually hindered by you going into the lower state of consciousness because this was part of the experience you needed in this world. It gave you a foundation for knowing the conditions that you wanted to change as you were engaging in the process of co-creating a better world.

Therefore, you see that when you reach a certain stage, there are no regrets about anything you have ever done or gone through. There is no sensation of the division between what is spiritual and what is not spiritual or even what is anti-spiritual. You suddenly begin to see that there is no phenomenon in this world that can oppose your growth, oppose your path. Even the dark forces, though they have a certain temporary existence, when you see them for what they are, they do not oppose your growth. They have no power over your mind when you are freed of these distinctions between what I 2,500 years ago called 'the pairs' but what we now call the dualistic extremes. They have no reality, they have no power and therefore you can see worldly phenomena without seeing them through the filter of these dualistic polarities and their value judgments. You see that every aspect of your life, every aspect of the world, is a vehicle for your growth, for your self-expression, for your co-creative process and ability.

My beloved, you may have heard the concept that "to the Buddha, time is not" and you may be realizing that I could go on like this indefinitely, for it gives me great enjoyment to give you these concepts. I also recognize that you are not yet at the point where time is not. Mindful of this, I will end this stream of consciousness expressed through words and once again express my gratitude and our gratitude for this wonderful gathering of us Above and you below. The Buddha I AM, Gautama is my name.

# 11 | YOUR SPIRITUAL

# MODUS OPERANDI

I AM the Ascended Master Jesus Christ, and I would like to begin by making a confession. We of the ascended masters are in some ways like used car salesmen who use a particular selling technique, called "bait and switch." The idea is you put a big sign on the car lot announcing some car model you are selling very cheap, and then, when the people come in, you say: "Unfortunately, we just sold the last one, but we have this other model that we can get you a good deal on." To some degree, that is what we have to do, and I want to explain to you why this is so.

## Why so few Christians listen to Jesus today

Now, you might ask a simple question. Here is a group of people who are not only believing that I am the Ascended Master Jesus Christ speaking through a human being, but you are experiencing in your hearts the living proof of this. Why is there not thousands or millions of those who call themselves Christians who are willing to listen to my Living Word? The reason for this is that they have created such images, such expectations, such conditions in their minds that for them to accept: 1) that I still exist in a higher realm; 2) that I am willing to speak to humankind; and 3) that *I am* speaking to humankind, they would have to overcome all of these conditions. However, they are not willing to let go of these conditions, and that means that their conditions form a filter. If I were to speak to them, I would have to live up to all of their conditions so that they could accept what I am saying, or even that I am saying anything.

Naturally, it would be completely impossible for me to live up to the conditions of Catholics, fundamentalist Christians or Lutherans and still be able to express anything new. They are so focused on the past, what they believe was said in the past, and what their churches for centuries have put on this of interpretations. There are so many layers of interpretations, or we might say distortions, on my original words and teachings that most Christians are so trapped in this that they will say that if I do not live up to the conditions defined by their church, then I cannot be the real Jesus Christ. If I were to live to all of these conditions, what could I say? Absolutely nothing, my beloved, for they do not need me or want me to say anything. They are satisfied with all the interpretations. You see, this is the basic dilemma we face on earth.

How are we, as ascended masters, going to help unascended human beings? If your present level of consciousness was sufficient for you to enter heaven, enter the spiritual realm, well, then we would have to do nothing. If your present level of consciousness was sufficient for you to enter heaven, then why are you not in heaven?

The simple fact is that your present level of consciousness is not sufficient. If we are to help you, we have to give you something that is beyond your present mental box, your present filter. If you use your present filter to reject anything that is beyond that filter, we are stuck. We are bound by the Law of Free Will. We cannot force you.

What this really means is that when we seek to help people – and of course we seek to help everyone in some way or another – we have to go in and we have to look at a specific group of people, we have to look at their level of consciousness. We have to look at their image of the world, their view of the world. We have to look at their expectations and then we are *not* trying to give them some highest or absolute truth. We are simply looking at what is the next step for them. What is the next step up in their evolution, and how can we help them make that leap, take that quantum leap, to the next level?

Never mind that there may be 143 levels above their level. This has no value for them because they cannot leap from the 1st to the 144th level— they have to leap from the 1st to the 2nd, or from the 48th to the 49th. We have to look at this, and this is where the bait and switch analogy comes in.

You understand that for anyone to do anything new, anything differently, for anyone to accept any kind of teaching – spiritual, mystical, what have you – they have to have a motivation. Their motivation will be based on their current level of consciousness, their current world view, their current expectations. What motivates these people? What is it they want that they do not have now? Can we then use that to give them that idea, that teaching, that can help them take the next step? This is what we have to do with everyone, my beloved.

As Lord Krishna expressed yesterday, there are people who are only ready for devotion, for a devotional path, and so he does not attempt to give them a teaching that they cannot grasp. He simply reflects back the devotion they send at him and this will in the long run help them grow to the next level. Then, in some future lifetime, they may be able to grasp the higher teaching, but we are not attempting to give people more than we evaluate that they can handle.

## Dealing with doubt on the path to Christhood

Now, the reason I am telling you this, as ascended master students, is that this can help you walk the path of Christhood. When you have walked the path for a while, you will have made progress, you will have raised yourself above the level of consciousness you were at when you found the teachings and started applying them. There comes a point where you can benefit from stepping back, looking at yourself, looking at your path, and saying: "What was it actually that motivated me to enter or to use the teachings of the ascended masters? What was it I wanted, what was my expectation, the expectation I had when I first entered the path?"

What you will find, if you do this, is that all of you will discover that you had some kind of motivation, something you wanted to get out of following the spiritual path. When you first found the teachings, it probably was not to make your ascension or to manifest your Christhood. There was probably some other motivation that you had—perhaps seeking understanding, perhaps seeking healing, perhaps seeking special powers, perhaps seeking abundance, this or that. People have many different kinds of motivation and I am not in any way criticizing, putting down or even evaluating it. You have to start where you are at and use the motivation you have at the time to then study and apply the teachings. When you have done this for a while, then you can step back and look at yourself and say:

"What was my original motivation, what did I expect would happen?" Then, you can say: "Based on the greater understanding I have today, the greater understanding of the path, based on the fact that I have now risen to a higher level of consciousness [and of course, you need to recognize that you have risen to a higher level of consciousness] what do I now think of my motivation? Is this really the motivation I have today, or have I developed a higher motivation where I now see that there is more to the path than I could see when I first started? There is a different goal, a higher goal that I see now, that I could not even see back then."

The reason this becomes important is that if you do not look at this, there will be somewhere in your four lower bodies an internal spirit, a matrix, a momentum that is still carrying that original motivation, that original expectation. After some time, what can happen to some students is that they are now actually beginning to realize that their original motivation was not the highest possible. In fact, it was unrealistic because it was a motivation that was not based on the reality of what the path is about. In some part of their being they recognize that their original motive and expectation was an impossible dream that cannot be fulfilled. Since they have not looked at that internal spirit (that is still holding on to the expectation, waiting for it to be fulfilled), they cannot resolve it and let it go.

There will be a spirit that is beginning to feel discouraged, disappointed or dissatisfied because it is also beginning to doubt that the original expectation will ever be fulfilled. It can come up with all kinds of thoughts and doubts, and of course the dark forces can use it to project doubt into your mind: "Does the path actually work? Is it really true? Does it work for me or does it only work for others? Or does it only work for very few people? Are there those who are so special but it doesn't apply to me?" All of these things can come up.

You probably all have some version of these doubts projected into your minds. What you can do is that you can look at the original motive, the original expectation, you had. Then, you can see: "Is it realistic based on what I now see, what I now understand, based on what I have experienced, based on the fact that I now see a new goal, and therefore really already have a new and higher expectation?" Then, you can look at that original spirit and you can recognize that it is still there. When you look at your particular personal motivation, you can see why it was either unrealistic or perhaps immature, perhaps incomplete. You can come to that point of resolution where you just realize: "But I am no longer looking at the path this way. Why should I expect a certain outcome of the path when I now know so much more about the path?" Then, you can allow yourself to actually go into that spirit and consciously dismiss it. You may say: "Get thee behind me Satan," or simply: "I don't need you anymore in my life." You can, of course, make the calls for this, when you become aware of it, to whatever masters: Astrea, Archangel Michael, or myself, or any other master, to dissolve the entity behind it. You can call to us to help you see the spirit, to see the expectation you had, and to see what that actually says about how you looked at the path back then.

## Teachings for different levels of consciousness

Why is this important? Well, it is important for yourself because, obviously, when you have that internal spirit that is holding on to a motivation that is no longer really relevant to you, you have a division in your psyche and it will pull you back. It is also important because most of you, before you came into this lifetime, had already reached a certain level of the path where you were not exclusively working on your personal issues, but you were willing and able to take on certain collective issues.

Many of you chose to be born in a certain environment whereby you took on a certain expectation about God, religion, spirituality that is one of these patterns that are in the collective consciousness. There is, of course, a spirit or beast behind the pattern, but you chose to take this on so that, by raising yourself above it and resolving the consciousness, the belief, the expectation, you could help raise the collective consciousness. Of course, until you have raised yourself above it, you have not actually raised the collective consciousness.

You can now take this further and realize that this is why I say that ascended masters are like used car salesmen. When we give a certain teaching, we are looking at a certain group of people. We are looking at where they at in consciousness: "What kind of teaching are they ready for, what are their expectations, what motivates them?" We know that in order to attract these people to our teaching, we have to give something that appeals to the motivation they have right now at their present level of consciousness. We also know that this is not the ultimate understanding about the spiritual path and the path to the ascension.

That is why we know that we have to bring people in and then gradually give them a higher teaching so that they can adapt and accelerate themselves, and switch their consciousness and gradually raise their motivation.

Then, they realize that what brought them into the teachings was what they could handle at the time, but now they are actually ready for something that is much more, because they now have the greater understanding of what the path is about. When you resolve the original expectation, you do not feel disappointed, you do not feel cheated. You actually recognize the need to take this approach on a planet like earth and therefore you simply say: "What is it that the masters want to give me now? What is it that I am ready for now?"

## Your psychological modus operandi

You can go even further with this, and you can recognize something else. In the criminal system of many nations, such as the United States, law enforcement officials attempt to categorize criminals based on what they call their "MO," or their modus operandi. This is because they have discovered that criminals are often creatures of habit, and when a certain criminal has committed one crime, he or she will tend to commit later crimes in much the same way. When they hear that a certain crime has been committed where there is some particular MO, they can often know which criminal is likely to have committed it. They can go and find out where that person was at the time, and they can often apprehend the criminal just based on this. Now, you are, of course, not criminals, my beloved, but all people have what we might call a psychological MO.

We have, of course, talked about this before in terms of the ego, in terms of internal spirits, but I am simply giving you this from another angle. What I am asking you to do to here is (not necessarily right now, but as you come home and process the experience you have had at this conference) to mentally step back and look at: "How do I relate to the material universe, to the matter realm? What is my MO in my interaction with the matter realm? What are my expectations? What do I think *can* happen or *cannot* happen? What do I think *should* happen or should *not* happen?" If you are willing to do this exercise, perhaps sometimes asking for our help if you like, then you can come to see that when it comes to relating to the physical world, you have a certain MO. In certain situations you encounter in the physical world, it is as if you are triggered into going into that MO, that reactionary pattern.

This messenger mentioned that he rarely gets irritated, but he did when he was dealing with the Russian visa or when he got a parking ticket. This says that he has certain expectations about what should not happen to him in the physical universe. When something like that does happen, instead of looking at the situation the way he looks at most other situations, instead of remaining non-attached, without even realizing it, he goes into a particular emotional reaction that this shouldn't have happened, this just isn't right, and he should be able to park outside a store for ten minutes without getting a ticket. My beloved, the expectations may be reasonable enough but the reality is that this is actually limiting you in your relationship with the mother realm.

You are taking certain conditions in society, certain conditions that are either man-made or are created by the fallen beings, and then you are projecting (creating) an expectation based on these conditions. You are projecting upon the mother realm that this is how the mother realm is, and this always happens. What does it do? It prevents you from following the teachings that Saint Germain gave because you cannot accept that something higher is possible. You are actually becoming what we have said before: a self-fulfilling prophecy. Your expectation of the mother realm is what you send into the cosmic mirror and as we have said so many times, what can the mirror do but reflect back what you are putting into it? You see that if you want to avoid these kinds of situations, you have to look at your MO. How do I relate to the matter realm? Then, you have to discover your expectations about what should or should not happen. Then, you have to ask yourself whether you want to carry these along with you, knowing that they can become self-fulfilled prophecies.

It boils down to: Are you living in a friendly universe or hostile universe? Are you living in a world that is out to get you or are you living in a world where there is at least some force that is eager to support you, to support your growth, to support your happiness, and to help you feel good about yourself? If you take the messenger's talk about him feeling that life is wonderful and having a positive expectation about the future, you may see that in most cases he does believe he lives in a friendly universe. But when it comes to applying for a Russian visa, he does not believe that the Russian visa authorities are friendly or there to support him, and that is why he manifested the trouble he had. Grant you, I am not saying the process is reasonable. It is, quite frankly, so complicated that it only hurts the Russian nation itself, but that is not the issue. The issue is that the reason the messenger had a reaction to it was that he does not believe, at some level of his being, that Russia is a friendly nation. This partly relates to some dramatic experiences he had in a past life, but nevertheless it shows you how you can have these MOs of what you expect. Now, when it comes to a parking ticket, well, he does not expect that certain authorities or bureaucracies are friendly and are there to support him. He has a certain expectation that bureaucracy is a difficult thing to deal with and often gives people unnecessary trouble. In a way you could say this is correct, my beloved. But the question for the messenger is: "Does he want to carry this with him for the rest of his life or does he want to leave it behind?" The question for you is: "What MO do I have? What expectation of the physical universe do I have? Is it friendly? Is it supporting me, or is there something that's out to get me?"

## The influence of dark forces

Now, I understand, of course, that it can always be confusing to people when I say something like this because we have taught you about dark forces, and they *are* out to get you, my beloved. But that is not what I am talking about; I am talking about making a distinction. You realize there are dark forces, you realize there are people who do not have good intentions, but what I am talking about is your view of the mother realm, the material universe in general. What I am saying is: Do not take the fact that there are fallen beings on the planet, do not take all of the troubles they have created, do not take that and project it onto the mother realm and say: "This is how the mother realm is." Do not say that the mother realm treats me like the fallen beings treat me. We have said before: Do not look at us as you look at the fallen beings. Do not think that we look at you like the fallen beings do. Do not think that we think like the fallen beings. Do the same with the mother realm. Do not put your expectations based on what the fallen beings have done onto the mother realm.

Of course, the fallen beings are still here, of course there are many things going on in the world that are not right and that we are having you make calls on. I am only talking here about your personal relationship to the mother realm, to the physical universe. Are you living in a friendly universe or do you think that this planet is so dark that the universe here, that the matter realm here, is hostile to you? I can assure you that regardless of how dark the planet is, the mother realm is still more than willing to support you and support your growth. It can only reflect back to you what you are projecting out. If you want something different to come back, you must change what you are projecting out. It can be no other way.

## Your relationship to the masters

Now, we can take this to an even higher level and have you look at what is your MO when you are relating to ascended masters? You may go back to when you first heard about ascended master teachings, and you may look at what it was that motivated you to enter these teachings. What does that motivation say about how you saw us, how you saw your potential to relate to us or not relate to us? Then, you may discover that you have certain expectations, you have a certain view of us. Many of you will actually discover that you have a view of us that is based on how a particular religion has portrayed God. Many of you have a view of ascended masters based on how Christianity has idolized me and put me way up there on the pedestal, way beyond your reach as the only son of God. Of course, for most of you this is not your own expectation. It is something you volunteered to take on in order to help raise the collective consciousness, but in order to raise the collective, you have to free your own mind from this. You may still have some expectations, some internal spirit, that you have not looked at and dismissed.

This, again, relates to the bait and switch. We know what expectations people have; we know how they are capable of looking at us. When we give an ascended master teaching, we must adapt the teaching to people's motivations and expectations, and we therefore present ourselves in a certain way. Those of you who are aware that over the last century we have sponsored several organizations and given several teachings, you will, if you care to go back and look at them, see that in the beginning we presented ourselves a certain way. There has been a progression up through the different movements and teachings. What we are giving you now is a higher level, a higher level of understanding of us, based on showing you that there is much less distance between you and us than most people tend to think.

In some of the past organizations the students had the ascended masters up there on a pedestal way above themselves. We, of course, understand people's needs, we understand their expectations. We understand that many people want to get closer to the spiritual realm but not too close. Why is it that 1.3 billion Catholics do not want to hear my Living Word but only want to listen to the Pope? Well, it is because they do not actually want to get close to the living spiritual being that I am. They do not want to encounter my Being because then they would have to change. We know also that many ascended master students are at a certain level of consciousness where they are open to the existence of ascended masters. They do want to study our teachings, they want to experience a dictation, but they do not want us to get too close.

It is as if these students want to maintain a certain distance where they say: "I would like to sit in the back and study you from a distance." What they are really saying is: "I want you to keep a distance because don't come and look at me. I don't want you to see me as I am right now. Just let me sit here in the dark so that I can pretend that you can't see me." This is all they are ready for, and I am making fun of it, but I am not putting these students down in any way. I understand their needs; I respect their needs. I am also giving a teaching for those who have already stepped up and those who are willing to step up, if you will look at your MO of how you look at ascended masters, how you can relate to us, what you expect and don't expect, what you expect can happen and what can't happen.

If you will look at this, you will see that you have actually risen to a higher understanding of the path to Christhood. Therefore, your original motivation, the original way you looked at ascended masters, is now a dead weight that you are dragging along. It is not relevant for your present level of understanding. If you will see this, you can dismiss that, and then you do not have that division in your being where something pulls you away from us and something pulls you towards us. Then, you take a step up and relate to us in a closer way.

This messenger has described how he followed an ascended master teaching and practiced it eagerly for over 15 years, and then one day suddenly came to the point where he looked at our pictures and spontaneously said: "I want more. I want a closer relationship to you. I want a more direct interaction with you." You all have the potential to make a similar decision. I am not telling you to make it with the outer mind, but I am telling you to, in your outer mind, look where you are at on the path. What are you ready for? Are you ready to step up to a higher level? Are you ready to step a little bit closer and say: "Jesus, it's okay that you look at me once in a while. Perhaps you can come and tell me a few things, but don't tell me too much, no more than I can handle." I assure you that we will respond to this because what are we actually really doing when we have students, and when you enter a student-master relationship with us? What is the spiritual path, the path to Christhood all about? It is all about coming into oneness.

## The Path of Oneness

In the end it is about the Conscious You coming into oneness with the I AM Presence. As an intermediary step, we offer you a path where we are the teachers that are, perhaps, easier for you to grasp when you have an outer teaching than your I AM Presence. The real path of the ascended masters is to come into oneness with us, or at least one of us that is closest to your heart. You see that when you first found the teachings, you may have carried with you this traditional Christian idolatry of putting the master up on the pedestal. Therefore, you might have thought that in order to interact with such an elevated master, you had to reach a certain level of perfection. You felt you had not reached that perfection, and that is why you just wanted to sit in the back so that the master could not see you and you could remain hidden because you would feel something – shame, guilt, embarrassment, whatever – if the master saw your imperfections. We, of course, allow you to do this, but many of you are at the point where you can make that switch in consciousness. You realize that it is not actually painful to have us look at you and point something out. We always do it for the purpose of helping you grow and helping you be more free. If you are more free, what happens? You feel better about yourself.

As long as you are sitting there in the distance, wanting to hide something from us, you are actually also hiding something from yourself. If you are hiding something from yourself, you cannot overcome it. What you are hiding will make you feel bad about yourself in some way. Only when you look at it and overcome it, will you feel better about yourself. This is simple, simple logic. I realize that 99.999999 percent of the people on earth do not think it is simple, but it really is, at least when you reach your level. You can come to that point where you look at your MO and you see you still have that original desire to keep the masters at a distance. You can say to it: "I just don't need you anymore. Why are you still hanging around? Get lost!"

Then, you can make that shift and you can begin to ask yourself a simple question: "What kind of master am I following? Is it a friendly master or hostile master?" Then, you will realize that the image that has been projected into the collective consciousness by the fallen beings now for thousands and thousands of years is that God is a hostile God.

Therefore, anyone who is up there in the spiritual realm and represents God must be a hostile being. You even have in some past ascended master organizations the concept that, for example, El Morya or Serapis Bey are strict disciplinarians. They are like the old-fashioned school teacher who is just looking for an excuse to spank the students. El Morya does not have a stick that he goes around hitting his students with. He never has had, and he never will have.

You see, this collective image of the hostile teacher who is somehow out to discipline you (or expose you and make you feel bad about yourself for having some imperfection), is not who we are. It is completely out of touch with the reality of who we are. When you recognize this in yourself, you can begin to separate yourself from it. You can step back and you can see it, and then you can truly let it go.

There will come that point – you may have to do some invocations and invoke some transformation of the energy, you may have to ask for our help to see it – where you just let it go. You feel that spontaneous release and suddenly you realize that we are not hostile. We are not out to get you. We are not out to expose you. We are not out to humiliate you.

## Why you fear the masters

I recognize that some people will take the teachings I have given and they will feel that I am exposing something in your psychology that is not the way it should be. They will, again, project this image that I am actually out to expose something in you. In a sense, of course I am, but I am not out to expose something that makes you feel shameful or embarrassed. I am out to set you free. Here is where you can take another step up, and when you look at the image you have had of spiritual masters and what you expect they will do or not do, you can probably identify that there is a negative aspect of this. You might think, for example, that we will expose something in you and then you might look at what is your fear in relation to this.

If I pulled one of you up here and told you that you had this tendency in your psychology, what would you feel? Now, all of you go through this exercise just for a second. Imagine that each of you were taken up here in front of the entire group and I told you very directly that you have this or that tendency in your psychology. What do you fear? What would you feel? Do you feel shame? Do you feel embarrassment? What is your feeling? Well, my beloved, that feeling is part of what holds you back on the path.

It is part of what prevents you from interacting with us. What I am saying here is this: You can step back and you can say: "Am *I* feeling this, or is this an internal spirit that defines my MO, my relationship to ascended masters, how I look at the masters, how I think I can relate to them? Is it the spirit that is feeling this, or is it me?" You can come to recognize: "But it's not me; it's the spirit!" Then, as you dismiss that spirit and make the calls on it, you can make that switch in the mind.

For example, if you would feel embarrassed if an ascended master exposed an imperfection in your psychology, you can say: "Why should I feel embarrassed about this? Why should I? It was the spirit that felt this, so why should I continue to look at the master, hoping that he won't come and embarrass me? I don't need to feel embarrassed about this, or shameful, or fearful, or whatever. Why do I need to feel this?" Then, you can gradually shift to where you recognize that we are not out to embarrass you. We are out to set you free so you feel better about yourself. Of course, you are not feeling good about yourself if you are constantly afraid of being embarrassed.

## Your positive expectations

Then, you can take another step further and you can look at that you probably also had some positive expectation of what might happen when you became an ascended master student. Many, many students have an expectation of somehow being acknowledged, recognized or honored by the ascended masters. We have, ironically, had a previous ascended master organization where most students had the masters way up there on a pedestal and they had a fear-based relationship to us. At the same time, many, many students had this compulsive desire to get recognized publicly and acknowledged by us.

It is a very complex psychology where you both have the fear and you have the hope of being acknowledged. Really, is it logical that you fear someone but you still want to be acknowledged by them? What is the likelihood that they will acknowledge you versus the likelihood that they will actually do what you fear most and put you down? It becomes this very, very artificial relationship that such students have to us, and it makes them virtually unreachable to us because we cannot approach them directly. We cannot give them an experience, we cannot give them inner direction because they are trapped in this push-pull. Of course, if you go to many Christian churches, that is how they look at God, that is how they look at me. That is why there are many Catholics that find they can relate to Mother Mary more freely than they can relate to me because she does not seem so threatening. You have this in many other religions.

Again, if you are an ascended master student and you recognize this pattern in you, why do you have it? Is it yours? Most likely it is something you have taken on from the collective consciousness. Just take a look at it, work on it, get to the point where you are neither fearing a direct encounter with an ascended master nor are you hoping for it so that it could boost your pride and make your ego feel special. When you come to the point where you can relate to us without any expectation either way, without any expectation motivated by fear or any expectation based on pride, then you can be neutral. You can be open. There are no expectations that are standing in our way. When you are just open, you will experience our Presence much more directly than you have ever done before, and this is, of course, what we desire for you.

## How the Holy Spirit can flow through you

Now, this is Pentecost time and you all know the story about how, after my departure from the physical realm, my disciples were all distraught, not knowing what to do, what was to come next. Then, they met and somehow there was a shift in their consciousness and they came into what is described as being "of one accord in one place." They actually came to what I have just described where instead of having these fear-based expectations (that this was the end of it and nothing would ever happen again), or instead of having the prideful expectations (that they would be elevated and they would be the ones who carried the movement forward), most of them (not all, but most) came to the point of just being neutral, just being open. It was that neutrality, that point of no expectation, that was the opening for what has been described as the descent of the Holy Spirit.

Now again, in a sense you could say: "What have we been doing with the teachings we have given through this messenger?" We have been deconstructing the images that people have of ascended masters based on previous dispensations. We have actually taken ourselves down from the pedestal. We have attempted to decrease the distance between you and us. Of course, we have not attempted to do this in real terms. We have been attempting to decrease the distance *in your minds,* the distance you think is there, that you project is there between you and us. We, of course, are beyond time and space and this means I am with you always if you want me, if you put your attention on me. It is not a matter of you crossing some distance. It is not a matter of me being way above you in distance or even in vibration, which of course I am, but I am still here with you. It is not a matter of you crossing this chasm. It is simply a matter of you getting rid of all the images and expectations in your minds.

We have ascended master students who, symbolically speaking, are standing there with their eyes glued to this giant telescope because they think that we are way, way, way out there in space. They need this giant telescope to see us, and the giant telescope is their elaborate intellectual understanding of the teaching. What we are doing is we are waiting for them to take their eyes away from the telescope and then say: "Oh there you are!" I have been there for the last 2,000 years next to them, and they have not bothered to pay attention because they have been looking for me way, way out there. This is, of course, what we desire for all of you, those who have followed our path for a long time, those who have applied yourselves to the path to Christhood.

## Christhood and miracles

Again, let us take the expectations down. You have the stories that when I was in embodiment, I performed all of these miracles. You have 2,000 years of humankind creating these very, very powerful, very, very elaborate collective spirits about how incredibly special it must have been if you had been there at the time of Jesus. If you go back there and look at the reality, you will see that most of my disciples were actually like the person with the eyes glued to the telescope. Even though they were following me and interacting with me physically every day, they hardly ever paid direct attention to me because they had so many expectations that they were looking at me through. You see this exemplified in the story of Peter where I said: "Get thee behind me, Satan." I was trying to shock him out of his expectations so that he could actually relate to me in a neutral way. Most of the people I encountered back then did not even really notice what kind of a being was standing there next to them. They did not recognize that I had a higher state of consciousness.

What I am saying is that this fantasy image that Christians have created later of how incredibly special it was, well, this never happened in reality.

There were many people who did not notice, there were even those who had seen me walk on water, for example, and who afterwards could not really believe what they had seen. As we have said before, the collective consciousness was so dense back then that it took much more of a dramatic event to even get people's attention.

Again, when you look at this situation of Pentecost, many Christians have created these elaborate images that the disciples were suddenly speaking in tongues. They were suddenly speaking in other languages so that other people could understand them. Even ascended master students tend to look at this as some dramatic event. They think, like the Pentecostals, that they were speaking in angelic tongues. Or they think, like some other Christians, that people fell over in the spirit and were shaking and had to be carried out of there and all of this. There is still this MO, this collective spirit that many ascended master students have, that they are longing for some dramatic event.

Some are longing for a dramatic event in their own lives, for them to have some dramatic encounter with us that suddenly changes everything. Some are longing for a dramatic event that makes other people see them as special. Many ascended master students over the decades have longed for some dramatic event where we appear in the sky or where the students themselves have the Holy Spirit and they can make people fall over and they can heal people. They can do all of these things so there is physical proof of the reality of ascended masters and therefore millions of people will be converted. Of course, these students will be the ones who brought it about so they will be elevated and honored. There is this mindset that has been created where ascended master students have carried what has been created by Christians over these 2,000 years where many Christians have also dreamed of being special, being elevated. You take this and you transfer this to ascended masters and you are projecting all of this upon us. You think that if you get the Holy Spirit, something dramatic must happen. It is possible that you could have an event where suddenly all people started speaking in tongues and all started taking a dictation or whatever people imagine. On the one hand, I do not want to limit what can happen. The Holy Spirit can manifest in various ways, but I want you to have a realistic assessment here. In the modern age, we are not performing miracles because humankind has risen to a higher level of consciousness where it is possible to get their attention in other ways. We are not looking to convert everybody to recognize ascended masters. We are not looking to create some undeniable manifestation because the Law of Free Will is clear:

There must be plausible deniability. It must be easy for people to deny our existence so we are not going to manifest some undeniable proof.

## Do you have the Holy Spirit?

Even when it comes to the descent of the Holy Spirit, we are not looking to create a spectacle, my beloved. We want you to recognize that each and every one of you have experienced that you have had the Holy Spirit. You most likely experience this when you are talking to others about something that you really care about, something that is dear to your heart. You can recognize that there are times where your voice might change a little bit, your vibration changes and you are just very, very sincere. My beloved, you are also in a neutral state of mind. You are not aggressively seeking to convert the other person, you do not have a desire to be acknowledged so you do not feel rejected. You are simply speaking from a higher level of your being, and this is a manifestation of the Holy Spirit.

Now, this whole idea that the disciples spoke in other languages, that they did not know, is not actually correct. It is all that people could project on the event based on the linear mindset. The deeper reality is that some of the disciples were infused with the Holy Spirit so that they could suddenly express the ideas of what Christianity was about in such a way that people from many different backgrounds could grasp the concepts and ideas. This is one of the primary manifestations of the Holy Spirit that I would like you to strive for. You would be able to go into that neutral state of mind and be able to speak to people from many different backgrounds. Instead of giving them some absolute truth, that with your outer mind you think they should have, you are giving them exactly what they need in order to take the next step on their path. You may not know this in the outer mind, you may not know why you are telling them this, but you just feel the flow and you go with the flow.

This is a much more valuable manifestation of the Holy Spirit than some kind of spectacle. Now, you may say: "Are you not putting on a spectacle now?" Well, yes, in a way. But is it as dramatic as many ascended master students expect, or as many Christians expect? Nay, it is not. We are attempting to give you something that still is beyond the normal level of consciousness but is not so far beyond that it reinforces your sense of distance. We realize that whatever we do will reinforce the sense of distance of some people, but you will notice how many teachings we have given over the years through this messenger that are actually specifically designed to help you decrease the distance that you project is there between you and us.

## Which master is closest to you?

I am with *you* always—*you* and *you* and *you* and *you*, each and every one of you. I am with you always, so is any ascended master that is close to your heart. Which master is closest to your heart? My beloved, I have no jealousy, I have no desire to be exclusive. It does not in any way affront me if there is another master that is closer to your heart. Why not? Because I am one with that master,

Find the master that is closest to your heart. Step back from your busy daily life. Step back from your busy-ness with the path, with your studies, with your giving invocations. Make some time where you can sit down and look at: "How am I relating to ascended masters? Here is the master that I feel closest to. How can I find a new way to relate to that master so that I decrease the distance, I come closer, I have a more direct experience?" Perhaps even ask yourself: "Am I ready for a more direct experience with an ascended master?" If you are not, again I do not criticize, I do not judge, I do not condemn. I fully understand that everyone needs to take a certain time before they are ready. You see my beloved, you are here because when you experience a dictation, you have a sense of reality that ascended masters exist. We can speak to you. I am just asking you to switch your mind so you recognize that as we exist and as we can speak through a messenger, we can also interact with you more directly, personally in your mind, in your heart.

If you are ready for this, then perhaps this would be a time for you to step up, to be more direct, and to find a different way to interact with us. Perhaps you could look at your MO, as I have called it, of how you interact with us. You could ask yourself: "Based on my current expectations, what do I think would happen if an ascended master came closer to me?" You will often find that there is a part of your mind, a part of your ego, that is actually afraid of what kind of changes you would have to make if that happened, and this might be a field where it could take you some time to deal with this issue.

## *What would you have to give up?*

This is not something that for most of you will happen in five minutes. When you reach a certain level, there is value in thinking about this, contemplating it: "What do I think would happen in my life?" There will be a part of your being that is afraid that certain outer changes would have to be made, certain things you would have to give up, and all of these things. If you will honestly look at this and examine it, you can gradually begin to see what is going on, see your unconscious expectations. You can begin to look at them. You could begin to maybe compare them to some of our teachings. You can begin to consider whether this is simply an expectation that you might have taken on from the collective consciousness, or whether it is a part of your ego. You can gradually come to the point where you become clear about where you stand right now. You may come to recognize that: Yes, there is a part of your ego that has a certain fear and that does not want to change because there is a particular thing in your life that you do not want to give up.

Now, just to give you a basic example, there was a student in Korea who asked whether you could be an ascended master student and still go to parties and drink in a social context. He was not willing to give up this because it was an important part of his family and culture to drink at these social events. This is just one example of an expectation you might have. If you are willing, you can take a look at this. You could approach it in various ways. You can even come a point where you realize that it is not a loss for you to give this up because you are actually ready to step up to a different level.

Some of you have come to this point of just spontaneously deciding that you are going to give up alcohol, but this is just an example. Do not fixate your mind on this because there are many other things that you might think you have to give up. There is always the possibility, my beloved, that you can find a different way to look at the issue so that you do not have to give up the outer activity.

To give you another example, in previous ascended master dispensations, there were many students who felt that when they entered the ascended master teachings, they could not relate to people who were not in the teachings. Many had difficulty relating to their spouses and many, many divorces have been created because of this. It has never been what we wanted to see happen, but this was how the culture was. The reason was that they had a much more black-and-white way of looking at the path: You are either in or you are out. You are either fully in, and then you have to follow the rules, or you are out. If you had a spouse that did not want to go in, then you could not relate to that spouse and so forth, and there would be conflicts and all of this stuff. The reality is that if you shift your consciousness, if you change your black-and-white view of the path and of the judgmental masters, then you can easily, or at least you can over time, find a way to relate to a spouse who is not on the spiritual path or not in the ascended master teachings.

## Your MO relating to sex

You see, it is not simply a matter of coming to a point where you think or recognize that there is a part to your ego that thinks: If you take a step closer to the masters, you will have to give up this or that. Many of you might fear you might have to give up sex, for example. This is probably the most common fear of students on the spiritual path, to be quite honest with you.

The alternative is always to look at yourself, look at your MO relating to sex. Look at your MO relating to sex and how it interacts with your MO about the spiritual path. See that you have two internal spirits that are clashing with each other. Then, recognize that there will be a spirit that is projecting that if you step up higher on the path, you have to give up sex. There will be the other spirit that screams: "No, no you can't do this!" Then you can come to the point where you realize that these are just spirits, these are not you—and you can transcend it, my beloved. You can transcend both of them and realize that by simply switching your mind, your attitude to spirituality and your attitude to sex and your attitude to the interaction between the two, you can still enjoy sexual activity and be on the spiritual path.

## Accept being here before you can leave

There can come a point where you have actually almost qualified for your ascension but you have followed an ascetic path of withdrawing from worldly activities. If you do not fully accept being in a physical body, and if you are not able to enjoy the activities you can do with the physical body, you cannot leave the earth behind, you cannot actually ascend. You could say that, surely, there are many dark forces, entities and demons that are attempting to use the sex drive to lure people into various downward spirals to drain their energy. Surely, there could be a time where you will have to discipline yourself so that you are not pulled into these negative spirals. This is why there has been, traditionally, all of this talk that spiritual people need to abstain from sex. Some of you have done this in past lifetimes and have needed to do so. It is always possible to step up to a higher view and say: "What kind of body am I living in? Is it a friendly body or a hostile body?"

You will find that many, many spiritual people actually think that their physical body is hostile to their spiritual growth. Then, you can work on this, process this, and you can come to accept that you live in a friendly universe, you live in a friendly body. While you are in this body, there are certain activities you can do with the body, and it really is not sinful or anti-spiritual to enjoy those activities. Be it sex, be it eating a good meal, be it interacting with people who are not in a spiritual teaching but who are nevertheless good people. They are your family and you enjoy being with them. What could possibly be unspiritual about this when you look at it from a neutral perspective that is not trapped in this black-and-white thinking?

You can even go on and look at your physical health and you can begin to ask yourself: "Am I living in a hostile body or a friendly body?" If you have some disease that is tormenting you, you can still (if you are willing) work on your attitude to the physical body. What is your MO? What are your expectations of what can and cannot happen? What do you really think of this body and especially in relation to your spiritual growth? You can come to a point where you can accept that you live in a friendly body that is capable of and willing to support your spiritual growth. Some of you will find that this can bring the healing of diseases that you have not been able to shake off. Others may not be healed of a physical condition but you will find a way to be at peace with it so that it does not hinder your spiritual growth.

## How to use this dictation

Again, this is one of these dictations where we throw an awful lot of ideas at you. We do this, of course, because it is not so often that you come together in a big group of people. We do this also because many of you in this particular group have reached a level on the path to Christhood where you are ready for this teaching or at least a certain element of it. Again, you do not need to go home afterwards and read this dictation and look at every element I have given you, and think that you have to study it and apply it all at once. You need to find something, one thing in there, that appeals to you at your present level. Then, you use it, you integrate it, and use it to step up to a higher level. Then, you may re-read this dictation and find that there is something else for you.

Now, I encourage you to study the dictation I gave in Korea about Christhood and the discourse by Gautama Buddha from Korea [Previous chapters] and see that they actually form sort of the Alpha whereas this dictation forms the Omega, a more practical down-to-earth approach.

## Being neutral allows the Spirit to flow

What I want to leave you with is this: The Holy Spirit bloweth where it listeth, it has been said. This is actually a statement that is not the highest view of the situation. The Holy Spirit does not blow where it listeth; it just blows, and it blows constantly and it flows constantly. Now, the reason the statement was given was that many people at the time could not understand why sometimes one person would have the flow of the spirit, other times another, and sometimes none would have it. They could not understand why because they looked at this with the outer mind.

Even my disciples tended to do this and create some sort of a hierarchy among the disciples, some sort of rank of who was at the top, who was the most advanced. Unfortunately, Peter often thought that he was at the top whereas in reality he had the lowest consciousness of any of the disciples. These outer evaluations actually block the flow of the spirit because the key to having the flow of the spirit is to be neutral, to be in the state that you have all experienced in glimpses and that you can cultivate. It is almost like you are standing still and there is nothing that pulls you in any direction. You can also call it pure awareness, but you are *neutral*. You are interacting with another person, but you do not have a judgment about what that person should be told or what that person should accept. You do not have a desire to convert that person. You do not even have a desire to help that person. You do not have a particular expectation of what should be said, what should happen or how the other person should react. You are just neutral and that is when you are the open door. That is when the spirit can flow through you, my beloved.

If you look at the phenomenon of giving dictations and the many channelers out there, you can see that the channelers who are not neutral always tune in to a lower level—the emotional, the mental, the lower identity realm. What may come through them may have some true ideas in it, but it also has some distorted ideas and there is not a vibration that sets people free. The more neutral the messenger or the channeler can be, the more pure will be the message coming through them. The more neutral you can be as you are listening to or reading a dictation, the more profound will be the insights you can get.

Another aspect of the Holy Spirit is not that you necessarily speak but also that you receive some insight that clearly comes from a higher level of your mind or from us. This is sort of the internal flow of the spirit and when you speak it is the external flow of the spirit, but both are very much part of your path.

There comes a point, as we have said, where Christhood that is not expressed is not Christhood. You must step up and instead of always studying the teaching and taking it in, you start giving it out. That is when you experience that Alpha and Omega flow of the Holy Spirit where you gain insights and you use them to help others. Many times you find that when you are actually speaking to others, you suddenly get ideas that you had never thought of before. You suddenly have an insight that you have never had before. This is the flow of the Holy Spirit. It is not a spectacle. It is not some dramatic event. It is actually something you have all experienced. I am simply saying that by becoming more conscious of this, by following some of the hints I have given you here, you can increase the frequency where you have this state of being in a neutral frame of mind.

## Do you have to have opinions?

This may take some work for some because it involves freeing yourself from the pull of some of these external things that are seeking to drag you into a reactionary pattern. It may actually mean that some of you will have to go through a certain process where you consider something very simple: "Do I, as a human being, have to have opinions?" Most of you have been brought up to think that you *should* have opinions. You should have opinions about *this* political party or *that* political party or *this* issue or *that* issue. You can come to a point where you recognize that the vast majority of the opinions that human beings have actually come from their internal spirits, which are then under the influence of collective spirits.

So many times you have two people who have opposite opinions on an issue, but it is simply because these are two spirits that are having an argument through the two people. You can come to the point where you ask yourself: "Is this really how I want to interact with other people, by always expressing my opinion and always seeking to change their opinion? Would it not be possible to come to a point where, when I interact with others, I am neutral and therefore I am open to saying something with no preconceived intention, something that comes from a higher source and can enlighten me and may actually enlighten the other person, but not with any intent from my conscious mind. I just allow it to happen?"

There are many people throughout the ages who have attempted to go through various efforts, various rituals, in order to get the Holy Spirit. There are black magicians who have attempted to create some kind of method, some kind of device, that will give them, mechanically, a flow of the spirit. They have never had a flow of the *Holy* Spirit. They may have a flow of some collective spirits that can seem powerful, but it is not the Holy Spirit. You cannot force the Holy Spirit. That is also why it was said that the Holy Spirit bloweth where it listeth. You cannot *force* it, my beloved, but you can *receive* it.

The thing is: for you to receive it, there must be room. If your mind is so filled up with opinions, there may not be room for the Spirit to express itself. I would like to set you free. I would like to give you permission to be free of all of these human opinions. You might actually feel that when you let go of some of these opinions, it is as if you are set free from some kind of treadmill. Your mind suddenly no longer has to feel that this opinion is constantly threatened and you are looking for threats. When you read something on the Internet that might threaten this opinion, then you feel agitated. Or when you meet people who have a different opinion, you have to go into an argument and try to change their minds. All of a sudden, you will feel that this is no longer draining your energy and you will feel so much better about yourself for having given up this human opinion.

I can assure you that you will probably encounter someone that you have known for a long time who will look at you and say: "What's wrong with you, you don't have any opinions anymore?" Look at how they feel about themselves and compare to how you feel about yourself and then say: "Where would I rather be, in that person's mind or in my mind?" Then, it is not so hard to give up all of these opinions that actually do not make you feel better about yourself, do not make you feel better about the world. They do not help you feel you are living in a friendly universe, they do not help you feel you are interacting with friendly masters, they do not help you feel you are in a friendly body.

Think about this: If your goal is to feel better about yourself, about the ascended masters, about the material world and about the physical body, then look at everything that pulls on your attention and ask yourself whether it helps you feel better or does not help you feel better. If it does not help you feel better, then you have my permission to give it up. I can assure you that if something does not help you feel better about yourself, the world you are living in and the masters, it is not helping your spiritual growth. It is not helping you move towards Christhood.

My beloved, if you will notice how some of you are shifting a little bit in your chairs and find it difficult to sit still, it is simply because we have now reached a point where I have given you as much as you can handle. Although I wish I could go on for another hour or two, I recognize the simple fact that the physical universe sets certain limitations for our interaction in this way. The physical universe sets no limitations for how you and I, or another master, can interact directly within your minds. We do not desire to have ascended master students who forever think that the only way they can interact with the ascended masters is through a messenger or an outer teaching. We want all of you to come to the point where you have direct interaction with us within your heart, within your mind.

With this, I thank you, I thank you from the bottom of my heart for coming together for this Pentecost celebration. I can assure you that Mother Mary's calls that these conferences were important was not given in vain, as she might tell you about after you have paid attention to the needs of the physical body.

Thus my beloved, I thank you once again. My gratitude, and I can assure you that it is a supreme joy for me to have a group of students who are willing to allow me to speak so freely and so openly. Had I only been able to do this constantly for these past 2,000 years, the world truly would have been a different place.

# 12 | INVOKING THE VISION OF MY MODUS OPERANDI

In the name I AM THAT I AM, Jesus Christ, I call to all representatives of the Divine Mother, especially Jesus, to help me see how I relate to myself, the ascended masters and the matter universe. Help me see any subtle expectations that are holding back my spiritual growth, including...

[Make personal calls.]

*Part 1*

1. Jesus, help me see how I relate to the material universe. Help me see my modus operandi, my MO, in my interaction with the matter realm. Help me see my expectations, what I think *can* happen or *cannot* happen, what I think *should* happen or *should not* happen?"

O Jesus, blessed brother mine,
I walk the path that you outline,
a great example to us all,
I follow now your inner call.

**O Jesus, let the Fire of Joy,
consume the devil's subtle ploy,
transfigured is our planet earth,
the golden age is given birth.**

2. Jesus, help me see my spiritual MO, help me see how, in certain situations in the physical world, I am triggered into going into that MO, that reactionary pattern.

O Jesus, open inner sight,
the ego wants to prove it's right,
but this I will no longer do,
I want to be all one with you.

**O Jesus, let the Fire of Joy,
consume the devil's subtle ploy,
transfigured is our planet earth,
the golden age is given birth.**

3. Jesus, help me see how I, without even realizing it, go into a particular emotional reaction that this shouldn't have happened, that this just isn't right.

O Jesus, I now clearly see,
the Key of Knowledge given me,
my Christ self I hereby embrace,
as you fill up my inner space.

**O Jesus, let the Fire of Joy,
consume the devil's subtle ploy,
transfigured is our planet earth,
the golden age is given birth.**

4. Jesus, help me see that even if my expectations are reasonable, the reality is that this is actually limiting me in my relationship with the mother realm.

O Jesus, show me serpent's lie,
expose the beam in my own eye,
as Christ discernment you me give,
in oneness I forever live.

**O Jesus, let the Fire of Joy,**
**consume the devil's subtle ploy,**
**transfigured is our planet earth,**
**the golden age is given birth.**

5. Jesus, help me see how I am taking certain conditions in society, certain conditions that are either man-made or are created by the fallen beings, and then projecting an expectation based on these conditions.

O Jesus, I am truly meek,
and thus I turn the other cheek,
when the accuser attacks me,
I go within and merge with thee.

**O Jesus, let the Fire of Joy,**
**consume the devil's subtle ploy,**
**transfigured is our planet earth,**
**the golden age is given birth.**

6. Jesus, help me see how I am projecting upon the mother realm that this is how the mother realm is, and this always happens. Help me see how this prevents me from accepting that something higher is possible.

O Jesus, ego I let die,
surrender ev'ry earthly tie,
the dead can bury what is dead,
I choose to walk with you instead.

**O Jesus, let the Fire of Joy,
consume the devil's subtle ploy,
transfigured is our planet earth,
the golden age is given birth.**

7. Jesus, help me see how this makes me a self-fulfilling prophecy. My expectation of the mother realm is what I send into the cosmic mirror and the mirror can only reflect back what I am putting into it.

O Jesus, help me rise above,
the devil's test through higher love,
show me separate self unreal,
my formless self you do reveal.

**O Jesus, let the Fire of Joy,
consume the devil's subtle ploy,
transfigured is our planet earth,
the golden age is given birth.**

8. I see that if I want to avoid these kind of situations, I have to look at my MO. I am willing to discover my expectations about what should or should not happen and ask myself whether I want to carry these along with me, knowing that they can become self-fulfilled prophecies.

O Jesus, what is that to me,
I just let go and follow thee,
with this I do pass ev'ry test,
to find with you eternal rest.

**O Jesus, let the Fire of Joy,
consume the devil's subtle ploy,
transfigured is our planet earth,
the golden age is given birth.**

9. I am willing to consider if I am living in a friendly universe or a hostile universe. Am I living in a world that is out to get me or am I living in a world where there is a force that is eager to support me, to support my growth, to support my happiness, and to help me feel good about myself?

O Jesus, fiery master mine,
my heart now melting into thine,
I love with heart and mind and soul,
the God who is my highest goal.

**O Jesus, let the Fire of Joy,**
**consume the devil's subtle ploy,**
**transfigured is our planet earth,**
**the golden age is given birth.**

## Part 2

1. Jesus, help me see that regardless of how dark the planet is, the mother realm is still more than willing to support me and support my growth. It can only reflect back to me what I am projecting out. If I want something different to come back, I must change what I am projecting out. It can be no other way.

O Jesus, blessed brother mine,
I walk the path that you outline,
a great example to us all,
I follow now your inner call.

**O Jesus, let the Fire of Joy,**
**consume the devil's subtle ploy,**
**transfigured is our planet earth,**
**the golden age is given birth.**

2. Jesus, help me see what is my MO when I am relating to the ascended masters. Help me see what motivated me to enter these teachings and what it says about how I saw my potential to relate to you or not relate to you.

O Jesus, open inner sight,
the ego wants to prove it's right,
but this I will no longer do,
I want to be all one with you.

> **O Jesus, let the Fire of Joy,**
> **consume the devil's subtle ploy,**
> **transfigured is our planet earth,**
> **the golden age is given birth.**

3. Jesus, help me see if I have a view of ascended masters that is based on how a particular religion has portrayed God. Help me free my own mind from this by discovering the expectations, the internal spirit, that I have not looked at and dismissed.

> O Jesus, I now clearly see,
> the Key of Knowledge given me,
> my Christ self I hereby embrace,
> as you fill up my inner space.

> **O Jesus, let the Fire of Joy,**
> **consume the devil's subtle ploy,**
> **transfigured is our planet earth,**
> **the golden age is given birth.**

4. Jesus, help me see if I am open to the existence of ascended masters, but I do not want you to get too close to me. Help me see if I am subconsciously saying: "I want you to keep a distance because I don't want you to see me as I am right now.

> O Jesus, show me serpent's lie,
> expose the beam in my own eye,
> as Christ discernment you me give,
> in oneness I forever live.

> **O Jesus, let the Fire of Joy,**
> **consume the devil's subtle ploy,**
> **transfigured is our planet earth,**
> **the golden age is given birth.**

5. Jesus, I am willing to step up and look at my MO of how I look at ascended masters, how I can relate to you, what I expect and don't expect, what I expect can happen and what can't happen.

O Jesus, I am truly meek,
and thus I turn the other cheek,
when the accuser attacks me,
I go within and merge with thee.

**O Jesus, let the Fire of Joy,
consume the devil's subtle ploy,
transfigured is our planet earth,
the golden age is given birth.**

6. Jesus, help me see how I have risen to a higher understanding of the path, and now my original way of looking at ascended masters is a dead weight that I am dragging along.

O Jesus, ego I let die,
surrender ev'ry earthly tie,
the dead can bury what is dead,
I choose to walk with you instead.

**O Jesus, let the Fire of Joy,
consume the devil's subtle ploy,
transfigured is our planet earth,
the golden age is given birth.**

7. Jesus, help me see this, dismiss it, and overcome the division in my being where something pulls me away from you and something pulls me towards you. I am willing to take a step up and relate to you in a closer way.

O Jesus, help me rise above,
the devil's test through higher love,
show me separate self unreal,
my formless self you do reveal.

**O Jesus, let the Fire of Joy,
consume the devil's subtle ploy,
transfigured is our planet earth,
the golden age is given birth.**

8. I say: "I want more. I want a closer relationship to you. I want a more direct interaction with you. Jesus, it's okay that you look at me and tell me something about myself."

O Jesus, what is that to me,
I just let go and follow thee,
with this I do pass ev'ry test,
to find with you eternal rest.

**O Jesus, let the Fire of Joy,
consume the devil's subtle ploy,
transfigured is our planet earth,
the golden age is given birth.**

9. Jesus, help me separate myself from the self that thinks that in order to interact with such an elevated master, I have to reach a certain level of perfection. Since I have not reached that perfection, this self wants to hide from you. Help me separate myself from the self that feels shame, guilt or embarrassment if the master sees my imperfections.

O Jesus, fiery master mine,
my heart now melting into thine,
I love with heart and mind and soul,
the God who is my highest goal.

**O Jesus, let the Fire of Joy,
consume the devil's subtle ploy,
transfigured is our planet earth,
the golden age is given birth.**

*Part 3*

1. Jesus, help me make the switch in consciousness where I realize that it is not actually painful to have you look at me and point something out. You always do it for the purpose of helping me grow and helping me be more free. If I am more free, I feel better about myself.

O Jesus, blessed brother mine,
I walk the path that you outline,
a great example to us all,
I follow now your inner call.

**O Jesus, let the Fire of Joy,
consume the devil's subtle ploy,
transfigured is our planet earth,
the golden age is given birth.**

2. Jesus, help me see my MO and see if I still have that original desire to keep the masters at a distance. I now say to that self: "I just don't need you anymore. Why are you still hanging around? Get lost!"

O Jesus, open inner sight,
the ego wants to prove it's right,
but this I will no longer do,
I want to be all one with you.

**O Jesus, let the Fire of Joy,
consume the devil's subtle ploy,
transfigured is our planet earth,
the golden age is given birth.**

3. The image that has been projected into the collective consciousness by the fallen beings for thousands of years is that God is a hostile God. Therefore, anyone who is up there in the spiritual realm and represents God must be a hostile being.

O Jesus, I now clearly see,
the Key of Knowledge given me,
my Christ self I hereby embrace,
as you fill up my inner space.

**O Jesus, let the Fire of Joy,
consume the devil's subtle ploy,
transfigured is our planet earth,
the golden age is given birth.**

4. Jesus, help me recognize this in myself, separate myself from it, step back and just let it go. Help me feel that spontaneous release and realize that you are not hostile. You are not out to get me. You are not out to expose me. You are not out to humiliate me.

> O Jesus, show me serpent's lie,
> expose the beam in my own eye,
> as Christ discernment you me give,
> in oneness I forever live.

> **O Jesus, let the Fire of Joy,**
> **consume the devil's subtle ploy,**
> **transfigured is our planet earth,**
> **the golden age is given birth.**

5. Jesus, help me step back and see the feeling and the internal spirit that defines my MO, my relationship to ascended masters, how I look at the masters, how I think I can relate to you. Help me see that it is the spirit that is feeling this, not me. Help me dismiss that spirit and make the switch in the mind.

> O Jesus, I am truly meek,
> and thus I turn the other cheek,
> when the accuser attacks me,
> I go within and merge with thee.

> **O Jesus, let the Fire of Joy,**
> **consume the devil's subtle ploy,**
> **transfigured is our planet earth,**
> **the golden age is given birth.**

6. I say: "Why should I feel embarrassed if an ascended master exposed an imperfection in my psychology? It was the spirit that felt this, so why should I continue to look at the master, hoping that he won't come and embarrass me? I don't need to feel embarrassed about this, or shameful, or fearful. Why do I need to feel this?"

> O Jesus, ego I let die,
> surrender ev'ry earthly tie,

the dead can bury what is dead,
I choose to walk with you instead.

**O Jesus, let the Fire of Joy,
consume the devil's subtle ploy,
transfigured is our planet earth,
the golden age is given birth.**

7. Jesus, help me see my positive expectation of what might happen when I became an ascended master student. Help me see any expectation of being acknowledged, recognized or honored by the ascended masters.

O Jesus, help me rise above,
the devil's test through higher love,
show me separate self unreal,
my formless self you do reveal.

**O Jesus, let the Fire of Joy,
consume the devil's subtle ploy,
transfigured is our planet earth,
the golden age is given birth.**

8. Jesus, help me see that it is not logical that I fear someone but I still want to be acknowledged by them. What is the likelihood that they will acknowledge me versus the likelihood that they will do what I fear most and put me down?

O Jesus, what is that to me,
I just let go and follow thee,
with this I do pass ev'ry test,
to find with you eternal rest.

**O Jesus, let the Fire of Joy,
consume the devil's subtle ploy,
transfigured is our planet earth,
the golden age is given birth.**

9. Jesus, help me rise above this artificial relationship that makes me unreachable to you because you cannot approach me directly. I want to receive a direct experience and inner direction from you.

O Jesus, fiery master mine,
my heart now melting into thine,
I love with heart and mind and soul,
the God who is my highest goal.

**O Jesus, let the Fire of Joy,
consume the devil's subtle ploy,
transfigured is our planet earth,
the golden age is given birth.**

*Part 4*

1. Jesus, help me get to the point where I am neither fearing a direct encounter with an ascended master nor am I hoping for it so that it could boost my pride and make my ego feel special.

O Jesus, blessed brother mine,
I walk the path that you outline,
a great example to us all,
I follow now your inner call.

**O Jesus, let the Fire of Joy,
consume the devil's subtle ploy,
transfigured is our planet earth,
the golden age is given birth.**

2. Jesus, help me relate to you without any expectation motivated by fear or any expectation based on pride so I can be neutral and open with no expectations that are standing in *my* way or *your* way.

O Jesus, open inner sight,
the ego wants to prove it's right,

but this I will no longer do,
I want to be all one with you.

**O Jesus, let the Fire of Joy,**
**consume the devil's subtle ploy,**
**transfigured is our planet earth,**
**the golden age is given birth.**

3. Jesus, help me decrease the distance between you and me, the distance *in my mind,* the distance I project is there between you and me.

O Jesus, I now clearly see,
the Key of Knowledge given me,
my Christ self I hereby embrace,
as you fill up my inner space.

**O Jesus, let the Fire of Joy,**
**consume the devil's subtle ploy,**
**transfigured is our planet earth,**
**the golden age is given birth.**

4. Jesus, help me know that you are beyond time and space so when I put my attention on you, you are here with me. It is not a matter of me crossing this chasm. It is simply a matter of me getting rid of all the images and expectations in my mind.

O Jesus, show me serpent's lie,
expose the beam in my own eye,
as Christ discernment you me give,
in oneness I forever live.

**O Jesus, let the Fire of Joy,**
**consume the devil's subtle ploy,**
**transfigured is our planet earth,**
**the golden age is given birth.**

5. Jesus, help me overcome any internal spirit that is longing for a dramatic event in my own life, for me to have some dramatic encounter with you that suddenly changes everything and makes other people see me as special.

O Jesus, I am truly meek,
and thus I turn the other cheek,
when the accuser attacks me,
I go within and merge with thee.

**O Jesus, let the Fire of Joy,**
**consume the devil's subtle ploy,**
**transfigured is our planet earth,**
**the golden age is given birth.**

6. Jesus, help me overcome any internal spirit that is longing for some dramatic event where you appear in the sky or where I have the Holy Spirit and have supernatural abilities.

O Jesus, ego I let die,
surrender ev'ry earthly tie,
the dead can bury what is dead,
I choose to walk with you instead.

**O Jesus, let the Fire of Joy,**
**consume the devil's subtle ploy,**
**transfigured is our planet earth,**
**the golden age is given birth.**

7. Jesus, help me recognize that I have experienced that I have had the Holy Spirit when talking to others about something that I really care about, something that is dear to my heart.

O Jesus, help me rise above,
the devil's test through higher love,
show me separate self unreal,
my formless self you do reveal.

**O Jesus, let the Fire of Joy,**
**consume the devil's subtle ploy,**
**transfigured is our planet earth,**
**the golden age is given birth.**

8. Jesus, help me be in a neutral state of mind where I am not aggressively seeking to convert another person and I have no desire to be acknowledged. I am speaking from a higher level of my being, and this is a manifestation of the Holy Spirit.

O Jesus, what is that to me,
I just let go and follow thee,
with this I do pass ev'ry test,
to find with you eternal rest.

**O Jesus, let the Fire of Joy,**
**consume the devil's subtle ploy,**
**transfigured is our planet earth,**
**the golden age is given birth.**

9. Jesus, help me be the open door for expressing ideas in such a way that people can grasp the concepts and ideas. Help me go into that neutral state of mind and be able to speak to people from many different backgrounds.

O Jesus, fiery master mine,
my heart now melting into thine,
I love with heart and mind and soul,
the God who is my highest goal.

**O Jesus, let the Fire of Joy,**
**consume the devil's subtle ploy,**
**transfigured is our planet earth,**
**the golden age is given birth.**

*Part 5*

1. Jesus, help me step back and discover which ascended master is closest to me. Help me see how I find a new way to relate to that master so that I decrease the distance, I come closer, I have a more direct experience.

> O Jesus, blessed brother mine,
> I walk the path that you outline,
> a great example to us all,
> I follow now your inner call.

> **O Jesus, let the Fire of Joy,**
> **consume the devil's subtle ploy,**
> **transfigured is our planet earth,**
> **the golden age is given birth.**

2. Jesus, I realize that I am ready for a more direct experience with an ascended master. I recognize that as you can speak through a messenger, you can also interact with me more directly in my mind and heart.

> O Jesus, open inner sight,
> the ego wants to prove it's right,
> but this I will no longer do,
> I want to be all one with you.

> **O Jesus, let the Fire of Joy,**
> **consume the devil's subtle ploy,**
> **transfigured is our planet earth,**
> **the golden age is given birth.**

3. Jesus, help me see my expectations of what I think would happen if an ascended master came closer to me. Help me see the part of my ego that is afraid of what kind of changes I would have to make and what I would have to give up.

> O Jesus, I now clearly see,
> the Key of Knowledge given me,

my Christ self I hereby embrace,
as you fill up my inner space.

**O Jesus, let the Fire of Joy,
consume the devil's subtle ploy,
transfigured is our planet earth,
the golden age is given birth.**

4. Jesus, help me recognize that one spirit is projecting that if I step up higher on the path, I have to give up something and there is another spirit that resists this. Help me see that these are just spirits, they are not me. Jesus, help me transcend both of them and realize that by simply switching my mind, I can still enjoy life and be on the spiritual path.

O Jesus, show me serpent's lie,
expose the beam in my own eye,
as Christ discernment you me give,
in oneness I forever live.

**O Jesus, let the Fire of Joy,
consume the devil's subtle ploy,
transfigured is our planet earth,
the golden age is given birth.**

5. Jesus, help me see that if I do not fully accept being in a physical body, and if I am not able to enjoy the activities I can do with the physical body, I cannot leave the earth behind, I cannot actually ascend.

O Jesus, I am truly meek,
and thus I turn the other cheek,
when the accuser attacks me,
I go within and merge with thee.

**O Jesus, let the Fire of Joy,
consume the devil's subtle ploy,
transfigured is our planet earth,
the golden age is given birth.**

6. Jesus, help me see if I think I am living in a friendly body or a hostile body. Help me see the spirit that thinks my physical body is hostile to my spiritual growth.

> O Jesus, ego I let die,
> surrender ev'ry earthly tie,
> the dead can bury what is dead,
> I choose to walk with you instead.

> **O Jesus, let the Fire of Joy,**
> **consume the devil's subtle ploy,**
> **transfigured is our planet earth,**
> **the golden age is given birth.**

7. Jesus, help me accept that I live in a friendly body that is capable of and willing to support my spiritual growth. Help me either heal a disease or make peace with it so that it does not hinder my spiritual growth.

> O Jesus, help me rise above,
> the devil's test through higher love,
> show me separate self unreal,
> my formless self you do reveal.

> **O Jesus, let the Fire of Joy,**
> **consume the devil's subtle ploy,**
> **transfigured is our planet earth,**
> **the golden age is given birth.**

8. Jesus, I want to be free and I accept that you give me permission to be free of all human opinions. I want to be free of the treadmill where an internal spirit feels that an opinion is constantly threatened and I am looking for threats and how to refute them.

> O Jesus, what is that to me,
> I just let go and follow thee,
> with this I do pass ev'ry test,
> to find with you eternal rest.

**O Jesus, let the Fire of Joy,**
**consume the devil's subtle ploy,**
**transfigured is our planet earth,**
**the golden age is given birth.**

9. Jesus, help me give up all of these opinions that actually do not make me feel better about myself or about the world. They do not help me feel I am living in a friendly universe, they do not help me feel I am interacting with friendly masters, they do not help me feel I am a friendly body.

O Jesus, fiery master mine,
my heart now melting into thine,
I love with heart and mind and soul,
the God who is my highest goal.

**O Jesus, let the Fire of Joy,**
**consume the devil's subtle ploy,**
**transfigured is our planet earth,**
**the golden age is given birth.**

## Sealing

In the name of the Divine Mother, I call to Mother Mary for the sealing of myself and all people in my circle of influence in the creative flow of the Divine Mother, the River of Life. I call for the multiplication of my calls by all representatives of the Divine Mother, so that we form the perfect figure-eight flow of "As Above, so below." Thus, I accept that this is fully manifest, because the mouth of the Lord, the Divine Mother that I AM, has spoken it. Amen.

# 13 | OVERCOMING THE FEAR OF MAKING DECISIONS

I AM the Ascended Master Mother Mary. It is my great joy to speak to you but more than that, to *be* with you in this beautiful gathering of your beautiful hearts in this beautiful place. My beloved, Archangel Michael has given you, so to speak, the marching orders for this conference. Therefore, I wish to give you some thoughts from my heart and a practical tool that can help you overcome the pain of making decisions.

## Avoidance decisions

We have spoken before here in Russia about this issue of making decisions, giving certain directions specifically for the Russian people, but I wish to give a tool that is universal. Truly, when you recognize the very basic teaching that we give, namely that everything in the entire universe revolves around free will, then you recognize also that the primary goal of the fallen beings (from the moment they came to this planet and for that matter from the moment they fell), has been to cause self-aware lifestreams who have not fallen to make decisions that the fallen beings can then later use to manipulate you in various ways.

First of all, their goal is, of course, to prove that God was wrong by giving you free will in the first place. They also want to trap you in all kinds of downward spirals where you make a decision that causes you intense pain. The pain, of course, is not caused by the decision but by the manipulation and reaction of the fallen beings. Nevertheless, they get you to make a decision, they cause you pain and then they seek to manipulate you into a never-ending spiral where you either seek to hide the pain of that first decision, you seek to justify it, you seek to explain it away or you seek to avoid making decisions again. Of course, the fallen beings are very skilled at manipulating you into practical situations on earth where you have to make decisions. In order to avoid making the same decision that caused you pain in the beginning, they seek to make you make other decisions that we might call "avoidance decisions." They are decisions aimed at, in your mind, avoiding the kind of decision that caused you so much pain.

You think that by making other types of decisions, you can avoid the pain. Of course, this leads to other kinds of pain and soon you are caught in this spiderweb where the more you move, the more you get rolled in and covered by the slimy substance, and the less you are able to move. Pretty soon, you sit there like a fly caught in a spiderweb and all you can do is buzz in the same place because you cannot truly move yourself out of that place. You then can keep doing this while the fallen beings milk you for your energy or until you decide that now it is enough and it is time to come up higher on the spiritual path.

## Avoiding avoidance decisions

My beloved, we know very well your situation on earth and we know how difficult it is to be in embodiment on earth. We also know the mechanism of making these avoidance decisions. We know that it is difficult to avoid making avoidance decisions, but we also know that you cannot actually enter the path of Christhood by making avoidance decisions.

Now, listen carefully. You can enter the spiritual path while you are still trapped in these avoidance decisions. You can make progress on the spiritual path because by studying spiritual teachings and practicing spiritual techniques, you can make progress. In order to step from what we might call the outer path (or the spiritual path) onto the inner path (or the path of Christhood), you have to be willing to make decisions that are not seeking to avoid a greater decision, that are not seeking to avoid pain. They are not actually a reaction to outer situations where, in a sense, you are making a decision to follow an outer teacher or practice an outer ritual. You are really doing it in order to avoid making the deeper decisions of what kind of being you are, what kind of world you want to live in, what you are willing to look at in yourself in order to change your outer situation and in order to change your inner situation and be free of these patterns that are programmed in there by the fallen beings.

Now, as was expressed by both the messenger and Archangel Michael, our only desire for you is to see you be free from whatever limits you, from whatever keeps you from, in the short run, feeling good about yourself and in the long run, qualifying for your ascension, manifesting your Christhood. In Holland we spoke at length about feeling good about yourselves and how important that is. Well, my beloved, may I ask you a simple question: "Do you think a Christed being is not feeling good about himself or herself?"

Naturally, if you think about this, you realize that as you walk higher and higher on the path, you express a higher and higher level of Christhood. You realize that it should be natural that you would feel better and better about yourself. After all, what did Jesus say? He said: "I and my Father are one." Well, if you are one with your Father, your I AM Presence, naturally you will feel good about yourself because your I AM Presence is not *in* this world or *of* this world, and it feels good about itself.

## An exercise for uncovering limiting decisions

I have had you give certain mantras and invocations in order to clear your chakras, and it is helpful to give this every time you go through the following exercise. I ask you to center in your hearts, to mentally go into the heart chakra, and I ask you to make a decision whether you want me to guide you in discovering the decision that is blocking your heart chakra, that is blocking the full expression of light in your heart chakra.

If your answer is "Yes," then I ask you to visualize that I am sitting in a chair and you are like a little child. You walk up to me and you reach up your hands. I bend down and pick you up and put you on my lap and I hold you in my arms. You are now completely surrounded by my loving arms, my loving aura, my loving vibration. You are protected against all the dangers of this world. Surely, the Divine Mother can protect you against anything from this world that is created out of the Being and substance of the Divine Mother. As you are lying on my lap, I ask you to formulate a simple question: "Mother Mary, show me the decision that is blocking my heart chakra." Then, as you go through this exercise on your own, you may take some time, you may play some music in the background if you desire, and you may meditate on my Presence, not with any forethought, not with any analytical, linear thinking or mantras or rituals or anything in your mind. Seek to calm the mind and to simply listen. I will not, in most cases, give you words but I might give you images, sensations that relate to what kind of decision you made. Naturally, you know that the heart chakra is the expression of love and so the decision for you individually, most likely, revolved around that you somehow felt your love was rejected and you decided not to express it again on this dark planet.

Now, it may be that as you give this exercise, you may get an impulse that you will want to meditate on or process. You may want to ask me to help you resolve this issue. Really, there must come a point where you see the issue clearly and you decide that you will undo that original decision because you now know that you have risen higher on the spiritual path, you have risen higher on the path to Christhood. Therefore, you will not again feel the pain that you originally felt when your love was rejected. Even if your love is rejected again, you still will not feel the same pain for you are a different being and therefore you do not need to be afraid of seeing the decision and changing it. You do not need to be afraid of expressing your love.

If you do not get a particular sensation, it may be because you need to work on a different chakra and therefore I ask you to move on with this exercise. For each chakra I go through, if you get a strong reaction, you can pause or stop the exercise and focus on that chakra. You can give calls on it, you can appeal to my heart, you can listen to music, whatever appeals to you, my beloved.

Now, I ask you to visualize that you are going up from the heart to the throat chakra. You are tuning in to your throat chakra, going into it and you are again asking me: "Mother Mary, help me to see the decision that blocks my throat chakra." You know, of course, that the throat chakra is related to expressing power and will. There was a time where you dared to express your power. Somehow, this decision caused you pain and you decided that you would never express your power again. You would never manifest that kind of a strong will, you would be less determined, less willing to take a stand, but kind of flow with things, whatever comes to you in order to avoid that pain. Again, you can ask me for my guidance in showing you the decision. You can know that you have risen higher and therefore, again, you can come to the point where you see the decision and you decide: "I am willing to express my God power, to use my willpower to take a stand and say: 'Thus far and no farther, I will go forward from here.'"

Next, I ask you to move down from the heart Chakra to the solar plexus. Again, you go into the solar plexus chakra and you ask me: "Mother Mary, help me to see the decision that blocks my solar plexus chakra." Naturally, the solar plexus revolves around peace, it revolves around service. There may have been a time where you decided to take a stand for peace and somehow this led the fallen beings to cause you pain. There may have been a time where you decided to give some service to life and again it was rejected and caused you pain. Again, mediate on my heart, see what comes to you. Apply the tools and teachings until you can see the decision clearly and can decide that you are willing to give service, you are willing to actually be at peace because you know that your peace is not as easily disturbed as it was in the past.

Then, we again move up from the heart chakra to the third eye, and you go into it and ask me: "Mother Mary, help me to see the decision that blocks my third eye chakra." This is the chakra of vision. It is the chakra of seeing truth. You may have taken a stand for truth and you were somehow hurt by the fallen beings. You may have expressed some higher vision and it was rejected. Again, when you come to see that decision, see it for what it is, you may decide that you dare again express your vision, take a stand for the highest truth that you see right now while knowing there may always be a higher truth for you to see. As you can let go of that decision, you will feel like a weight has been lifted from you, as you will feel in each case when you decide to again dare to express light through a particular chakra.

Now, we go down from the heart chakra to the seat of the soul chakra, the chakra that is related to creativity, playfulness, the joyfulness of the child. Just look at this planet and look at how those who have the child-like mind have often been brutally abused or hammered down by the fallen beings in some way, so that they dared not be the innocent children. Instead, they went into a fearful mode of always expecting that something bad would happen or they would somehow be punished.

Did not Jesus say: "Unless ye become as a little child, you cannot enter the kingdom of heaven?" Unless you dare to let the light flow through your seat of the soul chakra, how can you then truly make progress on the path to Christhood and dare to express yourself? You can again tune in to my Being, ask me to help you see the decision. If you get a strong impulse, then meditate on it, process it. Use the tools until you come to see why you decided to shut down your creative flow. As you decide to consciously change that decision again, another weight is lifted.

We now go up again to the Crown chakra, related to the Second Ray of God Wisdom. It is also the chakra that helps you connect to your I AM Presence to the spiritual realm, to a spiritual understanding. Again, I ask you to tune in and ask me to help you see the decision that blocks the flow through your Crown. Did not Jesus say: "Let no man take thy crown." Well, of course, it is almost impossible to embody on a planet like earth without having the fallen beings do something to destroy you or harm you when you dare to express your wisdom. Or you dare to express your intuition that you knew that something was true, even though there was no material proof of it. Once you tune in, once you are willing to open your mind and heart to receive an impulse from me, you can consciously begin to change that decision and therefore you can again have a weight lifted from you.

Now, we go to the last chakra, the base chakra, which has been called the Mother chakra, not in the sense that is particularly related to women or the Mother, or even sexuality. It is truly the chakra through which you express your creative drive to create and manifest something in the physical octave. It is this chakra that is the last in the chain when you are superimposing an image upon the Ma-ter light, seeking to bring it into manifestation. That is, of course, why the fallen beings are so intent, aggressively intent, on blocking it in as many people as possible.

Ask me again to help you see the decision of how you expressed something, manifested something, and it was rejected, put down, criticized, judged or perhaps it even was destroyed brutally in front of you. By tuning in to my heart, by opening your mind and heart, you can come to receive an impulse that gives you greater clarity and you can begin to change the decision.

## Using the exercise

Now, my beloved, this exercise for most of you is not something you give only once and then you have all your chakras cleared. It will be an exercise that most of you can benefit by repeating time and time again. You can, of course, combine it with giving my decrees for the clearing of the chakras [*www.transcendencetoolbox.com*], giving various rosaries and invocations for the clearing of the chakras. It is, of course, something you can combine with our Course in Self-Mastery where you work your way up through the seven rays and also thereby clear the corresponding chakra.

It is therefore an exercise that you can use in a recorded form or you can use in a written form and go through the various steps, perhaps giving some mantra, decree or invocations for each step, perhaps listening to music, whatever appeals to you. The key element is to tune in to your chakra, to ask me help you see the decision and then open your mind and heart as much as possible to receiving some impulse from me that helps you gain greater clarity on the decision that is blocking a particular chakra.

This is an exercise that can be used in connection with the other exercises I have given you, both for healing your original birth trauma and for healing other aspects of your psychology.

## Starting to make decisions again

You see, my beloved, there does come a point on the spiritual path where you need to start making your own decisions, you need to dare to make a decision that is not an avoidance decision. Now, all of you have already made such decisions (we might call them Christ decisions), or you would not be on the spiritual path and you would not be here. Nevertheless, most of you still have these patterns in your chakras, blockages in your chakras. In order to avoid the pain that you think will be associated with making a decision, you make these other decisions – the avoidance decisions – where you try to avoid making a real decision. You try to avoid expressing yourself in a way that will be judged and criticized by other people or by dark forces.

My beloved, as was expressed earlier by the messenger and by Archangel Michael, if you are willing to learn from a decision, it cannot be a mistake. Why is this so, my beloved? Because what is the purpose of your life on earth? It is *not* to live up to a certain standard of perfection defined by the fallen beings. Through so many religions and spiritual philosophies they have attempted to sell the idea that the only way to get to heaven is to live up to a standard that they have defined on earth. It is a complete lie. As has been said, you cannot enter heaven by living up to any standard on earth. You must go beyond all of them by making a Christ decision to leave behind one of the illusions that defines each of the 144 levels of consciousness, as Hilarion described in his book. You can make a certain decision that you have now found a spiritual teaching, a spiritual path, a spiritual group or a spiritual teacher and you will follow that teacher, follow that group. You will practice some ritual, you will study certain teachings, you will learn, you will apply yourself. As I said before, you can benefit from this, but it is still possible to do this as an avoidance decision. The entire idea of the outer path has found its way into so many places on earth, even spiritual teachings. Even some of the more experienced gurus and teachers have not quite seen this mechanism. There is this tendency for people, even teachers, to define an outer path and say that if you follow this outer path, you will one day make your ascension, be enlightened, reach a higher state of consciousness or whatever. You will, my beloved, make progress by following many of these paths but you will not make progress on the path of Christhood until you start making Christ decisions where you are not seeking to avoid the pain or avoid making what you see as dangerous decisions.

## Joining the path of Christhood

Truly, what you need to do in order to reach the path of Christhood, and walk the path of Christhood, is to somehow find a way, in your mind, to disconnect the process of making decisions with the fear of pain. My meditation I have just given you is one tool for this, but you can also make a general switch in your mind where you come to recognize that the real purpose of being on earth is not to live up to this outer standard. It is actually to be in embodiment and to go through the process that we have described as the immersion and the awakening process. You first immerse yourself in the physical octave, come to identify yourself with the body and with the physical octave, and then you awaken yourself.

In order to awaken yourself, you have to come to see that there is no pain, there is no shame, there is no condemnation from our side about anything you do, anything you have done, anything you could do in the material world. Whatever you do in the matter realm is done with the Mother's energy. Whatever you do in the matter realm can be erased again, there is no question about it. You could never do anything in the matter realm that you cannot undo by making a more enlightened, a more aware, decision. You recognize, my beloved, that even if you have made decisions that caused you to go into a lower state of consciousness and become identified with the material realm (or with your body, your four lower bodies, your soul vehicle, your ego, your pain), then this is just part of the entire process of immersion and awakening.

Therefore, every decision you made that caused you to be more immersed in the material world can be turned into a decision that actually builds your Christhood and therefore helps you awaken yourself. It even helps you come to the point where you can begin to express your Divine plan, be the open door for your I AM Presence, because now you know what you do *not* want to express. Now, you know that there is something higher, you know that you can be more than this. Once you have identified yourself with something in the material world and then awakened yourself from that identification, you know you can never again be trapped in that limitation. You have gone through it once and you do not need to go through it again. You have this awareness with you in your causal body, you can draw upon it and therefore you can avoid it.

## Going through the pain

You also know, my beloved, that there was a point where you were hurt by life on earth and it caused you pain. As we have said before, the first time this happened, the shock was the greatest it will ever be. Therefore, it will never be as painful to look at a decision as it would be in the situation where you felt the pain and made the original decision. It can never be that painful again. It may cause you pain to look at a decision you made that you, in your outer mind, might consider a mistake, but it will be a temporary pain. Once you go through it and undo the decision, you will be free of the pain. If you do not go through it and undo the decision, you will drag that pain with you as you have been doing for lifetimes.

You see, again, the fallen beings want to get you into this pattern and then they want to keep you trapped there forever. The ascended masters want to get you out of that identification with anything in the matter realm so that you can be free, unburdened, have no fears and again dare to be here below all that you are Above. How can you be here below all that you are Above unless you dare to make decisions?

## There are many right choices

My beloved, there is sometimes a certain consciousness among ascended master students that you want us or an outer guru to tell you what to do. You think that if some higher authority, some more evolved being, tells you what to do, then it could not be wrong. You are so afraid of making a mistake that you want to know ahead of time that you are making the right choice in any situation. You see, my beloved, it is an illusion to think that in a particular situation there is only one right choice. There are many, many situations in life that have many right choices. It is just a matter of which one is the one you want to make. You can have ten people and put them in a very similar situation. They might make ten different choices but they may be right for each person so that all ten are right because they lead to growth.

If you will honestly look at the situation I face as the representative of the Divine Mother, you might say that I am often repeating myself, talking about the same topic, saying the same thing in different ways. Why am I doing so? Partly, because I know that I cannot help everyone with a particular expression of this, and I truly desire to see you all free. I seek to give so many different things that they can appeal to many different people. You also need to be honest and recognize that for many of you, the reason I am saying it again was that you did not actually pay attention the first time I said it, or the second time I said it, or the third time or the fourth time or the fifth time. In some cases you are not ready, but in some cases you *are* ready, you are just not *willing.*

My beloved, there comes a point on the path where you need to recognize that when you created your Divine plan, it was not your ego that created your Divine plan. It was you in a very aware state of consciousness with your spiritual teachers and your I AM Presence. You decided what kind of growth you wanted to experience in this lifetime. You forget this when you come into embodiment, but the wheels are still turning in your three higher bodies. There are some times that your outer mind is not quite in tune with this. Therefore, you can actually be ready to make a certain decision (because you have done the work that has cleared your three higher bodies), but your outer mind has not caught up. Your outer mind is not *ready,* your outer mind is not *willing* to see the need to make this decision.

## Flowing with the River of Life

If you feel you have heard this before, then consider why you have heard it before but not truly *heard* it? Why have you not acted upon it, why have you not been able or willing to make the decision with the conscious mind to switch out of this limitation concerning making decisions. Thereby, you can set yourself free to flow with the River of Life, allow yourself to make decisions and simply see the result as a result that helps you adjust your course as you are flowing with the River of Life.

Flowing with the River of Life is not the same as making one decision to jump in the river and then the river carries you downstream. You are constantly changing course. You are making a decision, seeing the result, adjusting your course so you flow in the direction you want to go in and you keep doing this. That is why, my beloved, once you make that switch, you see that there are no wrong decisions. There is no decision that can stop you from flowing with the River of Life as long as you do not try to swim back to the point in the river where you made that decision in the past and think you have to undo something there. What you have to undo is the patterns in your four lower bodies of the energies. Then, you have to change the decision and you cannot change the decision in the *past,* you can only change it in the *present.* In order to change it in the present, you must connect to the decision you made in the past. This does not mean going back to the past, it means seeing it with the higher awareness you have now and then changing it, making a decision you could not make with the level of awareness you had in the past.

When you do this, you simply change your course in the river without stopping. You are constantly flowing and when you have done this a number of times, you realize that nothing can really stop you from flowing with the River of Life, no matter what decisions you make and how big of a mistake it might seem from the perspective of some people or the fallen beings. You allow yourself to become more and more like the little child who dares to express yourself, dares to look at life as something that is not a burden put upon you, that is not like walking in a mine-field where a wrong step can cause terrible consequences. It is something you can play with, and you can approach it with a playfulness of the little child. I now ask you to again visualize that you are sitting on my lap. I am holding you in my arms, I am looking at you, looking you deeply in the eye and radiating that unconditional love of the Divine Mother to you personally. I am asking you to consider in yourself whether you are willing to accept that love, accept that you are worthy of it? Then, are you willing to allow the bubbling joy of the child to spring up in your heart, to be expressed so that I can now put you down. Instead of standing there, being fearful of what step to take, you joyfully run out into the beautiful meadow, listening to the birds, looking at the flowers, playing with a ball, playing with whatever circumstances you face in life, looking at every decision as an experiment that will only help you make better decisions in the future.

I have said what I will say at this point. I may return to this in the future because I truly know it is one of the most difficult points to get on the spiritual path. If you, my beloved, are to have the maximum impact during this conference, on shifting the collective consciousness in Russia, then I ask you to consider this in your personal life and to dare to give yourself permission to make decisions and play with life like the innocent child that knows it can never lose its Mother's love.

You have my love with you wherever you go. I will never turn away from you, even if you turn away from *me*. You can at any time turn around and embrace me again. I will be there for you, for that is *my* Christ decision.

# 14 | INVOKING FREEDOM
# TO MAKE DECISIONS

In the name I AM THAT I AM, Jesus Christ, I call to all representatives of the Divine Mother, especially Mother Mary, to help me overcome any trauma related to making decisions. Help me see and overcome all spirals of making avoidance decisions, including...

[Make personal calls.]

*Part 1*

1. Mother Mary, I recognize that the primary goal of the fallen beings is to cause me to make decisions that the fallen beings can use to manipulate me.

O Blessed Mary's Song of Life,
consuming every form of strife.
As I attune to sound so fair,
each cell is healthy, I declare.

**O Mother Mary, generate,**
**the song that does accelerate,**
**my mind into a peaceful state,**
**God's perfect love I radiate.**

2. Mother Mary, help me see if the fallen beings have caused me to make decisions that caused me pain, and then I have gone into a never-ending spiral where I either seek to hide the pain of that first decision, I seek to justify it, I seek to explain it away or I seek to avoid making decisions again.

As life's own song I ever hear,
it does consume all sense of fear.
In tune with Mother's symphony,
from all diseases I AM free.

**O Mother Mary, generate,**
**the song that does accelerate,**
**my mind into a peaceful state,**
**God's perfect love I radiate.**

3. Mother Mary, help me see if the fallen beings have manipulated me into situations where I had to make decisions. In order to avoid making a decision that caused me pain, I made "avoidance decisions" that were aimed at avoiding the kind of decisions that caused me pain.

In Mother's love I do transcend,
and all my struggles hereby end.
For when with Mother's eye I see,
no imperfection touches me.

**O Mother Mary, generate,**
**the song that does accelerate,**
**my mind into a peaceful state,**
**God's perfect love I radiate.**

4. Mother Mary, I am determined to get out of this spider web of making avoidance decisions. Enough is enough and it is time to come up higher on the spiritual path.

I see that healing must begin
by finding Living Christ within.
For as I see with single eye,
each cell the light does amplify.

**O Mother Mary, generate,**
**the song that does accelerate,**
**my mind into a peaceful state,**
**God's perfect love I radiate.**

5. Mother Mary, I am willing to make decisions that are not seeking to avoid a greater decision and that are not seeking to avoid pain.

In Mother's music I am free,
from memories of a lesser me.
My vision in a perfect state,
that all my cells regenerate.

**O Mother Mary, generate,**
**the song that does accelerate,**
**my mind into a peaceful state,**
**God's perfect love I radiate.**

6. Mother Mary, I am willing to make the deeper decisions of what kind of being I am, what kind of world I want to live in, what I am willing to look at in myself in order to change my outer situation and in order to change my inner situation and be free of the patterns that are programmed by the fallen beings.

O Mother's Love, sweet melody,
from imperfections I AM free.
O Mother Mary, sound of sounds,
within my heart your love abounds.

**O Mother Mary, generate,**
**the song that does accelerate,**
**my mind into a peaceful state,**
**God's perfect love I radiate.**

7. Mother Mary, I am now making the decision that I want you to guide me in discovering the decisions that are blocking my chakras, that are blocking the full expression of light in my chakras.

> Through Mother's beauty so sublime,
> transcending bounds of space and time.
> All cells beyond the mortal tomb,
> as they are whole in Mother's womb.

> **O Mother Mary, generate,**
> **the song that does accelerate,**
> **my mind into a peaceful state,**
> **God's perfect love I radiate.**

8. Mother Mary, I visualize that you are sitting in a chair and I am like a little child. I walk up to you and I reach up my hands. You bend down, pick me up, put me on your lap and hold me in your arms.

> In resonance with life's own song,
> in life's harmonics I belong.
> The blueprint of my perfect state
> does every cell reconsecrate.

> **O Mother Mary, generate,**
> **the song that does accelerate,**
> **my mind into a peaceful state,**
> **God's perfect love I radiate.**

9. Mother Mary, I am now completely surrounded by your loving arms, your loving aura, your loving vibration. I am protected against all the dangers of this world.

> The tuning fork in every cell
> is now attuned to Mother's bell.
> From curse of death I AM now free,
> I claim my immortality.

**O Mother Mary, generate,**
**the song that does accelerate,**
**my mind into a peaceful state,**
**God's perfect love I radiate.**

## Part 2

1. Mother Mary, show me the decision that is blocking my heart chakra. I am tuning in to your Being and I am open to hearing you.

Hail Mary, we give praise
the Mother Light in all you raise.
In perfect balance light will stream,
in harmony our souls will gleam.

**Oh Mother Mary, we release**
**all thoughts and feelings less than peace,**
**releasing now all patterns old,**
**we leave behind the mortal mold.**

**River of Life, eternal flow,**
**we will to live, we will to grow.**
**We will transcend and be the more,**
**the joy of life we do adore.**

2. Mother Mary, help me see how I felt my love was rejected and I decided not to express it again on this planet.

All troubles in the heart now cease,
as Mary's love brings great release.
The rose of twelve in fullest bloom,
the soul is free to meet her groom.

**Oh Mother Mary, we release**
**all thoughts and feelings less than peace,**
**releasing now all patterns old,**
**we leave behind the mortal mold.**

**River of Life, eternal flow,
we will to live, we will to grow.
We will transcend and be the more,
the joy of life we do adore.**

3. Mother Mary, help me see the decision and resolve the issue. Help me see it clearly.

When Mother Light and Buddha meet,
the force of darkness they defeat,
with Jesus and our Saint Germain.
they bring the Golden Age again.

**Oh Mother Mary, we release
all thoughts and feelings less than peace,
releasing now all patterns old,
we leave behind the mortal mold.**

**River of Life, eternal flow,
we will to live, we will to grow.
We will transcend and be the more,
the joy of life we do adore.**

4. Mother Mary, I am undoing that original decision because I now know that I have risen higher on the path. I will not again feel the pain that I originally felt when my love was rejected.

I feel the Mother's gentle kiss,
as I am in eternal bliss,
floating in a space sublime,
in harmony with sacred chime.

**Oh Mother Mary, we release
all thoughts and feelings less than peace,
releasing now all patterns old,
we leave behind the mortal mold.**

**River of Life, eternal flow,**
**we will to live, we will to grow.**
**We will transcend and be the more,**
**the joy of life we do adore.**

5. Mother Mary, help me I recognize that I am a different being and therefore I am not afraid of seeing the decision and changing it. I am not afraid of expressing my love.

**By Mother Mary's endless Grace,**
**we conquer time, we conquer space.**
**The Buddha Nature is in all**
**and thus we rise to heed the call**
**to be the Christed ones on Earth,**
**the Golden Age is given birth.**

## Part 3

1. Mother Mary, show me the decision that is blocking my throat chakra. I am tuning in to your Being and I am open to hearing you.

Hail Mary, we give praise
the Mother Light in all you raise.
In perfect balance light will stream,
in harmony our souls will gleam.

**Oh Mother Mary, we release**
**all thoughts and feelings less than peace,**
**releasing now all patterns old,**
**we leave behind the mortal mold.**

**River of Life, eternal flow,**
**we will to live, we will to grow.**
**We will transcend and be the more,**
**the joy of life we do adore.**

2. Mother Mary, help me see how I felt I made a mistake by expressing power and I decided not to express it again on this planet.

> The throat is shining oh so blue,
> the will of God is always true.
> God's power is released in love
> through Christ direction from Above.
>
> **Oh Mother Mary, we release**
> **all thoughts and feelings less than peace,**
> **releasing now all patterns old,**
> **we leave behind the mortal mold.**
>
> **River of Life, eternal flow,**
> **we will to live, we will to grow.**
> **We will transcend and be the more,**
> **the joy of life we do adore.**

3. Mother Mary, help me see the decision and resolve the issue. Help me see it clearly.

> When Mother Light and Buddha meet,
> the force of darkness they defeat,
> with Jesus and our Saint Germain.
> they bring the Golden Age again.
>
> **Oh Mother Mary, we release**
> **all thoughts and feelings less than peace,**
> **releasing now all patterns old,**
> **we leave behind the mortal mold.**
>
> **River of Life, eternal flow,**
> **we will to live, we will to grow.**
> **We will transcend and be the more,**
> **the joy of life we do adore.**

4. Mother Mary, I am undoing that original decision because I now know that I have risen higher on the path. I will not again feel the pain that I originally felt when I expressed my power.

I feel the Mother's gentle kiss,
as I am in eternal bliss,
floating in a space sublime,
in harmony with sacred chime.

**Oh Mother Mary, we release
all thoughts and feelings less than peace,
releasing now all patterns old,
we leave behind the mortal mold.**

**River of Life, eternal flow,
we will to live, we will to grow.
We will transcend and be the more,
the joy of life we do adore.**

5. Mother Mary, help me I recognize that I am a different being and therefore I am not afraid of seeing the decision and changing it. I am willing to express my God power, to use my willpower to take a stand and say: "Thus far and no farther, I will go forward from here."

**By Mother Mary's endless Grace,
we conquer time, we conquer space.
The Buddha Nature is in all
and thus we rise to heed the call
to be the Christed ones on Earth,
the Golden Age is given birth.**

## Part 4

1. Mother Mary, show me the decision that is blocking my solar plexus chakra. I am tuning in to your Being and I am open to hearing you.

Hail Mary, we give praise
the Mother Light in all you raise.
In perfect balance light will stream,
in harmony our souls will gleam.

**Oh Mother Mary, we release
all thoughts and feelings less than peace,
releasing now all patterns old,
we leave behind the mortal mold.**

**River of Life, eternal flow,
we will to live, we will to grow.
We will transcend and be the more,
the joy of life we do adore.**

2. Mother Mary, help me see how I took a stand for peace and it caused me pain and I decided not to express it again on this planet.

The solar center is at peace,
as fear and anger we release.
The sacred ten will now unfold
a glow of purple and of gold.

**Oh Mother Mary, we release
all thoughts and feelings less than peace,
releasing now all patterns old,
we leave behind the mortal mold.**

**River of Life, eternal flow,
we will to live, we will to grow.
We will transcend and be the more,
the joy of life we do adore.**

3. Mother Mary, help me see the decision and resolve the issue. Help me see it clearly.

When Mother Light and Buddha meet,
the force of darkness they defeat,
with Jesus and our Saint Germain.
they bring the Golden Age again.

**Oh Mother Mary, we release
all thoughts and feelings less than peace,
releasing now all patterns old,
we leave behind the mortal mold.**

**River of Life, eternal flow,
we will to live, we will to grow.
We will transcend and be the more,
the joy of life we do adore.**

4. Mother Mary, I am undoing that original decision because I now know that I have risen higher on the path. I will not again feel the pain that I originally felt when I took a stand for peace.

I feel the Mother's gentle kiss,
as I am in eternal bliss,
floating in a space sublime,
in harmony with sacred chime.

**Oh Mother Mary, we release
all thoughts and feelings less than peace,
releasing now all patterns old,
we leave behind the mortal mold.**

**River of Life, eternal flow,
we will to live, we will to grow.
We will transcend and be the more,
the joy of life we do adore.**

5. Mother Mary, I recognize that I am a different being and therefore I am not afraid of seeing the decision and changing it. I am not afraid of expressing my peace and giving service to life.

**By Mother Mary's endless Grace,
we conquer time, we conquer space.
The Buddha Nature is in all
and thus we rise to heed the call
to be the Christed ones on Earth,
the Golden Age is given birth.**

*Part 5*

1. Mother Mary, show me the decision that is blocking my third eye chakra. I am tuning in to your Being and I am open to hearing you.

> Hail Mary, we give praise
> the Mother Light in all you raise.
> In perfect balance light will stream,
> in harmony our souls will gleam.
>
> **Oh Mother Mary, we release**
> **all thoughts and feelings less than peace,**
> **releasing now all patterns old,**
> **we leave behind the mortal mold.**
>
> **River of Life, eternal flow,**
> **we will to live, we will to grow.**
> **We will transcend and be the more,**
> **the joy of life we do adore.**

2. Mother Mary, help me see how I felt my vision was rejected and I decided not to express it again on this planet.

> The brow emits an emerald hue,
> Christ's perfect vision we pursue,
> and as we see God's perfect plan,
> we feel God's love for every man.
>
> **Oh Mother Mary, we release**
> **all thoughts and feelings less than peace,**
> **releasing now all patterns old,**
> **we leave behind the mortal mold.**
>
> **River of Life, eternal flow,**
> **we will to live, we will to grow.**
> **We will transcend and be the more,**
> **the joy of life we do adore.**

3. Mother Mary, help me see the decision and resolve the issue. Help me see it clearly.

> When Mother Light and Buddha meet,
> the force of darkness they defeat,
> with Jesus and our Saint Germain.
> they bring the Golden Age again.
>
> **Oh Mother Mary, we release**
> **all thoughts and feelings less than peace,**
> **releasing now all patterns old,**
> **we leave behind the mortal mold.**
>
> **River of Life, eternal flow,**
> **we will to live, we will to grow.**
> **We will transcend and be the more,**
> **the joy of life we do adore.**

4. Mother Mary, I am undoing that original decision because I now know that I have risen higher on the path. I will not again feel the pain that I originally felt when I took a stand for truth and my vision was rejected.

> I feel the Mother's gentle kiss,
> as I am in eternal bliss,
> floating in a space sublime,
> in harmony with sacred chime.
>
> **Oh Mother Mary, we release**
> **all thoughts and feelings less than peace,**
> **releasing now all patterns old,**
> **we leave behind the mortal mold.**
>
> **River of Life, eternal flow,**
> **we will to live, we will to grow.**
> **We will transcend and be the more,**
> **the joy of life we do adore.**

5. Mother Mary, help me I recognize that I am a different being and therefore I am not afraid of seeing the decision and changing it. I am not afraid
of expressing my vision and taking a stand for the truth I see.

> **By Mother Mary's endless Grace,**
> **we conquer time, we conquer space.**
> **The Buddha Nature is in all**
> **and thus we rise to heed the call**
> **to be the Christed ones on Earth,**
> **the Golden Age is given birth.**

## Part 6

1. Mother Mary, show me the decision that is blocking my seat of the soul
chakra. I am tuning in to your Being and I am open to hearing you.

> Hail Mary, we give praise
> the Mother Light in all you raise.
> In perfect balance light will stream,
> in harmony our souls will gleam.
>
> **Oh Mother Mary, we release**
> **all thoughts and feelings less than peace,**
> **releasing now all patterns old,**
> **we leave behind the mortal mold.**
>
> **River of Life, eternal flow,**
> **we will to live, we will to grow.**
> **We will transcend and be the more,**
> **the joy of life we do adore.**

2. Mother Mary, help me see how I felt my creativity was rejected and I
decided not to express it again on this planet.

> The soul is basking in delight,
> as violet flame is shining bright.

The soul is breathing God's pure air,
she feels so free in Mother's care.

**Oh Mother Mary, we release**
**all thoughts and feelings less than peace,**
**releasing now all patterns old,**
**we leave behind the mortal mold.**

**River of Life, eternal flow,**
**we will to live, we will to grow.**
**We will transcend and be the more,**
**the joy of life we do adore.**

3. Mother Mary, help me see the decision and resolve the issue. Help me see it clearly.

When Mother Light and Buddha meet,
the force of darkness they defeat,
with Jesus and our Saint Germain.
they bring the Golden Age again.

**Oh Mother Mary, we release**
**all thoughts and feelings less than peace,**
**releasing now all patterns old,**
**we leave behind the mortal mold.**

**River of Life, eternal flow,**
**we will to live, we will to grow.**
**We will transcend and be the more,**
**the joy of life we do adore.**

4. Mother Mary, I am undoing that original decision because I now know that I have risen higher on the path. I will not again feel the pain that I originally felt when my creativity was rejected.

I feel the Mother's gentle kiss,
as I am in eternal bliss,
floating in a space sublime,
in harmony with sacred chime.

Oh Mother Mary, we release
all thoughts and feelings less than peace,
releasing now all patterns old,
we leave behind the mortal mold.

River of Life, eternal flow,
we will to live, we will to grow.
We will transcend and be the more,
the joy of life we do adore.

5. Mother Mary, help me I recognize that I am a different being and therefore I am not afraid of seeing the decision and changing it. I am not afraid of being as the innocent child and playfully letting my creativity flow.

By Mother Mary's endless Grace,
we conquer time, we conquer space.
The Buddha Nature is in all
and thus we rise to heed the call
to be the Christed ones on Earth,
the Golden Age is given birth.

*Part 7*

1. Mother Mary, show me the decision that is blocking my crown chakra. I am tuning in to your Being and I am open to hearing you.

Hail Mary, we give praise
the Mother Light in all you raise.
In perfect balance light will stream,
in harmony our souls will gleam.

Oh Mother Mary, we release
all thoughts and feelings less than peace,
releasing now all patterns old,
we leave behind the mortal mold.

**River of Life, eternal flow,**
**we will to live, we will to grow.**
**We will transcend and be the more,**
**the joy of life we do adore.**

2. Mother Mary, help me see how I felt my wisdom was rejected and I decided not to express it again on this planet.

The crown is like a sea of gold,
as thousand petals now unfold.
We see the Buddha in the crown,
arrayed in his celestial gown.

**Oh Mother Mary, we release**
**all thoughts and feelings less than peace,**
**releasing now all patterns old,**
**we leave behind the mortal mold.**

**River of Life, eternal flow,**
**we will to live, we will to grow.**
**We will transcend and be the more,**
**the joy of life we do adore.**

3. Mother Mary, help me see the decision and resolve the issue. Help me see it clearly.

When Mother Light and Buddha meet,
the force of darkness they defeat,
with Jesus and our Saint Germain.
they bring the Golden Age again.

**Oh Mother Mary, we release**
**all thoughts and feelings less than peace,**
**releasing now all patterns old,**
**we leave behind the mortal mold.**

**River of Life, eternal flow,**
**we will to live, we will to grow.**
**We will transcend and be the more,**
**the joy of life we do adore.**

4. Mother Mary, I am undoing that original decision because I now know that I have risen higher on the path. I will not again feel the pain that I originally felt when my wisdom was rejected.

I feel the Mother's gentle kiss,
as I am in eternal bliss,
floating in a space sublime,
in harmony with sacred chime.

**Oh Mother Mary, we release**
**all thoughts and feelings less than peace,**
**releasing now all patterns old,**
**we leave behind the mortal mold.**

**River of Life, eternal flow,**
**we will to live, we will to grow.**
**We will transcend and be the more,**
**the joy of life we do adore.**

5. Mother Mary, help me I recognize that I am a different being and therefore I am not afraid of seeing the decision and changing it. I am not afraid of expressing my wisdom, my intuition, my inner knowing.

**By Mother Mary's endless Grace,**
**we conquer time, we conquer space.**
**The Buddha Nature is in all**
**and thus we rise to heed the call**
**to be the Christed ones on Earth,**
**the Golden Age is given birth.**

*Part 8*

1. Mother Mary, show me the decision that is blocking my base of the spine chakra. I am tuning in to your Being and I am open to hearing you.

> Hail Mary, we give praise
> the Mother Light in all you raise.
> In perfect balance light will stream,
> in harmony our souls will gleam.
>
> **Oh Mother Mary, we release**
> **all thoughts and feelings less than peace,**
> **releasing now all patterns old,**
> **we leave behind the mortal mold.**
>
> **River of Life, eternal flow,**
> **we will to live, we will to grow.**
> **We will transcend and be the more,**
> **the joy of life we do adore.**

2. Mother Mary, help me see how I felt my ability to manifest was rejected and I decided not to express it again on this planet.

> The base is of the purest white,
> four petals radiate your light.
> The Mother bows in purest love
> to God the Father from Above.
>
> **Oh Mother Mary, we release**
> **all thoughts and feelings less than peace,**
> **releasing now all patterns old,**
> **we leave behind the mortal mold.**
>
> **River of Life, eternal flow,**
> **we will to live, we will to grow.**
> **We will transcend and be the more,**
> **the joy of life we do adore.**

3. Mother Mary, help me see the decision and resolve the issue. Help me see it clearly.

> When Mother Light and Buddha meet,
> the force of darkness they defeat,
> with Jesus and our Saint Germain.
> they bring the Golden Age again.
>
> **Oh Mother Mary, we release**
> **all thoughts and feelings less than peace,**
> **releasing now all patterns old,**
> **we leave behind the mortal mold.**
>
> **River of Life, eternal flow,**
> **we will to live, we will to grow.**
> **We will transcend and be the more,**
> **the joy of life we do adore.**

4. Mother Mary, I am undoing that original decision because I now know that I have risen higher on the path. I will not again feel the pain that I originally felt when my manifestation was rejected.

> I feel the Mother's gentle kiss,
> as I am in eternal bliss,
> floating in a space sublime,
> in harmony with sacred chime.
>
> **Oh Mother Mary, we release**
> **all thoughts and feelings less than peace,**
> **releasing now all patterns old,**
> **we leave behind the mortal mold.**
>
> **River of Life, eternal flow,**
> **we will to live, we will to grow.**
> **We will transcend and be the more,**
> **the joy of life we do adore.**

5. Mother Mary, help me I recognize that I am a different being and therefore I am not afraid of seeing the decision and changing it. I am not afraid of manifesting my higher vision and true desire.

> **By Mother Mary's endless Grace,**
> **we conquer time, we conquer space.**
> **The Buddha Nature is in all**
> **and thus we rise to heed the call**
> **to be the Christed ones on Earth,**
> **the Golden Age is given birth.**

## Part 9

1. Mother Mary, help me disconnect the process of making decisions from the fear of pain. Help me make the switch and recognize that the real purpose of being on earth is not to live up to any outer standard.

> O Blessed Mary's Song of Life,
> consuming every form of strife.
> As I attune to sound so fair,
> each cell is healthy, I declare.

> **O Mother Mary, generate,**
> **the song that does accelerate,**
> **my mind into a peaceful state,**
> **God's perfect love I radiate.**

2. Mother Mary, help me see that there is no shame or condemnation from the ascended masters about anything I do. I could never do anything in the matter realm that I cannot undo by making a more enlightened, a more aware, decision.

> As life's own song I ever hear,
> it does consume all sense of fear.
> In tune with Mother's symphony,
> from all diseases I AM free.

**O Mother Mary, generate,**
**the song that does accelerate,**
**my mind into a peaceful state,**
**God's perfect love I radiate.**

3. Mother Mary, I accept that every decision I made that caused me to be more immersed in the material world can be turned into a decision that builds my Christhood and therefore helps me awaken myself and express my Divine plan.

In Mother's love I do transcend,
and all my struggles hereby end.
For when with Mother's eye I see,
no imperfection touches me.

**O Mother Mary, generate,**
**the song that does accelerate,**
**my mind into a peaceful state,**
**God's perfect love I radiate.**

4. Mother Mary, I recognize that although it may cause me pain to look at a decision I consider a mistake, it will be a temporary pain. Once I go through it and undo the decision, I will be free of the pain.

I see that healing must begin
by finding Living Christ within.
For as I see with single eye,
each cell the light does amplify.

**O Mother Mary, generate,**
**the song that does accelerate,**
**my mind into a peaceful state,**
**God's perfect love I radiate.**

5. Mother Mary, help me get out of my identification with anything in the matter realm so that I can be free, unburdened, have no fears and again dare to be here below all that I am Above.

In Mother's music I am free,
from memories of a lesser me.
My vision in a perfect state,
that all my cells regenerate.

**O Mother Mary, generate,**
**the song that does accelerate,**
**my mind into a peaceful state,**
**God's perfect love I radiate.**

6. Mother Mary, I give up the illusion that in a particular situation there is only one right choice. There are many situations in life that have many right choices. It is just a matter of which choice is the one I want to make.

O Mother's Love, sweet melody,
from imperfections I AM free.
O Mother Mary, sound of sounds,
within my heart your love abounds.

**O Mother Mary, generate,**
**the song that does accelerate,**
**my mind into a peaceful state,**
**God's perfect love I radiate.**

7. Mother Mary, I am willing to make the decision with the conscious mind to switch out of this limitation concerning making decisions. I set myself free to flow with the River of Life. I allow myself to make decisions and see the result as an opportunity that helps me adjust my course in the River of Life.

Through Mother's beauty so sublime,
transcending bounds of space and time.
All cells beyond the mortal tomb,
as they are whole in Mother's womb.

**O Mother Mary, generate,**
**the song that does accelerate,**
**my mind into a peaceful state,**
**God's perfect love I radiate.**

8. Mother Mary, I allow myself to become more and more like the little child who dares to express myself, dares to look at life as something that is not a burden put upon me. It is something I can play with, and I will approach it with the playfulness of the child.

> In resonance with life's own song,
> in life's harmonics I belong.
> The blueprint of my perfect state
> does every cell reconsecrate.

> **O Mother Mary, generate,**
> **the song that does accelerate,**
> **my mind into a peaceful state,**
> **God's perfect love I radiate.**

9. Mother Mary, I am sitting on your lap, and I am looking you deeply in the eye and accepting the unconditional love of the Divine Mother that you are giving to me personally. I allow the bubbling joy of the child to spring up in my heart, to be expressed as I play with life and look at every decision as an experiment that will only help me make better decisions in the future.

> The tuning fork in every cell
> is now attuned to Mother's bell.
> From curse of death I AM now free,
> I claim my immortality.

> **O Mother Mary, generate,**
> **the song that does accelerate,**
> **my mind into a peaceful state,**
> **God's perfect love I radiate.**

## Sealing

In the name of the Divine Mother, I call to Mother Mary for the sealing of myself and all people in my circle of influence in the creative flow of the Divine Mother, the River of Life. I call for the multiplication of my calls by all representatives of the Divine Mother, so that we form the perfect figure-eight flow of "As Above, so below." Thus, I accept that this is fully manifest, because the mouth of the Lord, the Divine Mother that I AM, has spoken it. Amen.

# 15 | THE SUBTLE DISCERNMENT BETWEEN CHRIST AND ANTI-CHRIST

I AM the Ascended Master Jesus Christ. I come to give you a teaching that has rarely been given on this planet, that has rarely been understood by students of various spiritual or religious movements. I give it because those of you who are students worldwide have reached the level of consciousness where you are able to begin to process this topic in your minds, perhaps, talking about it amongst yourselves based on your experiences with various spiritual teachings and movements.

## *The most severe expression of anti-christ*

Now, my beloved, let me begin by asking you to consider the most dense, the most serious, the most extreme expression of anti-Christ that you can imagine. Naturally, many of you will point to various manifestations of evil, such as large-scale killing and this or that atrocity that you have seen precipitated by human beings on earth. Of course, this is an outpicturing, an expression, of the mind of anti-Christ, but it is, actually, not the most severe expression of the mind of anti-Christ.

You see, my beloved, many people, when they hear the concept of Christ, Christhood or Christ-consciousness, they do what we have now talked about many times: They project their current understanding, their current state of consciousness, onto the concept. They see Christhood through the filter of their current understanding. This is, of course, natural; you can do nothing else. Those of you who are ready for it, can begin to recognize that Christ is a principle that has one purpose only, and that is to make sure that you can never be permanently or in any absolute way separated from your source, from your Creator.

Christ is necessary because you have been given free will. As Lanello so beautifully put it: "What a stroke of genius by our Creator!" Because you have been given free will, you have been given the opportunity to choose to walk away from Oneness. Therefore, there truly is no limit to how far away from Oneness you can go. Once you go into separation and you create your own worldview (that you believe is absolute), well, you can keep spiraling down, becoming more and more entrenched in your worldview. Christ is the principle that makes sure that when you have had enough of that experience, when you are ready and willing to move in the other direction (to start moving back to Oneness), then Christ will be there in whatever manifestation you can grasp with the level of consciousness you have when you finally turn around and want to come back to Oneness.

This means that Christ is the principle of growth, ongoing growth. As we have said several times, there is nothing final on earth, there is no state of consciousness that is final on earth. Christ and the Christ-consciousness is an ongoing process that ultimately leads you to the ascension, but, of course, you can continue to grow even in the ascended realm. This is the most important point you can understand about the Christ-consciousness: It is ongoingness. It constantly, continually and progressively pulls you to transcend your level of consciousness until you reach that level where the next transcendence leads to ascendance.

This is a principle that very few people have understood, that the vast majority of spiritual students, even ascended master students, are not ready to grasp. Many of you are ready to grasp it and that is why you are being given the teaching. Also, because you have the ability to hold the balance, so to speak, to be the electrodes who are sending it into the collective consciousness. You may remember the story of the angry mob that was ready to stone a woman, and I took a stick and drew a line in the sand. Well, in a sense, with this dictation I am drawing a line in the sand and saying: "It is now time to cross that line and come up to a higher understanding of what Christhood is about."

In order to illustrate what I mean here, let us go back to the idea of what is the most severe manifestation of anti-Christ known on earth. When I say "the most severe manifestation of anti-Christ," you can now understand that it actually means: "What is it that prevents people from growing, from continuing to grow?"

You will remember that in the Bible there is a quote, supposedly by me, where I said: "I wish you were either hot or cold, but because thou art lukewarm, I will spew thee out of my mouth." Well, there are those who are going in one direction and they are going away from Oneness. There are those who are going in the opposite direction and they are moving towards Oneness, but the majority of the people on earth are not going in either direction. They are simply not moving and this is the most severe manifestation of anti-Christ on earth when you consider what stops people's growth.

## People who are not moving

Now, Guru Ma talked about the possibility that you can have certain fixed points in your mind so that your mind might be moving and you are always taking in new information but you are not really shifting to a higher level because your mind is, so to speak, like a treadmill that is moving (perhaps, very fast) but is not getting anywhere. It is not moving away from that one spot and that is how so many people on earth are stuck in this point where they are not really moving. Now, this is when you look at it worldwide. There are, of course, many areas of the world where the majority of the population are moving in some way. It does not mean they are consciously on the path to Christhood, but they are moving.

The reason I said that it even was better if you were moving away from Oneness than you were standing still is that as long as you are moving, there is always the possibility that you can change direction. If you are moving away but change your direction enough, you will start moving back. If you are standing still, you cannot change direction because you are not going in any direction—there *is* no direction.

My beloved, what you see when you look at planet earth is that in many nations around the world, there are large groups of people who are in the state of consciousness where they simply are not moving. One way to acknowledge this is to look at how there are people who can live, they can be born into a certain lifestyle, a certain culture, a certain nation, they can grow up, find a job (often a rather mechanical job) and they simply just want to continue performing that job for the rest of their lives. They often live in the same house, the same apartment, they do very little to improve their outer environment. There is simply stalemate in their lives. They want some kind of stability, they want to stay where they are comfortable and keep doing the same thing over and over and over again.

Now my beloved, a lifetime is a precious opportunity. It is an opportunity to make sure that you are in a higher level of consciousness when you exit the physical octave than when you entered. They say popularly that you cannot take anything with you, meaning you come into the world naked and you leave the world naked and none of your material possessions you can take with you. It is not true, my beloved, because you can take with you the growth in consciousness. You take it with you to your next lifetime. Therefore, you can be born into a better circumstance where you have a better opportunity to grow. If you make use of that, you can continue to spiral upwards.

Not because this dictation is particularly focused on Russia, but since we are in Russia, I will use this as an example. If you go back to even before the communist revolution, the Bolshevik Revolution, you will see, as we have talked about, Peter the Great attempted to raise Russia to a higher level. Now, there were many among the noble class who resisted it but there were also many among the people who did not actively resist— they just did not move. They did not want to move. You will see that this was one of the big hindrances to growth. Now, Lanello gave his eloquent discourse about the last Tsar and how he failed to take the opportunities, but it must be said also that he faced a very difficult situation because many among the people were not willing to move. It was as if they were brought up in a certain station in life, they thought they had to be like their parents, strive for a certain kind of job, to live in a certain kind of dwelling. Once they had achieved that, they would just keep doing it for the rest of their lives.

## Even anti-christ can lead to growth

You see that all throughout the world, you have these large segments of populations that do not move and do not want to move. Now, you need to be very careful in seeking a higher understanding of what I am telling you. When you have a population that is frozen (frozen in time), what can bring them out of that coma, that hibernation? What, my beloved? Well, the ascended masters and those who represent us cannot because we respect free will. We will not force people, we will not violate them. Naturally, we have led you to the understanding that we do not consider the Bolshevik Revolution a positive development, and certainly not what followed after. *But listen carefully.* When you have a population that is so frozen in time, then even a violent change precipitated by fallen beings can actually for a short time serve in bringing the population closer to Christhood or at least giving them an opportunity.

You understand that when a population is not moving, there is nothing that can be done. They are not getting closer. Any change that happens that forces them to confront a new situation, that shakes them out of their old way of thinking, that may even force them to make changes in the way they live their lives, this is actually an opportunity for these people.

Now, I am not saying that Lenin and the Bolsheviks represented Christ. I am only saying that they did have the function of shaking the Russian population up more than the Tsar had done because the Tsar was not willing to kill so many of his own people as the Bolsheviks were willing to do. I am *not* sanctioning the killing. I am *not* excusing it. I am only pointing out that in a closed system, the people will attract something that will break down the system—which gives them an opportunity to move on because they have not been willing to do it on their own.

You need to recognize here a very important principle: Still-stand is the worst enemy of Christ because it is the opposite of growth. This means that there can actually be people who have a certain attunement that change needs to happen, and then they work for that change based on their own consciousness and the collective consciousness in a nation. In that attunement – *take care now* – they are not *representing* Christ, but they are actually in alignment with the Christ-mind because the Christ-mind also wants to bring change. It, of course, does not want to do it through force and violence, but when the people will not respond, then the Christ-mind steps back and allows those who are trapped in the consciousness of anti-Christ to do what they always want to do: either control, create chaos or create destruction.

This is not because the Christ-mind wants to see this happen but because the Christ-mind actually respects the free will of the people. When they are not willing to move based on their own choices, then the Christ-mind must step back and let the Second Law of Thermodynamics or the Law of Karma take its course. Then, the people are faced with a situation that forces them out of their mental box, out of their inertia, out of their unwillingness to change.

## The Bolshevik revolution and Stalin

There was a time where the people who precipitated the Bolshevik Revolution were in some way in alignment with the mind of Christ. This I know will be surprising to many people, to many ascended master students. Take care again: I do not say they *represented* Christ, but they were in alignment with the purpose of Christ, namely to put people in a situation where they were forced to grow when they were not willing to grow of their own accord. What you now need to recognize is that this period (where they were in alignment with the mind of Christ) did not last very long. You can actually see, if you study the Bolshevik Revolution, how they very quickly deteriorated into being more and more willing to use violence, more and more willing to suppress the people, to suppress dissent, to suppress any kind of free discussion. They did what fallen beings always do: They became very insensitive to the people. This, of course, led to the situation where Lenin went into this downward spiral that precipitated the bad health and his death and then Stalin took over.

Here is where you need to make a distinction: Stalin was *never* in alignment with the mind of Christ. He did not force the population to face a situation where they had to rethink the way they were living or rethink their approach to life. He simply consolidated the downward spiral that the others had taken the nation into, set himself up as the ultimate dictator and from there on, there was no growth. There was no potential for growth because he created such a reign of terror that it suppressed any desire for people to rethink, to think critically, to do things better. That is why you saw that very, very quickly after Stalin took power, the population went back into the state of inertia. In a sense, it became an even deeper inertia because they all reasoned that there was no point whatsoever in objecting to the system because you would just be killed. Then, they also made the decision (subconsciously, of course): there was no point in trying to improve anything, for life simply would not change. They were now in the Soviet Union and there was nothing the ordinary citizen could do about it other than try to have as tolerable of a life as possible.

You see that Stalin then forced people into an even deeper coma, inertia, of not wanting to change, not wanting to improve things. You see that there are still many people in Russia today who carry that attitude. You may simply go out and look at areas in Russia where you have apartment buildings or houses that are not well-maintained and where it is clear that those who live there have given up. They are not trying to even keep the environment clean, they are not trying to beautify or improve anything. They have accepted that they live a very static way of life, they have a completely static income and there is nothing they can do about it—or so they think. This is an example of how there is this very, very dense, very, very heavy inertia so that any effort to actually change Russia is pulled back, is pulled down, by this inertia of the people.

## The dissolution of the Soviet Union

Now, let me go forward to when the Soviet Union dissolved. Again, this was a shocking experience. Fortunately, this time there was not violence and large-scale bloodshed. It was possibly even more shocking for many people than the Bolshevik Revolution had been because there were truly people who thought that the Soviet Union would endure forever and certainly for the rest of their lifetimes. Therefore, there was nothing they could do to improve their lot in life and there was no point in even trying—just try to live a comfortable life within the system.

Now, it has, of course, been stated by previous ascended master dispensations that Gorbachev was a fallen being. Nevertheless, there was a time where he was, again, in alignment with the mind of Christ because he did see that change was needed and he tried to bring it about. I am not saying he *represented* Christ, but he was in alignment with the mind of Christ. Boris Yeltsin was also in alignment with the mind of Christ when he dissolved the Soviet Union. Again, I am not saying he had a particular level of Christ-consciousness or represented Christ. I am only saying he was in alignment by seeing the need for change that would force the people out of their coma.

Yeltsin, actually, realized something that Gorbachev never realized, namely that the people were in a coma and that the effect of communism had been to truly put the people in that coma where they were not doing what he suddenly realized that the average person in most of the western countries had been doing. *They* were seeking to improve their material life by working harder, by improving their living conditions, their houses, their apartments, buying bigger cars and this and that. There was a certain alignment there with the mind of Christ in the sense that these people saw that change was needed.

## The oligarchs

Now, look at the situation in the years right after the dissolution of the Soviet Union. You still had a large part of the population, the greatest majority of the population, who were in the state of coma, had been in this state of coma during the Soviet era. They had been in this state for all of their lives. They were now in a state of shock. They were forced to rethink certain things but they were in such state of shock that they still were not really moving and they did not know what to do with this new situation. Now, what did you see? You see that there were certain people who saw the opportunity and who stepped in and they started creating businesses. They started taking command over the oil industry and creating these larger and larger businesses and they became known as what you call "oligarchs."

You may look at the situation and see that these people have gathered incredible riches to themselves, they have disregarded the plight of the people to a large degree, they try not to pay taxes at all, they use corruption whenever they want to and they have set themselves up as mini Tsars who can get away with anything. If you go back to the early years, you will see that the majority of the people were not ready to take an initiative that could get the economy moving. The people in the government apparatus were not able to do this either because (as is proved by the Soviet economy going into a decline), the state and the people who made up the state apparatus were not able to reform the economy and put it on the upward track. They had all the power to do it but they could not do it. Gorbachev saw this, tried to change it, hoping he could bring the Soviet Union on a stable economic foundation without dissolving the Union, which never could have been done. Nevertheless, it was a move in *some* direction, it was an attempt to get the wheels turning but he could not do it, he could not overcome the resistance in the state apparatus and get them to take initiative.

What was the situation? The people could not take initiative. The state could not take initiative. Somebody needed to take an initiative to get the economy moving, and certain people were able to do this. Even the oligarchs, for a time, were in alignment with the mind of Christ because they brought change. When a population has been in this state of coma, almost any change is better than no change. You can always go back later and analyze the situation and you can go back and say: "Was the Bolshevik Revolution a good change?" Well, it was for a short time in the sense that it brought renewal and it forced people to think again. Then, of course, it went into a tailspin, and now it was not a good change. The same thing happened with the oligarchs.

There was a time where they were helping to get the economy moving. Then, there came a time where they had now reached this stage of feeling like they had control over the economy. What always happens to fallen beings or those who are trapped by fallen beings is that now they seek to consolidate their control. Instead of sharing the wealth with the people, they seek to consolidate their grip on the economy. Now, they are no longer in alignment with the mind of Christ, and they are not serving the growth of the country.

Fortunately, in the meantime many among the people had now risen to the point where they were able and willing to start taking an initiative. You have seen a movement in the Russian economy with new businesses springing up, smaller businesses springing up and so forth and so on. Still, it is a much slower movement than it could have been if there had not been the two factors of the inertia from large parts of the population, and the influence of the oligarchs who after that initial period of growth reverted into seeking to control the economy and now are actually holding back economic growth.

## The early capitalists

You see, my beloved, the same thing in the United Sates in the 1800's where the industrial revolution and technical improvements and inventions had brought a new opportunity to take the economy to a higher level.

Most of the people who had grown up on farms were not able to take this initiative. The state was not able to because in the United States' system the state does not have that kind of power. Somebody needed to take that initiative and that is what became known as the early capitalists.

You all know the names. You all know, probably, that these were fallen beings. There was a time where they were in alignment with the mind of Christ without representing the mind of Christ. They brought change the only way it could happen at the time. There, of course, again came a time where these capitalists (just like the oligarchs in Russia) reached the state where now they wanted to seek to control the economy. They wanted to create monopolies, and from that moment till the present day, they have been the force that has hindered and held back economic growth. Now, in the United States there quickly came a point where so many among the population were willing to take an initiative and start their own businesses that this is the only thing that has kept the economy from actually collapsing. This is what has maintained the economic growth you have seen.

## The principle of Christ as change

What I am pointing out to you here is a principle that Christ consciousness is not what most people see it as, including most ascended master students. Christ consciousness is that which brings change at a certain level. *This* is the Christ consciousness. It brings change because change gives people an opportunity to choose: Will they go into an upward spiral, or will they revert back into their coma and thereby actually having to consolidate it, so going into a downward spiral? The Christ consciousness brings this forth. Sometimes, when a population is in this stalemate, the Christ consciousness cannot do this through those people who represent the mind of Christ because they cannot violate free will. It can *only* do it through those who are in the mind of anti-Christ and are willing to violate free will.

You might say: "Well, how can this be the mind of Christ that brings this change?" Well, as I said, it is not truly the mind of Christ who actually does this, but the mind of Christ steps back and allows the mechanism we have called the Law of Karma or the Second Law of Thermodynamics to simply do its work. This is the safety mechanism built into the material universe, precisely to prevent that people can get themselves into a situation where they are comfortable and remain there indefinitely without growing.

## Ascended master students and Christhood

You now need to recognize that there is a certain mechanism that comes into play with ascended master students. From the time we have been talking about ascended masters, and especially the path to Christhood, we have been talking to students who were in a higher level of consciousness than the average population. Our students have not been in a coma, they have not been in this inertia where they were unwilling to grow. This does not mean, my beloved, that in order to recognize an outer ascended master teaching, you have to be at a high level of consciousness. You have to be at a higher level of consciousness than the average, but it does not mean you are anywhere close to the fullness of Christhood. Again, students will look at the concept of Christhood through the filter of their present level of consciousness and they will understand what they *can* understand. Then, they will create images and project those images upon it.

One of the images created by many, many students over the decades is that Christ consciousness is some state of perfection. This, of course, is partly brought about because the Catholic church, as I have explained many times, raised me up to be the *only* Son of God, to have been perfect from the beginning and therefore be up there on the pedestal beyond the reach of other human beings. Many ascended master students have taken over this concept, clearly created by the fallen beings, and have projected it upon the state of Christhood. They think that Christhood is an either-or thing. Either you do not have Christhood, or you have it—and if you have it, you are perfect.

What is truly non-constructive about this idea is that the image of perfection that is most common on earth is that perfection means something that does not have to change. Why would something that is perfect have to change? This means that perfection is a state of still-stand and that is why I tell you: Perfection seen from this perspective has nothing to do whatsoever with Christhood. Christhood is *ongoing* self-transcendence, *ever-moving* self-transcendence. It can never stand still. The Christ-mind never stands still and that is why it cannot be compatible with the current concept of perfection. Now, you can have another concept of perfection that is a dynamic perfection where you are perfect in the sense that you are constantly willing to look at yourself and transcend your state of consciousness. This is how you can, as Paul expressed it, "Be made perfect in Christ." The important point here is that Christhood never *can* be, never *will* be still-stand. There is no absolute state of Christhood.

## Spiritual students out of alignment with Christ

Now, why is this so important to understand? Well, because I have now given you the somewhat shocking realization – at least for some of you – that those that you consider to be fallen beings can actually in some cases be in alignment with the mind of Christ. We now need to go to the opposite side of the spectrum and look at the fact that many of the people who have actually reached some level of spiritual awareness, who may even have reached a certain level of Christhood, can actually in some cases be completely out of alignment with the mind of Christ.

If you are willing to be honest, you can look at the fact that many spiritual organizations have precipitated some rather serious atrocities. Again, we can go back to the Catholic church because it is the primary example. It is so obvious that it is hard not to refer to it. Was there a time when the Christian movement was in alignment with the mind of Christ? Well, yes, there was. Was there a time when the Catholic church was in alignment with the mind of Christ? Well, that is a much more subtle question. What we *can* say is that there certainly was a time when the Catholic church precipitated the massacre of the Cathars, the inquisition, the crusades and so on. Clearly, these actions were not in alignment with the mind of Christ. How is it possible that a movement started by me and in the beginning being in alignment with the mind of Christ, could deteriorate to the point where it precipitated these atrocities that are obviously expressions of the mind of anti-Christ?

How is it possible, for example, that there can be certain gurus who suddenly come to prominence, gain a large gathering of followers, and then suddenly their movement starts declining, various forms of abuses are exposed? An entire movement, that has been healthy and thriving a few years before, can now go into a decline and even completely disappear. Why is it possible that an ascended master organization (after having had the sponsorship of the ascended masters, after having had students who were eagerly walking the path of Christhood), can come to a point where we can no longer sponsor that organization and we must step back and watch as the organization goes into a decline? It becomes more and more closed-minded, more and more rigid, more and more focused on the outer path, more and more focused on rituals, rules and regulations. This goes to the point where the majority of the members of that organization are not actually growing in Christhood. They are comfortable, but they are not growing. They may feel holier than thou and feel they are better than those who are not ascended master students, but they are not growing in Christhood. They have stagnated, they are standing still.

How is it possible that a person who can have some alignment with the mind of Christ and seeing that change is needed, for example, and then, after a while, can go into being willing to use violence to bring about that change? You have seen many leaders throughout history who have seen the need to bring change, who have worked on bringing change, but then at some point a shift happened. Now, it was like they were willing to use force and power to consolidate their position and it all deteriorated into another downward cycle of violence.

The question here is really: "Is it possible that a person can reach a certain level of Christhood and still choose to go backwards, start a downward spiral that leads them far below the level of consciousness they had?" The answer is: "Yes." Up until you ascend, it is possible that you can start going backwards.

## Christed beings fooled by anti-christ

Now, I have talked about the fact that there is a stage where you reach the 96th level and you face this very important decision of can you truly get to the point where you recognize: "It's not about me." You start working selflessly to serve the whole. Or will you be even more focused on yourself, trying to expand your own growth for whatever desires you have, whether it be to feel that you have done something important or that you are more sophisticated than others or whatever it may be. Certainly, once you have made that decision and understood that Christhood is about overcoming the outer self, then it is more difficult for you to start going backwards. As I have said in several discourses now (in both Korea and Holland), there is that point between the 48th and the 96th level where you have some degree of Christhood, but it is still possible, at each of those levels, to suddenly come to a point where, for a personal reason, you are not now willing to grow, you are not willing to go beyond. There is a fixed point in your consciousness that you are not willing to look at and question and so you stagnate. You may even go backwards.

This also explains the phenomenon you have seen in history where you have certain leaders that have often been called charismatic leaders. Many people look at certain of these leaders and they think: "But that person has something. That person has some Light! There was something in this person's radiation that seemed genuine to us." They get taken in by this because they recognized there is something genuine. Then, later it is clearly seen that there came a point where that leader now took a downward turn and led his or her followers into the abyss. Many people have asked, and many more *should* ask: "How is this possible?"

Well, it is possible because, my beloved, Christhood is ongoingness but there can come a point where you have reached a certain level of Christhood, you have used the attainment you have at that level to precipitate a certain outer situation according to the vision you had, for example, to set yourself up as the leader of a country or spiritual movement. Then, since you set yourself up in that position, you are not willing to grow, you are not willing to move on. There is a fixed point in your consciousness you are not willing to look at. Then, what happens is, of course, that the earth is constantly being pulled upward by the acceleration of the entire universe, the collective consciousness is being raised.

The moment you are standing still, you are faced with this force that pulls on you to change and if you will not change, you have to resist the change. This means that from actually having and expressing a level of Christhood, you now become a closed system.

Then, you lose that Christhood because Christhood is a connection to the whole and the whole is always accelerating. The moment you refuse to accelerate, you must lose the connection to the Christ-mind. You then go into this spiral of seeking to maintain your power, having to become more extreme and more frantic in doing so. It is only a matter of time before this leads to a decline. There will be people who sense this, and they will leave. There will be others who will oppose and various things can happen. You see this many times in spiritual movements. You have seen it even in the recent century in many movements, even in some ascended master movements where there can be that initial growth cycle. Then, somehow, very subtly, the growth slows down and pretty soon inertia has set in. Well, inertia is another word for death.

## Looking at ascended master organizations

This is an important teaching for all those who are on the spiritual path. It is especially important for those of you who are or have been involved with an ascended master organization. You can use it to look at all these organizations and process what actually happened, process your own experience, gain a higher perspective. You can use this to help yourselves grow by turning around, looking at yourself and saying: "What fixed points do I have in my consciousness? Have I used an ascended master teaching to solidify these fixed points?"

As I said in Holland: "Have I used an ascended master teachings to solidify my view of ascended masters, my spiritual MO, and I am now stuck in it?" Then, you can look at the examples of these organizations, of these various leaders, and you can say: "I now see what happened and I do not want to fall into that trap myself. I want to continue to grow, and what is it going to take? Well, it is going to take that I'm continually willing to look at myself, to look for these fixed points, to look at where I'm stuck and I'll stop projecting out that it's anybody else's fault. I take responsibility and I recognize that my spiritual growth, my Christhood, is my personal responsibility."

"I can have a guru, I can have a teacher but the teacher cannot change my consciousness *for* me—only *I* can do that and so I'm not limited by any teacher, by any guru, by any teaching, by any outer organization. If I feel I'm not growing, then instead of projecting that it is someone else's responsibility that I am not growing, I can make the shift and take responsibility and say: 'But I'm not limited by anyone or anything on earth! There is nothing outside of me that can prevent me from shifting my consciousness, if only I am willing to look at myself.'"

## Christhood and the illusion of perfection

This means that you can now start shifting your view of Christhood so that you are not striving to attain some state of perfection. My beloved, let me make a very, very clear statement. There are many ascended master students who have become very sincere, very serious about walking the path, giving decrees, invocations, taking other steps, being very focused and very serious. Again, there is a time when doing this is precisely in alignment with the mind of Christ because you need to do this to break free of the collective consciousness and its downward pull. There also comes a point where this focus on doing the outer things can prevent you from going within, looking at your psychology and saying: "What is it in me that has to change?"

You can, for that matter, be so focused on changing the world that you are not looking at yourself. Take care to realize that there are many of these students who have a vision that there is a higher state of consciousness and they are very sincere about striving towards it, but they have not let go of this idea that Christhood means a state of perfection.

## Idolatry and hierarchy in spiritual organizations

Many of these have – as has happened in several ascended master organizations – idolized the messenger, thinking that in order to be a messenger you must have reached some state of Christhood and therefore you are "practically perfect in every way." Well, my beloved, only Mary Poppins is practically perfect in every way. No human being ever has been or ever will be. You need to recognize here that the real problem with idolizing the messenger or the guru, or even idolizing Jesus, is that it maintains this image that Christhood is the state of perfection.

We have seen many, many students who have been sincere about striving for Christhood, but their ego played a trick on them where they thought that once they have reached a certain level of Christhood, now they did not need to look at themselves and their own psychology. They did not need to change, they did not need to listen to anybody below them. In their mind, reaching a certain level of Christhood created a hierarchy where those who had reached a certain level of Christhood were now suddenly better than those who were below them and therefore they did not need to listen to those below them. They did not need to pay attention to them when they pointed out that there was something they needed to look at in themselves.

This is how your progress stops and, all of a sudden, inertia sets in because now you have reached some state in a spiritual organization, or even in your own mind, where you are comfortable and you think you do not need to grow. Many of these students recognized that they were not at the ultimate state of Christhood because only the messenger was. They have created this very subtle belief that: "Oh, the messenger was just in a different category, like Jesus." They could never reach that but now they had reached a certain level and therefore they certainly were higher than the other students in the organization.

When you have this kind of an earthly hierarchy, then an organization can be brought to a halt by this. This in itself is enough to bring a spiritual organization to a halt, if it is not recognized and addressed. There can be this attitude where those who are at lower levels, well, they feel there is no room to express their Christhood. They have two choices: Either they pause their growth towards Christhood so it does not disturb those above them and gets them into trouble, or they leave and they express their Christhood elsewhere. If those who are willing to express their Christhood leave, well, an organization cannot continue to grow. It is very simple and this is what has happened to several organizations that were sponsored by the ascended masters. I do not need to name names because those of you who know an ascended master organization, can clearly see the pattern if you are willing.

## Christhood defined by anti-christ

The real issue here is that the whole idea that Christhood is a state of perfection comes from the mind of anti-Christ. At the personal level it comes from your ego, and it is because the forces of anti-Christ are always seeking to prevent you from reaching your ascension. They know that they can potentially stop you at every level towards the 144th level. They are always trying to get you to a point where you think you do not have to grow, you do not have to transcend, you do not have to move on. Therefore, there is that last fixed point in your mind, that last illusion, as Hilarion said, that you will not look at. If you will not look at it, you cannot give it up, and therefore you are stuck in that illusion indefinitely.

My beloved, there is really not much honor in having reached the 143rd level of consciousness and then stopping there. It is a very, very sad state. Not that we have ever seen it, but if it were to occur, it would be a very sad state. It is, for that matter, almost as sad to have reached the 77th level of consciousness and stop there. What we always want to see for our students is, of course, that you make your ascension, and you do not make your ascension from the 77th level or the 143rd level! You can only make it from the 144th level but even there you have to transcend that last illusion. My beloved, this has been a long discourse. It has perhaps been a

shocking discourse. I have had my say, and I thank you for being willing to be the open doors for me radiating this into the collective consciousness. You may think I have not said much about Russia, but I assure you that I have radiated energies and impulses into the collective consciousness of this nation that is more than enough to shift Russia into an upward spiral—if enough people are willing to align themselves with those impulses coming from the mind of Christ. Thus, I have made my contribution to the upward spiral and the manifestation of the golden age in this beloved and beautiful nation.

# 16 | A MESSAGE TO ALL WHO HAVE COME ON A RESCUE MISSION

I AM the Ascended Master Sanat Kumara. I come with a message that is multifaceted. Truly, our messages are always multifaceted in the sense that they can be understood at different levels of consciousness. Nevertheless, mine is particularly multifaceted because I am not simply speaking based on the 144 levels of consciousness possible on earth. I am speaking for the many different people who have come to earth on what we might call a rescue mission.

You have all heard the story of how there was a point where the earth was in a very low state and it was thought that the planet could not be sustained. Then, I and 144,000 lifestreams from Venus decided to come to earth to help raise this planet. That meant that the 144,000 took physical embodiment on earth while I did not, but I set up a retreat here over the Gobi desert that has been known as Shamballa.

Now, we have said before, and I will say again, that, naturally, the lifestreams from Venus were not the only lifestreams to come to earth in order to help raise this planet, neither at that time, nor later. Both before and later, other lifestreams have come to this earth in order to help it be raised back up beyond the level of duality. The Venusians were the largest single group that have come to earth but other groups have come that were smaller, and individuals have come, and they have come from many different backgrounds.

## Natural and unnatural planets

We have hinted at the fact that you can divide planets up into two categories: natural and unnatural planets. Earth is an unnatural planet because the collective consciousness is fear-based. You have fallen beings embodying here, you have war, you have conflict, you have all these outer manifestations that clearly show that this could not be natural, in the sense that it was not created or designed by the Creator or by the ascended masters.

It is a phenomenon brought about by free will and by beings using their free will to go into duality, seeing themselves as separate beings. Therefore, they are creating all of these manifestations, that you see on the earth, that are only possible when people have forgotten the basic humanity that is in all people. Therefore, they do not see all people as being their spiritual brothers and sisters. They see them as "other" people and they fall prey to the illusion that they can do onto others without the universe doing onto themselves, without what they do to others being reflected back to them by the cosmic mirror.

This is an illusion that can exist only on an unnatural planet. In contrast to this, there are billions of planets in the material universe that are at the stage of being natural planets. Many of these planets are at very high levels of collective consciousness. They are therefore creating a tremendous magnetic pull that is pulling up on the entire universe, including, of course, planet earth. As this pull increases, what happens is that the unnatural planets are still being pulled up by the upward pull of the entire universe. Because of the low level of the collective consciousness, the threat is that the resistance created on these planets can actually create such a difference between the upper pull of the universe and the resistance on the planet that the physical planet cannot stay together, that it can literally be pulled apart.

In order to avoid this, it is necessary that lifestreams from some of these natural planets come to earth and embody here. Just by them being in physical embodiment, they are, so to speak, an anchor point for their home planet and the vibrations of their home planet. This can provide that last-ditch effort that is needed to hold the planet together for a longer period of time until hopefully the collective consciousness is raised so that the planet is no longer in danger of being pulled apart. Many, many lifestreams have come on a mission like this.

## It is time to know why you are here

Now, what you need to be careful to recognize here is that on one hand, I do speak to these lifestreams. It is my intention to send a strong signal into the collective consciousness, or perhaps we should even say into the individual consciousness of all of these lifestreams, that it is time to step up higher. It is time to come into a conscious recognition of why you are on this planet and that you are here not just to serve as an anchor point, but also to provide a positive frame of reference for the other inhabitants on the planet. It is high time that you start doing this.

However, in order to fulfill this mission, you need to recognize that even though you came from a natural planet, descending into embodiment on a planet as low as earth simply cannot be done while you maintain the full awareness of who you are and where you came from. It can only be done, as Hilarion explained, by taking on various illusions that correspond to the 144 levels. It is simply a matter of how low you descend before you can take embodiment here, and you need to recognize that you have taken on these illusions.

You also need to recognize a very simple fact: It does not matter where you came from and how high your consciousness was before you came to earth. Once you take on these illusions, you will be looking at life on earth through the filter of these illusions. This means that you are now in the same situation as the other inhabitants on earth. You are not superior, you are not more sophisticated, you are not more mature because you face the same initiations.

You have the potential to go down in consciousness, and indeed some of the lifestreams who have come from natural planets have gone below the 48th level of consciousness. Many have not, *most* have not, but still, you face the same initiations. You need to recognize that you cannot allow yourself to have this sense that you are different, you do not really belong here, this is a primitive planet, you cannot relate to these other people on the planet and all of these things. There are many of the lifestreams who have come here on a rescue mission who feel somehow distant from or superior to other people on earth. The reason for this is very simple. As you descend into the density of a planet like earth, you lose the connection to the awareness of what we have in recent dictations called the basic humanity. You become so shocked by being here, often by the treatment you have received here (where you have been brutally rejected, often in your very first embodiment on this planet) that you kind of lose the basic humanity in yourself. More than that, you fail to see it in the people on earth. You fail to see the basic humanity, so to speak, in the fallen beings who may have hurt you very brutally. You also fail to see it in the average population on earth because you see how many of them are not growing, they are not willing to grow.

You need to recognize here a very, very important dynamic, which is that many, in fact *most,* of the lifestreams who have come to earth from more highly evolved planets have gone into what we can term a negative frame of mind. You have become very critical of the earth, you have a sense that perhaps the matter universe itself is the enemy of your spiritual growth, it is somehow dirty, the people on this planet are primitive, societies are primitive. You have often been trapped into this selective criticism where you see specific groups of people as being very negative, backwards or not growing, and somehow not being worthy of your respect, your love or your consideration.

## Deceived by Nazism

It may shock you to realize, but it is a fact, that if you look at Nazi Germany, a certain number of these lifestreams who have come from higher planets were seduced by the Nazi ideology of the super race and the need to purify the human race. They actually gave their light to uphold the Nazi machine that ended up precipitating the Holocaust. I am not saying they were prison guards in the concentration camps or pushed people into the gas chambers, but they served at higher levels in the Nazi apparatus. Their light was a factor in helping to extend the lifespan of this war machine that Hitler had created.

You can actually see, if you look at some of these lifestreams, even if you look at pictures or movies from the time, that they had some spiritual light. There were these tall, blond, blue-eyed people who actually had spiritual light but they had been seduced into supporting this Nazi ideology. They thought that, given the low conditions on the earth and especially the low conditions of some groups of people, perhaps it was time to take drastic measures to raise the earth beyond what they saw as the madness that had overtaken the land. You need to recognize that when you are in embodiment on earth (and especially when you have descended, not necessarily below the 48th level, but certainly below the 96th level), even though you come from a higher planet, you can still be vulnerable to being pulled into falling in love with an idea, with an ideal. You actually can be seduced into thinking that in order to further this ideal, it is justified to kill certain people that are working against what you see as the ideal for this planet.

My beloved, the call I issue here is that it is time for those of you who have come from natural planets to raise yourself above this illusion once and for all. You can only do this by following the advice that we have given to: 1) Depersonalize your life and your path, and 2) Find what we have called the basic humanity in yourself.

## Raising yourself or the whole

Now, why do we call it "basic humanity?" Some will say why not "spiritual identity?" Well, it is because there is a time on the spiritual path, as we have said many times, where you need to raise yourself above the downward pull of the mass consciousness. We have attempted to give you a systematic path in the course of self-mastery where you can raise yourself up through the seven rays, from the 48th to the 96th level. We have also said that when you reach the 96th level, you face a specific initiation, and it is whether you will continue to focus on raising yourself or whether you will switch and begin to focus on raising the whole.

How can you make that switch and focus on raising the whole? Well, only by recognizing what we have in other contexts called the Christ consciousness. It is only when you begin to recognize the Christ consciousness in yourself, and when you begin to understand that the Christ consciousness is the connecting link between all life, that you can truly acknowledge why you are here.

You are not here, my beloved, to raise your own consciousness to a much higher level than the other inhabitants of the earth so that you can feel superior to them. You are here to raise the consciousness of the whole. You cannot do this if you use your progress on the path to decide that because you have risen to a certain level of the spiritual path, and because you came from a better world, you are superior to the other inhabitants of earth. You need to discover that element of the Christ consciousness that ties you to all life, including the inhabitants of earth, regardless of the level of consciousness they are at.

This is an element of the Christ consciousness that Jesus described when he said: "Those who have done it unto the least of these my brethren, have done it unto me." Jesus, when you look at his life, even the fragmentary account in the scriptures, you can see how he did not set himself apart. He did not do what many of the Jews did: feel superior to other people that lived in their land, such as the Samaritans and others. He reached out to all people and that is why we have said that this is the basic humanity.

## Avoiding superiority

Now, we have talked about the need that all people discover this basic humanity, that they can begin to cooperate based on trust and based on seeing themselves as equals. What you need to recognize, as the spiritual people, is that you face the same initiation, just in a slightly different way. Your primary challenge is not the same as it is for most people on earth. Your challenge is, first of all, to avoid feeling superior. How do you do this? Well, partly by locking in to that element of the Christ consciousness that is completely beyond the sense of hierarchy set up by the people on earth.

When you look at earth, you can look back into all of known history and you will see that every society has had this sense of hierarchy. Some are not only in a more powerful position than others, but they are often (at least by themselves, but often also by the people) considered to be in a separate class so they are inherently better, they are inherently superior. Some have even believed they were created that way by God. Unfortunately, many of the people who came from natural planets have been seduced by these thought systems because they have felt that they were more mature, more sophisticated than the inhabitants of this planet. I challenge you to make the distinction that can only be made with the Christ mind, namely that being at a higher level of the path and a higher level of consciousness does not make you superior to those who are at lower levels. In fact, the higher you go towards the 144th level of consciousness, the less superior you feel, the more you feel one with all life and the more you want to raise up all life. You can only, truly, meet this challenge if you understand the inner meaning of depersonalizing your life. You are not seeking in any way to reach some kind of position in an earthly hierarchy that makes other people or yourself think you are superior. Neither are you seeking to walk the spiritual path, and perhaps even reach some position in an ascended master organization, in order to gain recognition from the ascended masters. You understand, my beloved, that the entire concept of a hierarchy is valid in the sense that there *is* a hierarchy in the ascended realm. My beloved, the highest ascended being in the hierarchy that is working with this unascended sphere does not feel superior to the unascended beings inhabiting on earth. There is no superiority. There is hierarchy in the sense that there are certain positions that hold a higher office, but there is no value judgment, no sense of superiority associated with that hierarchy.

## A false hierarchy

You know very well that the fallen beings are experts at taking certain valid concepts and perverting them. All they needed to do on earth was to take the concept of hierarchy and pervert it with the value judgment of the duality consciousness. This led to two things. One is that those who are at the top of the hierarchy on earth are better than those who are at lower levels. You can even set up the condition seen in Nazi Germany of the Aryan race being superior to other races. You can even see in the Soviet Union how some felt that the true communists in the Soviet Union were superior to those in non-communist nations or even in the other Soviet Republics. You see many, many examples of this, both today and in history. My beloved, do you seriously believe that this consciousness can survive in the Golden age? *It cannot.*

The other aspect of this consciousness is that once you have established the hierarchy, those who are at the top can never be questioned or gainsaid by those who are below them in rank. Of course, this is what has led to these truly insane situations where, for example, if you look at the life of Adolf Hitler, you will see how he, in many cases, deliberately ignored the advice of his generals who told him how the war was actually going. He believed they were far too negative and limited and that his armies were able to do what his generals considered to be impossible. In the beginning of the war, this actually happened in several cases. The army generals had assessed that certain things could not be done, but Hitler gave the order to go ahead and it happened anyway. He lulled himself into this consciousness of feeling that he never needed to listen to the advice of others and he did not need to know what was actually happening on the battlefields. It was enough for him to go within and get the vision of what *should* happen, and then he would decree that and it *would* happen. Of course, you all know that it came to a point when he had simply run out of forward momentum and everything started collapsing. Instead of acknowledging this and making the necessary adjustments, he kept going in the same direction, which magnified the level of catastrophe that actually took place.

## The challenge of the Piscean age

My beloved, you need to recognize here that we of the ascended masters do not want to set up this kind of hierarchy on earth. You may then ask yourself why there have been several ascended master organizations who had precisely this kind of hierarchy? Well, because, again, we have to work with the level of the collective consciousness and we have to work with the level of those who are at higher levels and have more of the potential to follow our teachings. Who was it that gave the example that said: "Inasmuch you have done it unto the least of these my brethren, you have done it onto me?" Well, it was Jesus and Jesus was the one who inaugurated the Piscean age. What was the challenge that needed to be met at the end of the Piscean age? It was precisely to overcome this state of consciousness, this sense of superiority, this sense of rank, and to discover the basic humanity that ties you to all people.

There came a point in the 1900's where we recognized it was time to release a more direct teaching from the ascended level and we got the dispensation to anoint messengers and give direct dictations. We also recognized that the consciousness of the students in general, those who have the potential to follow our teachings, was simply not at a level where they had passed that initiation during the Piscean age. Many of them were not ready to pass that initiation because they were still so trapped in this need to feel that they were doing something important. We always face this dilemma that we want to appeal to a certain group of people by giving them a teaching that can take them higher, but in order to do so, we have to make a realistic assessment of their present level of consciousness.

We have to look at what exactly motivates them, and then we have to give them something that appeals to that motivation—in order to get them to even accept the teachings and start the path that we are offering. We had to give people teachings that contained the necessary keys that would help them transcend that level of consciousness, but they still contained certain elements that appealed to this motivation of feeling that they were doing something very important to improve planet earth.

## Stepping up to a higher motivation

What I am saying is that now for a number of years through this messenger we have given a higher level of teaching on duality, on the epic mindset, on the ego and overcoming the inferiority-superiority dynamic. It truly is my call, that I am sending to all of the lifestreams who came to earth from a higher planet, that it is time to awaken and get over this initiation, get over this hump and step up to a higher motivation. You are not seeking to walk the spiritual path or follow a certain spiritual teaching or practice in order to raise yourself up, to make yourself feel better than others, or to reinforce the sense you already have, or in order to make yourself feel that you are among the few who are saving the planet and doing something important for the ascended masters. You recognize that it is time to simply step beyond that level of consciousness and to acknowledge fully that this is not why you are here. Therefore, you need to do what we have given you the tools and the teachings to do: Go back and look at that initial birth trauma that you were exposed to when you took embodiment on this earth and were shocked by the conditions here.

You need to recognize that ever since then, you have maintained a certain attitude towards this planet of being critical, of feeling that this is a low planet, that the inhabitants here are far below you, that they are not really worthy to receive your light and your love, and perhaps even that the matter realm is an enemy of your spiritual growth. You may have developed a desire to just get out of here. It is time to recognize, my beloved, that you came to earth to make a positive difference, but you cannot make a positive difference while you are in a negative state of mind. You cannot make a positive difference on earth if you have a negative attitude to planet earth and the people on it.

You need to recognize that it is time, it is high time, to step beyond this entire consciousness and get to the point where you have looked at your personal motivation for walking the spiritual path. You have seen where it contains elements of negativity, elements of wanting to raise yourself up or elements of just wanting to get out of here. You need to recognize, my beloved, a simple fact, which other masters have said before, that until you are at peace with being on this planet, until you fully accept yourself as being on this planet and until you can feel good about being on this planet, you will not get out of here.

## Thinking the laws do not apply to you

There are some of you, my beloved, who have a very subtle (and often unrecognized) sense that because you came from a natural planet, where the laws of nature, so to speak, even the spiritual laws are different, then, even though you are now in embodiment on an unnatural planet, you should not be subject to the laws that apply here. You think that you should be able to come here and not have your garments soiled, and not have to face the consequences of your choices, not be held accountable for your reactions. My beloved, when you chose to come here, you knew full well that the moment you took embodiment, you would become subject to the laws that apply on this planet. You would face the same initiations as anyone else, and you would have to do exactly the same as anyone else in order to raise your consciousness and qualify for your ascension.

Get out of this dream, that some of you have, that you may find some shortcut, some magical formula where you can suddenly escape having to walk the path like anyone else. *Get rid of it!* It does not serve you, and it does not serve the cause that brought you here. Recognize the fact, my beloved, that the fallen beings have set up a very specific state on this planet. We have taught about the duality consciousness and the epic mind-set, but I wish to give you an even deeper teaching on this because some of you are ready for it.

## How to go beyond duality

I have said that fallen beings always want to set up a hierarchy and put themselves on top so they are untouchables, cannot be gainsaid or challenged by those below them. Of course, they cannot be challenged or gainsaid by anyone above them because they have attempted to shut off all knowledge of ascended masters on this planet. What they have actually done is to use the duality consciousness to create certain very subtle concepts. What the fallen beings would like to do on this planet is to set themselves up so that they are invincible, they are invulnerable. Now, you may think that there is some validity to this concept in a sense that, surely, Archangel Michael is invincible, he is invulnerable. He is not invincible in a dualistic way, he is invincible because he is beyond duality. The question is: "How do you get beyond duality?"

I said earlier that some of the people who came to earth on a rescue mission were seduced by Nazism and this ideology of the superior race. Well, one way to seek to raise yourself above the misery, the conflict, the struggle, the suffering on this planet is to try to make yourself invincible. Many of the more advanced lifestreams that came here have been seduced into thinking that they should use their spiritual attainment and power to try to set themselves up so that they were invincible. Some have been seduced by some warrior tradition, thinking they should be invincible warriors, others have attempted to do it in other ways. Some have even attempted to use the path of the ascended masters and the teachings to set themselves up to where they could be invincible. My beloved, the goal of the path of Christhood is not to become invincible in a dualistic way. Was Jesus invincible? Well, if he had been, why was he crucified?

You have to recognize that, when you are on a planet with duality, there are stages of the spiritual path. You grow, not by only pulling yourself away from duality. We have talked about an immersion phase and an awakening phase. You recognize that, while you are in the immersion phase, you are not only going down in the level of consciousness, you can also go up, but the way you go up is by experiencing these extreme contrasts that you find on earth. For some people, they have spent several lifetimes pursuing this goal of invincibility or superiority. They have attempted to make themselves invincible or put themselves in a certain station in an earthly hierarchy were they seem superior, but this can become a trap that is very difficult to break out of. How can people break out of it if they are not willing to do this consciously, if they are not willing to see the illusions of superiority and invincibility? Well, they have to experience a number of lifetimes where they are in the opposite extreme of being completely vulnerable and completely inferior. That is actually one of the reasons this planet precipitated the phenomenon of slavery.

Many times, you would see, for example in Roman society, that a soul had been for several lifetimes at the top of Roman hierarchy but then, suddenly, it went down and now embodied as a slave for several lifetimes. By experiencing both of these extreme contrasts on the planet, this eventually caused some lifestreams to recognize in themselves what we have called the basic humanity. They recognized that whether you are in a high position or in a low position, whether you are ultimately invulnerable or ultimately vulnerable, there was still a part of you that did not change. There was a part of you that was real and that would continue growing regardless of the outer situations you are in. These lifestreams began to, so to speak, depersonalize the extremes that you see on earth. They started to stop identifying themselves with this earthly spectacle and that is how they found more, what Gautama called the middle way, that is not so directed by the contrast. That is what has caused all of you to come to the point to be open to an ascended master teaching. What I am giving you now is simply the challenge to step up to a higher level of that teaching by seeing in yourself how you have, as a normal unavoidable part of your growth, had to go between these extremes.

It is now time to transcend them, to recognize, my beloved, that there is no ultimate security in being invulnerable on earth, nor is there any ultimate humiliation in being completely vulnerable. You come to a point where you recognize that compared to the ongoingness of your own being, to the basic humanity or the Christ mind in your being, all of these outer conditions do not matter. If they do not matter, why do you have to continue to walk the path of the ascended masters by being motivated by this need to feel superior, to feel better, to feel you have some kind of important rank or mission?

## A higher motivation for walking the path

Now, some will say: "But how can we then be motivated to walk the path when we don't have a sense that we are doing something important to save the earth or bring the golden age?" Well, my beloved, you can be motivated out of love—for that is what motivated you to come here. Reconnect to the original motivation that brought you here, and then you will be able to find an entirely new motivation for walking the path. You will not be pulled here and there by these extremes. You will not, for example, be pulled into these negative prophecies, thinking that you have to put your attention upon them.

You will find a more steady progression, a more steady growth. It will be an adjustment for you because many times you will not have the extreme experiences that some of you had on the path. There are lower levels of the path where you can have these, what people call "peak experiences." Many students have actually become trapped into a form of addiction, of seeking higher and higher peak experiences. You only have a peak when you have a valley, and you only have a high experience when you have the contrast of a low experience. When you find the true middle way, you go beyond the pairs, the extremes, and so you have less and less contrast on your path.

In the beginning, this will be confusing to you. As you continue to work with the teachings we have given, you can come to a point where you transcend it. You have no need to have this old motivation, this old sense of being important. You are being who you are, you are doing what you are doing, out of a love-based motivation.

## Infinite and unconditional patience

This also means that you develop something that many spiritual students fail to develop, namely infinite, unconditional patience. Many of you have felt a certain urgency to push hard on your personal path. Again, this is valid for a time because you need to raise yourself above the pull of the mass consciousness. There comes a time, my beloved, where you need to go beyond this. You are not seeking to set all of these goals, or set goals for what should happen on a planetary level, when a certain condition should change. Some of you, have gotten so preoccupied with your self-importance that you think that, if you give a large amount of invocations and decrees for a certain time, then the planet should change or specific nations should change. If they do not, you become disappointed, you start doubting whether the teachings work, and all these kind of things. You can transcend all of that and realize you are here to continue to raise your consciousness, to do what you feel prompted to do from within, and you are non-attached to the physical results. You rejoice when you see them, but you are not dissatisfied, angry or in doubt if you do not see them. You realize you must work within the constraints of free will, as we of the ascended masters do.

My beloved, it was a long time ago that I came to this earth. If I had had the impatience that many of you have, I would have destroyed myself psychologically long, long ago by the lack of progress on this planet. We of the ascended masters take an entirely different view. As we have said recently, our goal is not to produce specific outer changes but to raise the collective consciousness. This can only be done by working with people so that they come to the point where they can make a free, conscious choice to come up higher. This is our goal. Our goal is not to manifest these outer changes that so many spiritual students become attached to. When you can step beyond these things, that often pull you into this negative, critical state of mind, you can find peace with being on this planet. You can *accept* being on this planet. You can accept this planet for what it is, not that you are required to maintain its current state, but you accept it for what it is: an educational institution for the lifestreams that are here. You can respect what we have told you about free will and accept how it works. Therefore, you can come to the point where you are at peace with being here. You can allow yourself to feel good about being a human being in embodiment, not being beyond the laws of this planet, but being one with the people, identifying at the level of the Christ mind with them, seeing their basic humanity, and seeking to always raise it up.

This, my beloved, was my gift for today. As I said, it is a multi-faceted message that truly bears studying many, many times in order to extract the full value that is often half-way hidden between the words. Read between the lines. Connect to my Being beyond the words and I will give you, as you are willing, what could not be embedded in the words—at least, not at the level where your outer mind can grasp it through the words alone.

Thus, I thank you for, again, being the electrodes for radiating this into the collective consciousness. Make sure that you are not always looking at how those other people out there need to change. This was a dictation that put a mirror in front of you and said: "Now look at how *you* need to change."

# 17 | INVOKING PEACE WITH BEING ON EARTH

In the name I AM THAT I AM, Jesus Christ, I call to all representatives of the Divine Mother, especially Sanat Kumara, to help me overcome any negative attitude towards being on earth. Help me overcome everything that prevents me from accepting being here, including…

[Make personal calls.]

*Part 1*

1. Sanat Kumara, I am reconnecting to the basic humanity in myself and in all people. I see all people as being my spiritual brothers and sisters, I no longer see them as "other" people.

Sanat Kumara, Ruby Fire,
I seek my place in love's own choir,
with open hearts we sing your praise,
together we the earth do raise.

**Sanat Kumara, Ruby Ray,**
**bring to earth a higher way,**
**light this planet with your fire,**
**clothe her in a new attire.**

2. Sanat Kumara, I recognize that it is time to step up higher. It is time to come to a conscious recognition of why I am here. I am here to serve as an anchor point, and to provide a positive frame of reference for the other inhabitants on the planet.

Sanat Kumara, Ruby Fire,
initiations I desire,
I am for you an electrode,
Shamballa is my true abode.

**Sanat Kumara, Ruby Ray,**
**bring to earth a higher way,**
**light this planet with your fire,**
**clothe her in a new attire.**

3. Sanat Kumara, it does not matter where I came from and how high my consciousness was before I came to earth. Once I take on the illusions here, I will be looking at life on earth through the filter of these illusions.

Sanat Kumara, Ruby Fire,
I follow path that you require,
initiate me with your love,
the open door for Holy Dove.

**Sanat Kumara, Ruby Ray,**
**bring to earth a higher way,**
**light this planet with your fire,**
**clothe her in a new attire.**

4. Sanat Kumara, I am in the same situation as the other inhabitants on earth. I am not superior because I face the same initiations.

Sanat Kumara, Ruby Fire,
your great example all inspire,

with non-attachment and great mirth,
we give the earth a true rebirth.

**Sanat Kumara, Ruby Ray,**
**bring to earth a higher way,**
**light this planet with your fire,**
**clothe her in a new attire.**

5. Sanat Kumara, I will not allow myself to have the sense that I am different, I do not really belong here, this is a primitive planet or that I cannot relate to the people. I will not allow myself to feel distant from or superior to other people on earth.

Sanat Kumara, Ruby Fire,
you are this planet's purifier,
consume on earth all spirits dark,
reveal the inner Spirit Spark.

**Sanat Kumara, Ruby Ray,**
**bring to earth a higher way,**
**light this planet with your fire,**
**clothe her in a new attire.**

6. Sanat Kumara, I recognize that I was so shocked by what happened to me here on earth that I lost my sense of the basic humanity in myself. I also failed to see it in the people on earth and in the fallen beings.

Sanat Kumara, Ruby Fire,
you are a cosmic amplifier,
the lower forces can't withstand,
vibrations from Venusian band.

**Sanat Kumara, Ruby Ray,**
**bring to earth a higher way,**
**light this planet with your fire,**
**clothe her in a new attire.**

7. Sanat Kumara, I consciously raise myself above any negative frame of mind, of being critical of the earth, any sense that the matter universe is the enemy of my spiritual growth, any sense that the people on this planet are primitive, societies are primitive.

> Sanat Kumara, Ruby Fire,
> I am on earth your magnifier,
> the flow of love I do restore,
> my chakras are your open door.

> **Sanat Kumara, Ruby Ray,**
> **bring to earth a higher way,**
> **light this planet with your fire,**
> **clothe her in a new attire.**

8. Sanat Kumara, I raise myself above any selective criticism where I see specific groups of people as being negative, backwards, not growing, or not being worthy of my respect, my love or my consideration.

> Sanat Kumara, Ruby Fire,
> Venusian song the multiplier,
> as we your love reverberate,
> the densest minds we penetrate.

> **Sanat Kumara, Ruby Ray,**
> **bring to earth a higher way,**
> **light this planet with your fire,**
> **clothe her in a new attire.**

9. Sanat Kumara, I raise myself above the illusion that, given the low conditions on the earth, and especially the low conditions of some groups of people, it is necessary to take drastic measures to raise the earth.

> Sanat Kumara, Ruby Fire,
> you are for all the sanctifier,
> the earth is now a holy place,
> purified by cosmic grace.

**Sanat Kumara, Ruby Ray,**
**bring to earth a higher way,**
**light this planet with your fire,**
**clothe her in a new attire.**

## Part 2

1. Sanat Kumara, I raise myself above any tendency to be pulled into falling in love with an idea, with an ideal. I reject the illusion that in order to further an ideal, it is justified to kill or force certain people.

Sanat Kumara, Ruby Fire,
I seek my place in love's own choir,
with open hearts we sing your praise,
together we the earth do raise.

**Sanat Kumara, Ruby Ray,**
**bring to earth a higher way,**
**light this planet with your fire,**
**clothe her in a new attire.**

2. Sanat Kumara, I am willing to depersonalize my life and path in order to find the basic humanity in myself.

Sanat Kumara, Ruby Fire,
initiations I desire,
I am for you an electrode,
Shamballa is my true abode.

**Sanat Kumara, Ruby Ray,**
**bring to earth a higher way,**
**light this planet with your fire,**
**clothe her in a new attire.**

3. Sanat Kumara, I will not continue to focus on raising myself. I will switch and focus on raising the whole.

Sanat Kumara, Ruby Fire,
I follow path that you require,
initiate me with your love,
the open door for Holy Dove.

**Sanat Kumara, Ruby Ray,**
**bring to earth a higher way,**
**light this planet with your fire,**
**clothe her in a new attire.**

4. Sanat Kumara, I recognize the Christ consciousness in myself. I understand that the Christ consciousness is the connecting link between all life.

Sanat Kumara, Ruby Fire,
your great example all inspire,
with non-attachment and great mirth,
we give the earth a true rebirth.

**Sanat Kumara, Ruby Ray,**
**bring to earth a higher way,**
**light this planet with your fire,**
**clothe her in a new attire.**

5. Sanat Kumara, I am not here to raise my own consciousness to a much higher level than the other inhabitants of the earth so that I can feel superior to them. I am here to raise the consciousness of the whole.

Sanat Kumara, Ruby Fire,
you are this planet's purifier,
consume on earth all spirits dark,
reveal the inner Spirit Spark.

**Sanat Kumara, Ruby Ray,**
**bring to earth a higher way,**
**light this planet with your fire,**
**clothe her in a new attire.**

6. Sanat Kumara, I raise myself above the illusion that because I have risen to a certain level of the spiritual path, and because I came from a better world, I am superior to the other inhabitants of earth.

Sanat Kumara, Ruby Fire,
you are a cosmic amplifier,
the lower forces can't withstand,
vibrations from Venusian band.

**Sanat Kumara, Ruby Ray,**
**bring to earth a higher way,**
**light this planet with your fire,**
**clothe her in a new attire.**

7. Sanat Kumara, I discover the element of the Christ consciousness that ties me to all life, including the inhabitants of earth, regardless of the level of consciousness they are at.

Sanat Kumara, Ruby Fire,
I am on earth your magnifier,
the flow of love I do restore,
my chakras are your open door.

**Sanat Kumara, Ruby Ray,**
**bring to earth a higher way,**
**light this planet with your fire,**
**clothe her in a new attire.**

8. Sanat Kumara, I raise myself above any sense of superiority by locking in to that element of the Christ consciousness that is completely beyond the sense of hierarchy set up by the people on earth.

Sanat Kumara, Ruby Fire,
Venusian song the multiplier,
as we your love reverberate,
the densest minds we penetrate.

**Sanat Kumara, Ruby Ray,**
**bring to earth a higher way,**
**light this planet with your fire,**
**clothe her in a new attire.**

9. Sanat Kumara, I raise myself above the illusion behind the earthly hierarchy in which some people are considered to be in a separate class so they are inherently better, they are inherently superior.

Sanat Kumara, Ruby Fire,
you are for all the sanctifier,
the earth is now a holy place,
purified by cosmic grace.

**Sanat Kumara, Ruby Ray,**
**bring to earth a higher way,**
**light this planet with your fire,**
**clothe her in a new attire.**

*Part 3*

1. Sanat Kumara, I make the distinction that can only be made with the Christ mind, namely that being at a higher level of the path and a higher level of consciousness does not make me superior to those who are at lower levels.

Sanat Kumara, Ruby Fire,
I seek my place in love's own choir,
with open hearts we sing your praise,
together we the earth do raise.

**Sanat Kumara, Ruby Ray,**
**bring to earth a higher way,**
**light this planet with your fire,**
**clothe her in a new attire.**

2. Sanat Kumara, I see that the higher I go towards the 144th level of consciousness, the less superior I feel, the more I feel one with all life and the more I want to raise up all life.

> Sanat Kumara, Ruby Fire,
> initiations I desire,
> I am for you an electrode,
> Shamballa is my true abode.

> **Sanat Kumara, Ruby Ray,**
> **bring to earth a higher way,**
> **light this planet with your fire,**
> **clothe her in a new attire.**

3. Sanat Kumara, I raise myself above the need to seek a position in an earthly hierarchy that makes other people or myself think I am superior. I raise myself above the need to walk the spiritual path in order to gain recognition from the ascended masters.

> Sanat Kumara, Ruby Fire,
> I follow path that you require,
> initiate me with your love,
> the open door for Holy Dove.

> **Sanat Kumara, Ruby Ray,**
> **bring to earth a higher way,**
> **light this planet with your fire,**
> **clothe her in a new attire.**

4. Sanat Kumara, I raise myself above the need to be in the top position in a hierarchy, where I can never be questioned or gainsaid by those who are below me in rank.

> Sanat Kumara, Ruby Fire,
> your great example all inspire,
> with non-attachment and great mirth,
> we give the earth a true rebirth.

**Sanat Kumara, Ruby Ray,**
**bring to earth a higher way,**
**light this planet with your fire,**
**clothe her in a new attire.**

5. Sanat Kumara, I recognize that the ascended masters do not want to set up this kind of hierarchy on earth.

Sanat Kumara, Ruby Fire,
you are this planet's purifier,
consume on earth all spirits dark,
reveal the inner Spirit Spark.

**Sanat Kumara, Ruby Ray,**
**bring to earth a higher way,**
**light this planet with your fire,**
**clothe her in a new attire.**

6. Sanat Kumara, I am meeting the challenge of the Piscean age and overcoming all sense of superiority, all sense of rank. I am discovering the basic humanity that ties me to all people.

Sanat Kumara, Ruby Fire,
you are a cosmic amplifier,
the lower forces can't withstand,
vibrations from Venusian band.

**Sanat Kumara, Ruby Ray,**
**bring to earth a higher way,**
**light this planet with your fire,**
**clothe her in a new attire.**

7. Sanat Kumara, I am awakening and I am getting over this initiation, getting over the inferiority-superiority dynamic. I am not seeking to walk the spiritual path in order to raise myself up, to make myself feel better than others.

Sanat Kumara, Ruby Fire,
I am on earth your magnifier,

the flow of love I do restore,
my chakras are your open door.

**Sanat Kumara, Ruby Ray,**
**bring to earth a higher way,**
**light this planet with your fire,**
**clothe her in a new attire.**

8. Sanat Kumara, I raise myself above the feeling that I am among the few who are saving the planet and doing something important for the ascended masters. I recognize that it is time to step beyond that level of consciousness and to acknowledge that this is not why I am here.

Sanat Kumara, Ruby Fire,
Venusian song the multiplier,
as we your love reverberate,
the densest minds we penetrate.

**Sanat Kumara, Ruby Ray,**
**bring to earth a higher way,**
**light this planet with your fire,**
**clothe her in a new attire.**

9. Sanat Kumara, I raise myself above any critical attitude to this planet and the people here, and any desire to just get out of here.

Sanat Kumara, Ruby Fire,
you are for all the sanctifier,
the earth is now a holy place,
purified by cosmic grace.

**Sanat Kumara, Ruby Ray,**
**bring to earth a higher way,**
**light this planet with your fire,**
**clothe her in a new attire.**

*Part 4*

1. Sanat Kumara, I recognize that I came to earth to make a positive difference, but I cannot make a positive difference while I am in a negative state of mind. I cannot make a positive difference on earth if I have a negative attitude to this planet and the people on it.

> Sanat Kumara, Ruby Fire,
> I seek my place in love's own choir,
> with open hearts we sing your praise,
> together we the earth do raise.

> **Sanat Kumara, Ruby Ray,**
> **bring to earth a higher way,**
> **light this planet with your fire,**
> **clothe her in a new attire.**

2. Sanat Kumara, I recognize that it is high time to step beyond this entire consciousness and get to the point where my personal motivation for walking the spiritual path is free of all elements of negativity, elements of wanting to raise myself up or elements of wanting to get out of here.

> Sanat Kumara, Ruby Fire,
> initiations I desire,
> I am for you an electrode,
> Shamballa is my true abode.

> **Sanat Kumara, Ruby Ray,**
> **bring to earth a higher way,**
> **light this planet with your fire,**
> **clothe her in a new attire.**

3. Sanat Kumara, I recognize that until I am at peace with being on this planet, until I fully accept myself as being on this planet, until I feel good about being on this planet, I will not get out of here.

> Sanat Kumara, Ruby Fire,
> I follow path that you require,

initiate me with your love,
the open door for Holy Dove.

**Sanat Kumara, Ruby Ray,**
**bring to earth a higher way,**
**light this planet with your fire,**
**clothe her in a new attire.**

4. Sanat Kumara, I raise myself above the sense that I should not be subject to the laws that apply on earth. I give up the desire to avoid facing the consequences of my choices, to not be held accountable for my reactions.

Sanat Kumara, Ruby Fire,
your great example all inspire,
with non-attachment and great mirth,
we give the earth a true rebirth.

**Sanat Kumara, Ruby Ray,**
**bring to earth a higher way,**
**light this planet with your fire,**
**clothe her in a new attire.**

5. Sanat Kumara, I raise myself above the dream that I may find some shortcut, some magical formula, where I can suddenly escape having to walk the path like anyone else.

Sanat Kumara, Ruby Fire,
you are this planet's purifier,
consume on earth all spirits dark,
reveal the inner Spirit Spark.

**Sanat Kumara, Ruby Ray,**
**bring to earth a higher way,**
**light this planet with your fire,**
**clothe her in a new attire.**

6. Sanat Kumara, I let go of the desire to raise myself above the misery, the conflict, the struggle and the suffering on this planet by making myself invincible.

Sanat Kumara, Ruby Fire,
you are a cosmic amplifier,
the lower forces can't withstand,
vibrations from Venusian band.

**Sanat Kumara, Ruby Ray,**
**bring to earth a higher way,**
**light this planet with your fire,**
**clothe her in a new attire.**

7. Sanat Kumara, I raise myself above the illusion that I should use my spiritual attainment and power to set myself up so that I am invincible. I give up the attempt to use the path of the ascended masters to set myself up as being invincible.

Sanat Kumara, Ruby Fire,
I am on earth your magnifier,
the flow of love I do restore,
my chakras are your open door.

**Sanat Kumara, Ruby Ray,**
**bring to earth a higher way,**
**light this planet with your fire,**
**clothe her in a new attire.**

8. Sanat Kumara, I am willing to consciously see the illusions of superiority and invincibility. I raise myself above the need to go from one extreme of being superior to the other of being inferior.

Sanat Kumara, Ruby Fire,
Venusian song the multiplier,
as we your love reverberate,
the densest minds we penetrate.

**Sanat Kumara, Ruby Ray,**
**bring to earth a higher way,**
**light this planet with your fire,**
**clothe her in a new attire.**

9. Sanat Kumara, I take up your challenge to step up to a higher level of recognizing that there is no ultimate security in being invulnerable on earth, nor is there any ultimate humiliation in being completely vulnerable.

Sanat Kumara, Ruby Fire,
you are for all the sanctifier,
the earth is now a holy place,
purified by cosmic grace.

**Sanat Kumara, Ruby Ray,**
**bring to earth a higher way,**
**light this planet with your fire,**
**clothe her in a new attire.**

## Part 5

1. Sanat Kumara, I recognize that compared to the ongoingness of my own being, to the basic humanity or the Christ mind in my being, all of these outer conditions do not matter.

Sanat Kumara, Ruby Fire,
I seek my place in love's own choir,
with open hearts we sing your praise,
together we the earth do raise.

**Sanat Kumara, Ruby Ray,**
**bring to earth a higher way,**
**light this planet with your fire,**
**clothe her in a new attire.**

2. Sanat Kumara, I see that when outer conditions do not matter, I do not have to continue to walk the path of the ascended masters by being motivated by this need to feel superior, to feel better, to feel I have some kind of important rank or mission.

Sanat Kumara, Ruby Fire,
initiations I desire,

I am for you an electrode,
Shamballa is my true abode.

**Sanat Kumara, Ruby Ray,
bring to earth a higher way,
light this planet with your fire,
clothe her in a new attire.**

3. Sanat Kumara, I am motivated to walk the path out of love, the love that motivated me to come here. I am reconnecting to the original motivation that brought me here, and I am finding an entirely new motivation for walking the path.

Sanat Kumara, Ruby Fire,
I follow path that you require,
initiate me with your love,
the open door for Holy Dove.

**Sanat Kumara, Ruby Ray,
bring to earth a higher way,
light this planet with your fire,
clothe her in a new attire.**

4. Sanat Kumara, I raise myself above any addiction of seeking higher and higher peak experiences. I find the true middle way, I go beyond the pairs, the extremes, and I have less and less contrast on my path.

Sanat Kumara, Ruby Fire,
your great example all inspire,
with non-attachment and great mirth,
we give the earth a true rebirth.

**Sanat Kumara, Ruby Ray,
bring to earth a higher way,
light this planet with your fire,
clothe her in a new attire.**

5. Sanat Kumara, I am developing infinite, unconditional patience. I am not seeking to set all of these goals for myself or what should happen on a planetary level.

> Sanat Kumara, Ruby Fire,
> you are this planet's purifier,
> consume on earth all spirits dark,
> reveal the inner Spirit Spark.

> **Sanat Kumara, Ruby Ray,**
> **bring to earth a higher way,**
> **light this planet with your fire,**
> **clothe her in a new attire.**

6. Sanat Kumara, I realize I am here to continue to raise my consciousness, to do what I feel prompted to do from within. I am non-attached to the physical results. I rejoice when I see them, but I am not dissatisfied or in doubt if I do not see them.

> Sanat Kumara, Ruby Fire,
> you are a cosmic amplifier,
> the lower forces can't withstand,
> vibrations from Venusian band.

> **Sanat Kumara, Ruby Ray,**
> **bring to earth a higher way,**
> **light this planet with your fire,**
> **clothe her in a new attire.**

7. Sanat Kumara, I realize I must work within the constraints of free will, as the ascended masters do. I am working with people so that they come to the point where they can make a free, conscious choice to come up higher.

> Sanat Kumara, Ruby Fire,
> I am on earth your magnifier,
> the flow of love I do restore,
> my chakras are your open door.

**Sanat Kumara, Ruby Ray,**
**bring to earth a higher way,**
**light this planet with your fire,**
**clothe her in a new attire.**

8. Sanat Kumara, I raise myself above the negative, critical state of mind and I find peace with being on this planet. I *accept* being on this planet. I accept this planet for what it is: an educational institution for the lifestreams that are here.

Sanat Kumara, Ruby Fire,
Venusian song the multiplier,
as we your love reverberate,
the densest minds we penetrate.

**Sanat Kumara, Ruby Ray,**
**bring to earth a higher way,**
**light this planet with your fire,**
**clothe her in a new attire.**

9. Sanat Kumara, I respect free will and how it works. I am at peace with being here. I allow myself to feel good about being a human being in embodiment, not being beyond the laws of this planet, but being one with the people, identifying at the level of the Christ mind with them, seeing their basic humanity and seeking to always raise it up.

Sanat Kumara, Ruby Fire,
you are for all the sanctifier,
the earth is now a holy place,
purified by cosmic grace.

**Sanat Kumara, Ruby Ray,**
**bring to earth a higher way,**
**light this planet with your fire,**
**clothe her in a new attire.**

## Sealing

In the name of the Divine Mother, I call to Mother Mary for the sealing of myself and all people in my circle of influence in the creative flow of the Divine Mother, the River of Life. I call for the multiplication of my calls by all representatives of the Divine Mother, so that we form the perfect figure-eight flow of "As Above, so below." Thus, I accept that this is fully manifest, because the mouth of the Lord, the Divine Mother that I AM, has spoken it. Amen.

# 18 | SPIRITUAL ANGER MANAGEMENT THERAPY

I AM the Ascended Master Gautama Buddha. I come to give you some teachings that will add a few facets to the teachings of Sanat Kumara. Many of the spiritual people around the world, many of the religious people around the world, many of the ascended master students around the world have created a certain mechanism in their psychology that is holding them back on the path.

## The inevitability of reacting to earth

Now, we have several times said that when you descend into embodiment on a planet like earth, it is inevitable that you will be pulled into a reactionary pattern. It is also, my beloved, inevitable that when you encounter many of these situations that you cannot avoid on earth, such as violence, warfare and many other forms of struggle and abuse, you will have feelings about this.

It is quite simply inevitable that you will have a certain anger and resentment about what you have experienced on this planet. You may have some awareness, very subtle, very intuitive, often something you cannot formulate in words about how life *should* be. This is based on your sense of how life is on a natural planet. On a natural planet, anger and resentment are unnatural feelings. On an unnatural planet like earth, anger and resentment are, quite frankly, "natural." How can you possibly be in embodiment on a planet like this without feeling a certain anger and resentment about what is going on here?

However, based on the subtle sense that those of you who came here on a rescue mission have (about what life should be on a natural planet), you often have this sense that you should not be angry or resentful. This has been cleverly reinforced in many religious and spiritual movements by the fallen beings. Many spiritual people, including many ascended master students, have this sense that when you are a spiritual person, when you are an ascended master student, you should never feel anger or resentment. My beloved, deciding with your mental mind to adopt an idea that as an ascended master student you should not feel anger, is not going to resolve what is already in your emotional body and what has accumulated there for many lifetimes.

I therefore come to give you a tool and some teachings that can help you deal with this issue. First of all, you need to recognize that you have come here, my beloved, to immerse yourself in the consciousness of this planet. If you did not immerse yourself, how could you serve as an example for the people who were already on the planet, and how can you pull the collective consciousness up? Do you see, my beloved, that for those lifestreams who have lived on earth for much longer than you have, fear and anger seems so natural and unavoidable to them that they cannot see an alternative? For you to serve as an example, you need to go into a reactionary pattern, you need to feel the anger and resentment and then you need to rise above it. *Then,* you serve as an example. You cannot help these people if you have not experienced what they have experienced.

## Pulling up the collective consciousness

Now, my beloved, we have talked many, many times about pulling up the collective consciousness. How can you do this? Well, only if you are a part of that collective consciousness. Is this not eminently logical? Unless you go in and immerse yourself in the collective consciousness, react the way people on earth react, you do not build that tie to the collective consciousness that enables you to pull up on it, once you start the awakening phase and start raising yourself above the collective level.

If you had never connected to it, if you had never been part of it, you would just be a stranger on earth. You might come here, you might avoid going into a reactionary pattern, you might forever stay pure, and you might raise your consciousness to the ascended level, but how would that serve as an example, how would it pull up on the collective consciousness?

You see, precisely, what they have done to Jesus, and to a large extent to myself, portraying us as being so special from birth that we were never really part of the collective consciousness. Therefore, they have tried to destroy us as examples, but they have also tried to spread the illusion that we could not pull up on the collective consciousness because we were never part of it. Well, we *were*, my beloved. We went into duality, we reacted, we were in a lower state of consciousness for many lifetimes. Then, we awakened ourselves and we raised ourselves to higher levels and that is why we were able to pull up on the collective.

## The energy flow in your four lower bodies

Now, the secret, so to speak, that I want to give you here is that some of you will (especially when you start reaching higher levels where you have more attunement, more intuitive experiences) have a sense (and perhaps you have never verbalized it, but still many of you have had the sense) that on a natural planet there is a natural flow of energy through your lower bodies. In other words, the energy streaming from your I AM Presence flows into the identity body, into the mental body, into the emotional, then into the physical.

My beloved, on a natural planet you never experience the reverse, you never experience that there is something that affects you at the physical level that creates a response or a reaction in the emotional body, that then affects your thoughts and even your sense of identity. Many of you have this sense that you should have this flow from above to below and this means that you should be in command of your four lower bodies. Your identity body should be in command of your mental body, your mental body should be in command of your emotional body and your emotional body should be in command of your actions.

Of course, when you come to earth, what the fallen beings are experts at doing is exposing you to this initial trauma, this initial shock, that is so severe, so shocking to you, that you cannot avoid reacting to it emotionally. The emotional reaction is so strong that it goes up into the mental body, affects your beliefs about what life on this planet is. This even goes into your identity body and starts affecting how you see yourself in connection with this planet, what you *can* and *cannot* do, what you are *allowed* and *not allowed* to do on this planet. What you experience after this initial trauma is a reverse flow through your four lower bodies. The physical level starts affecting your emotions, which affect your thoughts, which affect your sense of identity—not the other way around.

## Suppressing anger

When you find a spiritual path, my beloved, you often come to a point where (whether it is based on the outer teachings or your intuition or a combination of both) you get this feeling that you should have command over your four lower bodies. Therefore, you should be able to decide: "My ideal for an ascended master student is a person who never gets angry and therefore I should never get angry." Then, when you find your emotional body reacting in a way you do not want, you do not know what to do about this. What many, many religious people, spiritual people and ascended master students have done is they have created a program in the mental mind that is designed to suppress the feelings that they have labeled "unwanted."

You now have, as we have talked about before, a certain reactionary program in the emotional body that causes you to react with anger in certain situations. Because you are so fixated on being a good ascended master student, you dare not even acknowledge when this happens. You immediately try to activate the program in the mental body, even sometimes a program in the identity body, to suppress the feeling of anger. This means that there are some people who have become so good at doing this that they do not even recognize consciously when they are feeling anger.

Of course, this does not mean that the anger is not there in the emotional body. You have many people (and you find them in all religious movements, in all spiritual movements and in all ascended master movements) who on the surface level seem to be very much in control, very harmonious. They often speak in a certain calm, measured way, perhaps even a slightly overbearing way as if they are speaking to children. You can feel (if you tune in) that there is a tension under the surface. If you could see their auras, you would see that some of them have like an erupting volcano in their emotional body where the hot magma, which is the anger energy, is always threatening to overflow the brim of the crater.

Somehow, in most situations they manage to hold it down, but there can come situations where they cannot hold it back and it may spill over and they may express that anger towards people that they feel are below them in a hierarchy they have set up. Or they may even come to a point where they feel so angry with the guru, because the guru left them (as happened in one previous organization that you know about) that they openly switch into this anger and express it.

Now, what I want you to recognize (as the more mature ascended master students that you are becoming) is that you do not overcome anger by suppressing it. You do not overcome *anything* by suppressing it. You need to recognize that there was a time (again a stage on the path) where it was constructive for you to suppress the anger because it prevented you from constantly going into these reactionary patterns and building more and more anger energy, or building more and more of a pattern of allowing yourself to respond with anger.

For a time, it is necessary and constructive to suppress the anger with a program in the mental body. There also comes a point where now this is no longer constructive. If you do not change it, you will go into a stalemate because you cannot free yourself from the emotional energy. You are dragging it along with you. As long as you have anger, well, you cannot move into what we have talked about: accepting that you are here, being at peace with being here, feeling good about being here.

## An exercise for transcending anger

You need to come to the point where you recognize that you have embodied on an extremely difficult planet. It is very unnatural, but precisely because it is so unnatural, it is "natural" for you to feel a certain anger and resentment about being here, about having experienced what you have experienced and about not being able to just walk out of here when you feel you have had enough. As Sanat Kumara said, you have become subject to the law and you must walk the path.

I need you to perform a little exercise, if you are willing to get over this. I need you to recognize that you need to discover whether you still have some reservoir of anger or resentment in your emotional body. In order to do this, I suggest the following exercise.

You go into a place where you know that nobody can hear you. If this is not in your home, then go somewhere else: out in nature, go somewhere in your car if you have one. Find a place where nobody can hear you, no matter how loudly you scream. Then, I want you to tune in and imagine that you are looking at this planet from outer space. Then, I want you to allow your mind to go to one of the most disturbing manifestations you see on this planet. What is it that mostly disturbs you, that you feel really should not be here? Then, I want you to recognize that because you feel so strongly about this issue, you have most likely been exposed to it in several lifetimes and it has inevitably caused you to feel anger.

Now, I want you to imagine that you are talking directly to the fallen beings or to the human beings in embodiment who are precipitating this problem, this issue. Then, I want you to feel free to say anything you want to say to them and say it with whatever feeling you have: anger, resentment, fear—whatever your feeling is that comes to you as you consider this issue. I do not care how loud you are, I do not care how much you have to express. I am setting you free to express this because I want you to get in tune with what is hidden in your emotional body. I am not necessarily telling you to do this for hours and hours. This is not primal scream therapy, but the purpose is to get in touch with what you have not quite seen or not seen clearly in your emotional body.

Once you acknowledge this, you also need to acknowledge that you have risen to a certain level of the spiritual path. Therefore, you can make the switch of seeing that this is a perfectly natural reaction, my beloved. There is nothing wrong with it, there is nothing unspiritual about it. None of us could embody on earth without reacting with anger, myself included—not in my last embodiment as the Buddha, but certainly in previous embodiments. Look at Jesus who expressed a certain anger at the money changers.

You recognize that you have now risen to a higher level of the path. Therefore, you do not need to condemn yourself for having this anger or whatever the feeling is. You just need to recognize that you have it and it is time to get beyond it.

You can use the tools we have given you, decrees to invoke light, you can use the invocations we have given you. First of all, I am asking you to give some decrees for protection, to give whatever invocation you feel, and then take some quiet time when you are back in your home where you can sit quietly. Then, again get in touch with the anger and then do something that many of you have never done before.

You see, many spiritual people build this facade of how they should be on the outer. Therefore, they do not see what is hidden below the level of

surface awareness. Some of them even think that we of the ascended masters do not see it, but this is, of course, a rather naive belief. You need to get to the point where you realize that we have already seen what is hidden in your subconscious. You do not need to be shy about seeing it yourself because you somehow think that if you see it, then we will suddenly see it and then we will condemn you.

The cat is already out of the bag as far as we are concerned. You cannot hide anything from us, my beloved. Get to the point, as Saint Germain said with the surveillance society, where you just accept: "There is no need for me to hide anything from the ascended masters, and therefore, there is no need to hide anything from myself. Because if I know the masters don't condemn me, I don't need to condemn myself. So I can now take a step that most people are afraid to take, I can connect to my anger, and then instead of not wanting to see it, wanting to run away from it, wanting to cover it over, I can acknowledge it and I can walk right into it."

## Facing your anger

You have heard the statement that the only way to overcome you fear is to face your fear. This is not something you can do at lower levels of the path because you might be absorbed in the anger, you might be overwhelmed by it because you might still be too identified with it. Those of you who are at the higher levels, who are ready for this message, *you* can do it.

You can walk into the anger, you can experience being in that maelstrom of anger. Then, you can reconnect consciously to what we have called your basic humanity, which is really the ongoingness of your being, that part of your being that is beyond anything on earth and cannot be defined by anything on earth. This even enabled some people in the concentration camps to maintain a certain sense of humanity that enabled them to survive psychologically and even lead constructive lives afterwards. You can recognize that beyond this anger is your basic humanity. It has not been changed by the anger and therefore, you can look at the anger and you can recognize: "This is not me. It is not even *my* anger, it was the reaction of my ego." Again, it was natural that you had the reaction, but now you can see that you have risen to a higher sense of identity where you do not need to react this way. You can truly "let it go."

## Establishing the natural energy flow

My beloved, I said that on planet earth there is the reverse energy flow through the four lower bodies. The fallen beings can force you into certain material situations that cause an emotional reaction that then goes up to the identity level. None of this has affected the Conscious You. When you connect to that basic humanity, that pure awareness, that point-like sense of identity, you can dissolve it. Once you dissolve it, you dissolve the inroad that the fallen beings have in your four lower bodies.

They can no longer force a reaction from the physical level into the three higher bodies. You may still be exposed to certain situations or you may still be confronted with certain conditions that affect other people, but you can avoid that reverse energy flow where (when you look at what is happening on this earth or experience it), it goes right up through your emotional, mental and identity bodies. Instead, you can re-establish the natural flow where you are in command of your identity body, you are in command of your mental body, you are in command of your emotional body.

Whatever happens at the physical level, you can consciously decide how you will react to it. This is Buddhahood, this is also the higher stages of Christhood. At the lower stages of Christhood you cannot yet do this. As you move higher, you need to come to that point where you are willing to acknowledge the feelings you have and where you are willing to neutrally examine whether you have any feelings in the emotional body. Then, you need to overcome them and leave them behind because only then are you free from that reverse energy flow. You can re-establish the natural energy flow that allows you to consciously choose your reactions to any physical condition or situation.

This means you can consciously choose to respond with love even in situations where most other people will respond with fear. This is how you fulfill the highest purpose for which you are here, this is how you show the example, this is how you pull up on the collective consciousness. Even though you have raised yourself above the collective consciousness, you still have some sense, some memory, some connection to it. It is not a connection that can overpower you, but it is a connection that allows you to pull up. You are, so to speak, one fiber in the carpet and as you pull yourself up, you pull up the entire carpet.

This, my beloved, is a higher vision of how you can use the teachings of Sanat Kumara and of other masters to get to the point where you know why you are here and you know you are fulfilling your reason for being here. You are at peace with being here, you have accepted being in embodiment on this planet at this time. Therefore, you feel good about yourself but more than that you feel what the Buddha feels about himself or herself. That feeling is beyond words, it is beyond peace, it is beyond being good, it is beyond love. It is a feeling that does not need to be described in words, but it is a feeling you can have. When you have it, you will know why it is beyond words.

My beloved, I also extend my gratitude to so many of you for having come to this conference, for having been willing to raise your consciousness. Therefore, it is my privilege, it is my joy, as the Buddha that I am, to seal all of you, each one individually, and to seal this conference in the heart and the peace of the Buddha that I am. Gautama I AM.

# 19 | INVOKING SPIRITUAL ANGER MANAGEMENT

In the name I AM THAT I AM, Jesus Christ, I call to all representatives of the Divine Mother, especially Gautama Buddha, to help me overcome any anger or other negative energy in my four lower bodies. Help me reestablish a natural energy flow and overcome all patterns that block this flow, including...

[Make personal calls.]


*Part 1*


1. Gautama, help me see if I have created a program in the mental mind that is designed to suppress the feelings that I have labeled "unwanted," such as anger.

> Gautama, show my mental state
> that does give rise to love and hate,
> your exposé I do endure,
> so my perception will be pure.

**Gautama, Flame of Cosmic Peace,**
**unruly thoughts do hereby cease,**
**we radiate from you and me**
**the peace to still Samsara's Sea.**

2. Gautama, help me see if I have a reactionary program in the emotional body that causes me to react with anger in certain situations.

Gautama, in your Flame of Peace,
the struggling self I now release,
the Buddha Nature I now see,
it is the core of you and me.

**Gautama, Flame of Cosmic Peace,**
**unruly thoughts do hereby cease,**
**we radiate from you and me**
**the peace to still Samsara's Sea.**

3. Gautama, help me see if I dare not acknowledge when this happens but instead activate the program in the mental body, even sometimes a program in the identity body, to suppress the feeling of anger.

Gautama, I am one with thee,
Mara's demons do now flee,
your Presence like a soothing balm,
my mind and senses ever calm.

**Gautama, Flame of Cosmic Peace,**
**unruly thoughts do hereby cease,**
**we radiate from you and me**
**the peace to still Samsara's Sea.**

4. Gautama, help me see if I have become so good at doing this that I do not even recognize consciously when I am feeling anger.

Gautama, I now take the vow,
to live in the eternal now,
with you I do transcend all time,
to live in present so sublime.

**Gautama, Flame of Cosmic Peace,**
**unruly thoughts do hereby cease,**
**we radiate from you and me**
**the peace to still Samsara's Sea.**

5. Gautama, help me see if I have created a facade that hides my anger, but it is still there in my aura, threatening to erupt like a volcano.

Gautama, I have no desire,
to nothing earthly I aspire,
in non-attachment I now rest,
passing Mara's subtle test.

**Gautama, Flame of Cosmic Peace,**
**unruly thoughts do hereby cease,**
**we radiate from you and me**
**the peace to still Samsara's Sea.**

6. Gautama, help me recognize that I do not overcome anger by suppressing it. I do not overcome *anything* by suppressing it.

Gautama, I melt into you,
my mind is one, no longer two,
immersed in your resplendent glow,
Nirvana is all that I know.

**Gautama, Flame of Cosmic Peace,**
**unruly thoughts do hereby cease,**
**we radiate from you and me**
**the peace to still Samsara's Sea.**

7. Gautama, help me recognize that there was a stage on the path where it was constructive for me to suppress the anger because it prevented me from constantly going into these reactionary patterns and building more and more anger energy.

Gautama, in your timeless space,
I am immersed in Cosmic Grace,

I know the God beyond all form,
to world I will no more conform.

**Gautama, Flame of Cosmic Peace,
unruly thoughts do hereby cease,
we radiate from you and me
the peace to still Samsara's Sea.**

8. Gautama, help me see that, for a time, it is necessary and constructive
to suppress the anger with a program in the mental body. Yet for me, this
is no longer constructive.

Gautama, I am now awake,
I clearly see what is at stake,
and thus I claim my sacred right
to be on earth the Buddhic Light.

**Gautama, Flame of Cosmic Peace,
unruly thoughts do hereby cease,
we radiate from you and me
the peace to still Samsara's Sea.**

9. Gautama, help me get out of any stalemate and free myself from the
emotional energy that I have been dragging along with me.

Gautama, with your thunderbolt,
we give the earth a mighty jolt,
I know that some will understand,
and join the Buddha's timeless band.

**Gautama, Flame of Cosmic Peace,
unruly thoughts do hereby cease,
we radiate from you and me
the peace to still Samsara's Sea.**

## Part 2

1. Gautama, help me see that as long as I have anger, I cannot move into accepting that I am here, I cannot be at peace with being here, I cannot feel good about being here.

> Gautama, show my mental state
> that does give rise to love and hate,
> your exposé I do endure,
> so my perception will be pure.

> **Gautama, Flame of Cosmic Peace,**
> **unruly thoughts do hereby cease,**
> **we radiate from you and me**
> **the peace to still Samsara's Sea.**

2. Gautama, help me see that I have embodied on an extremely difficult planet. It is very unnatural, but precisely because it is so unnatural, it is "natural" for me to feel a certain anger and resentment about being here and having experienced what I have experienced.

> Gautama, in your Flame of Peace,
> the struggling self I now release,
> the Buddha Nature I now see,
> it is the core of you and me.

> **Gautama, Flame of Cosmic Peace,**
> **unruly thoughts do hereby cease,**
> **we radiate from you and me**
> **the peace to still Samsara's Sea.**

3. Gautama, help me discover whether I still have some reservoir of anger or resentment in my emotional body.

> Gautama, I am one with thee,
> Mara's demons do now flee,
> your Presence like a soothing balm,
> my mind and senses ever calm.

**Gautama, Flame of Cosmic Peace,**
**unruly thoughts do hereby cease,**
**we radiate from you and me**
**the peace to still Samsara's Sea.**

4. Gautama, help me see what to me is the most disturbing manifestation on this planet, what I feel really should not be here.

Gautama, I now take the vow,
to live in the eternal now,
with you I do transcend all time,
to live in present so sublime.

**Gautama, Flame of Cosmic Peace,**
**unruly thoughts do hereby cease,**
**we radiate from you and me**
**the peace to still Samsara's Sea.**

5. Gautama, help me recognize that because I feel so strongly about this issue, I have most likely been exposed to it in several lifetimes and it has inevitably caused me to feel anger.

Gautama, I have no desire,
to nothing earthly I aspire,
in non-attachment I now rest,
passing Mara's subtle test.

**Gautama, Flame of Cosmic Peace,**
**unruly thoughts do hereby cease,**
**we radiate from you and me**
**the peace to still Samsara's Sea.**

6. Gautama, help me get in tune with what is hidden in my emotional body, what I have not quite seen or not seen clearly.

Gautama, I melt into you,
my mind is one, no longer two,
immersed in your resplendent glow,
Nirvana is all that I know.

**Gautama, Flame of Cosmic Peace,**
**unruly thoughts do hereby cease,**
**we radiate from you and me**
**the peace to still Samsara's Sea.**

7. Gautama, help me acknowledge that I have risen to a certain level of the spiritual path. Therefore, I can make the switch of seeing that this is a perfectly natural reaction. There is nothing wrong with it, there is nothing unspiritual about it.

Gautama, in your timeless space,
I am immersed in Cosmic Grace,
I know the God beyond all form,
to world I will no more conform.

**Gautama, Flame of Cosmic Peace,**
**unruly thoughts do hereby cease,**
**we radiate from you and me**
**the peace to still Samsara's Sea.**

8. Gautama, help me recognize that I have now risen to a higher level of the path. Therefore, I do not need to condemn myself for having this anger. I just need to recognize that I have it and it is time to get beyond it.

Gautama, I am now awake,
I clearly see what is at stake,
and thus I claim my sacred right
to be on earth the Buddhic Light.

**Gautama, Flame of Cosmic Peace,**
**unruly thoughts do hereby cease,**
**we radiate from you and me**
**the peace to still Samsara's Sea.**

9. Gautama, help me get in touch with the anger and then see what is hidden below the level of surface awareness.

Gautama, with your thunderbolt,
we give the earth a mighty jolt,

I know that some will understand,
and join the Buddha's timeless band.

**Gautama, Flame of Cosmic Peace,**
**unruly thoughts do hereby cease,**
**we radiate from you and me**
**the peace to still Samsara's Sea.**

## Part 3

1. Gautama, help me overcome any desire to hide my anger or any illusion
that if I don't look at it, you cannot see it either.

Gautama, show my mental state
that does give rise to love and hate,
your exposé I do endure,
so my perception will be pure.

**Gautama, Flame of Cosmic Peace,**
**unruly thoughts do hereby cease,**
**we radiate from you and me**
**the peace to still Samsara's Sea.**

2. Gautama, I accept that there is no need for me to hide anything from the
ascended masters, and therefore, there is no need to hide anything from
myself.

Gautama, in your Flame of Peace,
the struggling self I now release,
the Buddha Nature I now see,
it is the core of you and me.

**Gautama, Flame of Cosmic Peace,**
**unruly thoughts do hereby cease,**
**we radiate from you and me**
**the peace to still Samsara's Sea.**

3. Gautama, I know the masters don't condemn me, and therefore I don't need to condemn myself. I can now take a step that most people are afraid to take, I connect to my anger, and then instead of not wanting to see it, I acknowledge it and I walk right into it.

> Gautama, I am one with thee,
> Mara's demons do now flee,
> your Presence like a soothing balm,
> my mind and senses ever calm.

> **Gautama, Flame of Cosmic Peace,**
> **unruly thoughts do hereby cease,**
> **we radiate from you and me**
> **the peace to still Samsara's Sea.**

4. Gautama, help me walk into the anger, experience being in that maelstrom of anger.

> Gautama, I now take the vow,
> to live in the eternal now,
> with you I do transcend all time,
> to live in present so sublime.

> **Gautama, Flame of Cosmic Peace,**
> **unruly thoughts do hereby cease,**
> **we radiate from you and me**
> **the peace to still Samsara's Sea.**

5. Gautama, help me reconnect consciously to my basic humanity, which is the ongoingness of my being, that part of my being that is beyond anything on earth, that cannot be defined by anything on earth.

> Gautama, I have no desire,
> to nothing earthly I aspire,
> in non-attachment I now rest,
> passing Mara's subtle test.

**Gautama, Flame of Cosmic Peace,**
**unruly thoughts do hereby cease,**
**we radiate from you and me**
**the peace to still Samsara's Sea.**

6. Gautama, help me recognize that beyond this anger is my basic humanity. It has not been changed by the anger and therefore, I look at the anger and I recognize: "This is not me. It is not even *my* anger, it was the reaction of my ego."

Gautama, I melt into you,
my mind is one, no longer two,
immersed in your resplendent glow,
Nirvana is all that I know.

**Gautama, Flame of Cosmic Peace,**
**unruly thoughts do hereby cease,**
**we radiate from you and me**
**the peace to still Samsara's Sea.**

7. Gautama, help me see that it was natural that I had the reaction, but now I have risen to a higher sense of identity where I do not need to react this way. I am letting it go.

Gautama, in your timeless space,
I am immersed in Cosmic Grace,
I know the God beyond all form,
to world I will no more conform.

**Gautama, Flame of Cosmic Peace,**
**unruly thoughts do hereby cease,**
**we radiate from you and me**
**the peace to still Samsara's Sea.**

8. Gautama, help me see that even though the fallen beings have forced me into certain material situations that cause an emotional reaction going up to the identity level, none of this has affected the Conscious You.

Gautama, I am now awake,
I clearly see what is at stake,
and thus I claim my sacred right
to be on earth the Buddhic Light.

**Gautama, Flame of Cosmic Peace,**
**unruly thoughts do hereby cease,**
**we radiate from you and me**
**the peace to still Samsara's Sea.**

9. Gautama, help me connect to that basic humanity, that pure awareness, that point-like sense of identity, and then dissolve the anger, thereby dissolving the inroad that the fallen beings have in my four lower bodies.

Gautama, with your thunderbolt,
we give the earth a mighty jolt,
I know that some will understand,
and join the Buddha's timeless band.

**Gautama, Flame of Cosmic Peace,**
**unruly thoughts do hereby cease,**
**we radiate from you and me**
**the peace to still Samsara's Sea.**

## Part 4

1. Gautama, help me re-establish the natural flow where I am in command of my identity body, I am in command of my mental body, I am in command of my emotional body.

Gautama, show my mental state
that does give rise to love and hate,
your exposé I do endure,
so my perception will be pure.

**Gautama, Flame of Cosmic Peace,**
**unruly thoughts do hereby cease,**
**we radiate from you and me**
**the peace to still Samsara's Sea.**

2. Gautama, help me get to the point where I can consciously decide how
I will react to whatever happens at the physical level.

Gautama, in your Flame of Peace,
the struggling self I now release,
the Buddha Nature I now see,
it is the core of you and me.

**Gautama, Flame of Cosmic Peace,**
**unruly thoughts do hereby cease,**
**we radiate from you and me**
**the peace to still Samsara's Sea.**

3. Gautama, help me acknowledge the feelings I have and neutrally examine the feelings in the emotional body. Help me overcome them and leave
them behind so I am free from the reverse energy flow.

Gautama, I am one with thee,
Mara's demons do now flee,
your Presence like a soothing balm,
my mind and senses ever calm.

**Gautama, Flame of Cosmic Peace,**
**unruly thoughts do hereby cease,**
**we radiate from you and me**
**the peace to still Samsara's Sea.**

4. Gautama, help me re-establish the natural energy flow that allows me
to consciously choose my reactions to any physical condition or situation.

Gautama, I now take the vow,
to live in the eternal now,
with you I do transcend all time,
to live in present so sublime.

**Gautama, Flame of Cosmic Peace,**
**unruly thoughts do hereby cease,**
**we radiate from you and me**
**the peace to still Samsara's Sea.**

5. Gautama, help me consciously choose to respond with love even in situations where most other people will respond with fear.

Gautama, I have no desire,
to nothing earthly I aspire,
in non-attachment I now rest,
passing Mara's subtle test.

**Gautama, Flame of Cosmic Peace,**
**unruly thoughts do hereby cease,**
**we radiate from you and me**
**the peace to still Samsara's Sea.**

6. Gautama, help me fulfill the highest purpose for which I am here, namely to show an example and pull up on the collective consciousness.

Gautama, I melt into you,
my mind is one, no longer two,
immersed in your resplendent glow,
Nirvana is all that I know.

**Gautama, Flame of Cosmic Peace,**
**unruly thoughts do hereby cease,**
**we radiate from you and me**
**the peace to still Samsara's Sea.**

7. Gautama, help me get to the point where I know why I am here and I know I am fulfilling my reason for being here.

Gautama, in your timeless space,
I am immersed in Cosmic Grace,
I know the God beyond all form,
to world I will no more conform.

**Gautama, Flame of Cosmic Peace,**
**unruly thoughts do hereby cease,**
**we radiate from you and me**
**the peace to still Samsara's Sea.**

8. Gautama, help me be at peace with being here, help me accept being in embodiment on this planet at this time.

Gautama, I am now awake,
I clearly see what is at stake,
and thus I claim my sacred right
to be on earth the Buddhic Light.

**Gautama, Flame of Cosmic Peace,**
**unruly thoughts do hereby cease,**
**we radiate from you and me**
**the peace to still Samsara's Sea.**

9. Gautama, help me feel good about myself, help me feel what the Buddha feels, the feeling that is beyond peace, beyond being good, beyond love, beyond words.

Gautama, with your thunderbolt,
we give the earth a mighty jolt,
I know that some will understand,
and join the Buddha's timeless band.

**Gautama, Flame of Cosmic Peace,**
**unruly thoughts do hereby cease,**
**we radiate from you and me**
**the peace to still Samsara's Sea.**

## Sealing

In the name of the Divine Mother, I call to Mother Mary for the sealing of myself and all people in my circle of influence in the creative flow of the Divine Mother, the River of Life. I call for the multiplication of my calls by all representatives of the Divine Mother, so that we form the perfect figure-eight flow of "As Above, so below." Thus, I accept that this is fully manifest, because the mouth of the Lord, the Divine Mother that I AM, has spoken it. Amen.

# 20 | OVERCOMING ANGER

# AGAINST YOURSELF

I AM the Ascended Master MORE, and I am the ultimate way to overcome the consciousness of lack. By tuning in to my flame, you can know that there is no lack in my Being, there is no lack in my flame. Therefore, when you allow yourself to receive what I am more than willing to give you, there is no lack in you.

You are not an imperfect being! What have all of the systems that you see on this earth been programming into the collective mind now for eons of time? It is that human beings are inherently flawed or imperfect. This was, if you look at it honestly, the message behind Marxism and Communism, as it was the message behind the Catholic Church and all of the Christian churches building upon that foundation. You are sinners by nature, you are inherently limited and where does this consciousness come from?

## The anger of the fallen beings

Well, it comes, of course, from the fallen beings who have a (one might say) desperate need to feel superior to the people that they find themselves embodying amongst, much to their displeasure. They believe earth is such a low planet that they should not even have to be here. They should be on a much higher planet, a much bigger planet, where they could have a greater sense of power.

They feel that they have been degraded by coming to this planet. Therefore, many of them have a very deep-seated anger against the human beings that are on this planet, both the original inhabitants and those avatars who have dared to come here and embody and challenge their reign. You cannot explain this anger (which you clearly see in history, if you are willing to look) through any of these traditional thought systems. Why is that my beloved? Because the thought systems created by the fallen beings have one overriding need, plan or agenda and it is to hide the existence of the fallen beings. Therefore, of course, they cannot explain that there is such anger. They either leave it unexplained or they leave it up to some never really clearly stated ideas that this or that person was particularly evil and so forth and so on.

## Anger starts in the identity body

The reality is, of course, that the fallen beings have a very deep-seated, one might say *existential,* anger against human beings. They will do things to hurt, damage and eradicate human beings that are irrational, illogical, as all anger really is irrational and illogical. Anger is an emotion but anger is more than just a feeling, it is more than something in the emotional body. This has only been understood by very, very few people who have studied psychology.

The reality is that anger actually starts in the identity body. The fallen beings have in their identity bodies an anger against God. This is really (when you think about it) partly an anger against the external God that they have created, but it is more than that, it is actually an anger against *themselves.* After all, even though they have fallen, they started out as extensions of the Creators' being, as all of us have. There is an anger at the identity level, there is a certain intricate mental pattern that justifies this anger and gives it a certain direction. There is, of course, the emotional pattern, which often causes people to do things in anger that they never would have done if they were able to think more rationally or clearly about it.

You could say that for most of the human beings and the avatars on this planet, anger is mainly an emotional phenomenon but for the fallen beings it is more than that. That is why you can see that if you analyze the psychology of people like Hitler, Lenin, Stalin, Mao and all of these dictators you have seen in history, their anger is not purely emotional. They have a deeper anger at the mental and identity level. It is something that they often cannot control—it controls them. You can see that sometimes they have actually committed actions that were not done in an emotional rage but they were done in a more calculated anger, a more long-term, planned anger.

## The calculated anger of the fallen beings

Why am I bringing this up? Well, for a variety of reasons. One of the reasons is, of course, that you need to understand that what happened in the Soviet Block under Communism cannot be explained only as a matter of anger. You need to understand this very deep anger that the fallen beings have against human beings and their desire to either control them or to eradicate those who cannot be controlled. It is not so, my beloved, that Stalin or those who were in position in the Soviet apparatus were in an uncontrolled rage when they knocked on people's doors at four o'clock in the morning and shipped them off to Siberia. There was not the emotional anger behind this, even though in some cases, some of the henchman who carried out these acts had to put themselves in an emotional state in order to be able to do this to their own countrymen.

If you look at the leaders and especially at the top figure, you could see that it was not an emotional anger. You could see that during some of Hitler's speeches, he seemed to go off in this emotional anger. When he was dealing with his generals and others, he was not emotional, he was very calculated—one might even say *rational*. You can only understand this by this deeper level. You also need, as the avatars that we are addressing you as now, to recognize that while human beings, the original inhabitants of the earth, rarely have an anger that goes beyond the emotional level, as an avatar you can actually have built such an anger.

This does not mean that you have the same anger as the fallen beings have. In a certain sense, my beloved, you can look at the psychology of some fallen beings (not all but some) and you can look at the psychology of some avatars (not all but some) and you can see that they both have anger in their mental and identity bodies. If you look more closely, you can see that there is a fundamental difference. The anger of the fallen beings is always directed outwards. In many cases, it is also directed upwards as an anger against God. It is never in a fallen being directed inwards as an [conscious] anger against themselves. However, in many avatars you do find that they have an anger at the mental and identity level that is directed inwardly against themselves. It can have a variety of reasons at the mental level, there can be a variety of explanations that people have at the mental level. There can even be different explanations at the identity level but they all revolve around the same theme, namely that you are angry at yourself for voluntarily coming to this planet. You are angry at yourself for making the choice to come to this planet.

There may be some avatars that after they came here, after they went into duality, have taken on some of these subtle beliefs put out there by the fallen beings. They may feel a certain anger against God for creating a universe where the suffering that you see on earth is possible. Some avatars can have a certain sense of this, but it is not the same anger that fallen beings have against God. You do not feel the same as an avatar as you feel as a fallen being. I am not here going to describe how fallen beings feel, how their anger is against God because you do not need to even put your mind on this as an avatar. I am just telling you that even if you feel anger against God, it does not mean that you are a fallen being.

You do not have to come down on yourself for this. You recognize that this is not an anger you carried with you when you came to this planet. The fallen beings carried their anger against God with them when they came to this planet, even before they came into this sphere. You have taken it on here on earth, and as with everything else you have taken on here on earth, this means that you can come to see it, see that it is not yours and you can let it go, you can rise above it.

## Anger against the Mother realm

There may also be a certain anger against the Mother realm (the matter realm), for the fact that the matter realm, the Ma-ter light, will outpicture these physical conditions that create such intense suffering. Many avatars feel this, not because of what has happened to themselves, as Mother Mary said, but because of what they have seen happen to other people. You feel the compassion and therefore you have a certain anger: "Why does matter even allow this to happen, why doesn't the stones themselves cry out as Jesus said they were supposed to do?" Why don't the stones refuse to fall upon and crush people, is what you can sometimes feel. The reason for this is, of course, that we are talking about slightly different things. Jesus was talking about that the stones would cry out in recognition of the Christ even if human beings would not. This is not the same as matter creating these very severe physical consequences. Matter, as we have said, is just a mirror and must outplay what is projected into it. You understand this intellectually, I understand that. I am reminding you of this because it may be necessary for you to read or hear this dictation several times and work on this until you really come to see in yourselves that you have this anger and that it is really not yours but something you have taken on.

There are many of you who are spiritual people, many avatars, who have gone into this mindset (that the messenger has recognized in himself as well) where you feel that because you are a spiritual person, you should not feel anger. Therefore, you will not recognize your anger, but as Gautama Buddha said earlier this year, it is necessary sometimes for you to recognize the feelings you have in order for you to separate yourselves from them. He gave you an exercise where you can go in a remote location where nobody can hear you and you can speak out, you can verbalize your feelings towards the fallen beings but even towards God or the matter realm. You can verbalize your anger, put words on it. When you put words on it, it becomes easier to separate yourself from it, and I will give you a simple hint of why that is so, my beloved.

## Verbalizing who you are

Imagine now that you go out in a remote location and you verbalize your anger. I am angry against God because of this or that or the next thing. When you have done this, when you have emptied yourself and there are no more words coming, I am asking you to do a simple thing. Now, verbalize what you *are*. What are you really? Yes, you can say "I am a human being, I am a spiritual being," I am this I am that, but describe it. What are you really? You will find that it will be very difficult for you to put any deeper, meaningful words on this. You may have some superficial words that you can put on, based on whatever spiritual teaching or view of life you have, but it is very difficult for you to verbalize *what* you really are.

The reason for this is very simple. What you really are is the individuality anchored in your I AM Presence and that individuality is completely beyond words. It cannot be reduced to words. When you recognize that your anger could be expressed in words but your real Being cannot be expressed in words, then you can easily make the shift and realize that your anger is not the anger of your real Being—it is not *your* anger. It is just something you have taken on here in the physical octave on planet earth. My beloved, I have been in embodiment for a very long time on this planet. If there is any human nonsense, human indignity, human flaw, human idiocy that you could possibly imagine, then I have most likely experienced it.

Regardless of whatever image has been created by outer teachings or in the minds of previous ascended master students and previous organizations, let me tell you very honestly, my beloved, I have experienced just about everything that can be experienced on this planet in my many embodiments here. I have not always been some highly evolved spiritual teacher or some king or some philosopher king. I have many times been what you would call a very *human* being. I am not saying this to put myself down. I am simply saying it to make you realize that feeling anger because of what you have experienced on this planet is simply unavoidable.

## Feeling and co-creating

The only way you could come to this planet and not feel anger was if you were unable to feel anything at all. You could not be a self-conscious creative being if you were not able to feel because how can you be a co-creator if you are not able to feel? It is through your feeling body that you bring your creation into the physical realm, there is no other way.

You can have the most elaborate blueprint of a house in your mental body but you cannot lower it directly from the mental to the physical. You have to go through the emotional, and it is that way with everything you create. By the very fact that you came here as an avatar, you are able to feel. Why would you have come here if you did not feel compassion for the people on earth? When you come here and you experience the intense suffering that people go through, how could you not react with anger?

I had many embodiments where I reacted with anger, and every being that ever ascended from earth had those kind of embodiments. There is a certain tendency among some spiritual students that they want to maintain this idolatrous image that even though El Morya, Saint Germain or Jesus had embodiments on earth, we were always somehow cool, calm and collected. We were always above reproach, we never did anything really bad, we never lost it, we never lost our temper. My beloved, have we not explained to you that the role of us coming to earth (all of us, you who are here now, us who have been here but have ascended) was to go through the process of immersion and awakening?

## What do you take seriously?

I can assure you that all of us who have gone through the immersion phase have gone into all kinds of human actions, feelings and beliefs and that is just the way it is. There comes a point where you recognize who you are as a spiritual being, where you simply have to look at this and say: "Okay," I did this, I felt this, I thought this way but it was just something I took on as a reaction to this very difficult planet." Then, you have to step back and say: "What is there on this planet that I take seriously, what is there that I feel has power over me as a spiritual being?" It may help you to go through an exercise and look at many of the human activities out there, many of the activities that people are engaged in. Then, recognize with yourself: "Do I take this seriously? Does this have any pull on me? Does it have any power over me?"

You may look at, for example, how people are fighting in this or that part of the world and how they have been fighting for generations. Nobody can remember what they are fighting about but they are still fighting. You may say: "Do I take this seriously, does this have any pull on me." You may look at some of the activities that people engage in (in your own culture) and say: "The quest to accumulate billions of Dollars, do I take that seriously, does it have any pull on me?" You will discover that there are so many things on this earth that you do not take seriously. You have transcended it, it has no pull on you, it has no pull on your emotional, mental or identity body. It is simply something you can look at and say: "So what, this means nothing to me." Then, you can look at why do you take it so seriously, why does it have such a pull on you, if you felt anger about something. If you reacted with negative feelings, why do you take that so seriously, my beloved? Of course, there are legitimate reasons for why you take it seriously and there are some not so legitimate reasons.

## Being hard on yourself

The legitimate reason is that as a spiritual being, who is walking the path, as an avatar, you are always looking at yourself. You are always evaluating yourself and you are always seeking to do better. This is legitimate, we all have had to do this. We have tried to explain to you before in various ways, sometimes subtle but now I will be very direct: Why is it that you who are the most spiritual people, who are not truly aggressive, who are not bad people according to any standard, why is it that you are so hard on yourselves?

Why is it that your natural, legitimate tendency to look at yourself and evaluate where you could have done better is so often accompanied by this overlay where you feel so bad about yourself if you have made a mistake, if you have done something that you thought you should not have done as a spiritual person? Why is there that, often very strong, emotional feeling, even (if you look at it) a certain mental overlay, even in some cases in the lower parts of your identity body? There can be this sense that you should not have gone into this, you should not have been angry, you should not have really done what other human beings do. You should have kept yourself above it. Why do you have that sense, why does there come that value judgment on top of your natural and constructive self-evaluation?

Why is it, then, that some of you have overcome it but many of you are still in it? Many people, when they first find the spiritual path, go through a phase of dealing with this. Suddenly, their spiritual teaching becomes just another way for them to condemn themselves and to feel that they have come up short. We have talked about earlier this year that all we want as ascended masters is for you to feel good about yourselves, but so many times the spiritual teachings we give you actually cause you to feel worse about yourselves than you felt before.

Why is there that mechanism? My beloved, this is, of course, partly inserted by the fallen beings. They have come up with these elaborate theories of how you are flawed and how you are this and how you are that. Recognize, my beloved, that the fallen beings have not just created, for example, the concept of original sin according to which all people are flawed. They have also created some very, very subtle concepts that you cannot really find in writing anywhere but they are floating around in the collective consciousness. They say that if you are a spiritual person, you must not be angry for this is very, very bad. If you are angry and if you lose your temper, you should feel very bad about yourself.

This is a creation by the fallen beings. It is not – *not* – a creation of the ascended masters. We do not want you to judge yourself that way. Why is it, then, that even many of you who are ascended master students actually respond to the fallen beings and what they have put upon you and you do not respond to *us,* even though you know about us? Why do you still have that mechanism in your four lower bodies (that you cannot quite get over) that causes you to feel so bad about yourself? I will tell you why! It is because you have this anger against yourself. You have for many, many embodiments directed anger against yourself because you have retained, or at least you have reclaimed as you started climbing the path, some sense that the way things are on earth is not the only way things *can* be.

## Stopping the downward spiral

You have, many of you, come from natural planets where you did not have these manifestations seen on earth. Therefore, there was never an outer condition that was so severe that you felt angry about it. Then, you had retained in your being (or you had reconnected to the sense in your being) that you should not feel angry. As I have said, things are so much worse on earth than on a natural planet that it is inevitable that you will feel anger.

Because you have this tendency to evaluate yourself (which is needed, for otherwise you cannot grow), because you have this sense of what you should not have done, then you end up feeling angry with yourself for having felt angry with conditions on earth. This creates a spiral and your anger against yourself is accumulated in your emotional, mental and lower identity body. This means that in your next embodiment, when you encounter another severe condition on earth, you are more likely to feel angry with that condition. Then, of course, you feel anger with yourself for having felt angry and the spiral can just keep building and building and building.

My beloved, it is not – it is *not* – my intention to make you feel even worse about having this spiral. It is my intention to have you recognize that you have this spiral and that it is just time to transcend it. How do you, then, transcend it? Well, my beloved, this may require a process for you individually. It involves what I already said: recognizing that it is not *your* anger. You did not have it when you came here, you did not have anger against yourself when you came here. It is something you have taken on in response to the conditions on earth. You may need to go through the exercise I gave you on looking at the conditions on earth and saying: "Do they really have any pull on me anymore? Why then do I feel angry with myself for having felt angry about those conditions?" You may be able to go through this process of gradually letting go of some of the anger.

## Anger cannot exist on its own

I am not saying there is one thing you can do where you can snap your fingers and get rid of the anger. You *can* come to the point where you recognize that anger is not a feeling or a thought pattern that can exist on its own. We have talked about true desires and false desires. We can also say there are true feelings, false feelings, higher feelings and lower feelings. We have talked about love-based feelings and fear-based feelings. Well, my beloved, the difference is very simple, or at least it can be expressed very simply.

A love-based feeling can exist on its own. A love based feeling is a spiritual form of energy that originates in a higher realm and flows through you. It can exist entirely on its own. A fear-based feeling, and anger is a fear-based feeling, cannot exist on its own. It may take on a life of its own and become an entity or a demon, but the feeling cannot exist on its own.

It must have an object. You are not simply afraid of an unspecified something, you are not afraid of *nothing*. There must be something you are afraid of. Yes, anger or fear can become a general feeling that fills up your emotional body to the point where you are not aware of the object of your fear, but it started with you fearing something. Likewise, anger starts with you being angry at an object. There was a reason you were angry and this is why I am telling you that you can overcome your feelings by being willing to do what Jesus said: "Let us reason together." This is a motto of the ascended masters: "Let us reason together."

## Reasoning about anger

If you are willing, you pick a certain ascended master. I volunteer my services, but choose any master who is close to you. Then, you say: "Let us reason together about my anger." If you are willing to go through this process, you can come to the point where you gradually see what was the object that originally caused you to feel anger with this planet. Then, you can gradually come to see that this really does not mean so much to you any more as it did in the beginning. As it says in the new book, your original birth trauma, your first trauma, could never be repeated because you could never again have the contrast between what caused the trauma and your innocence. When you reconnect to what originally made you angry with earth, it will not mean as much to you. This means you can come to a point of saying: "Okay, I can let this go; I no longer feel angry at this" Then, when you have done this to some degree about the objects that made you feel angry on earth, you can come under the guidance of the master to see that: "Why do I then feel angry with myself?"

Then, you will realize, once again, that there is something illogical here. As I said, it is difficult to put words on what you are, and you realize that if you are angry with yourself, you must have turned yourself into an object. You can only be angry with an object, as you were angry with certain conditions on earth or angry at the fallen beings. If you are angry with yourself, it means that there is an object that you are angry with.

What is that object? Well, it is what we have called (in various teachings we have given) an aspect of your ego, an internal spirit or a separate self. You can come to the point where you recognize that maybe you have a self that feels that as a spiritual person you should never be angry. Therefore, when you are angry, this separate self is shooting an arrow into your emotional body and now you feel bad. You feel bad in an unspecified way about yourself. You feel you are no good, you are inferior, you made a mistake, you can never be redeemed. Because this self is making you feel bad, you become angry with the self, you feel anger towards the self. Then, you recognize that the object of your anger with yourself is not actually with *you*, with yourself, it is with *a self that is not you.*

It is just a separate self that you have created as a reaction to the conditions on earth. Then, you have separated yourself, you have realized that the anger you have at yourself is not really so different from the anger you feel over seeing people killed in a war or whatever you have experienced in your past. You can separate yourself from the anger and say: "But if there are certain conditions on earth that I no longer feel so angry over, why am I feeling so angry over this self?" I see that this self is unreal, it is not really me, so why am I feeling angry at this self?

## Exercise for dissolving anger

When you come to recognize that the self you are feeling angry with is separate from you, then you may do another little exercise. Based on what you now know about the spiritual side of life and about yourself, I am asking you to, in your mind, envision that now you are looking at this anger you have towards your self (the separate self) and then you are saying: "Okay, but I no longer want to direct that anger at my separate self, now

I want to direct it at my real self. So what is my real self, where is my real self, can I pinpoint it." You will find that if you do this, your mind will go blank. You cannot create a mental image or verbalized image of your real self because your real self – even though we have called it your I AM Presence and given you some concepts – is beyond what you can imagine and envision with your outer mind.

Your outer mind cannot fathom your I AM Presence. The Conscious You can in a glimpse experience the I AM Presence but your outer mind cannot. It is not the Conscious You that is directing anger; it is your outer mind, your outer self. When you realize that you cannot find a real self to direct your anger at, then you also see that it is not your real self that is angry. It is not even your real self that is angry at the separate self that is making you feel bad. What is it that is angry at the separate self? Well, it is *another* separate self.

Now, you have one separate self that is making you feel bad and another separate self that is making you angry at the first separate self. When you begin to see this, you see that this is ridiculous. It is not that the selves are not there. You can actually come to see that there is this little gnome-like figure that is looking very burdened and very crippled and that is constantly projecting that you should feel bad for being imperfect. There is this other gnarled-up self that is projecting that you are angry with the first self. You can see that those selves are there. Then, you can come to see that: "They are not me. They are in my four lower bodies." It is not that you have not created them, but they are not you and then you can say: "Why do I want to drag these selves around with me? Why?"

If you can come up, my beloved, with a good reason for why you want to continue dragging these selves around with you, then I have no issue with that. I respect your free will. If you want to carry this with you, go ahead and carry it with you. I am just here to offer my assistance if you want to be free of them. Then, you simply need to make a decision. What is the decision you need to make? It is: "I am willing to let these selves die."

## The missionary syndrome

Now, this may require a little bit of contemplation. Once again, I am trying to use your minds, your, logical, rational, reasoning minds, to out-reason themselves by having you see that sometimes reason becomes unreasonable by creating contradictions. What you need to recognize here is what

Mother Mary said in her dictation: "As an avatar you are not on earth to create specific physical changes." Why is that so? Because what happens on this planet is not up to you; it is up to the original inhabitants.

If there are to be specific physical changes, for example that war is banished and there is no more war on this planet, then you as an avatar cannot make the decision that will make this physical. There needs to be a critical mass of the original inhabitants that make this decision and then it can become physical. What you *can* do is help them make that decision. How do you do that? Not by forcing them because then you are just doing what the fallen beings are doing—not even by forcing them emotionally, mentally or at the identity level.

This is where you need to recognize something that many, many religious and spiritual people (but even many people who have believed in a political ideology) have been trapped in, namely what we might call the "missionary syndrome." It is that you think that you have to go out and convert everybody to your belief system by somehow using their emotions, their mental bodies or their sense of who they are, to make them switch into now believing your belief system. They are taking this belief system on as an overcoat and saying: "Now I belong to this religion and therefore I will behave accordingly." This is *not* why you are here as an avatar. You are here to demonstrate the process, as we have said, of awakening from your identification with the material realm. You are here to show that it is possible for any human being to rise above the sense of identity as a human being and recognize that we are all spiritual beings.

You are here to *demonstrate* the awakening and even if you could, my beloved, convert other people to a certain belief system—*that* is not awakening. This will be hard for many people to understand, but you can see it yourselves. If you could convert every person on the planet to being a faithful Catholic, would that mean they had come any closer to Christhood? Well, of course, you know it would not because the Catholic church has perverted the concept of Christhood.

You can say: "If you could convert everybody to believe in an ascended master teaching, would that bring them closer to Christhood"? Here, we have a little bit more tricky question because it *would* actually bring them closer to Christhood in the sense that it is a more valuable teaching for raising your consciousness. You cannot really embrace an ascended master teaching without somewhat raising your consciousness. As we have said many times, many ascended master students have demonstrated that you can follow an ascended master teaching for decades and *not* truly understand what the inner path is about. You see what I am saying? It is not a matter of making people believe in a certain teaching. The only way to bring people closer to Christhood, to raise the collective consciousness, is that you *demonstrate* in yourself the process of awakening. Then, of course, you can help people lock in to that but awakening is not a matter of accepting an outer teaching with your outer mind. It is, as you all know, an inner process. When you recognize this, my beloved, you can recognize that if you are not here to affect a specific change on earth, then there is absolutely no reason for you to have any regrets about what you have done and specifically what you have *not* done in this or past lifetimes.

## Having no regrets

Now, we are in Eastern Europe, an area that was under the communist yoke. Mother Mary said that many people in Eastern Europe feel a lack of nurturance but they also feel a sense of lost opportunity. If you look at the nations that were under the communist yoke, many people have a sense that because they did not have an opportunity to express their personal creativity, their lifetime was a lost opportunity. Some of you may even feel this way, but you will know that many in your parents' generation felt that way. There are even nations where the national consciousness (and this is certainly the case in this nation of Estonia) feels this lost opportunity of where we could have been in our national growth if we had not been suppressed by the Soviet Union.

Many, many avatars have that same sense of the lost opportunity. Whereas many human beings have the sense that it was someone else, some external force, that destroyed their opportunity, many avatars have the sense that: "It was myself that destroyed the opportunity because I reacted the way I reacted. I was angry, I went into a negative spiral, I fought the fallen beings, I did this, I did that and therefore I have wasted so many lifetimes." As this messenger was receiving the latest book, he had to go through a period where he processed this sense of: "But if I did what the protagonist in the book went through of fighting the fallen beings for a million years, think of all the time I wasted in this dualistic struggle." My beloved, when you recognize what I have said: That you are not here to affect specific physical changes, you are here to demonstrate the process of awakening, then you can see that from a higher perspective you never have lost the opportunity. You cannot lose the opportunity, my beloved. You may say: "But I haven't been spiritual in this lifetime, I haven't been doing anything spiritual. It was only after I found the teachings but for decades I was doing nothing spiritual." I would say: "And how did that cause you to lose an opportunity?"

## Never a lost opportunity

What are you here to do? You are here to demonstrate that a person who in the past was not spiritual has now awakened. If you had not been unspiritual in the past, how could you demonstrate how to awaken? If you had come into embodiment having the same mastery that many of you think Jesus had, they would have done to you what they did to Jesus: turn you into an idol. We have said it before and I will say it again. If *one* person demonstrates the Christ Consciousness, the fallen beings will immediately turn him or her into an exception and say: "The rest of you could never attain this." If ten thousand or millions of people demonstrate it, they cannot do this and that is precisely the plan that we have for this age. It was the plan that Jesus had 2,000 years ago when he said: "Those who believe on me, shall do the works that I did and greater works."

My beloved, yes, perhaps it could have happened earlier. But it did not happen earlier and it does not matter now that it did not happen earlier, because it can happen now if you are willing to switch your mind and simply look at the angry self and say: "This is not me, I am willing to let it die." You can look at any kind of self that is holding you back, any kind of self that is hindering you and you can say: "I see that this is not me, I am willing to let this self die" Then, you let it die, my beloved. How do you let it die? Well, I will leave that for one of my esteemed colleagues to expound upon, for I have said what I wanted to say for now and I have given you what you can handle and a little more, as I always do.

## Master MORE does not take himself too seriously

Since I am Master MORE, how could I not give you more than you can handle? By giving you more than you can handle *now,* you can handle more next time and then I can give you even more than you can handle *then.* That is the game I will play because that is my flame. My beloved, in a previous ascended master dispensation the students took El Morya, as was the name they used then, very seriously. I never took myself as seriously as the students did. Why is that? Well, the students were not ascended but *I* was ascended. They are not ascended because they took me and themselves too seriously. I ascended because I stopped taking myself and anything on earth too seriously. It is the only way to ascend, my beloved.

As long as there is something on earth that you take seriously and think it has power over you (it has power to hold you here on earth), then you cannot ascend. Ascending means leaving everything on earth behind. You can only leave something behind when you come to the point where you can look at it and you do not take it seriously, it has no pull on you. You can just say: "Well, so what, this means nothing to me, I have transcended it. It used to mean something to me." It was fine that things meant something to you because that is part of your process of immersion and awakening. You immerse by takings things seriously so they mean something to you. My beloved, you awaken by overcoming this tendency to take something on earth seriously.

You might say that in order to ascend, you have to take the path, your I AM Presence or your ascension seriously. How can you take your I AM Presence seriously when you cannot really pin-point what it is? Again, you take things seriously because they have become an object for you, but your I AM Presence can never fully be turned into an object. You may, as some ascended master students have done, create such a concept of what the I AM Presence is that it almost takes on the role of an object for you. If you really start looking at this, reasoning about it, you will see that you cannot turn your I AM Presence into an object. Why not? Because it is not *external* to you. You may say you have a concept of your I AM Presence but that is *not* your I AM Presence. You may take the concept seriously, but that is *not* your I AM Presence. You cannot objectify what is not separate from you and you cannot truly grasp your I AM Presence until you no longer have a sense of separation.

I could not resist the temptation to give your more than I said I would give you. Now, I will take my leave of you and bid you a very fond adieu because I have truly enjoyed interacting with your beings. I would enjoy interacting with each and every one of you on a personal level, as you apply yourself to me.

My gratitude, my love and my Flame of MORE.

# 21 | INVOKING FREEDOM FROM ANGER AGAINST MYSELF

In the name I AM THAT I AM, Jesus Christ, I call to all representatives of the Divine Mother, especially Master MORE, to help me overcome any anger against myself. Help me separate myself from all angry selves so I can liquefy those selves and rise above my past selves, including...

[Make personal calls.]

*Part 1*

1. Master MORE, help me see any anger at the mental and identity level that is directed inwardly against myself. Help me see if I am angry at myself for making the choice to come to this planet.

Master MORE, come to the fore,
we will absorb your flame of MORE.

Master MORE, our will so strong,
our power centers cleared by song.

**Master MORE, your Sacred Heart,
from this we will no more depart,
we are forever in your flow,
of Diamond Will that you bestow.**

2. Master MORE, help me see any anger against the Mother realm for the fact that the Ma-ter light will outpicture physical conditions that create such intense suffering.

Master MORE, your wisdom flows,
as our attunement ever grows.
Master MORE, we have a tie,
that helps us see through Serpent's lie.

**Master MORE, your Sacred Heart,
from this we will no more depart,
we are forever in your flow,
of Diamond Will that you bestow.**

3. Master MORE, help me see if I have gone into the mindset where I feel that because I am a spiritual person, I should not feel anger.

Master MORE, your love so pink,
there is no purer love, we think.
Master MORE, you set us free,
from all conditionality.

**Master MORE, your Sacred Heart,
from this we will no more depart,
we are forever in your flow,
of Diamond Will that you bestow.**

4. Master MORE, I am willing to verbalize my anger by saying the first thing that comes to my mind: "I am angry because . . ."

Master MORE, we will endure,
your discipline that makes us pure.
Master MORE, intentions true,
as we are always one with you.

**Master MORE, your Sacred Heart,
from this we will no more depart,
we are forever in your flow,
of Diamond Will that you bestow.**

5. Master MORE, I am willing to verbalize *what* I am. "I am . . ."

Master MORE, our vision raised,
the will of God is always praised.
Master MORE, creative will,
raising all life higher still.

**Master MORE, your Sacred Heart,
from this we will no more depart,
we are forever in your flow,
of Diamond Will that you bestow.**

6. Master MORE, I recognize that beyond superficial things, it is very difficult for me to verbalize *what* I really am. The reason is that what I really am is the individuality anchored in my I AM Presence and it is beyond words.

Master MORE, your peace is power,
the demons of war it will devour.
Master MORE, we serve all life,
our flames consuming war and strife.

**Master MORE, your Sacred Heart,
from this we will no more depart,
we are forever in your flow,
of Diamond Will that you bestow.**

7. Master MORE, I recognize that my anger could be expressed in words but my real Being cannot be expressed in words. Help me make the shift and realize that my anger is not the anger of my real Being—it is not *my* anger. It is just something I have taken on here in the physical octave on planet earth.

> Master MORE, we are so free,
> eternal bond from you we see.
> Master MORE, we find rebirth,
> in flow of your eternal mirth.

> **Master MORE, your Sacred Heart,**
> **from this we will no more depart,**
> **we are forever in your flow,**
> **of Diamond Will that you bestow.**

8. Master MORE, help me realize that feeling anger because of what I have experienced on this planet is unavoidable. I could not be a self-conscious creative being if I was not able to feel because it is through my feeling body that I bring my creation into the physical realm.

> Master MORE, you balance all,
> the seven rays upon our call.
> Master MORE, forever MORE,
> we are the Spirit's open door.

> **Master MORE, your Sacred Heart,**
> **from this we will no more depart,**
> **we are forever in your flow,**
> **of Diamond Will that you bestow.**

9. Master MORE, help me see that I would not have come here if I did not feel compassion for the people on earth. When I came here and experienced the intense suffering that people go through, how could I not react with anger?

> Master MORE, your Presence here,
> filling up the inner sphere.

Life is now a sacred flow,
God Power we on all bestow.

**Master MORE, your Sacred Heart,
from this we will no more depart,
we are forever in your flow,
of Diamond Will that you bestow.**

## Part 2

1. Master MORE, help me recognize who I am as a spiritual being. Help me look at my anger and say: "Okay I did this, I felt this, I thought this way but it was just something I took on as a reaction to this very difficult planet."

Master MORE, come to the fore,
we will absorb your flame of MORE.
Master MORE, our will so strong,
our power centers cleared by song.

**Master MORE, your Sacred Heart,
from this we will no more depart,
we are forever in your flow,
of Diamond Will that you bestow.**

2. Master MORE, help me step back and say: "What is there on this planet that I take seriously, what is there that I feel has power over me as a spiritual being?"

Master MORE, your wisdom flows,
as our attunement ever grows.
Master MORE, we have a tie,
that helps us see through Serpent's lie.

**Master MORE, your Sacred Heart,**
**from this we will no more depart,**
**we are forever in your flow,**
**of Diamond Will that you bestow.**

3. Master MORE, help me look at many of the activities people are engaged in and see: "Do I take this seriously? Does this have any pull on me? Does it have any power over me?"

Master MORE, your love so pink,
there is no purer love, we think.
Master MORE, you set us free,
from all conditionality.

**Master MORE, your Sacred Heart,**
**from this we will no more depart,**
**we are forever in your flow,**
**of Diamond Will that you bestow.**

4. Master MORE, help me see that there are many things I do not take seriously. I have transcended it, and it has no pull on my emotional, mental or identity body. It is something I can look at and say: "So what, this means nothing to me."

Master MORE, we will endure,
your discipline that makes us pure.
Master MORE, intentions true,
as we are always one with you.

**Master MORE, your Sacred Heart,**
**from this we will no more depart,**
**we are forever in your flow,**
**of Diamond Will that you bestow.**

5. Master MORE, help me see why I take it so seriously if I felt anger about something, if I reacted with negative feelings. Why do I take this so seriously?

Master MORE, our vision raised,
the will of God is always praised.
Master MORE, creative will,
raising all life higher still.

**Master MORE, your Sacred Heart,
from this we will no more depart,
we are forever in your flow,
of Diamond Will that you bestow.**

6. Master MORE, help me see why – as a spiritual person, a person who is not truly aggressive – I am so hard on myself.

Master MORE, your peace is power,
the demons of war it will devour.
Master MORE, we serve all life,
our flames consuming war and strife.

**Master MORE, your Sacred Heart,
from this we will no more depart,
we are forever in your flow,
of Diamond Will that you bestow.**

7. Master MORE, help me see why my natural, legitimate tendency to evaluate myself has this overlay where I feel so bad about myself if I have made a mistake, if I have done something that I thought I should not have done as a spiritual person.

Master MORE, we are so free,
eternal bond from you we see.
Master MORE, we find rebirth,
in flow of your eternal mirth.

**Master MORE, your Sacred Heart,
from this we will no more depart,
we are forever in your flow,
of Diamond Will that you bestow.**

8. Master MORE, help me see the overlay in my mental and identity body that says I should not have been angry, I should not have done what other human beings do, I should have kept myself above it. Help me see why there is this value judgment on top of my natural and constructive self-evaluation.

> Master MORE, you balance all,
> the seven rays upon our call.
> Master MORE, forever MORE,
> we are the Spirit's open door.
>
> **Master MORE, your Sacred Heart,**
> **from this we will no more depart,**
> **we are forever in your flow,**
> **of Diamond Will that you bestow.**

9. Master MORE, help me see if I have used a spiritual teaching as another way for me to condemn myself and to feel that I have come up short.

> Master MORE, your Presence here,
> filling up the inner sphere.
> Life is now a sacred flow,
> God Power we on all bestow.
>
> **Master MORE, your Sacred Heart,**
> **from this we will no more depart,**
> **we are forever in your flow,**
> **of Diamond Will that you bestow.**

## Part 3

1. Master MORE, help me see that this self-condemnation is partly inserted by the fallen beings. They have come up with elaborate theories of how a spiritual person must not be angry. They say that if I lose my temper, I should feel very bad about myself.

Master MORE, come to the fore,
we will absorb your flame of MORE.
Master MORE, our will so strong,
our power centers cleared by song.

**Master MORE, your Sacred Heart,
from this we will no more depart,
we are forever in your flow,
of Diamond Will that you bestow.**

2. Master MORE, help me see that this is a creation by the fallen beings. It is not a creation of the ascended masters. You do not want me to judge myself that way.

Master MORE, your wisdom flows,
as our attunement ever grows.
Master MORE, we have a tie,
that helps us see through Serpent's lie.

**Master MORE, your Sacred Heart,
from this we will no more depart,
we are forever in your flow,
of Diamond Will that you bestow.**

3. Master MORE, help me see that the mechanism that makes me feel so bad about myself is caused by my anger against myself.

Master MORE, your love so pink,
there is no purer love, we think.
Master MORE, you set us free,
from all conditionality.

**Master MORE, your Sacred Heart,
from this we will no more depart,
we are forever in your flow,
of Diamond Will that you bestow.**

4. Master MORE, help me see that for many embodiments I have directed anger against myself because I have a sense that the way things are on earth is not the only way things *can* be.

Master MORE, we will endure,
your discipline that makes us pure.
Master MORE, intentions true,
as we are always one with you.

**Master MORE, your Sacred Heart,**
**from this we will no more depart,**
**we are forever in your flow,**
**of Diamond Will that you bestow.**

5. Master MORE, help me see that I have a sense that I should not feel angry. Because of my tendency to evaluate myself, then I end up feeling angry with myself for having felt angry with conditions on earth.

Master MORE, our vision raised,
the will of God is always praised.
Master MORE, creative will,
raising all life higher still.

**Master MORE, your Sacred Heart,**
**from this we will no more depart,**
**we are forever in your flow,**
**of Diamond Will that you bestow.**

6. Master MORE, help me see that this creates a spiral and my anger against myself is accumulated in my emotional, mental and lower identity body. I feel anger with myself for having felt angry and the spiral can continue building.

Master MORE, your peace is power,
the demons of war it will devour.
Master MORE, we serve all life,
our flames consuming war and strife.

**Master MORE, your Sacred Heart,**
**from this we will no more depart,**
**we are forever in your flow,**
**of Diamond Will that you bestow.**

7. Master MORE, help me see that it is not your intention to make me feel even worse about having this spiral. It is your intention to have me recognize that I have this spiral and that it is time to transcend it.

Master MORE, we are so free,
eternal bond from you we see.
Master MORE, we find rebirth,
in flow of your eternal mirth.

**Master MORE, your Sacred Heart,**
**from this we will no more depart,**
**we are forever in your flow,**
**of Diamond Will that you bestow.**

8. Master MORE, help me recognize that it is not *my* anger. I did not have anger against myself when I came here. It is something I have taken on in response to the conditions on earth.

Master MORE, you balance all,
the seven rays upon our call.
Master MORE, forever MORE,
we are the Spirit's open door.

**Master MORE, your Sacred Heart,**
**from this we will no more depart,**
**we are forever in your flow,**
**of Diamond Will that you bestow.**

9. Master MORE, help me look at the conditions on earth and see that they do not have any pull on me anymore. Why then do I feel angry with myself for having felt angry about those conditions?

Master MORE, your Presence here,
filling up the inner sphere.

Life is now a sacred flow,
God Power we on all bestow.

**Master MORE, your Sacred Heart,
from this we will no more depart,
we are forever in your flow,
of Diamond Will that you bestow.**

## Part 4

1. Master MORE, I say: "Let us reason together about my anger." Help me recognize that anger is not a feeling or a thought pattern that can exist on its own. It must have an object. I am angry at something.

Master MORE, come to the fore,
we will absorb your flame of MORE.
Master MORE, our will so strong,
our power centers cleared by song.

**Master MORE, your Sacred Heart,
from this we will no more depart,
we are forever in your flow,
of Diamond Will that you bestow.**

2. Master MORE, help me come to the point where I see what was the object that originally caused me to feel anger with this planet. Help me see that this does not mean so much to me anymore as it did in the beginning.

Master MORE, your wisdom flows,
as our attunement ever grows.
Master MORE, we have a tie,
that helps us see through Serpent's lie.

**Master MORE, your Sacred Heart,
from this we will no more depart,
we are forever in your flow,
of Diamond Will that you bestow.**

3. Master MORE, help me reconnect to what originally made me angry with earth and see that it does not mean as much to me now. Help me come to a point of saying: "Okay, I can let this go; I no longer feel anger at this"

Master MORE, your love so pink,
there is no purer love, we think.
Master MORE, you set us free,
from all conditionality.

**Master MORE, your Sacred Heart,**
**from this we will no more depart,**
**we are forever in your flow,**
**of Diamond Will that you bestow.**

4. Master MORE, help me see that if I am angry with myself, I must have turned myself into an object. I can only be angry with an object, as I was angry with certain conditions on earth or angry with the fallen beings. If I am angry with myself, it means that there is an object that I am angry with.

Master MORE, we will endure,
your discipline that makes us pure.
Master MORE, intentions true,
as we are always one with you.

**Master MORE, your Sacred Heart,**
**from this we will no more depart,**
**we are forever in your flow,**
**of Diamond Will that you bestow.**

5. Master MORE, help me see that this object is a separate self. This self is shooting an arrow into my emotional body, making me feel bad. Because this self is making me feel bad, I become angry with the self, I feel anger towards the self.

Master MORE, our vision raised,
the will of God is always praised.
Master MORE, creative will,
raising all life higher still.

**Master MORE, your Sacred Heart,**
**from this we will no more depart,**
**we are forever in your flow,**
**of Diamond Will that you bestow.**

6. Master MORE, help me see recognize that the object of my anger with myself is not actually with *me,* with myself, it is with *a self that is not me.* It is just a separate self that I have created as a reaction to the conditions on earth.

Master MORE, your peace is power,
the demons of war it will devour.
Master MORE, we serve all life,
our flames consuming war and strife.

**Master MORE, your Sacred Heart,**
**from this we will no more depart,**
**we are forever in your flow,**
**of Diamond Will that you bestow.**

7. Master MORE, help me separate myself from the anger and say: "But if there are certain conditions on earth that I no longer feel so angry over, why am I feeling so angry over this self? I see that this self is unreal, it is not really me, so why am I feeling angry at this self?"

Master MORE, we are so free,
eternal bond from you we see.
Master MORE, we find rebirth,
in flow of your eternal mirth.

**Master MORE, your Sacred Heart,**
**from this we will no more depart,**
**we are forever in your flow,**
**of Diamond Will that you bestow.**

8. Master MORE, help me recognize that the self I am feeling angry with is separate from me. Help me look at the anger I have towards my self and say: "Okay, but I no longer want to direct that anger at my separate self, now I want to direct it at my real self. So what is my real self, where is my real self?"

> Master MORE, you balance all,
> the seven rays upon our call.
> Master MORE, forever MORE,
> we are the Spirit's open door.

> **Master MORE, your Sacred Heart,**
> **from this we will no more depart,**
> **we are forever in your flow,**
> **of Diamond Will that you bestow.**

9. Master MORE, help me see that I cannot direct anger against my real self because I cannot create a mental image or verbalized image of my real self. My real self is beyond what I can imagine and envision with my outer mind.

> Master MORE, your Presence here,
> filling up the inner sphere.
> Life is now a sacred flow,
> God Power we on all bestow.

> **Master MORE, your Sacred Heart,**
> **from this we will no more depart,**
> **we are forever in your flow,**
> **of Diamond Will that you bestow.**

## Part 5

1. Master MORE, help me realize that because I cannot find a real self to direct my anger at, it is not my real self that is angry. It is not even my real self that is angry at the separate self that is making me feel bad. What is angry at one separate self is another separate self.

Master MORE, come to the fore,
we will absorb your flame of MORE.
Master MORE, our will so strong,
our power centers cleared by song.

**Master MORE, your Sacred Heart,
from this we will no more depart,
we are forever in your flow,
of Diamond Will that you bestow.**

2. Master MORE, help me see that I have one separate self that is making
me feel bad and another separate self that is making me angry at the first
separate self. I now see that this is ridiculous.

Master MORE, your wisdom flows,
as our attunement ever grows.
Master MORE, we have a tie,
that helps us see through Serpent's lie.

**Master MORE, your Sacred Heart,
from this we will no more depart,
we are forever in your flow,
of Diamond Will that you bestow.**

3. Master MORE, help me see the gnome-like figure that is looking very
burdened and crippled and that is constantly projecting that I should feel
bad for being imperfect. Help me see the other gnarled-up self that is projecting that I am angry with the first self.

Master MORE, your love so pink,
there is no purer love, we think.
Master MORE, you set us free,
from all conditionality.

**Master MORE, your Sacred Heart,
from this we will no more depart,
we are forever in your flow,
of Diamond Will that you bestow.**

4. Master MORE, help me see that those selves are there, but they are not me. They are in my four lower bodies and I have created them, but they are not me. I now say: "Why do I want to drag these selves around with me?"

Master MORE, we will endure,
your discipline that makes us pure.
Master MORE, intentions true,
as we are always one with you.

**Master MORE, your Sacred Heart,
from this we will no more depart,
we are forever in your flow,
of Diamond Will that you bestow.**

5. Master MORE, I want to be free of them. I am now making the decision that I am willing to let these selves die.

Master MORE, our vision raised,
the will of God is always praised.
Master MORE, creative will,
raising all life higher still.

**Master MORE, your Sacred Heart,
from this we will no more depart,
we are forever in your flow,
of Diamond Will that you bestow.**

6. Master MORE, help me see that I am not on earth to create specific physical changes. Therefore, there is absolutely no reason for me to have any regrets about what I have done and what I have not done in this or past lifetimes. Help me overcome all sense of lost opportunity.

Master MORE, your peace is power,
the demons of war it will devour.
Master MORE, we serve all life,
our flames consuming war and strife.

**Master MORE, your Sacred Heart,**
**from this we will no more depart,**
**we are forever in your flow,**
**of Diamond Will that you bestow.**

7. Master MORE, help me see that I am here to demonstrate that a person who in the past was not spiritual has now awakened. Help me see that my awakening can happen now, when I am willing to switch my mind and look at the angry self and say: "This is not me, I am willing to let it die."

Master MORE, we are so free,
eternal bond from you we see.
Master MORE, we find rebirth,
in flow of your eternal mirth.

**Master MORE, your Sacred Heart,**
**from this we will no more depart,**
**we are forever in your flow,**
**of Diamond Will that you bestow.**

8. Master MORE, help me look at any kind of self that is hindering me and say: "I see that this is not me, I am willing to let this self die."

Master MORE, you balance all,
the seven rays upon our call.
Master MORE, forever MORE,
we are the Spirit's open door.

**Master MORE, your Sacred Heart,**
**from this we will no more depart,**
**we are forever in your flow,**
**of Diamond Will that you bestow.**

9. Master MORE, help me see anything on earth that I take seriously. Help me come to the point where I can look at it and I do not take it seriously, it has no pull on me. I can say: "Well, so what, this means nothing to me, I have transcended it. It used to mean something to me but now I am free of it."

Master MORE, your Presence here,
filling up the inner sphere.
Life is now a sacred flow,
God Power we on all bestow.

**Master MORE, your Sacred Heart,
from this we will no more depart,
we are forever in your flow,
of Diamond Will that you bestow.**

## Sealing

In the name of the Divine Mother, I call to Mother Mary for the sealing of myself and all people in my circle of influence in the creative flow of the Divine Mother, the River of Life. I call for the multiplication of my calls by all representatives of the Divine Mother, so that we form the perfect figure-eight flow of "As Above, so below." Thus, I accept that this is fully manifest, because the mouth of the Lord, the Divine Mother that I AM, has spoken it. Amen.

# 22 | FREEING YOURSELF

# FROM IMPOSSIBLE

# DESIRES

I AM the Ascended Master Jesus Christ and I am here to give you some teachings about self-esteem that are specifically designed for those of you whom we have chosen to call avatars. We have chosen this name for a variety of reasons, as you have demonstrated by the fact that some of you have had a reaction to the word or the concept. Everything we do has the aim of raising people's consciousness, and sometimes we must do this by being provocative, challenging some of the images and beliefs that people have. Indeed, you saw me do this many times when I walked the earth and encountered the scribes and the Pharisees and other closed-minded individuals and groups of people.

My beloved, truly, it is necessary that the nations that were under the communist yoke do something to increase the self-esteem of their people, but I wish to go beyond here and talk to those of you who have come to this earth for a particular purpose, not because you had to do so for karma or because your own planet ascended and you could not rise with it. You have come here for the particular purpose, in a broad sense, of being the open door, being an example, showing that there is an alternative to the consciousness that dominates this planet. When you came here, you may

have had a certain intent, a certain goal, a certain sense of what you wanted
to change on earth.

## Relative self-esteem

What I desire you to recognize here is that when we talk about self-esteem
in an outer way, for people in the world, it is, of course, very important
that all people have a sense of self-esteem because they generally function
better in their lives than if they have no or a very low sense of self-esteem.
Now, in some way we could say that all people have self-esteem, it is just
a matter of how they see the self, how they define the self. Do they define
it in a positive way or a negative way? Nevertheless, what we can say about
most people in the world is that they have a *relative* sense of self-esteem
because it is related to something in this world. If you are an athlete who
does the long jump, then your sense of self-esteem may be related to how
far you can jump. If you are a businessman, your sense of self-esteem may
be related to how much money you have or how much money you are
making.

You see that many people in the world have created a relative sense
of self where there is a scale related to some kind of performance in the
world. Now, there is not necessarily anything wrong or bad about this. It
is a necessary stage in the unfoldment of a being. We have said that one of
the basic desires people have is to make an effort and receive some kind of
positive outcome, some kind of reward for their effort. You can say that
as an expression of this basic desire, you create the sense of self-esteem
where there is a scale for your own performance. Naturally, the higher you
can perform on that scale, the more sense of self-esteem you will have.
This is what we might call a higher form of self-esteem, again in a worldly
sense.

Now, there are other people who have a lower form of self-esteem
where, instead of comparing their own performance to the goals they have
set, they are always comparing themselves to others. Are they doing better
or worse than other people? Do they have more or less than other people?
This can still be seen as an expression of this basic desire to make an effort
and to reap the rewards. Again, clearly a lower sense of self-esteem than
when you are working on your own and comparing yourself only to yourself, but still not a destructive sense of self-esteem.

## Self-esteem and status

Now then, you have another type of self-esteem that is not related to your performance but to your status in some human, artificially created hierarchy. You may have, for example, the sense that because you are the emperor or the king, you are superior to other people because of your position. You may have the sense that because you have some position in the state apparatus, you are superior to ordinary people. You see that this form of self-esteem is not tied to performance but to a certain position.

Now, in some cases, of course, it may require an effort to attain this position but the lowest level of this form of esteem is tied to a position that you have somehow gotten, either through inheritance, by claiming some kind of authority or by using force, deceit or whatever it may be. Once you have this status, you think that there is nothing that can challenge your status, that the people below you cannot challenge that status. You see that this form of self-esteem is the self-esteem of the fallen beings. They can, of course, also have a certain sense of self-esteem where being able to exercise great power gives them the self-esteem. Although this, in some sense, is tied to their performance, it is still, when your performance is measured on how well you can exercise power over others, clearly a lower source of self-esteem.

## Contradiction in the word self-esteem

If we go beyond this level, we can see that when we talk about avatars, when we talk about spiritual people who are consciously walking a spiritual path (a true inner path towards their ascension), we need to take these considerations to a higher level. We need to ask ourselves if there is not a certain contradiction in the word "self-esteem." Now, as Master MORE was talking about last night: "Can you really feel anger in a non-specific way, or do you need an object?" In the same way, you can say: "Can you really feel esteem for anything if you do not have an object that you are esteeming?"

What is *self*-esteem? Many people have not defined the word. They somehow think they know what it means. You are appreciating yourself. You think you are a good or capable person. You are feeling good about yourself, whatever it is. What is the self that is being esteemed? As spiritual people you can clearly see that for most people in the world, it is not their inner beings, their Conscious Yous, their real beings that are being esteemed because their self-esteem is related to something in this world. Their inner being is not defined by anything in this world so when your self-esteem is related to anything in this world, it cannot be your true self. It can only be an outer self, an element of your outer self.

You may say, for example, the athlete who does the long jump, he has defined and created a self and when he performs well, this self feels good, feels capable, feels superior, feels whatever—but it is an outer self. Really, does it have any significance in a spiritual sense how far you can jump on the field? You see that so many other people out there have created these outer selves, these relative selves, selves that are related to a specific condition in the world. When they live up to that condition to some degree, then they can feel good about themselves and they can feel they have some value. They have some esteem in their own minds and perhaps even in the minds of others.

Naturally, we do not desire you who are direct students to be limited to this form of self-esteem. We desire you to reach a much higher level of self-esteem that truly comes from within and is not related to how you perform or what status you have on earth. Truly, when you consider the message of the new book of the contrast between a natural planet and earth, you can see that it really is not a very high form of self-esteem you can have if your self-esteem is related to anything on such a low planet.

## A spiritual form of self-esteem

We desire you to go beyond this relative, worldly, outer self-esteem and gain a higher form of self-esteem. Now, it is natural that when you first find the spiritual path, you do not have a completely clear vision and understanding of what the goal of the path is and where it leads. In many cases, you may be more focused on the outer path than on the inner path. In many cases, spiritual students have created a different form of outer self. Instead of being related to something in the material world, it is related to how well they perform on the spiritual path as they understand it.

Now again, this is not particularly negative. It is just an expression of the fact that when you first find the spiritual path, you use this drive to make an effort and reap a reward to define what it means to be a good student, what it means to make progress on the path, what it means to make an effort to apply yourself. You use this to define a self and a way to evaluate where you are at in your performance, and then you can feel good about yourself or not so good about yourself according to this standard. This is, of course, a phase that you need to go through and then you transcend into a higher form of self-esteem.

## Negative self-esteem

Before I talk about that, I want to talk about the fact that there are also people who have defined what I call a negative self and that leads them to have negative self-worth. In other words, you can have what we might call a positive sense of self where your performance can be higher or lower, but it is not so that you are a complete failure. On the other hand, you see, of course, in the world many people who have defined a negative sense of self where there is something wrong with them. It is not a matter of being higher or lower, it is a matter of being low or much lower.

One of the effects of a communist system is that many people have this negative sense of self-worth but it can only be bad or worse. Many Christians have had the same thing, feeling as sinners and therefore defining a negative sense of self. This may, again, have a certain scale where you can feel that you are a sinner, but some sinners are worse than others so maybe you are not quite as bad as those other people who are doing this or that. This is still very relative. You see examples of this in the world, but what I want to point out to you is that there are some of you who are avatars and spiritual people who also have, most often in past lives, defined these negative selves where you feel in some way bad about yourself. You feel that you have made a mistake in the past or that there is something wrong with you, and therefore you could not really, on that scale, go into the positive territory. You are always in the negative territory and it is just a matter of how low you are, how bad you feel about yourself.

Many of you have created these selves because you have been exposed to situations where you felt you had failed in your goals. In other words, you had a certain goal but you completely failed to attain that goal and therefore you decided that there was something inherently flawed or wrong about you. This then created these negative selves that cannot give you self-esteem but can only give you the opposite. There are, of course, many ways that you can create these negative selves, but what I really want to talk about is that in many cases, you have created these negative selves because you have interacted with fallen beings. Here is where you need to understand the dynamic between an avatar and a fallen being. Naturally, the new book gives a very, very good and detailed description about this, but it does not go so much into the deeper psychology, at least not in the aspect I want to talk about here.

## Seeking approval of fallen beings

Now, on a more superficial level, we can say that when you are on a natural planet, you have never, ever encountered anyone who criticized you or put you down. You have only encountered people who encouraged you and gave you positive feedback. It does not mean that your teachers or even your peers on a natural planet always agree with what you have been doing or think it was the best it could be. They always give you positive feedback of how you could do better, not that there is something wrong with you or what you did. You have never encountered this. What you have built up on a natural planet is an expectation that when you do something positive for other people, they will at least not be negative about it, but they will most likely appreciate it. In other words, when you have the best of intentions, they will not put you down because they realize that what you are doing is done with the best of intentions.

In a sense, this gives you a certain expectation and even a certain desire for receiving approval and acceptance of who you are and that you have good intentions. We can even say that this is not really what we call a "desire" on earth. It is just that because of what you have encountered on a natural planet, you have a natural expectation that when you do something for others with the best of intentions (and, of course, you only have good intentions on a natural planet), then they will accept you and accept your effort in a positive way. They may suggest a better way you can do it, but they will not put you down and criticize you for having good intentions.

When you then come to a planet like earth and you encounter the fallen beings, you again come here with the best of intentions. What you do is done with the best of intentions, but then you experience that the fallen beings do not accept you, do not accept your intentions, do not appreciate anything you are doing. They are putting you down for every-thing you do, and even for being who you are. Even if you are not exposed to this extreme form of torture that is described in the book, you will still encounter this phenomenon. You will encounter the fallen beings on the planet, and you will encounter that they do not accept you, they do not approve of you. At first, you are bewildered. You cannot understand this, but there are many avatars who then gradually, perhaps over several lifetimes, build this desire to win the approval of the fallen beings. You see, my beloved, Portia was saying that there are few efforts you can make on this planet that are more futile than seeking the approval of the male ego, but there is one effort that is more futile, and that is seeking the approval of the fallen beings. Many of you have these deep scars in you of seeking this approval, not getting it but instead getting the opposite. This has, in many cases, made you even more eager to seek their approval, to come to understand the fallen beings. How can you actually please them, how can you do something they approve of, how can you help them?

## The impossible quest

You can go into this spiral of seeking this, and you are not realizing in the beginning that it is an impossible quest. This can give you these scars and burdens that then gradually grow into these negative selves. The self is not responding rationally, but it is responding to your feelings about being put down again and again and again. This is a very emotional self that can only have a negative self-esteem and it is just a matter of how negative it is. In other words, there may be times where the fallen beings were just ignoring you and that led you to some level of negative self-esteem. There may be others where they directly criticized you, put you down or killed you and that gave you an even deeper level of self-esteem on this negative scale.

Many of you have these selves that are still lingering in your four lower bodies, very often in the emotional body. This can be selves that are very raw, that are very sensitive. You can maybe see in this lifetime how you have been very sensitive to the approval and disapproval from other people, your parents, your teachers, your siblings, whatever. Therefore, you have been wounded many times by what people have done or not done to you. You may not have encountered fallen beings in this lifetime, or you may have, but they may not have been the extreme evil that is described in the book. Still, they have, in some way, ignored you or put you down. These selves, of course, can be hurt not only by fallen beings. They are so sensitive to this approval of others that anybody can stir up the self and give you a negative self-esteem.

Naturally, our desire as ascended masters is to help you overcome this, to let go of these selves and to come to see that they are just separate selves. They are simply outer selves that are created and they are not (as Master MORE said) *you*. They are objects, they are objects that exist in your four lower bodies. When you recognize them for the objects they are (you can call them aspects of the ego, you can call them "internal spirits," you can call them "selves," it does not matter), but when you see this and you can separate yourself from them, you can begin to let them go.

Of course, there may be some energy stored there and you can benefit from giving invocations and decrees to transform the energy. At the bottom line, you need to come to that point where you recognize that these selves were created out of an illusion. What was the illusion that led you to create these selves in response to the encounter of the fallen beings? Well, the primary illusion that you had was this expectation that when you do something for others with the best of intentions, they will accept you. They will approve of you, even if they do not approve of everything you are doing.

## Fallen beings will never approve avatars

You have to come to recognize, my beloved, that it is fundamentally impossible for an avatar to win the approval of a fallen being. *It cannot be done.* The fallen beings will never, as long as they are in the fallen state of consciousness, accept or approve of an avatar. They can only see an avatar as a threat because they subconsciously sense that the avatar has more light than they do and they feel threatened by this. By their very nature, they must feel threatened and therefore, they will never give you their acceptance or their approval. What you need to come to is the realization that the pattern you had from natural planets and that you took with you to earth, simply is not appropriate on a planet like this. Therefore, you need to make a conscious effort to come into this acceptance that you will simply let this desire, this expectation, go in terms of being on earth.

It really does not matter at all in a cosmic sense (in a sense of your spiritual growth and your ascension) whether you have the approval of fallen beings. The fallen beings have absolutely no power over your ascension. Their disapproval of you cannot hinder your ascension. Their approval of you cannot further your ascension. Their disapproval can hinder your ascension in a sense, if you take it in and accept it and feed this separate self you have created. This is not the fallen beings determining this; it is your own reaction to them. No fallen being can hinder your ascension directly. They can only do it if you give them some kind of power in your being by creating these selves in reaction to them.

## Your unrealistic expectations about earth

When you come to see this, you can see that it is almost inevitable, as described in the book, that when you are on a natural planet and you look at earth and decide to come to earth, you will have some unrealistic expectations, not only about what life is like on this planet, but also about how you will respond to earth. You need to recognize that these were unrealistic expectations and therefore you need to let them go. They were based on life on a natural planet. On a natural planet they would be reasonable expectations but you are not on a natural planet, are you? None of you are in doubt of this, I assume. You can see that these expectations are not realistic here. You must simply let them go, and you can do this when you consciously see them for what they are and understand the teachings we have been giving you, both in the new book and in these dictations we have given you here.

This is a matter of the unrealistic expectation of how the fallen beings will react to you. Now, there comes another level of this because you, of course, also have expectations of how you are going to react to the fallen beings and to life on earth in general. These are far more subtle, and they relate to what I talked about earlier, namely that you had some desire, some reason for coming here. You wanted to affect a positive change on this planet. Do you see, my beloved, that just as you can have people who have created a scale for how far they can jump on the field and they have created a self that measures its self-esteem based on how well they are performing, you, as an avatar, can have created a self that measures your performance on how well are you fulfilling the reason you had in mind before you came here?

For example, many of you had the expectation that even though you knew this was a low planet and there was war and torture and all kinds of murder and mayhem going on, you would still be able to stay in a positive frame of mind and not go into a negative, reactionary spiral with the fallen beings or with conditions on earth. Like Master MORE said, you thought you would not become angry, would not become afraid, would not react in a negative way, would not fight the fallen beings, and so on. Since all of us, as Master MORE says, who have come to earth have gone into a reactionary pattern with the fallen beings, have been shocked, then it is safe to say that all of us have failed according to these expectations. We all reacted in ways we did not think we would react before we came here—myself no exception, as is hopefully demonstrated by the book.

## Your hopes for coming to earth

Again, you have to look at this and say: "This was clearly an unrealistic expectation and I need to let it go." Then, there is a more subtle one, and that is related to what you were hoping to accomplish, what result you were hoping to see here on earth, what change you were hoping to produce. There, again, it is almost inevitable you have created a self that feels that you have failed in your reason for coming here. You have not produced the result that you were hoping to produce, you have not seen the positive change.

You have this self that is somewhat parallel to what many people have in the world for measuring their performance according to some standard. It is just that your standard is very, very different. You may say that the ascended masters want to raise the earth and the only way the earth could really be raised is that there were some of us avatars who took embodiment on earth and helped raise the collective consciousness. "So aren't we here to affect a positive change? Isn't it reasonable to expect that we should affect a positive change?"

In a certain sense, we could say: "Yes, yes, yes, it is reasonable." The problem is that if you have a created a self that feels that until you have affected the change you envisioned, you will have failed, then you have a self that prevents you from attaining the true self-esteem that we would like you to attain. This self simply pulls you down into a negative view of yourself, of earth, your reason for coming here, your performance here and therefore you cannot attain true self-esteem. What is more is that as long as you have this self, you cannot leave this planet because you will feel that you cannot leave with a negative view of why you came here. Until you have fulfilled your reason for coming here, you cannot leave.

## Expectations that block your ascension

Where this becomes a real problem, in terms of your ascension and your spiritual growth, is because the change you envisioned before you came here was in a general sense a raising of the consciousness. You also, most of you, had a certain goal for coming here of what negative manifestation you would like to help the earth transcend. For many of you it was war, for others it was torture. For each negative manifestation, there were some avatars who desired to come here and see the earth rise above this.

Now, my beloved, again you can say: "But the ascended masters want to remove war from the earth, do they not?" Yes, we do—of course we do. But we do not look at this process the same way you tend to look at it when you are in embodiment. You see, my beloved, as we have attempted to explain, we respect free will. We realize that if war is going to be banished from the earth, this requires certain fallen beings to be taken from the earth. They cannot be taken until a critical mass of the original inhabitants of the earth – those who invited the fallen beings here in the first place (unconsciously, of course, but nevertheless) – have raised their consciousness and abandoned the consciousness that caused the fallen beings to come here because there was an opening.

We know very well that banishing war from the earth involves the free-will choices of many among the original inhabitants of the earth. What we are giving you is a teaching that will help you come to that same realization, and therefore you can see something very, very simple. I said it is completely impossible to win the approval of the fallen beings, but at the same time it is completely impossible to make the fallen beings abandon their warring ways. You can see that if you were to have the effect of removing war from the earth, it would be futile to expect that you could do this by changing the fallen beings.

On the other hand, you also saw before you came here that most of the original inhabitants of the earth were at a far lower level of consciousness than you were. Again, you can see that what you are doing when you have the expectation that you can help remove war from the earth is that you are making the success or failure of your mission dependent on the free-will choices of beings who are in a much lower state of consciousness than you were when you came here. My beloved, is it wise to do this? Is it wise to tie your performance, and therefore your self-esteem, to the choices made by anyone outside yourself? This is, of course, not wise.

Your self-esteem should depend *only* on factors inside yourself, namely the way you look at yourself, the way you look at your performance or behavior on earth. You see that because you have created this unrealistic expectation that, just by coming here, you would instantly pull up people and create a change (or whatever you envisioned in your mind), you have inevitably become disappointed by realizing that this planet was so much denser and that it was impossible, even though you had the best of intentions, for you to just come here and affect this change.

You have been disappointed because you tied your expectation of what you could do on earth to the free-will choices of people who were in a very low, very dualistic, state of consciousness. The disappointment was inevitable, and you need to come to see this so that you can separate yourself from these selves and say: "I cannot allow my self-esteem to depend on these selves that are tied to the choices made by beings in a lower state of consciousness. Why would I want to have my self-esteem tied to the choices of people in the duality consciousness?"

Of course, there is no blame in telling you that you created these selves because, as we have said now several times, it was part of your mission on earth to go into the immersion phase and come to identify yourself as a human being. As part of this process, it was inevitable that you created these selves. What you need to recognize is that now that you are at a higher level of consciousness and you are contemplating the possibility of your ascension in this lifetime, you need to look at these selves. You need to see why they were created, you need to see that they were based on an illusion and an unrealistic expectation so that you can see that these are not the kind of selves that you want to carry with you. You can use the tools to let them go, but first of all, you can come to the realization that they *need* to go.

## Self-esteem comes from who you are

My beloved, what is true self-esteem? Well, it must be a self-esteem that does not depend on anything outside yourself. As we have said now many times, your outer being, your four lower bodies, is not your real self. Even if you have certain conditions, certain selves, in your four lower bodies, true self-esteem cannot depend on these. Where does self-esteem come from? Well, you need to then contemplate that the world has a view of self-esteem, a concept of self-esteem, that is not higher self-esteem because it is, as I have said, related to something in this world. Even the selves you have created based on your expectations for coming here are related to this world and what you have accomplished or have not accomplished. You need to recognize here that as an avatar, as a spiritual student that has reached the beginning stages of Christhood, you cannot strive for (you cannot have the expectation that you should have) the kind of self-esteem that people have in the world.

Then what *can* you do? Well, you can ask yourself: "What is the self, the real self, the core of my being?" We have given you many teachings on this. We have given you beautiful teachings in Guru Ma's book about drinking your own Kool-Aid [*Don't Drink Your own Kool-Aid*]. You can contemplate and use these teachings to very gradually come to look beyond the sense of identity, the sense of self, you have built in this world.

You can come to the point where you have gone into your identity body and you are beginning to question and challenge the sense of self you have built in your sojourn on this planet, realizing more and more: "This is not the real me, it is not who I really am." Then, you can come to this sense of connection where, as we have said many times, the Conscious You is pure awareness. You can begin to contemplate what this means and there are some very important keys in the new book [*My Lives with Lucifer, Satan, Hitler and Jesus*] that, as the messenger has described, even helped him understand this better. Even though he had received all the previous teachings on it, there were still things that helped him grasp it.

Really, the real self cannot be defined by anything in this world. That is why you can recognize that the real self does not need anything from this world – any approval, any performance, any result – in order to feel good about itself. The real you, the Conscious You, has an ability to feel good about itself when it recognizes who and what it is. You are an extension of the I AM Presence, a spiritual being, however you can see it right now, however you can conceive of it. I know that this is tricky. It is not easy to conceptualize because the whole idea of giving you the concept of the Conscious You is to trick your linear, analytical mind, to confuse it, because it cannot conceptualize what it is. It cannot relate it to anything it is familiar with here on earth. When you recognize that you are not anything that can be defined on earth, you can see that your self-esteem is not tied to anything on earth, it comes from the very fact that you exist. By the very fact that you exist, you are worthy. You are esteemed. You are esteem-able. You see, my beloved, true self-esteem cannot come as long as you have an object, a self, and you are esteeming that object.

## How to fulfill a desire

Therefore, we can say that when you come to this level of awareness, the concept of self-esteem fades away. When you see that there is no self, there is no need for esteem. You are just experiencing your self for who you are. You are not even concerned about any form of self-esteem, any scale of a high and a low, any dualistic comparison. It just fades away.

I know that I am setting you a goal that for some of you may take some time to realize. I want you to know that not only with self-esteem, but with many other concepts that you have on the spiritual path, that as you go to these higher levels of Christhood, the concepts fade away. They lose their meaning because you see that they only had meaning at a lower level of consciousness. At a higher level of consciousness, they no longer have any specific meaning, they do not have any importance, they have no pull on you. You could say, in order to again confound the linear mind, that the only way to gain true self-esteem is to come to the point where you have no need for self-esteem. You have no need to be esteemed.

In a sense, we could say that the only way to truly fulfill your desires is to come to the point where you have transcended the desire and you no longer have the desire. It is not a matter of filling it—it is a matter of transcending it. What the fallen beings want you to think – and one of the primary ways they keep you trapped in a reactionary pattern – is that you have a desire and you need to attain the object of the desire. If you have a desire for self-esteem, you need to attain self-esteem. How do you attain self-esteem? By being able to jump further than anybody else. When this criteria is fulfilled, *then* you will have self-esteem.

This is not the case. You can never, *ever,* feel true self-esteem by fulfilling any desire whatsoever—you can never actually have any desire filled. You can only be truly whole, feel truly good about yourself, when you *transcend* the desire and you are no longer experiencing lack. You will have self-esteem when you no longer experience a lack of self-esteem, but *that* can only be accomplished by transcending the desire, even the desire to have a self that can be esteemed.

The Conscious You, when it realizes it is pure awareness, does not need to be esteemed. It actually does not even see itself as a self anymore. Yes, I am giving you tricky, subtle concepts. The only way to overcome this is to trick the linear, analytical mind so you are tricked out of it and you have an experience of something higher. It is this experience I desire you to have. I am, of course, as any ascended master, willing to guide you step-by-step until you are ready to have that experience because the illusions have gradually fallen away until there is no more illusion and then you snap out of that limited sense of self and it just is no more.

My beloved, I have given you what I wish to give you in this install-ment, but I have more to say about some of the topics that have been brought up at this conference. I will fulfill the promise made by Master MORE that I will give you some thoughts on how to let a self die. *This* I will reserve for tomorrow so that you can ask, if you are willing, to be taken to whichever retreat of the master, but I suggest the retreat over Arabia. I will be guiding those who are willing to come there in order to integrate the concepts I have been giving you so that you are more prepared to receive what I will give you tomorrow.

I bid you good night, and I thank you for your always joyous attention. It is always my great joy to interact with students at your level of willing-ness to learn.

# 23 | BEING FREE OF YOUR

# PRIMAL SELF

I AM the Ascended Master Jesus Christ. I ask you to consider the many Christians who sit around the world on a Sunday morning worshiping in their sanctuaries. Many of them belong to a specific church and they believe that *their* church has the true or perhaps even the *only* true interpretation of my life.

Many of these Christians consider themselves to have a literal interpretation of the Bible. They claim that the way they interpret the scriptures is the literal way. Now, my beloved, I can in just a few sentences prove this claim wrong. You all know that there is a quote in the scriptures where I supposedly said: "He who is willing to save his life shall lose it but he who is willing to lose his life for my sake shall find true life, eternal life." My beloved, if you claim to interpret the scriptures literally, the question is: "Why then haven't you killed yourself?"

If you are still alive, then the simple truth is that you are not taking everything that was said in the Bible literally. If there is *one* statement that you do not take literally (because you have not lost your life in order to find this eternal life), then why is it that you do not take that statement literally? It is because you realize, of course, that it could not be meant to be taken literally. If there is *one* sentence that is not meant to be taken literally, then is it not possible that there might be others? Is it not even possible that *all* of my statements were never meant to be taken literally?

As is even demonstrated in the scriptures, I gave a lower teaching for the general public and a higher teaching for my own disciples. Is it that difficult to see that I gave teachings that can be understood at different levels because you are meant to use the teachings to increase your understanding, to raise your awareness? When you do so, you will understand deeper meanings behind my statements. Thus, those who are taking the Bible literally are not following the path, the Way, that I outlined. Is that so difficult to see, my beloved?

## Your selves are stuck in a specific perception

I know, of course, that all of you can see this or you would not be in ascended master teachings. I am bringing it up because even those of you who are open to our teachings do indeed realize that there are certain elements of your consciousness that are taking certain things literally. I have talked about these selves that you have created in reaction to your experiences in this world. My beloved, such a self is in a sense stuck in the same state of consciousness that you see in many fundamentalist Christians.

The self was created for a specific purpose, and it can only look at life (or look at a specific aspect of life) the way it was created. It is like a machine that simply keeps repeating the same pattern over and over. The teaching we are giving here is, of course, not for beginners on the path, not even for beginners in ascended master teachings. It is given specifically for those who have risen to the higher levels. The teaching I will give in this release is specifically for people who have read the book we have given [*My Lives with Lucifer, Satan, Hitler and Jesus*] and who, therefore, are ready to deal with these initiations because you realize you are an avatar who came to earth. I am asking you, if you do not feel you are at this level, then you put this teaching aside and study some of the other teachings until you feel you are ready for it. Many of you are ready for it and that is why we will not hold back the teaching.

We have given you various teachings about the selves you have created, the aspects of the ego, the internal spirits. I have talked earlier this year about your modus operandi, how you look at the ascended masters. We have talked about how you look at the material world and these are all tools to help you uncover that you have created some kind of self inside of you that is still there, that you are still carrying with you. It is burdening you, holding you back in various ways. It may, for example, cause your thoughts to go into certain repetitive patterns. It may cause an emotional reaction where in certain situations you feel a certain reaction. It can be fear; it can be a sense of embarrassment or shame. It can be anger; it can be many other things. It is individual for each one, but the point is that you see there is a pattern here that is repeated. My beloved, notice, this: The Conscious You, the core of your being is a *creative* being.

It wants to continually move on and experience something new. That is why you came here in the first place. After having lived on natural planets for a long time, you desired to experience something new, something different. Again, nothing wrong with this. Curiosity may have killed the cat but you are not cats. Curiosity is perfectly natural for a being who is expanding its self-awareness. How else would you expand your self-awareness if you were not curious about what is outside your current sense of self?

You recognize here that the core of your being is curious, likes to move on, experience new things. This means that anytime you see that there is a pattern in your four lower bodies that repeats, then you know this is not the real you. You also know that it is holding you back and it is making the real you, perhaps, have a certain sense of frustration, feeling unfulfilled, feeling unhappy about being here.

## The creation of your first separate self

Now, when I say this, we, of course, need to make a distinction. We need to ask ourselves: "If the Conscious You is pure awareness, can the Conscious You actually feel unhappy, angry, frustrated?" This is a question that does not have a straightforward, linear answer. The reason for this is that you have been in embodiment for a very long time and therefore you have created certain selves that are so subtle that you cannot at present tell the difference between the Conscious You and these selves.

That is why we have started out talking to you about certain selves that are at a more superficial level and that you can very easily see are related to specific situations or specific aspects of life. It is easier to see these more superficial selves and to identify them as a separate self, to realize this is not the real you. As we have previously given the teaching about the birth trauma that you received when you first came into embodiment on earth, we are now ready to give you the understanding that when you went through this birth trauma, you created a self. It really is not the basic way that you relate to the earth but the basic way that you related to the earth as a result of your trauma. In other words, in order to deal with the trauma, you created this first separate self. In a sense, we can say that what happened was that the sense of self you had before then, the sense of self you had created as you created your four lower bodies, it died as a result of the birth trauma.

Take note that we have said it before but I will summarize. In order to take embodiment on a dense-matter planet like earth for the first time, you created (with the awareness you had before you came here) your identity body, your mental body, your emotional body and then eventually the physical body [Meaning the mind associated with the physical body]. These three higher bodies were created based on the view of life on earth that you had before you had actually experienced life on earth. It was a somewhat theoretical self. Then, you came down with the best of intentions, with this self you had created that had some expectations about what you wanted to do and what you were likely to encounter, what might happen as a result of you being here. Then, you experienced the birth trauma of encountering the fallen beings, and the original self dies. A new self is created in response to the fallen beings, to conditions on earth. In a certain sense, it is true that the Conscious You cannot feel unhappy, frustrated or fulfilled when it realizes it is pure awareness. In pure awareness there are no *negative* feelings, there are none of what you call *positive* feelings on earth. In pure awareness you are simply observing. If you can center yourself in the pure awareness of the Conscious You, you can just observe earth. You are not evaluating, judging. There is no value judgment, there is no *should* or *should not:* You are just observing.

This is the state of consciousness demonstrated by the Buddha, as he made his final initiation where he was sitting in meditation under the Bo tree, and he was approached by the demons of Mara who attempted to get him to react to them in some way. He stayed non-attached, he stayed out of a reactionary pattern, by being in his pure awareness where he was not blind to what was happening on earth but he was just observing without reacting.

Now, of course my beloved, you are not here to sit under a tree and just observe. You are here to take part in life on earth. What do you need in order to take part in life? You need an identity body, a mental body, an emotional body and a physical body. As a result of that, you have a self and that means that you can step back from this self, go into the pure awareness of the Conscious You and only observe. This, of course, is not what you do in your practical everyday life. The moment your attention

is directed out towards actually engaging in life on this planet, you (as the Conscious You) are experiencing life through the self you have created. That is why the Conscious You can experience frustration, disappointment, a sense of being rejected.

From a theoretical point it is not the Conscious You. These feelings are not *in* the Conscious You but the Conscious You is experiencing life through this self. That is why it is such a deep sense of self that most people cannot see it. Even many people who have been of the path for some time cannot see it because it is really the basic self they created after they came here. It was the self that was born after the first self died. It is so ingrained, it is so deep, it is so subtle that you take it for granted. You think this is the only way to experience life on earth.

## You have let other selves go

We have given you the concept of these more superficial selves that are related to a specific condition. The purpose is to help you see that you have already seen some of these selves. You have walked the spiritual path, even if you have walked it for a short time (and I am not here talking about finding these particular teachings because many of you have been on the path for many years before you found these teachings). If you have followed the path for some time, you have already seen some of these outer selves, you have separated yourself from them and you have let them go.

You are already familiar with the process. Once you start thinking about it and considering your path, you realize you have already (maybe without being consciously aware of it) let go of some of these selves. You are not reacting today the way you did before you found the spiritual path. There are some reactionary patterns that you have transcended, that you have left behind, and that is because you have overcome these outer selves. What I want to bring up here is that an outer self is an outer self. You may have an outer self that is related to how you deal with people who are angry at you. This is, of course, a more specific outer self than the self you created as a result of your birth trauma, but they are created in fundamentally the same way.

They are both based on an illusion and therefore the way to overcome them is really the same way. It is that you come to identify that there is an outer self and you make a choice that you no longer want to carry this with you. Then, you can let it go. However when it comes to the cosmic birth trauma self that you created, we might call it the *primal* self, then this, of course, is more difficult to do because it is more subtle.

## The self you had in your first embodiment

What does it actually mean when I say that you came down into embodiment with a self you had created before you had experienced earth, and that self dies and then you created another self? Well, what it means is, my beloved, that when the previous self died, you lost the frame of reference that this self could give you. In other words, the self with which you descended was created based on the perspective you had from a higher realm, based on your life on a natural planet. It was, of course, an incomplete self because it did not know what life here is like. What it *did* know was that there is an alternative to life on earth, there is a better form of life; there is something else. When you experienced the trauma and that self dies, you lose that frame of reference at least at the conscious level.

This means that you now begin to think or experience that the only way to look at life is the way you now look at life through this new self that was created, the primal self, that was created in reaction to your birth trauma and conditions on earth. Therefore, it is more difficult to identify this self than the more superficial selves. It will take more work for you, but we have given the teachings, we have given the tools. Mother Mary's tool for getting in contact with your birth trauma is a magnificent tool for helping you gain some awareness, some greater awareness, of the self you created so that you can begin to separate yourself from it. You can, in a sense, begin to see the self from the outside instead of seeing life through that self, from inside the self.

## Letting go of the deeper self

It should be obvious, I trust, that as long as you are inside a self, you cannot see the self. If you are wearing yellow glasses and you are not aware of this, you cannot see the glasses. In order to see a self, you must step outside of it. Of course, what we are aiming to take you through is a process where you gradually let go of all the more superficial selves and spirits until you get down to a point where the only self you have left is the primal self. When you have gone through this process, then it is possible for you to make this shift where you can realize that you have a primal self. It is more subtle than the other selves but it is still a self that is created the same way. What you can then do is that you can begin to recognize that this is not the real you. It was a self that was created in response to a very difficult, very traumatic, situation that you encountered on earth.

Again, there is absolutely no blame from our side here. We have been in embodiment; we created this primal self in response to our own birth trauma on this planet. We are only here to demonstrate to you that as we have overcome that primal self, so can you. What one has done, all can do.

How do you, then, overcome it? Well, as we have said before, the key is to recognize that any self you have is created for a specific purpose, with a specific view. Therefore, in essence the self has, we can say, a certain problem. It has a built-in problem and when you are looking from inside the self, it must be resolved somehow. We have talked about how you may have come here with the intent to affect a certain outer change on earth. Then, when you create a certain self based on what you encountered on this earth, this self may project or may see that there is a specific problem here on earth and it absolutely must be solved. As I said, if it is war, then war must be removed from the earth before you have solved the problem.

Of course, this is not the way you can overcome such a self. Even if you solved the problem that the self projects, such as removing all war, you would not automatically overcome the outer self. The trick is to begin to see that you will *not* overcome the primal self by solving the problem or changing the condition that the primal self was created in reaction to.

You will overcome it only by recognizing that it is a separate self, that it is based on an illusion and that there is no problem to solve. This, of course, is tricky. Yes, there is war on the earth. Yes, the ascended masters want to remove war from the earth as do all of you. There *is* a real problem, but for you to be free of your primal self, this cannot be done by solving the outer problem. It can *only* be done by resolving the mechanism in you that makes you think that your life on this planet, your sense of self and your exit from this planet, depends on any condition here.

We could, again to reference the scriptures, look at where I said: "The Prince of this world comes and has nothing in me." What does this mean? It means that there is no force on earth who has any pull on you that you have to do something, change something, solve something here. There is no force dictating that you have to react a certain way, that you have to feel a certain way.

## The feeling of the primal self

Now, it is, of course, not so that all of you have created a primal self that is aimed at solving a particular problem. Some of you have created a primal self that feels completely rejected by the fallen beings. Some of you have created selves that have a general unhappiness about life, feel so disappointed so shocked about conditions here, feel so powerless to change it that you feel it was senseless, it had no purpose, for you to come here. It was a mistake for you to come here.

You need to, each one, use our tools, use Mother Mary's exercise, contemplate what your primal self is. What is the core of it? What is the reaction? What is the belief? Then, you need to recognize that the primal self has given you a certain primal feeling, a primal sense of what earth and life on earth is like. It is, of course, unpleasant so you know it is not the way it should be. As I said, some of you, even though your original self died, can still have a certain sense that there is an alternative to life on earth, there is a different realm where war, for example, is not present.

You feel it as a discomfort, as a tension. There is something that is not right, something you are not comfortable with. You need to come to identify exactly what is the feeling, what is the belief because, as we have told you, when you were exposed to this birth trauma, you made a decision. It can be a decision that can be difficult to pin-point in words. As it says in the book, you made the decision: "I never want to experience this again." What was it exactly that you did not want to experience again? You also made a decision about what you *could* do or what you *would* do from that point on here on earth—how you would approach life. Here, you need to recognize a fundamental dynamic.

## Fallen beings aborting your mission

There are many fallen beings who are in physical embodiment, and that you may have encountered in physical embodiment, who are not conscious of this. The fallen beings in the identity realm are certainly conscious of this. They know about avatars, they know that many beings have come to earth to help raise this planet. They know that their reign on earth, their domination of earth, depends on aborting the mission of these avatars or at least postponing it. What they really want to do is to shock you so much that you feel that the original mission you had for coming here could not be fulfilled. Therefore, you feel that coming here was a mistake because you just cannot make a difference. You cannot change anything on earth.

Many of you, when you went through this cosmic birth trauma, the shock that you went through was because you came here with the best of intentions. That means you saw how all people on earth are suffering, for example because there is war on earth. You *assumed* that if people are suffering, they want to overcome the suffering and therefore they want to overcome war. You come down here and you are thinking that it is self-evident that people want to overcome war. When you make a proposal for how this could be done, you expect that people will respond positively.

You are used to, from a natural planet, that people want to improve their lives. Then, you come down here on earth and you realize two things. First of all, there are people on earth who do not want to change, they do not want to overcome their suffering; they do not want to abandon war or whatever it may be. They do not want to change. Then, when you are down here, you fully experience the absolute, unchanging reality of free will. Before, when you were looking down on earth from above, you did not quite grasp it. All of us, we did not quite grasp that if the people on earth do not want to abandon war, you cannot make them. When you are down here, you realize (and it is often the greatest shock) that even though you know how to overcome human problems and limitations, there is nothing you can do about it because people are not responding.

## The shock of encountering resistance to change

You, of course, cannot go against their free will. It is not that you really have a desire to go against free will, but before you came here, you were just thinking that when you show them there is a way out of misery, they will want to follow that way. You realize, as a shock, that there are certain beings, the fallen beings, and not only do they *not* want to change but they will attempt to destroy you. In some cases, you can deal with this, but what you also realize is that the vast majority of the people on this planet, they do not want to destroy you, they just do not want to have anything to do with you. They do not want to listen to you, they do not want to change.

When you experience this, it is so easy for us (and we have all done it) to somehow make a decision (whatever it is for us individually) that: "I shouldn't have come here, this was a mistake, there is nothing I can do here, there is no point for me being here, I can't change the fallen beings, I can't even change the human beings because they don't want to change, they don't want to overcome their suffering, they don't even want to listen to me. They actually don't want me here."

It gives you a sense of deep frustration. Why am I here? What am I doing here? In the moment where you experience this frustration full force, that is when you make some kind of decision about how you will approach life from now on. It can be, again, very individual how you formulate this in words and that is why you need to discover it individually. As a general example, you may make a decision that: "I will not interfere with people's free will." Or: "I will never force anyone. I will never make decisions that affect other people because I do not want to force anyone." Or: "I will not challenge the fallen beings." Or you may make the decision, as is described in the book, that you will fight the fallen beings; or the decision that you want to understand the fallen beings and why they are reacting the way they do.

## Being born again in Christ

This creates a self that now colors how you see yourself as a being on earth. This is the last self, the primal self, that you can let go of, but you *can* let go of it. You can let go of it in increments. You can come to the point where you let this self die and then you are reborn into a new sense of identity based on the understanding you now have and based on establishing some contact with your I AM Presence. Therefore, you can be born again in Christ because this is not the outer fear-based self that is in reaction to earth. It is a self in reaction to or as an extension of your I AM Presence, the individuality of your I AM Presence and the Christ reality that you are a spiritual being, a pure awareness that cannot be affected or changed by anything on earth.

Then, it is possible to overcome this primal self and be reborn into a sense of identity where you look at life on earth as a positive thing. You now have a positive view, a positive goal, a positive sense. It does not mean that you have a problem you absolutely have to solve. You realize there is a meaning in being here because just in being here, you are shining a light in the darkness. You are giving people an example that there is an alternative to the duality consciousness, an alternative to suffering, an alternative to this agitated state of mind that everyone is in.

## When the abnormal becomes normal

It is perfectly true that everyone on earth is unhappy and dissatisfied and agitated. It is just that in order to be able to function, there can come a point where a state of imbalance becomes seen as normal. That is why communism survived for as long as it did. Most people accepted that this is normal so they could live with it and then they can function that way. It does not mean they are happy about it. It does not mean they are growing but they can function. Of course, you have done the same: created some kind of norm that allows you to function. You have found a way to live here on earth so that you avoid situations that stir up the feeling you had when you received that original birth trauma.

It is almost like you have found a way to put the primal self to sleep, put it in a coma, because you have learned to create outer situations that do not stir it up. You can actually live this way for several lifetimes and you may make progress by getting rid of some of the outer selves but you are never really touching that primal self. There are examples of people who are ascended master students, who have followed an ascended master teaching for decades, and they have made some progress but they have not even started to look at the primal self.

Again, this is not necessarily wrong. You cannot look at it until you are ready for it. There comes that point where, if you do not start looking at the primal self, you will actually stagnate. You will not grow, potentially for the rest of that lifetime, because there is that sense in you that there is something here that you do not want to touch, you do not want to deal with it—this is too much.

## The shift in identification

You can have the sense that you know you have let go of many other selves and it has not been a problem. *This* self you do not feel you can let go of because you feel that if you do, you will die. *You* will die. My beloved, it is true. You *will* die. The "you" through which you look at yourself as a being on earth, *that* self will die. It does not mean that the real you will die because you will be reborn into a new self that you must gradually create, of course. You see that we are perfectly aware, my beloved, that what we are asking you to do here (in these latest teachings about the birth trauma and your sojourn on earth) is a very, very complicated task. It cannot be done with a snap of your fingers. It will take a long time, maybe years, maybe decades because you are gradually breaking down the old self and you are at the same time creating a new.

It is a complicated task, but it is a task that can be done and that you are already in the process of doing. What I am describing here may sound very dramatic but it is not quite that dramatic. As you are walking the path, as you are giving up some of the more superficial selves, you are also creating a new sense of self based on a positive view, based on your understanding of the teachings. It is not that you have to completely break down the primal self and then that dies and you have nothing—and then you can start building a new self. That is not the way it works. You are breaking down the old and building the new at the same time.

What is it that can bring a shift to you? Well, it is simply this. I am not saying all of you can do this right now, but there comes that point where you have broken down most of the primal self. You have created a new self, but there is a point in your being where you are still identified with the primal self. You are still looking at life on earth through that primal self. When I talk about letting the primal self die, it is when you finally come to that point where you see it, you see the self and then you can let it go. You can let the primal self die. *That* is when I say you are reborn.

What actually happens is that the focus of your identity, the center of your identity, shifts from the primal self to the new self you have been building. Suddenly, you snap out of this negative view of earth and life on earth and now you are seeing life through the positive. You are seeing yourself through the positive. You do not anymore have a negative view of what you can or cannot do on earth, why you are here and that you were stupid for coming here—this and that. It is gone. It is dead.

## When death becomes your ally

You understand, my beloved, that there is a quote in the scriptures that the last enemy that shall be conquered is death. It does not mean physical death. You are all spiritual people, you all recognize that you have lived before so you have experienced many times that the physical body dies but you go on. Bodies may come, bodies may go but *I* go on forever. What happens here is not that *you* die (not that the real you dies) but there is a "you," a self that literally dies. This self, of course, will resist dying. It does not have self-awareness but it has enough consciousness that it will resist dying. It will project upon you, of course, that *you* will die when *it* dies. That is why you have to come to this point where you reconsider your view of death. Is death really an enemy?

When you recognize that the core of your identity is your I AM Presence, which is in the spiritual realm, a realm that is beyond time and space, you know that your I AM Presence cannot die. We have told you many times that the Conscious You is an extension of the Presence and it cannot die. When you begin to connect to that sense of pure awareness (the sense that you are more than the outer self, that you are more than anything on earth), you can make that switch where you realize that you cannot die. It is only your sense of "you," your sense of self, your sense of who you are that can die. Since your sense of self is limited, is the death of this self really a loss for you? Or is it a gain for you because now the negative view of yourself dies, and you are reborn into a positive view? You are, in other words, more free after the self has died.

What does it mean to conquer death as the last enemy? It means to recognize that death is not your *enemy*. Death is your *friend*. Death is a tool for letting the limited self die and gaining freedom from that. Naturally, most people resist death because they are so identified with their bodies, and even the body has a certain awareness, the survival instinct as it is called, that causes it to resist death. You know that you will not die when the separate self dies. We are not here talking about physical death. Certainly, this is not a suicide cult. My beloved, we are talking about coming to the point where instead of fearing death, the death of the separate self and resisting it, you are letting it happen. You are welcoming it because you realize that you will be more free after the death of this separate self. *That* is the true meaning of the resurrection.

## The true resurrection

The resurrection is not really a bodily resurrection, as some Christians have started to fantasize about. It is primarily a spiritual initiation. It is what you saw in the situation where I was hanging on the cross and I first called out:

"My God, my God, why have you forsaken me?" Why did I do this? It was because up until that point, I had a certain self where I thought that God would somehow create a miracle, send angels to rescue me so that I would not have to die on the cross. Then I am hanging there and I am realizing this was an illusion. It was a separate self that had this illusion. It was actually the separate self that I had built as a result of my birth trauma. It was my primal separate self.

Before I came to my first embodiment on earth, I was very aware that I can of my own self do nothing. I was very aware that someone needed to take embodiment on earth in order to be an open door for the power of God to work in the material realm on this planet. I volunteered to do this, but I also had an expectation I had built that when I did something for God, then God would prevent something really bad from happening to me. Therefore, when things were really bad, God would come and save me through some kind of miracle.

This was the self that I built, this was the self I had when I descended into embodiment. Then, when I received my birth trauma, I actually realized that this would not happen. God would not save me through a miracle from this very difficult situation I faced that led to my original birth trauma. I reacted to this by creating a primal self that could explain why God had not saved me in that situation. At the same time, I would not really accept the reality of free will and that God cannot interfere with free will and therefore in some cases cannot save me. I would not accept this so I still had the expectation that if I really, really needed it, then God would save me.

My primal self had to believe that, well in *that* situation, even though it was very traumatic for me, I did not really need to be saved because I could deal with this. But if there came a situation where I *really* needed it, then God would save me. Many, many years later, in my last embodiment, I am hanging on the cross physically and I suddenly am confronted with this primal self and this expectation that this is one of those situations where I really, really need it and now God will save me.

I see the reality, the full reality, of free will for the first time. I *truly* see it and I realize that God will not save me. Then, instead of creating another self to deal with this, I suddenly see that this is an unreal self. This is just a complete illusion and I see it from the outside, and that is when, as it says in the scriptures, I "give up the ghost." I give up the self that I am somehow special and therefore I am entitled to some miracle from God because I have done something for God on this earth. I give it up. I let it go and then my body dies but the real importance of this situation is that I was spiritually reborn. The separate self, the primal self, died and I was reborn. Then, I did not need to re-embody on earth. I could let go of earth. Even though I was given the dispensation to materialize a physical body, this was primarily to get the Christian movement going and to overcome certain outer desires that did not have anything to do with my primal self. The process was really that of letting one self die, and in a sense, my beloved, when you let the primal self die, you have to go through that experience where you feel *you* will die. You feel you are dying.

## Embracing death

Now, you will see, if you read some of these near-death experiences, that there are many people who have had a near-death experience in a very dangerous, traumatic situation. For a time, their survival instinct causes them to resist leaving the body. Then, there can come a point where they suddenly feel an inner peace and now they just let go of the body and say: "Come what may." In that surrender, they then leave the body. Then, they have an out-of-body experience, come back into the body to tell the story. You can actually come to a point where you have identified the primal self, you know it needs to die, you know the time is there now. Then, instead of resisting the death of the primal self, you submit to it. You surrender to it. You feel at peace and you say: "Let it die; come what may" or "Not my will but thine be done."

You just allow it and you allow yourself to go through this process that can feel like death, like you are letting go of something. It is because you *are* letting go. Of course, you experience that after you have let go of this separate self, you have not disappeared, you still have self-awareness. *That* is when you can then shift your identity to the new self, to the self that is built in Christ and you become, as Paul expressed it, "a new being in Christ."

Not all of you can do this in an instant. I am not asking you to do it as a result of hearing or reading this dictation. I am asking you to contemplate the process, be aware of the process. When you come to that point where you are ready because you have demolished most of your primal self, you have built a new self and it is really not such a dramatic thing anymore (it is just a matter of making that shift in consciousness where you take the focus of your identity away from the primal self onto the new self), then

·you do not resist the process. You sense: "Oh, I'm ready" and you just let go. You embrace death. You embrace the death of the primal self. You embrace death as your friend. You stop fighting it. You stop resenting or resisting it. You embrace it, not as a death but as a rebirth, as a new beginning.

## Fulfilling your reason for coming to earth

*That,* my beloved, is when you can actually start fulfilling your original reason for coming to earth. You are not doing it by doing anything, by changing anything, by changing other people. You are fulfilling your reason just by being who you are and radiating the light, the being, the consciousness, the matrices of your individuality. There is no specific problem you have to solve or goal you have to accomplish. You realize that just being here is doing what you came here to do. You feel fulfilled in this because being who you are is not in any way dependent on the choices of other people. You do not need to change the choices of other people in order to be who you are.

You recognize, perhaps, that what did the primal self do? What is the core belief of the primal self? It is, my beloved, that being yourself, being who you are, is not good enough. Or it is wrong on this planet. It is not welcomed on this planet. In other words, before you came here, you expected that by just coming here and being who you were, people would embrace this. Then, you recognized that neither the fallen beings nor most people will embrace you, welcome you, accept you. You decided that apparently you are not allowed or you are not supposed to be who you are on this planet. Or it is not enough to be who you are.

In a sense, everything that you have done, everything that has happened to you since that birth trauma, you have suppressed being who you are. This is what you can reclaim, and when you reclaim it, you will have an impact on the planet. You will be non-attached to what that impact is because you are not being who you are in order to change anything on earth. You are being who you are because this is what gives you the greatest sense of joy and fulfillment.

You recognize that the greatest joy you can have on earth is being who you are in the face of all the conditions that are on this planet. You can stand there and be untouched by all of this, like the Buddha under the Bo tree, facing the demons of Mara, tempting him to react to them in some way. You can look at the circus on earth, you can look at the demons of Mara, without reacting. You are still shining your light, still functioning in your normal daily life, interacting with other people, going to work, raising your children, whatever. You are feeling that flow, that joy, that you are expressing who you are in everything you do. Suddenly, the barrier between spiritual activities and non-spiritual activities has become meaningless for everything is a spiritual activity.

Everything is an expression of who you are. Everything gives you a sense of joy and fulfillment, there is no right or wrong or this or that. This is how you can really have a maximum impact on this planet because this will pull up on the collective consciousness. It will shock people, those who are open for it, into realizing there is an alternative to what they see as normal human life

Again, you are not attached to what other people do or do not do. You are not attached to it. You are just focused on being who you are and enjoying this. Then, you have the attitude that whatever happens, just "Come what may." You have no intent, you have no outer will. You are just allowing life to unfold. *That* is, as we have said before, being in the River of life. *That* is flowing with the River of Life. My beloved, that is truly demonstrating Christhood. It may not seem as dramatic as what many Christians or even ascended master students have come up with, namely that you are supposed to do all of these miracles or do all of these other visible manifestations.

My beloved, a very important, a very high, aspect of Christhood (and there are, of course, several) is to be able to engage in everyday life with a completely positive attitude and view of life. Is this not demonstrating Christhood, my beloved? Truly, it *is*.

It is not what I did in my last embodiment, I grant you. But did I not say that you should do greater works than I did? This is an example of the greater works that I did not have the mastery to do 2,000 years ago—you see.

# 24 | INVOKING FREEDOM FROM MY PRIMAL SELF

In the name I AM THAT I AM, Jesus Christ, I call to all representatives of the Divine Mother, especially Jesus, to help me overcome my primal self. Help me see how my primal self colors the way I look at life, including…

[Make personal calls.]

*Part 1*

1. Jesus, help me reconnect to the trauma I received when I first came into embodiment on earth. Help me see that I created a separate self in order to deal with this trauma.

> O Jesus, blessed brother mine,
> I walk the path that you outline,
> a great example to us all,
> I follow now your inner call.

**O Jesus, let the Fire of Joy,**
**consume the devil's subtle ploy,**
**transfigured is our planet earth,**
**the golden age is given birth.**

2. Jesus, help me see that the primal self is such a deep sense of self that most people cannot see it. It is so ingrained, it is so deep, it is so subtle that we take it for granted. We think this is the only way to experience life on earth.

O Jesus, open inner sight,
the ego wants to prove it's right,
but this I will no longer do,
I want to be all one with you.

**O Jesus, let the Fire of Joy,**
**consume the devil's subtle ploy,**
**transfigured is our planet earth,**
**the golden age is given birth.**

3. Jesus, help me see that my primal self is just like any of the other selves I have already overcome. It is based on an illusion and the way to overcome it is to identify that there is an outer self and then to make the choice that I no longer want to carry this with me.

O Jesus, I now clearly see,
the Key of Knowledge given me,
my Christ self I hereby embrace,
as you fill up my inner space.

**O Jesus, let the Fire of Joy,**
**consume the devil's subtle ploy,**
**transfigured is our planet earth,**
**the golden age is given birth.**

4. Jesus, help me gain a greater awareness of the primal self so that I can begin to separate myself from it. Help me begin to see the self from the outside instead of seeing life through that self, from inside the self.

O Jesus, show me serpent's lie,
expose the beam in my own eye,
as Christ discernment you me give,
in oneness I forever live.

**O Jesus, let the Fire of Joy,
consume the devil's subtle ploy,
transfigured is our planet earth,
the golden age is given birth.**

5. Jesus, help me make the shift where I realize that my primal self is not the real me. It is a self that was created in response to a very difficult, very traumatic, situation that I encountered on earth. I did not bring it with me when I came here.

O Jesus, I am truly meek,
and thus I turn the other cheek,
when the accuser attacks me,
I go within and merge with thee.

**O Jesus, let the Fire of Joy,
consume the devil's subtle ploy,
transfigured is our planet earth,
the golden age is given birth.**

6. Jesus, help me see that my primal self was created for a specific purpose, with a specific view. Therefore, the self has a built-in problem and when I am looking from inside the self, it seems like I must solve it.

O Jesus, ego I let die,
surrender ev'ry earthly tie,
the dead can bury what is dead,
I choose to walk with you instead.

**O Jesus, let the Fire of Joy,
consume the devil's subtle ploy,
transfigured is our planet earth,
the golden age is given birth.**

7. Jesus, help me see that solving the problem is not the way to overcome the primal self. Even if I solved the problem that the self projects, I would not automatically overcome the outer self.

> O Jesus, help me rise above,
> the devil's test through higher love,
> show me separate self unreal,
> my formless self you do reveal.

> **O Jesus, let the Fire of Joy,**
> **consume the devil's subtle ploy,**
> **transfigured is our planet earth,**
> **the golden age is given birth.**

8. Jesus, help me begin to see that I will *not* overcome the primal self by solving the problem or changing the condition that the primal self was created in reaction to.

> O Jesus, what is that to me,
> I just let go and follow thee,
> with this I do pass ev'ry test,
> to find with you eternal rest.

> **O Jesus, let the Fire of Joy,**
> **consume the devil's subtle ploy,**
> **transfigured is our planet earth,**
> **the golden age is given birth.**

9. Jesus, help me see that I will overcome the primal self only by recognizing that it is a separate self, that it is based on an illusion and that there is no problem to solve. I need to resolve the mechanism in me that makes me think that my life on this planet, my sense of self and my exit from this planet depends on any condition here.

> O Jesus, fiery master mine,
> my heart now melting into thine,
> I love with heart and mind and soul,
> the God who is my highest goal.

**O Jesus, let the Fire of Joy,**
**consume the devil's subtle ploy,**
**transfigured is our planet earth,**
**the golden age is given birth.**

## Part 2

1. Jesus, help me see if I have created a primal self that feels rejected by the fallen beings. Help me see if my primal self has a general unhappiness about life, feels disappointed and shocked about conditions here, feels powerless to change anything and therefore makes me feel it was a mistake for me to come here.

O Jesus, blessed brother mine,
I walk the path that you outline,
a great example to us all,
I follow now your inner call.

**O Jesus, let the Fire of Joy,**
**consume the devil's subtle ploy,**
**transfigured is our planet earth,**
**the golden age is given birth.**

2. Jesus, help me see what my primal self is, what is the core of it, what is the reaction, what is the belief behind it. Help me recognize that the primal self has given me a certain primal feeling, a primal sense of what earth and life on earth is like.

O Jesus, open inner sight,
the ego wants to prove it's right,
but this I will no longer do,
I want to be all one with you.

**O Jesus, let the Fire of Joy,**
**consume the devil's subtle ploy,**
**transfigured is our planet earth,**
**the golden age is given birth.**

3. Jesus, help me identify what is the feeling and belief so I can see the decision I made when I was exposed to the birth trauma, the decision that: "I never want to experience this again."

> O Jesus, I now clearly see,
> the Key of Knowledge given me,
> my Christ self I hereby embrace,
> as you fill up my inner space.

> **O Jesus, let the Fire of Joy,**
> **consume the devil's subtle ploy,**
> **transfigured is our planet earth,**
> **the golden age is given birth.**

4. Jesus, help me see what I did not want to experience again. Help me see the decision I made about what I *could* do or what I *would* do from that point on here on earth—how I would approach life.

> O Jesus, show me serpent's lie,
> expose the beam in my own eye,
> as Christ discernment you me give,
> in oneness I forever live.

> **O Jesus, let the Fire of Joy,**
> **consume the devil's subtle ploy,**
> **transfigured is our planet earth,**
> **the golden age is given birth.**

5. Jesus, help me see that the birth trauma shocked me so much that I felt that the original mission I had for coming here could not be fulfilled. I felt that coming here was a mistake because I could not make a difference, I could not change anything on earth.

> O Jesus, I am truly meek,
> and thus I turn the other cheek,
> when the accuser attacks me,
> I go within and merge with thee.

**O Jesus, let the Fire of Joy,**
**consume the devil's subtle ploy,**
**transfigured is our planet earth,**
**the golden age is given birth.**

6. Jesus, help me see that I came here with the best of intentions. I *assumed* that if people are suffering, they want to overcome the suffering. When I came down here, I experienced the absolute, unchanging reality of free will. I realized that even though I knew how to overcome human problems and limitations, there was nothing I could do about it because people were not responding.

O Jesus, ego I let die,
surrender ev'ry earthly tie,
the dead can bury what is dead,
I choose to walk with you instead.

**O Jesus, let the Fire of Joy,**
**consume the devil's subtle ploy,**
**transfigured is our planet earth,**
**the golden age is given birth.**

7. Jesus, help me see how it was a great shock to me that there are certain beings, the fallen beings, who do not want to change and who will attempt to destroy me.

O Jesus, help me rise above,
the devil's test through higher love,
show me separate self unreal,
my formless self you do reveal.

**O Jesus, let the Fire of Joy,**
**consume the devil's subtle ploy,**
**transfigured is our planet earth,**
**the golden age is given birth.**

8. Jesus, help me see if this caused me to make a decision that: "I shouldn't have come here, this was a mistake, there is nothing I can do here, there is no point for me being here, I can't change the fallen beings, I can't even change the human beings because they don't want to change, they don't want to overcome their suffering, they don't even want to listen to me. They actually don't want me here."

O Jesus, what is that to me,
I just let go and follow thee,
with this I do pass ev'ry test,
to find with you eternal rest.

**O Jesus, let the Fire of Joy,
consume the devil's subtle ploy,
transfigured is our planet earth,
the golden age is given birth.**

9. Jesus, help me see how this gave me a sense of deep frustration. In the moment when I experienced this frustration full force, I made a decision about how I would approach life from then on.

O Jesus, fiery master mine,
my heart now melting into thine,
I love with heart and mind and soul,
the God who is my highest goal.

**O Jesus, let the Fire of Joy,
consume the devil's subtle ploy,
transfigured is our planet earth,
the golden age is given birth.**

## Part 3

1. Jesus, help me see if I made the decision that: "I will not interfere with people's free will." Or: "I will never force anyone. I will never make decisions that affect other people because I do not want to force anyone." Or: "I will not challenge the fallen beings."

O Jesus, blessed brother mine,
I walk the path that you outline,
a great example to us all,
I follow now your inner call.

**O Jesus, let the Fire of Joy,**
**consume the devil's subtle ploy,**
**transfigured is our planet earth,**
**the golden age is given birth.**

2. Jesus, help me see if I made the decision that I will fight the fallen beings; or the decision that I want to understand the fallen beings and why they are reacting the way they do.

O Jesus, open inner sight,
the ego wants to prove it's right,
but this I will no longer do,
I want to be all one with you.

**O Jesus, let the Fire of Joy,**
**consume the devil's subtle ploy,**
**transfigured is our planet earth,**
**the golden age is given birth.**

3. Jesus, help me see that such decisions create a self that now colors how I see myself as a being on earth. This is the last self that I can let go of, but I *can* let go of it. I can let go of it in increments.

O Jesus, I now clearly see,
the Key of Knowledge given me,
my Christ self I hereby embrace,
as you fill up my inner space.

**O Jesus, let the Fire of Joy,**
**consume the devil's subtle ploy,**
**transfigured is our planet earth,**
**the golden age is given birth.**

4. Jesus, help me see that I can come to the point where I let the primal self die. Then, I am reborn into a new sense of identity based on the understanding I now have and based on establishing contact with my I AM Presence.

O Jesus, show me serpent's lie,
expose the beam in my own eye,
as Christ discernment you me give,
in oneness I forever live.

**O Jesus, let the Fire of Joy,**
**consume the devil's subtle ploy,**
**transfigured is our planet earth,**
**the golden age is given birth.**

5. Jesus, help me see that I can be born again in Christ, creating a self that is not the outer fear-based self that is in reaction to earth. It is a self in reaction to or as an extension of my I AM Presence. It is based on the Christ reality that I am a spiritual being, and as pure awareness I cannot be affected or changed by anything on earth.

O Jesus, I am truly meek,
and thus I turn the other cheek,
when the accuser attacks me,
I go within and merge with thee.

**O Jesus, let the Fire of Joy,**
**consume the devil's subtle ploy,**
**transfigured is our planet earth,**
**the golden age is given birth.**

6. Jesus, help me see that it is possible to overcome the primal self and be reborn into a sense of identity where I look at life on earth as a positive thing. I now have a positive view, a positive goal, a positive sense. I no longer have a problem I absolutely have to solve.

O Jesus, ego I let die,
surrender ev'ry earthly tie,

the dead can bury what is dead,
I choose to walk with you instead.

**O Jesus, let the Fire of Joy,
consume the devil's subtle ploy,
transfigured is our planet earth,
the golden age is given birth.**

7. Jesus, help me see if I have created some kind of norm that allows me to function. Help me see if I have found a way to live here on earth so that I avoid situations that stir up the feeling I had when I received my original birth trauma.

O Jesus, help me rise above,
the devil's test through higher love,
show me separate self unreal,
my formless self you do reveal.

**O Jesus, let the Fire of Joy,
consume the devil's subtle ploy,
transfigured is our planet earth,
the golden age is given birth.**

8. Jesus, help me see if I have found a way to put the primal self to sleep because I have learned to create outer situations that do not stir it up. Help me see that this does not bring me closer to being free of the primal self.

O Jesus, what is that to me,
I just let go and follow thee,
with this I do pass ev'ry test,
to find with you eternal rest.

**O Jesus, let the Fire of Joy,
consume the devil's subtle ploy,
transfigured is our planet earth,
the golden age is given birth.**

9. Jesus, help me come to the point where I am ready to look at the primal self because I have overcome the sense that there is something in me that I do not want to deal with because it is too much.

> O Jesus, fiery master mine,
> my heart now melting into thine,
> I love with heart and mind and soul,
> the God who is my highest goal.

> **O Jesus, let the Fire of Joy,**
> **consume the devil's subtle ploy,**
> **transfigured is our planet earth,**
> **the golden age is given birth.**

## Part 4

1. Jesus, help me see that I feel that if I let go of the primal self, I will die. Help me see that it is only the "me" through which I look at myself as a being on earth that will die.

> O Jesus, blessed brother mine,
> I walk the path that you outline,
> a great example to us all,
> I follow now your inner call.

> **O Jesus, let the Fire of Joy,**
> **consume the devil's subtle ploy,**
> **transfigured is our planet earth,**
> **the golden age is given birth.**

2. Jesus, help me come to the point where I have broken down most of the primal self and I have created a new self. Help me see the primal self and let it go. Help me let the primal self die.

> O Jesus, open inner sight,
> the ego wants to prove it's right,

but this I will no longer do,
I want to be all one with you.

**O Jesus, let the Fire of Joy,**
**consume the devil's subtle ploy,**
**transfigured is our planet earth,**
**the golden age is given birth.**

3. Jesus, help me shift the focus of my identity from the primal self to the new self I have been building. Help me snap out of the negative view of life and see life through the positive. Help me let the negative self die.

O Jesus, I now clearly see,
the Key of Knowledge given me,
my Christ self I hereby embrace,
as you fill up my inner space.

**O Jesus, let the Fire of Joy,**
**consume the devil's subtle ploy,**
**transfigured is our planet earth,**
**the golden age is given birth.**

4. Jesus, help me see that what happens is not that the real me dies but there is a "me," a self that literally dies. This self will resist dying. It will project upon me that *I* will die when it dies. Help me reconsider my view of death as an enemy.

O Jesus, show me serpent's lie,
expose the beam in my own eye,
as Christ discernment you me give,
in oneness I forever live.

**O Jesus, let the Fire of Joy,**
**consume the devil's subtle ploy,**
**transfigured is our planet earth,**
**the golden age is given birth.**

5. Jesus, help me recognize that the core of my identity is my I AM Presence, which is in the spiritual realm. Therefore, my I AM Presence cannot die and since the Conscious You is an extension of the Presence, it cannot die either.

> O Jesus, I am truly meek,
> and thus I turn the other cheek,
> when the accuser attacks me,
> I go within and merge with thee.

> **O Jesus, let the Fire of Joy,**
> **consume the devil's subtle ploy,**
> **transfigured is our planet earth,**
> **the golden age is given birth.**

6. Jesus, help me connect to the sense of pure awareness, the sense that I am more than the outer self, I am more than anything on earth. Help me make the switch and realize that I cannot die.

> O Jesus, ego I let die,
> surrender ev'ry earthly tie,
> the dead can bury what is dead,
> I choose to walk with you instead.

> **O Jesus, let the Fire of Joy,**
> **consume the devil's subtle ploy,**
> **transfigured is our planet earth,**
> **the golden age is given birth.**

7. Jesus, help me see that it is only my sense of "me," my sense of self, my sense of who I am that can die. My sense of self is limited so the death of this self is not a loss for me. It is a gain because now the negative view of myself dies, and I am reborn into a positive view.

> O Jesus, help me rise above,
> the devil's test through higher love,
> show me separate self unreal,
> my formless self you do reveal.

**O Jesus, let the Fire of Joy,**
**consume the devil's subtle ploy,**
**transfigured is our planet earth,**
**the golden age is given birth.**

8. Jesus, help me see that conquering death as the last enemy means to recognize that death is not my enemy. Death is my friend. Death is a tool for letting the limited self die and gaining freedom from that self.

O Jesus, what is that to me,
I just let go and follow thee,
with this I do pass ev'ry test,
to find with you eternal rest.

**O Jesus, let the Fire of Joy,**
**consume the devil's subtle ploy,**
**transfigured is our planet earth,**
**the golden age is given birth.**

9. Jesus, help me come to the point where instead of fearing the death of the separate self and resisting it, I am letting it happen. I am welcoming it because I realize that I will be more free after the death of this separate self. *This* is the true meaning of the resurrection.

O Jesus, fiery master mine,
my heart now melting into thine,
I love with heart and mind and soul,
the God who is my highest goal.

**O Jesus, let the Fire of Joy,**
**consume the devil's subtle ploy,**
**transfigured is our planet earth,**
**the golden age is given birth.**

*Part 5*

1. Jesus, help me see that the resurrection is not a bodily resurrection. It is a spiritual initiation of letting go of the primal self in order to be spiritually reborn.

> O Jesus, blessed brother mine,
> I walk the path that you outline,
> a great example to us all,
> I follow now your inner call.
>
> **O Jesus, let the Fire of Joy,**
> **consume the devil's subtle ploy,**
> **transfigured is our planet earth,**
> **the golden age is given birth.**

2. Jesus, help me see that before I came into my first embodiment on earth, I was aware that someone needed to take embodiment on earth in order to be an open door for the power of God. I volunteered to do this, but I also had an expectation that when I did something for God, then God would prevent something really bad from happening to me.

> O Jesus, open inner sight,
> the ego wants to prove it's right,
> but this I will no longer do,
> I want to be all one with you.
>
> **O Jesus, let the Fire of Joy,**
> **consume the devil's subtle ploy,**
> **transfigured is our planet earth,**
> **the golden age is given birth.**

3. Jesus, help me see that when I received my birth trauma, I realized that this would not happen. God would not save me through a miracle from this very difficult situation. I reacted to this by creating a primal self that could explain why God had not saved me in that situation.

O Jesus, I now clearly see,
the Key of Knowledge given me,
my Christ self I hereby embrace,
as you fill up my inner space.

**O Jesus, let the Fire of Joy,**
**consume the devil's subtle ploy,**
**transfigured is our planet earth,**
**the golden age is given birth.**

4. Jesus, help me see the full reality of free will and that God will not save me. Then, instead of creating another self to deal with this, I see that this is an unreal self. This is just a complete illusion and I see it from the outside, and that is when I "give up the ghost."

O Jesus, show me serpent's lie,
expose the beam in my own eye,
as Christ discernment you me give,
in oneness I forever live.

**O Jesus, let the Fire of Joy,**
**consume the devil's subtle ploy,**
**transfigured is our planet earth,**
**the golden age is given birth.**

5. Jesus, I give up the self that I am somehow special and therefore I am entitled to some miracle from God because I have done something for God on this earth. I give it up. I let it go and then I am spiritually reborn.

O Jesus, I am truly meek,
and thus I turn the other cheek,
when the accuser attacks me,
I go within and merge with thee.

**O Jesus, let the Fire of Joy,**
**consume the devil's subtle ploy,**
**transfigured is our planet earth,**
**the golden age is given birth.**

6. Jesus, help me accept that when I let the primal self die, I have to go through the experience where I feel I will die. I feel I am dying, but I will not disappear.

> O Jesus, ego I let die,
> surrender ev'ry earthly tie,
> the dead can bury what is dead,
> I choose to walk with you instead.

> **O Jesus, let the Fire of Joy,**
> **consume the devil's subtle ploy,**
> **transfigured is our planet earth,**
> **the golden age is given birth.**

7. Jesus, help me come to the point where I have identified the primal self, I know it needs to die, I know the time is there now and then, instead of resisting the death of the primal self, I submit to it. I surrender to it. I feel at peace and I say: "Let it die; come what may. Not my will but thine be done."

> O Jesus, help me rise above,
> the devil's test through higher love,
> show me separate self unreal,
> my formless self you do reveal.

> **O Jesus, let the Fire of Joy,**
> **consume the devil's subtle ploy,**
> **transfigured is our planet earth,**
> **the golden age is given birth.**

8. Jesus, help me go through this process even though it can feel like death. Help me shift my identity to the new self, to the self that is built in Christ so I become "a new being in Christ."

> O Jesus, what is that to me,
> I just let go and follow thee,
> with this I do pass ev'ry test,
> to find with you eternal rest.

**O Jesus, let the Fire of Joy,**
**consume the devil's subtle ploy,**
**transfigured is our planet earth,**
**the golden age is given birth.**

9. Jesus, help me come to the point where I have demolished most of my primal self, I have built a new self, and it is really not such a dramatic thing anymore to let the primal self die.

O Jesus, fiery master mine,
my heart now melting into thine,
I love with heart and mind and soul,
the God who is my highest goal.

**O Jesus, let the Fire of Joy,**
**consume the devil's subtle ploy,**
**transfigured is our planet earth,**
**the golden age is given birth.**

## Part 6

1. Jesus, help me embrace death, the death of the primal self. Help me embrace death as my friend and stop fighting it, stop resenting or resisting it. Help me embrace it, not as a death but as a rebirth, as a new beginning.

O Jesus, blessed brother mine,
I walk the path that you outline,
a great example to us all,
I follow now your inner call.

**O Jesus, let the Fire of Joy,**
**consume the devil's subtle ploy,**
**transfigured is our planet earth,**
**the golden age is given birth.**

2. Jesus, help me see that there is no specific problem I have to solve or goal I have to accomplish. Just being here is doing what I came here to do. Being who I am is not dependent on the choices of other people. I do not need to change the choices of other people in order to be who I am.

> O Jesus, open inner sight,
> the ego wants to prove it's right,
> but this I will no longer do,
> I want to be all one with you.

> **O Jesus, let the Fire of Joy,**
> **consume the devil's subtle ploy,**
> **transfigured is our planet earth,**
> **the golden age is given birth.**

3. Jesus, help me see that the core belief of the primal self is that being myself, being who I am, is not good enough or is wrong. It is not welcomed on this planet.

> O Jesus, I now clearly see,
> the Key of Knowledge given me,
> my Christ self I hereby embrace,
> as you fill up my inner space.

> **O Jesus, let the Fire of Joy,**
> **consume the devil's subtle ploy,**
> **transfigured is our planet earth,**
> **the golden age is given birth.**

4. Jesus, help me see that before I came here, I expected that people would embrace me. When I recognized that neither the fallen beings nor most people will embrace me, I decided that I am not allowed to be who I am on this planet. It is not enough to be who I am.

> O Jesus, show me serpent's lie,
> expose the beam in my own eye,
> as Christ discernment you me give,
> in oneness I forever live.

**O Jesus, let the Fire of Joy,**
**consume the devil's subtle ploy,**
**transfigured is our planet earth,**
**the golden age is given birth.**

5. Jesus, help me see that since my birth trauma, I have suppressed being who I am. Help me reclaim this and be non-attached to what impact I have on the planet because I am not being who I am in order to change anything on earth. I am being who I am because this is what gives me the greatest sense of joy and fulfillment.

O Jesus, I am truly meek,
and thus I turn the other cheek,
when the accuser attacks me,
I go within and merge with thee.

**O Jesus, let the Fire of Joy,**
**consume the devil's subtle ploy,**
**transfigured is our planet earth,**
**the golden age is given birth.**

6. Jesus, help me recognize that the greatest joy I can have on earth is being who I am in the face of all the conditions that are on this planet. I can stand there and be untouched by all of this, like the Buddha under the Bo tree, facing the demons of Mara, tempting him to react to them in some way.

O Jesus, ego I let die,
surrender ev'ry earthly tie,
the dead can bury what is dead,
I choose to walk with you instead.

**O Jesus, let the Fire of Joy,**
**consume the devil's subtle ploy,**
**transfigured is our planet earth,**
**the golden age is given birth.**

7. Jesus, help me look at the circus on earth, look at the demons of Mara, without reacting. I am shining my light, still functioning in my normal life, interacting with other people. I am feeling the flow, the joy, that I am expressing who I am in everything I do. The barrier between spiritual activities and non-spiritual activities has become meaningless for everything is a spiritual activity.

> O Jesus, help me rise above,
> the devil's test through higher love,
> show me separate self unreal,
> my formless self you do reveal.

> **O Jesus, let the Fire of Joy,**
> **consume the devil's subtle ploy,**
> **transfigured is our planet earth,**
> **the golden age is given birth.**

8. Jesus, help me focus on being who I am with the attitude that whatever happens just "Come what may." I have no intent, I have no outer will. I am allowing life to unfold. *That* is being in the River of life. *That* is flowing with the River of Life.

> O Jesus, what is that to me,
> I just let go and follow thee,
> with this I do pass ev'ry test,
> to find with you eternal rest.

> **O Jesus, let the Fire of Joy,**
> **consume the devil's subtle ploy,**
> **transfigured is our planet earth,**
> **the golden age is given birth.**

9. Jesus, help me express the aspect of Christhood where I am able to engage in everyday life with a completely positive attitude and view of life.

> O Jesus, fiery master mine,
> my heart now melting into thine,
> I love with heart and mind and soul,
> the God who is my highest goal.

**O Jesus, let the Fire of Joy,**
**consume the devil's subtle ploy,**
**transfigured is our planet earth,**
**the golden age is given birth.**

## *Sealing*

In the name of the Divine Mother, I call to Mother Mary for the sealing of myself and all people in my circle of influence in the creative flow of the Divine Mother, the River of Life. I call for the multiplication of my calls by all representatives of the Divine Mother, so that we form the perfect figure-eight flow of "As Above, so below." Thus, I accept that this is fully manifest, because the mouth of the Lord, the Divine Mother that I AM, has spoken it. Amen.

# 25 | FEELING GOOD

# ABOUT BEING ON EARTH

I AM the Ascended Master Gautama Buddha and in the joy of the Buddha, I Am. Many may not have associated the Buddha with joy, seeing him as being more serious, sitting there, seeming aloof to the world and the people of the world. Of course, my beloved, if I *were* aloof to the people of the world, would I have come out of Nirvana to minister onto them? Would I have vowed to hold the flame of the Buddha, to hold space for earth, if I *were* aloof. Certainly not, and so I am not aloof but neither am I attached. The Middle Way is to be found, not necessarily *between* these extremes but *beyond* them.

It is a very difficult balance to find on a planet as dense and as dark as earth. Certainly, those of you who have come here as avatars have faced this challenge. All of us, who have come here as avatars, have faced this challenge of how you remain *in* the world but not *of* the world. Of course, all of us have had a period where we went into immersing ourselves in the world, identifying ourselves with the world, and why did we do this? We did this as an extension of the desire that brought us here originally. We came here to affect a positive change and help the earth rise above some of the manifestations that we clearly saw were not natural and did not belong on a natural planet.

## The desire for supernatural abilities

This is what brought us here and therefore, as a result of this coming to the earth and feeling how our good intentions were rejected and put down, we then went into a reactionary pattern. In many cases, we became even more eager, even more attached, to doing something that could not be ignored, that could not be denied, either by the dark forces, the fallen beings, or by the people of earth—the original inhabitants. You see, my beloved, many of us, when we received that initial birth trauma, we built some kind of expectation that since the fallen beings and the people of earth had ignored us or put us down, we desired to have the ability, even a supernatural ability, to make some kind of manifestation that they could not ignore, that they could not deny.

You see even many spiritual people today who have this desire that somehow there should be some undeniable manifestation that would demonstrate the validity of the spiritual outlook on life and that there is a spiritual side to life. Many have a desire to attain some kind of clairvoyant or supernatural ability so they can do something that people cannot ignore, deny or explain away. Many religious people have the same desire, either for some kind of ability, speaking in tongues, healing (whatever it may be) or for the Christ to come back as some undeniable manifestation in the sky where nobody can deny that this is happening.

## Doubting God's existence

Over the ages, many people have asked: "Why doesn't God prove that he exists, why doesn't he remove the evil and darkness from the earth?" When they see that the darkness continues and God is seemingly not there and is seemingly aloof, then they begin to doubt whether there even *is* a God. This is, of course, when the fallen ones feel that they have truly accomplished some of their greatest works—when they have caused an avatar to doubt the existence of God. Truly, that is probably the lowest point you can sink to as an avatar who came here having some sense of the oneness of all life, came here in a desire to raise up all life. Now, you have come to the point where you doubt that there is any higher being, there is any higher purpose and there is any purpose for you coming here.

This is what they truly want to accomplish. They want to get us into that state, and we have all gone into it, as now several of my esteemed brothers have said. My beloved, I certainly went into it myself. I went also so low that those who have an idolatrous view of the Buddha would refuse to believe it. They would say that this cannot be the real Buddha speaking if he says that the Buddha ever went low, for surely he was born perfect. I was not born perfect, neither in my last embodiment nor in any previous embodiments. My beloved, I made the same mistakes that many of you have made.

## What if you had extra-ordinary abilities?

I also had a desire for some kind of ability that would awaken people so that they could not deny that there is a spiritual side to life. I had to overcome that in my last embodiment. Indeed, the last initiation I had to face, as I was being tempted by the demons of Mara, was to actually use the ability of the mind, that I had attained, in my reaction to the demons of Mara. As a result of attaining that level of consciousness of Buddhahood, then I actually had certain abilities that I could have used in my reaction to the demons of Mara. The thing is, my beloved, what would have been the point? What would I have accomplished? What would have been accomplished for the ongoing progression of life by demonstrating this?

You need to consider this in yourselves if you can recognize that you have this desire to have some extraordinary ability. You need to consider what would actually be accomplished if you had the ability that you sometimes imagine yourself having. If you used it, what would actually be accomplished?

First of all, you need to recognize that there are some beings, some people, who would immediately deny the manifestation, even if they saw it with their own eyes. There were people who saw Jesus walk on water or who drank the wine he had precipitated from water, and they did not believe it. They did not believe what their own senses had experienced. After the experience had passed, their intellectual, analytical minds started doubting that this had actually happened. They started doubting that this was actually a sign of some spiritual mastery on Jesus' part. They thought it was some kind of trickery. They thought it was some kind of trickery of the devil and therefore Jesus was not a true spiritual teacher, he was not the Messiah and so forth and so on. Of course, the fallen beings immediately tried to counteract this demonstration of a higher power by Jesus by making the people also believe that this was the dark forces and the devil who had tricked them or who had somehow taken over Jesus and performed these tricks.

If you transfer this to the modern age, even the materialists would immediately start doubting that this could have happened. Many of the materialists would say that even though people had seen this outer manifestation, it was simply their minds and the group mind that had tricked them into thinking they had seen this, but it was not actually real. You recognize, when you ponder this, that there is absolutely nothing that the outer mind (the carnal mind, the human mind, the intellectual, analytical, linear mind) cannot cast doubt upon.

The thing is, my beloved, you can never prove anything on a dense-matter, dense-consciousness planet as earth. Why is that? Because the primary function of a dense-matter planet is to give people an immersion experience where they can experience themselves as separate beings.

## The purpose of dense-matter planets

In order to have that experience, you cannot have the frame of reference that you have on a natural planet where you have some sense of connection to something bigger than your current sense of self, you have some sense of the oneness of all life. This is not an intellectual understanding you have on a natural planet. It is an experience, an inner – what you today would call "intuitive" – experience, but which on a natural planet is seen as a natural experience. It is as natural as you opening your eyes and seeing the sun.

You cannot have this ability in order to have the immersion experience. Those people who are in the immersion phase, they do not have any sense of the oneness of all life. *That* is precisely why they do not have a frame of reference that allows them to have any undeniable sense that there is more to life than what they experience through the separate self. They cannot see what you have seen when you awaken to the spiritual side of life. My beloved, there is *nothing* you could say, nothing you could do that would give people in the immersion phase the experience of a higher reality that you have—and that many of you have come to take for granted, for you have had it so long and it seems to be so obvious to you.

Many of you have had this inner sense of a connection to something greater in this entire lifetime. Even as children you could not understand that other people did not have it. You have later in life sometimes wondered how it could be that you could tell somebody about the spiritual side of life and it seems so obvious to you, but they could not grasp it. It did not seem obvious to them, they felt threatened by it and felt they had to reject it.

Well, you understand, my beloved, that as long as someone is in the immersion phase, they *have* to reject it. Otherwise, they could not stay immersed, stay identified with the earth and the outer self. Naturally, we all know there are many people on earth who are not voluntarily staying in that immersion phase. They have been fooled, they have been manipulated by the fallen beings into these reactionary patterns that keep them immersed.

If you look at an ideal scenario, you could say that long ago all of the original inhabitants of the earth that are still in embodiment should actually have ascended based on an ideal scenario. Nevertheless, we also recognize that because of free will, an ideal scenario is just a guideline because free will must be allowed to outplay itself. In a sense, you could say that when a planet is created, when certain lifestreams are embodying for the first time on this planet, there may be an ideal scenario for how they could grow. Because of free will, this ideal scenario is not set in stone and it is not so that the ascended masters say that if the ideal scenario is not fulfilled, then something has gone horribly wrong on this planet.

## Demonstrating an alternative

We allow people to go into whatever detour they need to go into. Of course, there does come a point where it is also valid to say that the fallen beings have had the impact of causing people to go into these reactionary patterns. People do not have an alternative to the reactionary patterns so it is valid that avatars take embodiment on a planet to demonstrate that there is such an alternative. My beloved, the entire point of what we have been telling you (including in the new book) about taking embodiment as an avatar is that you are not here to affect a particular change on this planet. You are only here to demonstrate the alternative.

This means that for those people who are not ready or who are not willing to start moving out of the immersion phase, you need to allow them to reject you and reject what you are saying. My real point for bringing this up is to build upon what Jesus has said, namely that when you came down and you received your initial birth trauma and you created that primal self (the first separate self you created), many of you did not fully grasp the reality of free will. You did not fully accept that your role was only to give an example and not to affect a particular change. You created the primal self out of this desire to affect some change, and that is what gave you this desire to have some special ability to manifest some special manifestation that people could not ignore or deny. In order to fully let go of this self, to see it as an unreal self, you need to recognize that because of free will, what you had was an inordinate, an *unlawful*, desire. You had a desire to force people to awaken for their own good.

## The what and the how

My beloved, what do the fallen beings have? They have a desire to force people *not* to awaken for *their* own good—the good of the fallen beings. What you need to recognize here is that, naturally, it is not appropriate that as an avatar you have the desire to force people to awaken for the good of the people. That is why you need to take the next step and look at this primal self you have created that has the desire to somehow force a change on earth, to somehow force people to change, force them to awaken. You need to realize that even though this is born from good intentions, it is born from what we have talked about before, namely that many people have an understanding of *what* should happen, but where they fail is that they have an unrealistic understanding or view of *how* this should happen. You came here with a correct understanding that change should happen on earth and that people should eventually be awakened. You had an unrealistic understanding of how this could be brought about, including thinking that since the fallen beings had used force to put people asleep, it was acceptable for you to use a milder kind of force to awaken them.

## A self-centered altruistic desire

Now, you need to take the next step and look at this separate self that you have created and realize that even though the separate self firmly believes, is firmly convinced, that it only wants to awaken people for their own good, the reality is that the separate self actually wants to awaken people for *your* good, for *its own* good. In other words, the desire you have to awaken people, after you created this separate self, is actually so that you feel that you could accomplish what you came to earth to accomplish but what you have not so far have been able to accomplish.

Do you see that the separate self is absolutely convinced that it is doing this for people's good, but it is actually for your own sake, for the accomplishment of the goal that you have defined? As long as you are seeing through that separate self, that primal self, you think that you want to awaken people for *their* own good but it is for *your* own "good," for your own sake, for you to feel good about having come to earth.

It is, of course, understandable, it is even "natural" we might say, that you have come to earth, you have experienced this initial trauma, you have been so shocked that you do not feel good about being here, you do not feel good about coming here. Therefore, it is natural that you have a desire to come to a point where you can feel good about being here, you can feel good about coming here. You think, as long as you have this separate self, that the only way to come to feel good about being here is to accomplish the purpose that you had in mind when you came.

What it did say in the new book, both indirectly and between the lines, is that you have to come to that point where you realize that the understanding, the awareness you had before you came here was not the highest awareness. Surely, you were in a higher state of consciousness than most of the inhabitants of the earth, but you were not in the highest understanding of free will and how it works itself out. As long as you are holding on to that original vision, that original purpose, you cannot feel good about being here until that purpose is fulfilled. Since that purpose, you must realize now, can *never* be fulfilled because of free will, then that means that as long as you are holding on to this, you cannot feel good about being on earth.

The change we are putting before you, that you need to go through, is that you let this self die. Therefore, you come to accept, as Jesus so eloquently said, that you are here just to be who you are, to shine your light, to give people an example, a frame of reference. When you make this switch, which we have all had to make (or at least most us had to make, except those who have created another primal self), then you will feel free of this entire burden of feeling bad about being here and feeling that if only this or that change would happen, then you could feel good about being here. Or even this entire burden of blaming yourself for coming here, feeling: "How stupid could I be to volunteer to come to a planet like this." This can all fall away from you when you go through the gradual process until you come to that point where you can finally let go. Then, my beloved, you can feel good about being here simply by being who you are.

## Feeling good about who you are

You see my beloved, when you create this self that wants to do something on earth, you cannot be who you are. This is not who you are. Through this self, even if this self felt it had accomplished its goals, you could never feel good about yourself or about being here. You can only feel good about being here when you feel good about yourself, and that feeling can only come from inside. It cannot be tied to any outer performance, any outer result that you could ever achieve on this or any other planet. Even on a natural planet, you could not feel ultimately good about yourself through your outer accomplishments. You had to develop that inner sense of feeling good about yourself simply based on who you are.

What does this say about those of us who chose to become avatars? It says that we chose to come to a lower planet because we had not developed that sense of fully appreciating who we are from inside ourselves. We still thought that our self-worth, our feeling good about ourselves, was somehow tied to our accomplishments, our performance. That is why we decided to give ourselves another goal, put ourselves through another cycle, and this time setting a more difficult goal for ourselves where we could accomplish something you cannot accomplish on a natural planet, namely affecting change on an unnatural planet.

The challenge we face for us to ascend is to come to this point where we finally let go of this desire to feel good about ourselves based on our accomplishments and achievements, based on something we have done. We come to the point of feeling good about ourselves based on who we are, *what* we are, the Being we are.

## The initiation of using extra-ordinary abilities

That is the initiation I faced under the Bo tree, facing the demons of Mara. I had the ability to use some extraordinary power to do something that would shock them or impress them. I had that second of temptation where I was "this close" to using that power. I was able to hold back, to be non-attached, to use the earth-touching mudra [A movement of touching the earth with the fingers of one hand] to touch the ground and exclaim: "Vajra!" I have the right to be here without doing, but only (which is not only) by being. *You* can come to that point as well where you have given up the desire to do anything on earth.

This does not mean you will sit under a tree for the rest of your life and do nothing. You can very well live an active life. You can even, as Jesus said, live a "normal" life and express your higher being in that seemingly normal life. You may also do certain things that accomplish something in the world and improve conditions in the world, but you are not doing it from the separate self that always feels a sense of lack, a sense of unfulfillment. You are just being who you are and letting the light of the River of Life flow through you. You are letting the light do its work instead of you with the outer mind having this sense of what *should* be done or the sense that you have accomplished it. You recognize with Jesus: "I can of my own self do nothing."

My beloved, it has been our great joy to give you these teachings at this conference that will allow this messenger to create a book that is sort of the Omega companion to the new book. You have some tools and teachings that can allow you to use a practical step-by-step procedure to overcome some of these attachments that you have as avatars. This means that you can gradually come to that point where you can sit there, facing the demons of Mara, resisting the temptation to act through that separate self that wants to do, that wants to impress, that wants to force. Instead, you can be centered, you can touch the earth and you can state your right to be here in a state of pure being that is not the dualistic "wanting to do."

Even though some of you may not yet have gone through this process and are not quite at that point, I am asking you to go through this exercise with me. Take your right hand, reach down, I recognize you cannot touch the ground as you are sitting, but you can imagine, envision that you are touching the ground. Then, we say together: "Vajra, Vajra, Vajra, Vajra, Vajra, Vajra, Vajra, Vajra, Vajra, Vajra, Vajra, Vajra, Vajra," and one last time: "Vajra."

Thus, it is fulfilled and I seal you, I seal this conference in the love and the joy of the Buddha that I AM.

# 26 | INVOKING FREEDOM FROM INORDINATE DESIRE

In the name I AM THAT I AM, Jesus Christ, I call to all representatives of the Divine Mother, especially Gautama Buddha, to help me overcome any inordinate desires of wanting to force a certain change on earth. Help me overcome all desires that are based on the limited vision I had when I came to earth, including…

[Make personal calls.]

*Part 1*

1. Gautama, help me see how, as a result of coming to the earth and feeling how my good intentions were rejected and put down, I went into a reactionary pattern.

Gautama, show my mental state
that does give rise to love and hate,

your exposé I do endure,
so my perception will be pure.

**Gautama, Flame of Cosmic Peace,**
**unruly thoughts do hereby cease,**
**we radiate from you and me**
**the peace to still Samsara's Sea.**

2. Gautama, help me see if I became even more eager, even more attached to doing something that could not be ignored, that could not be denied, either by the fallen beings or by the people of earth.

Gautama, in your Flame of Peace,
the struggling self I now release,
the Buddha Nature I now see,
it is the core of you and me.

**Gautama, Flame of Cosmic Peace,**
**unruly thoughts do hereby cease,**
**we radiate from you and me**
**the peace to still Samsara's Sea.**

3. Gautama, help me see if I have a desire for a supernatural ability, to make some kind of manifestation that people or the fallen beings cannot ignore or deny.

Gautama, I am one with thee,
Mara's demons do now flee,
your Presence like a soothing balm,
my mind and senses ever calm.

**Gautama, Flame of Cosmic Peace,**
**unruly thoughts do hereby cease,**
**we radiate from you and me**
**the peace to still Samsara's Sea.**

4. Gautama, help me see if I have a desire for an undeniable manifestation that would demonstrate the validity of the spiritual side to life. Help me see if I have a desire for a clairvoyant or supernatural ability so I can do something that people cannot ignore, deny or explain away.

Gautama, I now take the vow,
to live in the eternal now,
with you I do transcend all time,
to live in present so sublime.

**Gautama, Flame of Cosmic Peace,**
**unruly thoughts do hereby cease,**
**we radiate from you and me**
**the peace to still Samsara's Sea.**

5. Gautama, help me see if I have a subtle doubt that because there is evil on earth, God may not exist. Help me see that the fallen beings feel they have accomplished some of their greatest works when they can get an avatar to doubt the existence of God.

Gautama, I have no desire,
to nothing earthly I aspire,
in non-attachment I now rest,
passing Mara's subtle test.

**Gautama, Flame of Cosmic Peace,**
**unruly thoughts do hereby cease,**
**we radiate from you and me**
**the peace to still Samsara's Sea.**

6. Gautama, I see that the lowest point I can sink to as an avatar is to doubt that there is any higher being, there is any higher purpose and any purpose for me coming here.

Gautama, I melt into you,
my mind is one, no longer two,
immersed in your resplendent glow,
Nirvana is all that I know.

**Gautama, Flame of Cosmic Peace,**
**unruly thoughts do hereby cease,**
**we radiate from you and me**
**the peace to still Samsara's Sea.**

7. Gautama, help me recognize if I have a desire to have some extraordinary ability. Help me consider what would actually be accomplished if I had such an ability. If I used it, what would actually be accomplished?

Gautama, in your timeless space,
I am immersed in Cosmic Grace,
I know the God beyond all form,
to world I will no more conform.

**Gautama, Flame of Cosmic Peace,**
**unruly thoughts do hereby cease,**
**we radiate from you and me**
**the peace to still Samsara's Sea.**

8. Gautama, help me recognize that there is absolutely nothing that the outer mind, the carnal mind, the human mind, the intellectual, analytical, linear mind cannot cast doubt upon.

Gautama, I am now awake,
I clearly see what is at stake,
and thus I claim my sacred right
to be on earth the Buddhic Light.

**Gautama, Flame of Cosmic Peace,**
**unruly thoughts do hereby cease,**
**we radiate from you and me**
**the peace to still Samsara's Sea.**

9. Gautama, help me accept that I can never prove anything on a dense-matter, dense-consciousness planet like earth. The primary function of a dense-matter planet is to give people an immersion experience where they can experience themselves as separate beings.

Gautama, with your thunderbolt,
we give the earth a mighty jolt,
I know that some will understand,
and join the Buddha's timeless band.

**Gautama, Flame of Cosmic Peace,**
**unruly thoughts do hereby cease,**
**we radiate from you and me**
**the peace to still Samsara's Sea.**

## Part 2

1. Gautama, help me see that in order to have that experience, people cannot have the frame of reference that I have on a natural planet where I have a sense of my connection to something bigger than my current sense of self, I have a sense of the oneness of all life.

Gautama, show my mental state
that does give rise to love and hate,
your exposé I do endure,
so my perception will be pure.

**Gautama, Flame of Cosmic Peace,**
**unruly thoughts do hereby cease,**
**we radiate from you and me**
**the peace to still Samsara's Sea.**

2. Gautama, help me see that people who are in the immersion phase do not have any sense of the oneness of all life. *That* is why they do not have a frame of reference that allows them to have any undeniable sense that there is more to life than what they experience through the separate self.

Gautama, in your Flame of Peace,
the struggling self I now release,
the Buddha Nature I now see,
it is the core of you and me.

> **Gautama, Flame of Cosmic Peace,**
> **unruly thoughts do hereby cease,**
> **we radiate from you and me**
> **the peace to still Samsara's Sea.**

3. Gautama, help me accept that people cannot see what I have seen when I awaken to the spiritual side of life. There is *nothing* I could say or do that would give people in the immersion phase the experience of a higher reality. They cannot see what seems so obvious to me.

> Gautama, I am one with thee,
> Mara's demons do now flee,
> your Presence like a soothing balm,
> my mind and senses ever calm.

> **Gautama, Flame of Cosmic Peace,**
> **unruly thoughts do hereby cease,**
> **we radiate from you and me**
> **the peace to still Samsara's Sea.**

4. Gautama, help me accept that as long as people are in the immersion phase, they have to reject my higher perspective. Otherwise, they could not stay immersed, stay identified with the earth and the outer self.

> Gautama, I now take the vow,
> to live in the eternal now,
> with you I do transcend all time,
> to live in present so sublime.

> **Gautama, Flame of Cosmic Peace,**
> **unruly thoughts do hereby cease,**
> **we radiate from you and me**
> **the peace to still Samsara's Sea.**

5. Gautama, help me see that because people do not have an alternative to the reactionary patterns, it is valid that avatars take embodiment in order to demonstrate that there is such an alternative.

Gautama, I have no desire,
to nothing earthly I aspire,
in non-attachment I now rest,
passing Mara's subtle test.

**Gautama, Flame of Cosmic Peace,**
**unruly thoughts do hereby cease,**
**we radiate from you and me**
**the peace to still Samsara's Sea.**

6. Gautama, help me accept that the entire point for an avatar taking embodiment is that I am not here to affect a particular change on this planet. I am only here to demonstrate the alternative.

Gautama, I melt into you,
my mind is one, no longer two,
immersed in your resplendent glow,
Nirvana is all that I know.

**Gautama, Flame of Cosmic Peace,**
**unruly thoughts do hereby cease,**
**we radiate from you and me**
**the peace to still Samsara's Sea.**

7. Gautama, help me accept that for those people who are not ready or willing to start moving out of the immersion phase, I need to allow them to reject me and reject what I am saying—without reacting to this.

Gautama, in your timeless space,
I am immersed in Cosmic Grace,
I know the God beyond all form,
to world I will no more conform.

**Gautama, Flame of Cosmic Peace,**
**unruly thoughts do hereby cease,**
**we radiate from you and me**
**the peace to still Samsara's Sea.**

8. Gautama, help me see that when I came down and received my initial birth trauma and created my primal self, I did not fully grasp the reality of free will. I did not fully accept that my role was only to give an example and not to affect a particular change.

> Gautama, I am now awake,
> I clearly see what is at stake,
> and thus I claim my sacred right
> to be on earth the Buddhic Light.
>
> **Gautama, Flame of Cosmic Peace,**
> **unruly thoughts do hereby cease,**
> **we radiate from you and me**
> **the peace to still Samsara's Sea.**

9. Gautama, help me see that I created the primal self out of this desire to affect some change, and that is what gave me the desire to have some special ability that people could not ignore or deny.

> Gautama, with your thunderbolt,
> we give the earth a mighty jolt,
> I know that some will understand,
> and join the Buddha's timeless band.
>
> **Gautama, Flame of Cosmic Peace,**
> **unruly thoughts do hereby cease,**
> **we radiate from you and me**
> **the peace to still Samsara's Sea.**

## Part 3

1. Gautama, help me see that in order to let go of my primal self, I need to see it as an unreal self. Help me recognize that because of free will, what I had was an inordinate, an *unlawful,* desire. I had a desire to force people to awaken for their own good.

Gautama, show my mental state
that does give rise to love and hate,
your exposé I do endure,
so my perception will be pure.

**Gautama, Flame of Cosmic Peace,**
**unruly thoughts do hereby cease,**
**we radiate from you and me**
**the peace to still Samsara's Sea.**

2. Gautama, help me see that the fallen beings desire to force people for the good of the fallen beings. Help me recognize that it is not appropriate that an avatar has a desire to force people to awaken, even if it is for their own good.

Gautama, in your Flame of Peace,
the struggling self I now release,
the Buddha Nature I now see,
it is the core of you and me.

**Gautama, Flame of Cosmic Peace,**
**unruly thoughts do hereby cease,**
**we radiate from you and me**
**the peace to still Samsara's Sea.**

3. Gautama, help me take the next step and look at the primal self that has the desire to force a change on earth, to force people to change, force them to awaken.

Gautama, I am one with thee,
Mara's demons do now flee,
your Presence like a soothing balm,
my mind and senses ever calm.

**Gautama, Flame of Cosmic Peace,**
**unruly thoughts do hereby cease,**
**we radiate from you and me**
**the peace to still Samsara's Sea.**

4. Gautama, help me see that I came here with a correct understanding that change should happen on earth and that people should eventually be awakened. Yet, I had an unrealistic understanding of *how* this could be brought about.

> Gautama, I now take the vow,
> to live in the eternal now,
> with you I do transcend all time,
> to live in present so sublime.

> **Gautama, Flame of Cosmic Peace,**
> **unruly thoughts do hereby cease,**
> **we radiate from you and me**
> **the peace to still Samsara's Sea.**

5. Gautama, help me see if I was thinking that since the fallen beings had used force to put people asleep, it was acceptable for me to use a milder kind of force to awaken them.

> Gautama, I have no desire,
> to nothing earthly I aspire,
> in non-attachment I now rest,
> passing Mara's subtle test.

> **Gautama, Flame of Cosmic Peace,**
> **unruly thoughts do hereby cease,**
> **we radiate from you and me**
> **the peace to still Samsara's Sea.**

6. Gautama, help me look at this separate self and realize that even though the separate self firmly believes that it only wants to awaken people for their own good, the reality is that the separate self actually wants to awaken people for *its own* good.

> Gautama, I melt into you,
> my mind is one, no longer two,
> immersed in your resplendent glow,
> Nirvana is all that I know.

**Gautama, Flame of Cosmic Peace,**
**unruly thoughts do hereby cease,**
**we radiate from you and me**
**the peace to still Samsara's Sea.**

7. Gautama, help me see that the desire I have to awaken people is actually so that I feel that I can accomplish what I came to earth to do but what I have not so far have been able to achieve.

Gautama, in your timeless space,
I am immersed in Cosmic Grace,
I know the God beyond all form,
to world I will no more conform.

**Gautama, Flame of Cosmic Peace,**
**unruly thoughts do hereby cease,**
**we radiate from you and me**
**the peace to still Samsara's Sea.**

8. Gautama, help me see that the separate self is absolutely convinced that it is doing this for people's good, but it is actually for its own sake, for the accomplishment of the goal that the self has defined.

Gautama, I am now awake,
I clearly see what is at stake,
and thus I claim my sacred right
to be on earth the Buddhic Light.

**Gautama, Flame of Cosmic Peace,**
**unruly thoughts do hereby cease,**
**we radiate from you and me**
**the peace to still Samsara's Sea.**

9. Gautama, help me see that as long as I am seeing through this primal self, I think that I want to awaken people for *their* own good but it is for *my* own "good," for my own sake, for me to feel good about having come to earth.

Gautama, with your thunderbolt,
we give the earth a mighty jolt,
I know that some will understand,
and join the Buddha's timeless band.

**Gautama, Flame of Cosmic Peace,**
**unruly thoughts do hereby cease,**
**we radiate from you and me**
**the peace to still Samsara's Sea.**

## Part 4

1. Gautama, help me see that it is natural that I have a desire to come to a point where I can feel good about being here. Yet as long as I have this separate self, it seems that the only way to come to feel good about being here is to accomplish the purpose that I had in mind when I came.

Gautama, show my mental state
that does give rise to love and hate,
your exposé I do endure,
so my perception will be pure.

**Gautama, Flame of Cosmic Peace,**
**unruly thoughts do hereby cease,**
**we radiate from you and me**
**the peace to still Samsara's Sea.**

2. Gautama, help me recognize that the awareness I had before I came here was not the highest awareness. I was in a higher state of consciousness than most of the inhabitants of the earth, but I did not have the highest understanding of free will and how it works itself out.

Gautama, in your Flame of Peace,
the struggling self I now release,
the Buddha Nature I now see,
it is the core of you and me.

**Gautama, Flame of Cosmic Peace,**
**unruly thoughts do hereby cease,**
**we radiate from you and me**
**the peace to still Samsara's Sea.**

3. Gautama, help me see that as long as I am holding on to that original vision, I cannot feel good about being here until that purpose is fulfilled. Since that purpose can *never* be fulfilled because of free will, then as long as I am holding on to this, I cannot feel good about being on earth.

Gautama, I am one with thee,
Mara's demons do now flee,
your Presence like a soothing balm,
my mind and senses ever calm.

**Gautama, Flame of Cosmic Peace,**
**unruly thoughts do hereby cease,**
**we radiate from you and me**
**the peace to still Samsara's Sea.**

4. Gautama, help me truly see and accept the need to let this self die. Help me accept that I am here just to be who I am, to shine my light, to give people an example, a frame of reference.

Gautama, I now take the vow,
to live in the eternal now,
with you I do transcend all time,
to live in present so sublime.

**Gautama, Flame of Cosmic Peace,**
**unruly thoughts do hereby cease,**
**we radiate from you and me**
**the peace to still Samsara's Sea.**

5. Gautama, help me make this switch and be free of the entire burden of feeling bad about being here. Help me overcome the illusion that if only this or that change would happen, then I could feel good about being here.

Gautama, I have no desire,
to nothing earthly I aspire,
in non-attachment I now rest,
passing Mara's subtle test.

**Gautama, Flame of Cosmic Peace,**
**unruly thoughts do hereby cease,**
**we radiate from you and me**
**the peace to still Samsara's Sea.**

6. Gautama, help me be free of this entire burden of blaming myself for
coming here, feeling: "How stupid could I be to volunteer to come to a
planet like this." Help me go through a gradual process until I come to the
point where I can finally let go.

Gautama, I melt into you,
my mind is one, no longer two,
immersed in your resplendent glow,
Nirvana is all that I know.

**Gautama, Flame of Cosmic Peace,**
**unruly thoughts do hereby cease,**
**we radiate from you and me**
**the peace to still Samsara's Sea.**

7. Gautama, help me see that as long as I have a self that wants to do something on earth, I cannot be who I am. Even if this self accomplished its
goals, I still could not feel good about myself or about being here.

Gautama, in your timeless space,
I am immersed in Cosmic Grace,
I know the God beyond all form,
to world I will no more conform.

**Gautama, Flame of Cosmic Peace,**
**unruly thoughts do hereby cease,**
**we radiate from you and me**
**the peace to still Samsara's Sea.**

8. Gautama, help me see that I can only feel good about being here when I feel good about myself, and that feeling can only come from inside. It cannot be tied to any outer performance, any outer result that I could ever achieve on this or any other planet.

> Gautama, I am now awake,
> I clearly see what is at stake,
> and thus I claim my sacred right
> to be on earth the Buddhic Light.

> **Gautama, Flame of Cosmic Peace,**
> **unruly thoughts do hereby cease,**
> **we radiate from you and me**
> **the peace to still Samsara's Sea.**

9. Gautama, help me see that even on a natural planet, I could not feel ultimately good about myself through my outer accomplishments. I had to develop that inner sense of feeling good about myself simply based on who I am.

> Gautama, with your thunderbolt,
> we give the earth a mighty jolt,
> I know that some will understand,
> and join the Buddha's timeless band.

> **Gautama, Flame of Cosmic Peace,**
> **unruly thoughts do hereby cease,**
> **we radiate from you and me**
> **the peace to still Samsara's Sea.**

## Part 5

1. Gautama, help me see that as an avatar, I chose to come to a lower planet because I had not developed that sense of fully appreciating who I am from inside myself. I still thought that my self-worth was tied to my accomplishments, my performance.

Gautama, show my mental state
that does give rise to love and hate,
your exposé I do endure,
so my perception will be pure.

**Gautama, Flame of Cosmic Peace,**
**unruly thoughts do hereby cease,**
**we radiate from you and me**
**the peace to still Samsara's Sea.**

2. Gautama, help me see that I decided to give myself another goal, put myself through another cycle, and this time setting a more difficult goal for myself where I could accomplish something I cannot accomplish on a natural planet.

Gautama, in your Flame of Peace,
the struggling self I now release,
the Buddha Nature I now see,
it is the core of you and me.

**Gautama, Flame of Cosmic Peace,**
**unruly thoughts do hereby cease,**
**we radiate from you and me**
**the peace to still Samsara's Sea.**

3. Gautama, help me see that the challenge I face is that for me to ascend, I have to come to the point where I finally let go of this desire to feel good about myself based on my accomplishments and achievements, based on something I have done.

Gautama, I am one with thee,
Mara's demons do now flee,
your Presence like a soothing balm,
my mind and senses ever calm.

**Gautama, Flame of Cosmic Peace,**
**unruly thoughts do hereby cease,**
**we radiate from you and me**
**the peace to still Samsara's Sea.**

4. Gautama, help me come to the point of feeling good about myself based on who I am, *what* I am, the Being I am.

> Gautama, I now take the vow,
> to live in the eternal now,
> with you I do transcend all time,
> to live in present so sublime.

> **Gautama, Flame of Cosmic Peace,**
> **unruly thoughts do hereby cease,**
> **we radiate from you and me**
> **the peace to still Samsara's Sea.**

5. Gautama, help me see that when you were being tempted by the demons of Mara, you had an extraordinary ability but you chose not to use it.

> Gautama, I have no desire,
> to nothing earthly I aspire,
> in non-attachment I now rest,
> passing Mara's subtle test.

> **Gautama, Flame of Cosmic Peace,**
> **unruly thoughts do hereby cease,**
> **we radiate from you and me**
> **the peace to still Samsara's Sea.**

6. Gautama, help me come to the same point of having given up the desire to do anything on earth.

> Gautama, I melt into you,
> my mind is one, no longer two,
> immersed in your resplendent glow,
> Nirvana is all that I know.

> **Gautama, Flame of Cosmic Peace,**
> **unruly thoughts do hereby cease,**
> **we radiate from you and me**
> **the peace to still Samsara's Sea.**

7. Gautama, help me see that this does not mean I will sit under a tree for the rest of my life and do nothing. I can still live a normal life and express my higher being in that seemingly normal life.

Gautama, in your timeless space,
I am immersed in Cosmic Grace,
I know the God beyond all form,
to world I will no more conform.

**Gautama, Flame of Cosmic Peace,
unruly thoughts do hereby cease,
we radiate from you and me
the peace to still Samsara's Sea.**

8. Gautama, help me see that I may also do certain things that accomplish something in the world and improve conditions in the world, but I am not doing it from that separate self that always feels a sense of lack, a sense of unfulfillment.

Gautama, I am now awake,
I clearly see what is at stake,
and thus I claim my sacred right
to be on earth the Buddhic Light.

**Gautama, Flame of Cosmic Peace,
unruly thoughts do hereby cease,
we radiate from you and me
the peace to still Samsara's Sea.**

9. Gautama, help me be who I am and let the light of the River of Life flow through me. Help me let the light do its work instead of me with the outer mind having this sense of what *should* be done or the sense that I have accomplished it. I recognize with Jesus: "I can of my own self do nothing."

Gautama, with your thunderbolt,
we give the earth a mighty jolt,
I know that some will understand,
and join the Buddha's timeless band.

**Gautama, Flame of Cosmic Peace,
unruly thoughts do hereby cease,
we radiate from you and me
the peace to still Samsara's Sea.**

Gautama, in oneness with you, I touch the earth and I say:

**VAJRA!**

(33 times)

## Sealing

In the name of the Divine Mother, I call to Mother Mary for the sealing of myself and all people in my circle of influence in the creative flow of the Divine Mother, the River of Life. I call for the multiplication of my calls by all representatives of the Divine Mother, so that we form the perfect figure-eight flow of "As Above, so below." Thus, I accept that this is fully manifest, because the mouth of the Lord, the Divine Mother that I AM, has spoken it. Amen.